STRAUSS'
Life of Jesus
volume one

from
George Eliot

Edited/Designed/Introduced by Yoesh (the Priest) Gloger

text originally known as
The Life of Jesus Critically Examined
by David Friedrich Strauss; translated by George Eliot

Gloger Family Books
A Division of Gloger Family Products
New York   Tokyo   Antwerp

ISBN 1-878632-53-1
Library of Congress
Catalog Card Number 92-75332

In the library, *Strauss' Life of Jesus from George Eliot* should be shelved in "literature" with the complete works of George Eliot, since this finest example of translation is a literary work in itself created by GE. A second copy belongs with the biographies of George Eliot, since mastering its 1,550 pages was her primary occupation and preoccupation during the years 1843-46. A third copy should be shelved in "religion," with the other quests for the historical Jesus, since Strauss' *Life* is one of the best.

Predecessors

● *Das Leben Jesu, kritisch bearbeitet* by David Friedrich Strauss, 1835 German in two volumes, 1,550 pages, revised for the last time by the author in 1840 as the 4th German edition, which restored the greatness of the first and second editions. The watered down third edition was Strauss' unsuccessful attempt to appease critics until he could get a university professorship. The masterful "first" *Life of Jesus* (1st or 4th edition) should not be confused with another book about Jesus that Strauss would write years later, the uninspired *Life of Jesus for the German People*.

● *The Life of Jesus Critically Examined* by David Friedrich Strauss, 1846 English translation of the 4th German edition, in three volumes. The 1892 London edition was exactly the same, except that the type was reset for one volume (784 pages) instead of three, and George Eliot was given credit as the translator.

● *Strauss' Life of Jesus volume one from George Eliot*, a 1993 edition, specially edited, designed and introduced by Yoesh (the Priest) Gloger. The text is a photographic reprint magnified 125% of *The Life of Jesus Critically Examined* (1892), pages i-205, from a rare copy (784 pages total) owned by Gloger Family Books. New material is added and the classic type is repaired. ISBN 1-878632-53-1; Library of Congress Catalog Card Number 92-75332.

Design

While laboring over Strauss' translation, George Eliot sadly predicted it would only reach the select few; that the millions of people who need to read the book will not (letters of April 6, 1845 and May 20, 1846). This present volume attempts to honor the memory of George Eliot by bringing her work to the millions. This is done by making the book user-friendly:

(1) large type is easier to read; (2) paperback brings the price down; (3) quality notch/burst binding prevents pages from coming loose; (4) three manageable volumes eliminate a heavy, thick, academic-looking book; (5) three volumes make each affordable to millions; (6) three volumes let three library users read George Eliot's Strauss at the same time; (7) a slim volume is more tempting to take on a weekend vacation or to read on the bus.

Signatures

The 784 pages (London 1892 printing) were printed in 16-page booklets or sections that were bound together with thread and glue. To prevent a section from being bound upside down or in the wrong order, the printer put an isolated capital letter on the bottom right of the first page of the section. The title page is so obviously the beginning of the first section, that "A" is not used on it. "B" is on the bottom of page xvii (17), "C" on the bottom of page xxxiii (33), "D" on page 49, "E" on 65, "F" on 81, "G" on 97, "H" on 113, "I" on 129, "K" on 145 ("J" as well as "V" and "W" were not used because they could be misread), "L" on 161, "M" on 177, and "N" on 193. The bookbinder would read the printer's "signatures" that told him the correct way to place the sections together. The modern name for a section as well as the letter that introduces it is "signature."

Illustrations

(1) Young Strauss, 29 years old, from Strauss-Nachlass in Dillenburg, reproduced from the frontispiece of an 1856 New York edition; (2) older Strauss, 44, from Universitätsbibliothek, Tübingen; (3) teenager GE silhouette, from collection of Miss Druce, printed in *George Eliot and Her Times* by Elizabeth S. Haldane, 1927; (4) left profile of GE head, age 27, drawn from a shadow of a cast and filled in by Sara Hennell, 1846, from Coventry Library; (5) GE, 31 years, front head and bodice, from an 1850 portrait painting by Francois D'Albert Durade; (6) austere young GE, 23 years old, water-color portrait by Cara Bray, 1842 — the last two by courtesy of the National Portrait Gallery, London.

Otto Pfleiderer

The Rev. Dr. Otto Pfleiderer (1839-1908) followed in the footsteps of his countryman, David Friedrich Strauss. Both were born in Württemberg, both graduated from Tübingen University where they were taught by Ferdinand Baur, both became Lutheran ministers and New Testament scholars. Pfleiderer cultivated an interest in the English, where six of his books were popular in translation. As a distinguished visiting professor of theology from Berlin University, Pfleiderer lectured in London and Edinburgh, and wrote a book in English for the English: *The Development of Theology since Kant, and its Progress in Great Britain since 1825*. The article about Pfleiderer in the distinguished 11th edition of the Encyclopaedia Britannica concludes, "All his work shows a judicial tone of mind, and is remarkable for the charm of its style." He provided a special introduction to the 1892 London edition of Strauss' *Life of Jesus* that is here reproduced.

Gloger

Yoesh (the Priest) Gloger, B.S. University of New Hampshire, M.S. New York University, was born in White Plains, NY and graduated from the city's public schools. Before entering graduate school, he was a case worker for the Dutchess County (NY) Welfare Dept. Gloger taught 7th grade science plus 12th grade chemistry at Mohanason High School, Schenectady, NY, and anatomy & physiology at Hudson Valley Community College, Troy, NY. Retiring to San Francisco after the death of his parents, Gloger published *I Love Radio: The Complete AM/FM Guide to the Bay Area* and was the radio columnist for the *Richmond Independent/Berkeley Gazette* daily newspapers. Gloger later taught English as a second language in Israel for a year before settling in Crown Heights, Brooklyn, NY, to write the biographical study, *Jesus Mishegahs: The Jewish Xmas Book*.

Young Strauss: Good Christian

David Friedrich Strauss was born in the German-speaking town of Ludwigsburg on January 27, 1808, and died there 66 years later. He was showered with the best that God and Christian Europe had to offer: intelligence, a loving family, the religion of the majority, a supportive hometown that he never strayed far from, a first-rate education and life-long friends. He was a decent person with a keen sense of humor and a great desire to find truth. His was a charmed life until the age of 27, when *The Life of Jesus* was published. Afterwards, his life continued to be richly eventful, which means "happy," to an intellectual.

Duchy of Württemberg

Strauss' hometown was in the beautiful Duchy (or Kingdom) of Württemberg (enclosing medieval Swabia), still unspoiled by the industrial revolution that was polluting England. (Württemberg did not even have a railroad yet; fast travel was by horse-drawn coach.) An independent state of forests, warm springs, clean rivers and picturesque castles, Württemberg was in the southwest of what is now Germany, nudging like an elbow into France and Switzerland, with the wild Black Forest to the west, and the towering Alps to the South. The duchy had a prosperous capital (Stuttgart), a charming university town (Tübingen) and a summer resort for royalty (Ludwigsburg).

It was quite fitting that in the same year Strauss was born into that idyllic setting, Ludwig Beethoven gave the world his *Pastoral Symphony*.

Lutheran Church

Strauss was baptized in the local Lutheran Church by Pastor Vischer, whose son became Strauss' friend for 60 years.

Strauss' gentle mother, Christiane, was the daughter of a local Lutheran minister. She loved her hymn book, Bible, working in the garden, walking in the woods and doing good deeds. To her, Christianity meant helping others.

Strauss' father, proprietor of a spice & tea shop that his father owned before him in more prosperous times, was a devout Christian who had perfect faith that Jesus died to atone for everyone's sins. He kept bees, *grew fruit trees*, wrote poems and read Latin classics for pleasure. Both parents taught Strauss that the Bible was God's Word.

Jewish Misfortune

Strauss and his classmates grew up on stories about the duchy's famous Court Jew, Joseph Oppenheimer (Jew Suess), who was hanged 75 years earlier; and when David Friedrich was eleven years old (1819), anti-Jewish riots in economically depressed neighboring states produced a battle cry that was an easy rhyme for children to sing:

> Hep HEP,
> Jude verRECK.
> Hep HEP,
> Jude verRECK.

German-speaking people knew that "Hep hep!" was the victory cry of hunters as they closed in on the tired beast, minutes before the kill. The novelty that turned it into a catchy tune was the addition "Jude verreck" that had a Jewish person be the animal about to be slaughtered.

Inquisitive David Friedrich must have noticed some of the Jews (1% of the population) who lived as second-class citizens in 79 villages throughout his Duchy of Württemberg, where they bought and sold agricultural products, loaned money to small farmers, butchered, baked, wove, sewed, made shoes and soap. As a literate Lutheran, Strauss would have read Martin Luther's anti-Jewish commands to: Burn synagogues! Destroy Jewish houses! Take away their Talmud! Forbid rabbis from teaching! Deny Jews travel protection! Confiscate Jewish valuables! Force them to do manual labor! And if these things don't make the Hebs love Jesus, then kick them out of our sacred Christian land!

As he was growing up to manhood, Strauss witnessed the fact that almost all wealthy, educated German Jews were converting (Graetz 420f, 587; Katz 1973, 120-22; Katz 1986, 37, 54), and he might have taken that as proof of triumphant Christianity's superiority over Judaism. Also, Strauss lived during continental Europe's restoration of Jewish degradation (after Napoleon's defeat).

Blaubeuren Seminary

Young David Friedrich mastered Latin at the local elementary school, which helped him win a full scholarship to the excellent boarding school that turned out Lutheran pastors and university-bound scholars.

Strauss spent four happy years between the ages of 13 and 17 (1821-25) at Blaubeuren's Royal Protestant Theological Lyceum, cloistered in an 11th century monastery near a bubbling warm spring, flowing streams, wooded hills, and freedom from parents 50 miles away. Some of the 40 boys who entered with Strauss kept in touch with him for a lifetime.

The teachers were excellent and approachable. One of them, Ferdinand Baur, became a long-time acquaintance. He taught the boys the prose classics: Herodotus, Thucydides, Plato, Livy and Tacitus. But what made Baur very special was that while teaching them, he became a published author with his 1824 *Symbolism and Mythology: The Nature Religion of Antiquity*, and when the boys graduated to the university, Baur went with them as a professor.

Strauss was tall, slim, full of fun and clever. He wrote school plays, attended masquerades, dances, and flirted with local girls. Each weekday morning began with Christian prayer services while Sunday meant going to church and taking religious instruction.

On his final report card—reflecting four years at the school—young Strauss was given "outstanding" grades in poetry, history, German style, religion; and "excellent" grades in Latin, Greek, Hebrew. It was noted that Strauss was very sociable, persevering, thorough. One observer called Strauss "too sensitive" (Cromwell 22) which is a label the crudely insensitive stick on any decent person properly outraged by injustice.

Tübingen University (17-22 years old)

Strauss won a full five-year scholarship (1825-1830) to the state university, Tübingen. As was expected of future Lutheran Church leaders, Strauss concentrated on ancient languages plus philosophy during the first two years, and Christian theology in the last three.

Renowned for its Christian theology department, the university in Tübingen was founded in 1477, an event that was celebrated by expelling all Jews from the town. By the time Strauss entered, the university had both a Protestant and a Catholic division, representing the mixed population co-existing in the easy-going (liberal) Duchy of Württemberg. With special permission from the duke (king), a few Jewish students could attend.

Life was good for Strauss at picturesque Tübingen with its castle on the hill, the Neckar River flowing below and the impressive St. George's Church with its tombs of the dukes. After mastering his lessons, he could visit the taverns at night with his friends to drink wine, discuss life and flirt with girls. In his search for truth, Strauss even investigated faith healers and fortunetellers.

Strauss' favorite philosopher of reason was G. W. F. HEGEL, whose *The Spirit of Christianity and its Destiny* contains "one of the most inimical descriptions of Judaism extant in literature" (Katz 1980, 70). The disgusting anti-Jewish writings of young Hegel (Jews are parasites et cetera et cetera) provided the philosophical basis for anti-Semitism. Strauss' hunger for Hegelian philosophy was so great that he organized an extracurricular class to master it.

The Synoptic Gospels course of Professor FRIEDRICH KERN highlighted the many inconsistencies that Strauss would later strip away from Jesus' life to make for a better Christianity, *just as his father pruned trees to improve the fruit.*

In his third year, Strauss won an essay contest on the topic, "The Resurrection of the Dead," and later presented his doctoral thesis on "The Summing Up of All Things," from Acts of the Apostles 3:21. He graduated first in his class.

Tübingen University Professor of Theology FERDINAND BAUR tried to accommodate the modern philosophy of Hegel with accepted Christian theology. He was an early supporter of Strauss' book for he correctly understood that it was the logical development of Protestant thinking. Strauss attended Baur's university classes on Christian symbolism, Acts of the Apostles, Epistles of Paul to Romans and Corinthians. Baur's 51-year tenure at the university was not continuous: For nine years he taught the prose classics at the Blaubeuren lyceum when Strauss was a student there.

While Strauss was at the university, Felix Mendelssohn revived Bach's *St. Matthew's Passion*, and Württemberg granted some civil rights to its Jews: Those born in the duchy could move around, but not enter the professions; Jews could be craftsmen, but only if the Christian guilds agreed; Jewish cattle traders could marry, but not before they were 35.

During this period, Professor H. E. G. PAULUS of Heidelberg University, 75 miles north, published a rationalist biography of Jesus. Paulus applied natural explanations to gospel contradictions. He believed that there was a truthful historical core to the Jesus stories that enthusiastic disciples embellished.

(Strauss' *Life of Jesus* would expose the flaws of this naturalist approach.) When he was not researching Jesus, Paulus was arguing against Jewish emancipation. To be a real German, the Jew must give up his Jewish nationality by converting to Christianity. Resistance to his logical plan, Paulus believed, came from the strong sense of Jewish community which could be weakened by targeting individual Jews for missionary work. If this were not done, Paulus warned, the entire Jewish community in Germany would eventually be exiled or even exterminated.

Clergyman at 22

Strauss was given a job close to home in the village of Klein-Ingersheim on the Neckar River as acting vicar, who baptized, taught Sunday school, led services, married, buried, and—after the local grape crop was ruined by a hailstorm—preached that the field of God's Word can never be destroyed. Strauss was considered a great success by his parishioners who were sad when he was reassigned the next year to Maulbronn Theological Seminary, a few miles west of his hometown.

Train Future Pastors

At Maulbronn, Strauss gave the Hebrew, Latin and history lessons for a year. Students and headmaster praised Strauss as an excellent teacher.

Berlin (1832)

Strauss went to Berlin University for two semesters of intensive postdoctoral studies, paid for by his father when the state scholarship was withheld as punishment for the young man's interest in *pruning the Gospels*. Berlin, an exciting cultural and intellectual center, was the capital city of the independent kingdom of Prussia when the German language was spoken by 38 million Europeans. (English was native to less than half that.) Berlin was the city of famous salons, where both Jewish and Christian intellectuals openly discussed all matters.

The Jewish presence in Germany was a favorite topic at the salons as well as in the many circulating pamphlets. There were pamphlets on every shade of anti-Jewish opinion, which caused the appearance of pro-Jewish pamphlets. Are Jews German or not? Will conversion make them German? Is Judaism a religion or a nation? Should Jewish ritual be modernized? Does Jewish Law come from God or man? Must Sabbath services be only in Hebrew?

In Berlin, Strauss learned from the renowned Christian theologian, F.D.E. SCHLEIER-MACHER, who tried to merge modern philosophy with Christianity. He was a staunch defender of the Gospel of John as an eyewitness account, partly because he realized that the Synoptic Gospels hopelessly contradicted each other. (His lecture notes on the historical Jesus stimulated Strauss to develop his own version, which turned out to be as critical of John as of Matthew, Mark and Luke.) Schleiermacher enjoyed the hospitality of Jewish ladies at their famous Berlin salons, then turned around to warn fellow Christians that converts from Judaism would contaminate the Church. He believed that Judaism was not a legitimate religion because Christianity had made it obsolete, and since it was not a religion, reasoned Schleiermacher, then Judaism was a nation—an alien nation within Germany.

At Berlin, Strauss was also influenced by the leading Christian historian, Professor AUGUST NEANDER (born David Mendel), who would defend the Gospel of John against its criticism by Strauss. Neander would also defend contemporary Jews against blood libel accusations, even though he wanting them kept out of his university.

Berlin University Professor of Hebrew and Aramaic, E. W. HENGSTENBERG, was opposed to the study of Hebrew Scriptures as mythology, which was popular then. He warned that this dangerous practice would spill over into the New Testament, challenging the very foundation of Christian belief (Harris 74). His worst fears came to be when a young Strauss—there in Berlin with him—developed the hypothesis that all of the gospel stories of Jesus came from the myth-making imagination of early Christians.

An earlier (1816) Berlin professor, historian FRIEDRICH RUHS, blamed the Jews for the disunity of a potentially great Christian German nation. He recommended that the Jewish population be severely limited, and that each Jew pay a head tax and wear a yellow badge. Ruhs began the flood of anti-Jewish pamphlets by professors that brainwashed Germany's university students.

The likable Strauss made personal contact with his teachers. He visited Hegel, Schleiermacher, and listened to music with Professor of Hebrew Scriptures, WILHELM VATKE, who showed Strauss that the Gospel of John was too Greek philosophically to be from a Holy Land witness.

Strauss was almost one of them now—that elite group of German philosophy/theology intellectuals who had similar backgrounds and academic aspirations.

University Instructor for 3 Years

Strauss was called back to his alma mater (Tübingen U.) at the age of 24 to teach logic, the history of modern philosophy, and ethics (1832-35). Strauss was joined by a group of friends from teenage days, who had the same assignment, and was their leader in a merry social life that included an affair with the innkeeper's daughter.

Strauss was a very dynamic teacher in the philosophy department, attracting more students than the other lecturers could draw. One of his admiring students was BERTHOLD AUERBACH, a former rabbinical student. Some jealous philosophy professors banded together to deny Strauss the large lecture hall he needed and even tried to withhold credit from any student taking his course by claiming Strauss was not a qualified philosophy professor. This was a hint of what would motivate future critics of his great book: Mediocrity jealous of genius.

Although protected by the theology department as one of the family, Strauss had his troubles there also. When he wove his *positive criticism* (pruning the Gospels to get a better fruit) into the regular lecture, his supervisor censored him in front of the students, putting an end to that. A periodical then refused to publish those thoughts, so that Strauss turned to book writing as the way to make his contribution to Jesus scholarship.

During his last year at Tübingen, Strauss sat in the teachers' lounge by a window overlooking a campus gate and the Neckar River to write his magnum opus. Strauss analyzed over 90 gospel incidents, *pruning away all their contradictions with a patient gardener's thoroughness*. A talent for writing and a keen sense of humor led to his use of comic *irony* (a legitimate literary devise) to persuade. He would show the emptiness of both rational and supernatural explanations for a gospel inconsistency by ridiculing those untenable positions. Strauss believed that fiction was created unintentionally because the Evangelists had impatient faith in Jewish messianic prophecies and because they were seduced by a charismatic personality.

Publication Day: June 1, 1835

Das Leben Jesu, kritisch bearbeitet was David Friedrich Strauss' masterpiece, just as eleven years later, its English version, *The Life of Jesus Critically Examined*, would be George Eliot's masterpiece of translation. The big German book was published in two parts by Osiander Press, Tübingen—volume I being 730 pages. The rest of the 1,550 pages would appear six months later as volume II. Strauss was 27 years old.

High School Latin Teacher (1836)

Strauss' sudden fame for unorthodox ideas beautifully written had the kingdom's Ministry of Church & School remove Strauss from impressionable Christian students. But the young men rallied to Strauss' support. They were about to organize the biggest protest demonstration that Tübingen had ever experienced when the university head pleaded with Strauss to stop it and Strauss obeyed, telling the students to accept his removal. Rector Robert von Mohl was grateful for Strauss' cooperation, and this was a pattern that continued throughout his life: being criticized and respected at the same time, as loving relatives might do with each other.

Strauss was reassigned to his quiet hometown of Ludwigsburg (1836) to teach harmless Latin in the local high school and live at home with his proper Lutheran parents. The book became a sensation throughout Europe, making him a celebrity superstar the likes of which the duchy had never seen. In a lively literary style, Strauss' *Life of Jesus* brought into the open everybody's secret thoughts about his Christianity. It became the center of conversation in every little church of every little town at a time when the social life of religious people revolved around that little church. Lovers and haters of democracy discussed the book in every coffee house, beer hall, salon, and bureaucratic office, for it undermined the divine right of kings. (Central Europe was then a patchwork of semi-feudal Teutonic states ruled by arrogant aristocrats who justified their inherited power as coming from Jesus himself.)

Strauss met the great demand for his book by approving a second edition which also sold well.

Strauss paid a heavy price for his fame. Professional friendships that meant a lot to him, came to a sudden end when it became evident that *The Life of Jesus* was feared by the powerful establishment that gave jobs and promotions. Strauss' colleagues abandoned him to protect their careers. Almost unanimously, they wrote unfavorable reviews of the book whose ideas they had favorably discussed before.

Stuttgart Free-lance Writer (1837-42)

Since he was anxious to reply to critics with essays of his own, and his hometown lacked a good library, he resigned his teaching job the next year and moved five miles away to Württemberg's capital city, Stuttgart, where he rented a garden apartment that suited him until he married six years later. Strauss lived the good life of a celebrated man of letters. When he was not reading, writing or researching, Strauss enthusiastically supported the performing arts, and enjoyed the company of actors, artists, musicians and the ladies—one being the famous Bohemian opera star, Agnese Schebest, his future wife, as she performed in Stuttgart while on international tour.

Strauss loved music and literature, especially the inspiring composers of sacred (Christian) works:

Mozart (Masses, vespers, *Requiem*); Beethoven (*Missa Solemnis, Christus am Ölberge, Mass in C*); and Haydn (*Missa Sanctae Caeciliae, The Seven Words of the Savior on the Cross, Missa in Augustiis, Stabat Mater,* and *Te Deum*). His favorite authors were: F.G. Klopstock, the poet of religion, whose epic poem of Jesus, *Der Messias* (the Messiah), is not anti-Jewish; C.M. Wieland, proponent of Jewish emancipation, son of a Württemberg Lutheran pastor, whose early poems were devoutly Christian; playwright G.E. Lessing, son of a famous Lutheran pastor, author of *Die Juden* and *Nathan der Weise*; J.G. Herder, Lutheran theologian who called anti-Jewish laws barbaric; J.W. Goethe; and Württemberg playwright-poet J.C.F. Schiller.

While in Stuttgart, Strauss approved a third (1838) and finally a fourth edition (1840: the last, best revision) of his great book. His beloved mother died (1839), and then his father (1841).

Zürich

Strauss was offered a professorship (1839) at the new University of Zürich, 100 miles south, but important people who feared reform had the appointment cancelled before he could begin. In compensation, Strauss was given a half-salary pension for life. (His friends were not without influence.) This pension plus the inheritance from his father plus book royalties, allowed Strauss to continue being an uncompromising seeker of truth. He became a hero to religious reformers fed up with an unbelievable Jesus, and a hero to political reformers fed up with the unfair system of divine right of Christian princes to rule.

At this time, Christian theologian BRUNO BAUER was teaching in Berlin. Like Strauss, Bauer wanted to cleanse the Gospels of their errors. He developed the idea that Jesus never existed, but was invented by early Christians in love with Greek (not Hebrew) culture. Bauer was consumed with a deep intellectual and emotional hatred of Judaism (Jewish money controls nations et cetera et cetera) which came out in his 1843 *Die Juden Frage* (The Jewish Question/Problem). There was no such thing as a Jewish nation, Bauer insisted, so that there should be no attempt to reform Judaism as if it were—just do away with it. He wished for a rational German state free of irrational Jews. Bauer proudly showed off his knowledge of the latest scientific research by declaring that Jewish blood was different from, and stronger than Christian blood, so that intermarriage would "Jewify" Europe (Rose 273). Strauss finally labeled Bauer a scoundrel in all ways (Low 274ff; Katz 1980, 159f). Bauer's Jew-hatred was admired by his Bonn University student, Karl Marx, who wrote his own *On*

The Jewish Problem that promised Utopia when society would free itself from the Jewish yoke of money worship.

LUDWIG FEUERBACH (Meyer 1990, 40) published *Das Wesen des Christentums* (1841) which George Eliot would translate into English 12 years later as *The Essence of Christianity*. In it, Judaism is dismissed as being not only inferior to Christianity but also inferior to polytheism, for Jewish monotheism was invented by egoistic people needing a god to reflect their self-love (Katz 1980, 163ff).

During this period, young Queen Victoria of England married Prince Albert from a northern German kingdom, and Strauss married the Catholic Agnese Schebest in a Lutheran church 20 miles north of his hometown, on the Neckar River near Heilbronn. Dominating the skyline of the city of Heilbronn was a 210-foot church tower belonging to the High Renaissance St. Killan's, noted also for a spring bubbling up from beneath the carved wood high altar. The newlyweds began married life in a rented castle in the nearby village of Sontheim where Jews built a synagogue in 1702 because they were chased out of Heilbronn. Until 1828, a Jew could only be in Heilbronn during daylight, and then only by paying a toll.

Strauss' Jewish Connection

While Strauss lived in Stuttgart (1837-42), the city got its first state-recognized rabbi, and neo-orthodox SAMSON RAPHAEL HIRSCH published *Nineteen Letters*, an intellectual justification of Orthodox Judaism as a religion, not a nation. Hirsch argued that religious Jews could and should participate in modern society without having to assimilate, for it was the Jewish mission to be a light unto the Gentiles.

Available from Frankfurt, 100 miles to the north, was GABRIEL RIESSER's pamphlet for Jewish readers on how to fight anti-Semitism (1830); and another (1831) to be read by Christians, pleading for Jewish advancement without having to convert. Since religion was a private matter of the citizen, and the state should respect the privacy of its citizens, then a Jew was as much a citizen of his German state as was a Christian resident. Riesser was a civil-rights lawyer for the oppressed, and the oppressed then and there were the Jews struggling for emancipation. He even admonished upper class Jews for being ashamed of the Jewishness of their poor cousins recently from Poland.

Strauss probably came across *Sermons of the Jews* (1832) by the Jewish historian, LEOPOLD (Yomtov Lipman) ZUNZ, that analyzed great Jewish literature (Aggada, Targum, Midrash) in connection with the history of Jewish worship from Ezra to the Middle Ages. Zunz aimed for a "Science of Judaism," that would investigate the Jewish past as systematically as Strauss investigated Jesus. Zunz liked the way Strauss *pruned* the Gospel stories to reveal Jewish messianic expectations (Wallach 65). To help repeal an anti-Jewish law, Zunz published, "About Jewish Names" (1837) proving with documented research that Jews of ancient times had Greek, Roman and Arabic names. This project was to undo the Prussian law that prohibited Jews from taking so-called Christian names.

Strauss would have been pleased that his former philosophy student, BERTHOLD AUERBACH, published a first novel (1837) about the life of Spinoza, and a second about the German Jewish poet, Ephraim Moses Kuh (1840). Growing up in a Black Forest village, Auerbach studied to be a rabbi at Karlsruhe (1827-29), 35 miles west of Strauss' hometown. (Karlsruhe was a center for Hebrew printing and home of 700 Jews.) He hoped that Judaism would be reformed the way he thought Strauss was reforming Christianity, and he wanted Judaism to be considered only a religion and not a nationality. Auerbach thought it would help if the words "Jewish & Judaism" would disappear, to be replaced by "Mosaic & Mosaism." His 1836 pamphlet called upon Germans to end their view of Jews as inherently evil beings. Auerbach and Strauss corresponded: 33 letters from Strauss have been discovered. Auerbach became famous for social novels and *Black Forest Village Stories* (1843-54), which became very popular, but not with Bruno Bauer who called Auerbach a Court Jew injecting pro-Jewish propaganda into his fiction (Rose 224, 252; Rosenbloom 35).

LUDWIG BOERNE (born Loeb Baruch in the Frankfurt ghetto) wrote brilliant essays favoring Jewish equality. He pointed to the shame of the Hep Hep Riots of 1819, hopefully predicting that never again would German people be guilty of anti-Jewish hate crimes (Katz 1980, 155). Boerne, like Strauss, was a student of Schleiermacher. His clever use of *irony* would have been appreciated by Strauss, who used that literary devise to *prune deadwood from the Gospels.* When Boerne—a new Lutheran—wanted to irritate bigoted Germans who continued to call him a Jew, he proclaimed pride in his Jewish background, for that made him a citizen of the world who did not have to bear the shame of being a German.

Since Strauss was a voracious reader and a poet himself, he must have been familiar with the great lyric poetry and ballads of HEINRICH (Chayyim) HEINE, whose four volumes of essays (from 1826) satirized religious bigotry.

Strauss probably read about the first reform rab-

binical conference (1837) in Wiesbaden to the north, organized by ABRAHAM GEIGER, who was impressed by Strauss' *Life of Jesus* (Katz 1980, 159f; Meyer 1988, 92), although disappointed with its mistakes about Judaism. Geiger thought Judaism would benefit from scientific study, just as Christianity was being improved by Strauss. He believed that the traditions of the Jewish religion evolved, each historical period contributing something that stayed. Geiger would strip Judaism of those additions.

Strauss was considered a decent, honorable man having no ill-feelings towards Jews. He was a good goy (Katz 1980, 160; Low, 331; Poliakov, 416). Yet scholarly Strauss, who knew so much about other matters, chose to remain blind to Judaism's influence on the development of Christianity and even blind to the importance of the Pharisees. Rabbi Abraham Geiger accused Strauss of "ignoring all modern research in Jewish literature, and it is apparent how he delights in coloring Judaism with the darkest shades" (Geiger Appendix).

Future Look

The second half of Strauss' life was richly eventful. From the time of his marriage until he died 32 years later in the town of his birth, Strauss was a popular lecturer, journalist, patron of the arts, politician and patriot, publishing volumes of essays, reviews, poems, books (religious, philosophical and biographical). He may have been the greatest living nonfiction German prose writer. His style was superb. In his *Life of Jesus*, Strauss not only exposed both rational and supernatural arguments as flawed, but he played them against each other, weaving thoughts in and out, as would a great composer construct a symphony.

Strauss lived in several places, almost all connected by the one Neckar River that flowed through his home duchy of Württemberg and north.

1843: a daughter, Georgine, was born on St. George's day, and properly baptized according to the Lutheran customs of Württemberg. Strauss was a loving father who guided her education (an excellent girl's college in Heidelberg) until she married a mining businessman from Bonn.

1845: a son, Fritz, was born. He went to a private boarding school near Heidelberg, studied medicine at Tübingen University, and, as a Stuttgart physician, lovingly cared for his famous father during his terminal illness. Also in 1845, Leopold Zunz published a *History of the Medieval Rabbinical Literature in Europe* highlighting the ethics of Judaism, and Abraham Geiger published his commentary on the Mishneh.

1846: George Eliot's excellent English translation of Strauss' *Life of Jesus* appeared, for which Strauss contributed a preface in Latin. He was 39 years old; she was 27.

1848: Strauss ran for election in the new all-German Parliament, and all the Jewish voters voted for him (Harris 164). Unfortunately, the powerful country vote went to someone else. The leaders of his hometown of Ludwigsburg then asked Strauss to be their representative in the state assembly, to which he agreed—another case of critics showing him respect. Also in 1848, Strauss stained his "good goy" reputation with two published articles blaming the peasant riots on the Jewish victims who, Strauss wrote, antagonized the peasants by their separateness and financial dishonesty (Rose 252).

1854: Strauss met his English translator, George Eliot (known then as Marian Evans or Mrs. George H. Lewes) in Cologne during her summer vacation. He was 47; she was 35. He wrote that when saying goodbye, he gallantly kissed the hand that did the writing.

1858: Strauss met George Eliot for a second time, in Munich. Of the occasion, Strauss wrote that there existed a mystical marriage between the writer and his lady translator.

1859: George Eliot won fame as the author of *Adam Bede*, and when she revealed her real identity, Strauss must have been happily surprised to find his translator now as famous as he. Strauss was 52; she, 40.

1861: Strauss lectured in honor of the 80th anniversary of Gotthold Ephraim Lessing's *Nathan der Weise*, a great dramatic poem about an admirable human being who happened to be a German Jew. Strauss pleaded with his audience to learn the story's powerful lesson of tolerance. The brilliant lecture was printed in a journal, then made into a 79-page book (Low 280, 310). Seven years earlier, George Eliot saw a *Nathan* performance in Berlin that made her cry and finally overcome a deep-seated prejudice against Judaism.

1872: Strauss published his last book—a financial success—and George Eliot published her big moneymaker, *Middlemarch*, which borrowed from the time she translated Strauss. (Young Dorothea Brooke seems to be part young Mary Anne Evans; the older Edward Casaubon could be part Dr. Brabant, her connection to Strauss.)

1874: David Friedrich Strauss died at 66.

Bibliography

Brazill, William J., *The Young Hegelians*. New Haven: Yale Univ Press, 1970.

Cahnman, Werner Jacob, *German Jewry: Its History and Sociology*. New Brunswick, NJ: Transaction Publ, 1989.

Cromwell, Richard S., *David Friedrich Strauss and His Place in Modern Thought*. Fairlawn, NJ: R.E. Burdick, 1974.

Dubnov, Simon, *History of the Jews*, volumes IV & V revised, translated from the Russian. Cranbury, NJ: T. Yoseloff, 1973.

Geiger, Abraham, *Judaism and its History*, translated from the 1865 German. NY: M. Thalmessinger, 1865.

Graetz, Heinrich, *History of the Jews*, volume 5, translated from the German. Phila: Jewish Publ Society, 1895.

Harris, Horton, *David Friedrich Strauss and his Theology*. Cambridge: C. Univ Press, 1973.

Katz, Jacob, *From Prejudice to Destruction: Anti-Semitism, 1700-1933*. Cambridge: Harvard Univ Press, 1980.

Katz, Jacob, *Out of the Ghetto: Social Background of Jewish Emancipation 1770-1870*. Cambridge: Harvard Univ Press, 1973.

Katz, Jacob, *Jewish Emancipation and Self-Emancipation*. Phila: Jewish Publ Society, 1986.

Kissinger, Warren S., *The Lives of Jesus: A History and Bibliography*. London: Garland Publ, 1985.

Lawler, Edwina G., *David Friedrich Strauss and His Critics: The Life of Jesus Debate in Early Nineteenth-Century German Journals*. NY: Peter Lang, 1986.

Low, Alfred D., *Jews in the Eyes of the Germans: From the Enlightenment to Imperial Germany*. Phila: ISHI Institute for the Study of Human Issues, 1979.

Lowenthal, Marvin, *The Jews of Germany: A Story of 16 Centuries*. Phila: Jewish Publ Society, 1936.

Massey, Marilyn Chapin, *Christ Unmasked: The Meaning of 'The Life of Jesus' in German Politics*. Chapel Hill: Univ of N. Carolina Press, 1983.

Meyer, Michael A., *Jewish Identity in the Modern World*. Seattle: Univ of Washington Press, 1990.

Meyer, Michael A., *Response To Modernity: A History of the Reform Movement in Judaism*. NY: Oxford Univ Press, 1988.

Neusner, Jacob, *Stranger at Home*, Chapter 7: "Jubilee in Tübingen." Chicago: Univ of C. Press, 1981.

Poliakov, Leon, *The History of Anti-Semitism, volume III: From Voltaire to Wagner*, translated from the 1968 French. NY: Vanguard Press, 1975.

Reinharz, Jehuda and W. Schatzberg, editors, *The Jewish Response to German Culture: from the Enlightenment to the Second World War*. London: Univ Press of New England, 1985.

Rose, Paul Lawrence, *Revolutionary Anti-Semitism in Germany from Kant to Wagner*. Princeton: P. Univ Press, 1990.

Rosenbloom, Noah H., *Tradition in an Age of Reform: The Religious Philosophy of Samson Raphael Hirsch*. Phila: Jewish Publ Society, 1976.

Schweitzer, Albert, *The Quest of the Historical Jesus: A Critical Study of its Progress from Reimarus to Wrede*, translated from 1906 German. London: 1911.

Stepelevich, Lawrence, S., editor, *The Young Hegelians*. Cambridge: C. Univ Press, 1983.

Wallach, Luitpold, *Liberty and Letters: The Thoughts of Leopold Zunz*. London: Leo Baeck Institute, 1959.

George Eliot + D.F. Strauss = A Perfect Match, for Mary Anne Evans and David Friedrich Strauss had much in common: (1) loving Christian homes; (2) taught to love Jesus; (3) siblings died in infancy; (4) he grew up with a brother, she with a brother and sister; (5) the best education; (6) studied Latin, Greek, Hebrew, French, German; (7) excellent grades; (8) expert knowledge of the Christian Bible; (9) voracious readers; (10) curious about all subjects; (11) investigated unconventional items such as fortunetelling and phrenology; (12) fathers were conservative Christians; (13) fathers were businessmen; (14) mothers believed that Christianity meant doing good deeds; (15) he loved his home duchy, she wrote about her home county; (16) she preferred older men, he was 11 years

(continued on page "r")

Young George Eliot: Good Christian

The great English novelist with the pen name "George Eliot" was born November 22, 1819, in Warwickshire County of the English Midlands, into a family of conventional Anglicans. She was christened Mary Anne Evans at Chilvers Coton parish church, and became a life-long communicant of the Church of England.

Her paternal grandfather was a High Anglican Christian, attending the elaborate church service with full sacramental worship. Her father had been a choirboy, had dabbled in Methodism as a young man, but matured into a conventional Church of England member, in tune with the conservative people he worked for. He was a wealthy country real estate manager and advisor to the landed aristocracy. He attended church every Sunday with his family, then visited the neighbors. He would not work on Sunday.

Mary Anne's maternal grandfather was a church warden, helping with the business of his parish church. Both her mother and sister (five years older) were named Christiana, in honor of Jesus Christ.

As a little girl, Mary Anne loved reading the Authorized (King James) version of the Christian Bible.

Mary Anne's uncle, Samuel Evans, and his wife Elizabeth, were devout Methodists. They met when both were field preachers spreading the enthusiasm of John Wesley's social holiness. Mary Anne enjoyed their company.

Her brother Isaac, three years older, grew up to be a High Anglican Church Christian.

Mary Anne's father encouraged her to learn. He thought it a good investment to spend whatever it cost to give her the best education that was proper.

Mrs. Moore's (1824) at 4

Several mornings a week, 4-year-old Mary Anne went with her adored brother to nearby Mrs. Moore's Dame School, while back at the house, Mary Anne would notice those few books there that she would get to know very well: *Pilgrim's Progress* by John Bunyan; *Vicar of Wakefield* by Oliver Goldsmith; King James Christian Bible; and *Political History of the Devil* by Daniel Defoe, who had the Devil spend most of his time chasing Jews because they resisted him the most. Defoe devoted a chapter to Jewish biblical history.

Miss Lathom's, 5 to 8

For four years, Mary Anne attended a boarding school with her older sister Christiana (Chrissey): Miss Lathom's Seminary for Young Ladies in Attleborough, a weaving village three miles from home. She was looked upon as a very serious child who preferred the company of older people. At this time, the Church of England gave the area an Evangelical as bishop who assigned another Evangelical as local minister.

Mrs. Wallington's, 9 to 13

From the age of nine, Mary Anne joined 30 other children for five years (1828-32) at The Elms: Mrs. Wallington's Ladies Boarding School in Church Lane, Nuneaton, whose principal teacher was an enthusiastic young Irish-born Evangelical Anglican, Maria Lewis, destined to be Mary Anne's friend for 19 years. Miss Lewis seriously studied the Christian Bible, and little Mary Anne imitated her new role model by reading and rereading her own Bible. The Rev. John Edmund Jones stirred up religious feelings in Nuneaton with his controversial sermons that packed the church with both Conservatives and Evangelicals.

Reading, writing and reciting the English language were emphasized at the school. In addition, little Mary Anne studied French and practiced playing the piano. She read a lot and listened to Evangelical preaching.

Miss Franklins', 13 to 16

Mary Evans studied (1832-35) in Mary and Rebecca Franklin's school, Warwick Row, in the larger city of Coventry, to acquire feminine social graces, learn to play religious music on the piano (taught by Edward Simms, the organist of St. Michael's Church), improve her French (she won a prize for translation), write English well, appreciate art, Shakespeare and Milton. Her intellectual curiosity was awakened to all subjects: astronomy, biology, geology, anthropology, politics, the historical novels of Walter Scott, even hypnotism and phrenology.

Mary Franklin had been a student teacher in Essex, and Rebecca had studied for a year in Paris. With that experience and the support of their father, the Franklin sisters developed an excellent school that drew students from London, India and New York.

The father of the Franklin sisters was the Rev. Francis Franklin, minister of the Cow Lane Baptist Church, Coventry, whose congregants believed that they were the elect, chosen by God for eternal salvation. Franklin's brother-in-law was an important official of the Baptist Missionary Society who had a missionary daughter in India and a son who died preparing for the same work. On Sundays, Mary Anne and her classmates attended church to hear the Rev. Franklin preach, while on weekdays, Mary Anne organized school prayer meetings. She was much more learned than any of her classmates and they knew it. When visitors came, it was Mary Anne Evans who was called upon to recite from the Bible or play the piano—honors that caused inner conflict: pride in demonstrating her abilities versus guilt for not being humble.

On her fifteenth birthday, (November 22, 1834), Mary Anne Evans had a sudden religious experience that made her neglect her personal appearance for the sake of saving the soul, which may explain her austere look in the watercolor by Cara Bray.

17-24 years old (1836-43)

This period marked the beginning of the Victorian Era (Princess Victoria was crowned Queen in 1838) and adult responsibilities for Mary Anne, whose mother died from painful cancer (February 3, 1836). Mary Anne left school to run the household and care for her father who suffered from kidney stones.

With her father and soon-to-marry sister, Mary Anne received the Sacrament (eating bread consecrated as the body of Jesus) in church on December 25, 1836. It was her first Holy Communion.

Mary Anne continued her education at home, her father agreeing to pay for books and things. He hired Coventry's leading language teacher, Joseph Brezzi, to tutor his daughter in Italian and German while she continued Latin with self-help books and advice from the Reverend Thomas Sheepshanks, Rector of St. John's Church, Coventry, and Headmaster of the Free Grammar School.

London

On a week's visit to London (1838), Mary and brother Isaac went to St. Bride's Church on Sunday to hear the Reverend Thomas Dale, whose religious verse Mary Anne knew, and in the afternoon they went to St. Paul's Church where less serious churchgoers upset the girl. When Isaac went to the theater, Mary Anne stayed in her room reading what she bought in a bookstore: *War of the Jews* by Josephus Flavius (Baker 16).

Blasphemous Jew

Back home, Mary Anne attended a concert that displeased her. The elderly organist at St. Michael's Church was being honored with a performance of Haydn's *Creation*, Handel's *Jephtha*, and Felix Mendelssohn's new oratorio, *Paul*, sung by John Braham, a famous tenor from London. Mary Anne Evans thought it was inappropriate to sing holy words in concert, and for sure, sacred New Testament words should not be sung by the Jew, John Braham! She thought that was blasphemous (letter to Maria Lewis, November 6-8, 1838).

Lady of the Manor

Mrs. Charles Newdegate, a philanthropic Evangelical Anglican, feminist, and trustee of the area's dominant 7,000-acre estate, let the future George Eliot use the great library at Arbury Hall. They became friends when Mary Anne helped the lady collect clothes for unemployed ribbon weavers and manage a local circulation library of religious books.

Serious Reading

Mary Anne read a lot of religious books, poems and essays at this time: *Theological Letters* and *A Practical Commentary upon I Peter: 1-2* by Archbishop Leighton; *Schism as Opposed to Unity of the Church* by John Hoppus; *The History of the Church of Christ* by Joseph Milner; *Portrait of an English Churchman* by William Grisley; *The Christian Year* by Keble; *Ancient Christianity* by Isaac Taylor; *Doctrine of the Deluge* by L. Vernon Harcourt; *An Inquiry into the Origin of Christianity* by Charles C. Hennell; *Das Wesen des Christentums* (1841) by Ludwig A. Feuerbach, which Mary Anne would translate—with its disgusting anti-Jewish passages—in 1854 as *The*

Essence of Christianity; *On the Morning of Christ's Nativity*, John Milton's first great English poem; *Childe Harold's Pilgrimage*, which made Lord Byron famous as a poet; and *Holy Living and Holy Dying* by Jeremy Taylor who was called the "Hebraic" writer because he denied original sin. Mary Anne liked the words of Ryland's hymn, "Sovereign Ruler of the Skies" so much that she wrote them down in a letter to share.

Mary Anne became a member of two English mail order religious book clubs: "Ward's Library of Standard Divinity" and "The Christian Family Library."

All the while, she continued to read her King James Christian Bible every day, studying it ever more carefully. She bought a multiple-language Bible and Alexander Cruden's biblical concordance.

Prophecy Scroll

Mary Anne Evans spent months (1839-40) developing a chart of ecclesiastical history from the birth of Jesus to the Protestant Reformation, showing, side by side, the Roman emperors, bishops, important Christians, and Jewish historical events that linked prophecy with prophecy fulfilled. Her father was proud of Mary Anne for the work, even though it was not publishable—similar charts were available.

Poet

When 19 years old, she wrote a religious poem that was published in *The Christian Observer* (January, 1840), signed "M.A.E." The poem was about a dying Christian saying farewell to all the good things on earth: birds, trees, stars and books. But she would not say farewell to her Bible which she would take to heaven with her. The poem was inspired by "Knowing that shortly I must put off this my tabernacle" (1 Peter 1:14) and began with "As O'er the Fields." The stanzas near the end that gave up books but not the Bible read:

> Books, that have been to me as chests of gold,
> Which, miser-like, I secretly have told,
> And for you love, health, friendship, peace, have sold,
> Farewell!

> Blest tome, to thee, whose truth-writ page once known,
> Fades not before heaven's sunshine or hell's moan,
> I say not of God's earthly gifts alone,
> Farewell!

Bird Grove Mansion, Folleshill

In January 1841, her 68-year-old, semi-retired and wealthy father bought a mansion five miles to the south, in the outskirts of Coventry, a ribbon manufacturing city of 30,000, where 22-year-old Mary Anne might have a better chance of getting married. It would be her home until she moved to London ten years later. The family home at Griff that he and Mary

Anne left, he left to his recently married son Isaac.

Mary Anne received Easter Day (1841) Communion with her father at Trinity Church, a mile from the mansion, in the center of Coventry, where they became regular attendants. They would go almost every Sunday morning and return in the evening for another sermon. They sometimes drove to a neighboring town to hear a preacher.

Mary Anne liked being with people. Her extended family alone provided her with lots of conversation and laughter. She frequently visited her old home where lived brother Isaac, his wife Sarah—whose brother was the Reverend Richard Rawlins of Nottinghamshire County—and their four children. Sister Chrissey, her husband and their three children lived five miles to the west. Mary Anne would sometimes borrow a few nieces and nephews for a week at the mansion. Also dear to her were the families of her older half-siblings, as well as her Methodist aunt and uncle who visited several times.

Her reputation as a learned woman spread through Coventry society, leading to friendships with the educated, accomplished gentry who let her use their private libraries.

Among the nice people who befriended Mary Anne Evans were Caroline (Cara) Bray, a Unitarian, whose husband was a successful ribbon manufacturer; Cara's sister, Sara Hennell; and their brother, Charles Christian Hennell, author of a popular book, *An Inquiry into the Origin of Christianity* (1838), whose 1840 translation into German had an introduction by David Friedrich Strauss. Mary Anne Evans' copy was dated January 1, 1842.

Rebel

The next day, Sunday, January 2, 1842, 22-year-old Mary Anne did not go to church. She told her father (letter of February 28, 1842) that while she cherished Jesus, she rejected the doctrines that were built on his life because they were Jewish ideas not pleasing to God. After four months of rebellion, she agreed to conform outwardly and resume going to church with her father.

Her friendship with the freethinking Brays and Hennells grew deeper. With her father's permission, Mary Anne went with them on several vacations. New friends, the Brabants, joined the group. Dr. Brabant, M.D., made it his business to befriend Charles Hennell after reading his book, just as he arranged to meet Strauss in Germany after reading his *Life of Jesus*. Dr. Brabant had a daughter, Rufa.

Charles Hennell fell in love with Rufa Brabant.

Translates Strauss

Some wealthy liberals thought that an English translation of Strauss' book would make a good companion volume to Charles Hennell's *Inquiry*, so they asked Hennell to make the arrangements. Hennell first asked his sister, Sara, if she wanted the job (no, too difficult), then convinced his fiancée, Rufa Brabant, to do it. However, soon after she married Charles (November 3, 1843), Rufa transferred that very time-consuming assignment to Mary Anne Evans.

January 1844

Rufa had a rough translation of the two chapters she had done (up to the magi story) to show Mary Anne. They both went over it together and then the job was Mary Anne's. Sara wrote to Rufa: "It is remarkably difficult, but we both think it very interesting." While on holiday in Germany that summer, Dr. Brabant told Strauss that a young lady was translating his book.

Mary Anne wrote to Mrs. (Cara) Bray, June 18, 1844: "I do not think it was kind to Strauss (I knew that he was handsome) to tell him that a young lady was translating his book. I am sure he must have some twinges of alarm to think he was dependent on that most contemptible specimen of the human being for his English reputation."

Mary Anne translated in a small study connected to her bedroom in the mansion. It was upstairs above the south entrance with a window looking out over meadows, gardens and the church spires of Coventry. On a wall, Mary Anne placed an engraving of French artist Hippolyte Delarouche's *Head of Christ* that was newly popular in English homes. Mary Anne also kept in the study a 20-inch high model of *Risen Christ* by the Danish sculptor, Bertel Thorvaldsen. Those religious items helped her reshape her faith rather than abandon it when Strauss' words successfully challenged her early beliefs. Mary Anne's solution was to accept the symbolic value of the Gospels, for she saw the need to connect with ancestral roots and have guidelines for civilized behavior. This newfound maturity led to respect for Judaism, with its emphasis on roots and behavior—a respect which expressed itself in her novel, *Daniel Deronda* (Redinger 147).

Her plan for the 1,550 pages of condensed German type, was to translate six pages a day within the hours of 9 a.m. and 1 p.m. When Mary Anne finished a batch of pages, she would post it to Sara Hennell for proofreading. Mary Anne weighed every German word and phrase for just the right English word and phrase. Her letters to Sara accompanying the translated pages testify to her meticulous care in creating a faithful English *Life of Jesus*. The following letters quoted are from the John Cross collection published in 1885:

Strauss Letters

● June 13, 1845: "There is one word I must mention,—Azazel is the word put in the original of the Old Testament for the *scape-goat*: now I imagine there is some dubiousness about the meaning, and that Strauss would not think it right to translate *scape-goat*, because, from the tenor of his sentence, he appears to include Azazel with the evil demons. I wonder if it be supposed by any one that Azazel is in any way a distinct being from the goat."

● Probably November, 1845: "Please to tell Mr. Hennell that 'habits of thought' is not a translation of the word *particularismus*. This does not mean national idiosyncrasy, but is a word which characterises that idiosyncrasy. If he decidedly objects to *particularism*, ask him to be so good as substitute *exclusiveness*, though there is a shade of meaning in *particularismus* which even that does not express. It was because the word could only be translated by a circumlocution that I ventured to anglicize it."

● Probably March 1846: "I am not altogether satisfied with the use of the word 'sacrament' as applied specifically to the *Abendmahl*. It seems like a vulgarism to say, *the* sacrament, for one thing, and for another it does not seem *ab*original enough in the life of Jesus; but I know of no other word that can be substituted. I have altered passover to paschal meal, but [Greek word] is used in the New Testament of the eating of the lamb, *par excellence*. You remember in the title of the first section in the Schluss—which I had been so careless as to omit, the expression is 'Nothwendiger Uebergang der Kritik in das Dogma.' Now Dogmatism will not do, as that would represent *Dogmatismus*. 'Dogmatik' is the idea I believe—i.e. positive theology. Is it allowable to say *dogmatics*, think you?"

● January 1, 1846: "I could easily give the meaning of the Hebrew word in question, as I know where to borrow a lexicon. But observe there are two Hebrew words untranslated in this proof. I do not think it will do to give the English in one place and not in another where there is no reason for such a distinction,—and there is not here, for the note in this proof sounds just as fee-fo-fumish as the other without any translation. I could not alter the 'troublesome,' because it is the nearest usable adjective for *schwierig*, which stands in the German. I am tired of inevitable *importance*, and cannot bear to put them when they do not represent the German."

● Probably May 1846: "I will leave the title-page to you and Mr. Hennell. . . . I should like if possible to throw the emphasis on *critically* in the title-page.

Strauss means it to be so. . . . I have written to Mr. Hennell anent the title-page and have voted for *critically examined*, from an entire conviction of its preference."

● November 1846: "The expression 'granite' applied to the sayings of Jesus, is nowhere used by Strauss, but is an impudent addition of mine to eke out his metaphor."

More Strauss Letters

More letters throwing light on Mary Anne's careful translation of Strauss were published by biographer Gordon S. Haight in 1954:

● August 1844: She decides to translate the quotes from the Bible not literally (word for word) from German, but as King James phrases, because the English world was familiar with the latter.

● April 6, 1845: Should she use "finally" or "lastly?" Mary Anne found that "finally" was used by King James in Ephesians 6:10 ("Finally, my brethren, be strong in the Lord . . .") but felt that Strauss' "firstly, secondly, thirdly, fourthly and LASTLY" was better because in the church sermons she remembered, the preacher always used "lastly" in similar series.

● April 6 & 29, 1845: "As if" is interchangeable with "as though," Mary Anne decided.

● December 1845: Should "hellenistische" be translated "Greek" or "Hellenistic?"

● Probably March 1846: She reluctantly picked "The Lord's Supper" over "The Sacrament" because there are many sacraments, even though it is awkward to say that Jesus instituted the Lord's (his own) supper.

● May 20, 1846: She agrees with Sara that "cold-bloodedness" is better than "insensibility."

Discipline

Self-disciplined Mary Anne kept to the translation job for two and a half years (until spring 1846), even though she suffered from headaches and depression. (Strauss' dissection of the crucifixion story had her looking up at the Jesus statue and engraving for solace.)

Besides the German, she translated the numerous Greek, Latin and Hebrew phrases that Strauss used.

While an ordinary reader would skim chapters and skip paragraphs, the translator cannot. Mary Anne stopped at every word, considered every phrase, thought about every idea. No reader of a book gets to know that book as well as the author—except for the translator, especially if the translator is a financially secure 24-year-old, eager to learn and please. When Strauss met Mary Anne, he felt that there was a mystical marriage between them—the author and his lady translator.

Ten years later, in a book review for *The Leader* (Oct. 20, 1855), Mary Anne reflected on the translator's job: "Though a good translator is infinitely below the man who produces good original works, he is infinitely above the man who produces feeble original works. We had meant to say something of the moral qualities especially demanded in the translator—the patience, the rigid fidelity, and the sense of responsibility in interpreting another man's mind."

Strauss' *Life of Jesus* entered her very being and mixed with her other learning experiences that together would make possible the George Eliot fiction to come—those great novels that featured the religious and irreligious.

Recess

Strauss time was not a prison term, for Mary Anne Evans was an intellectual stimulated by Strauss' ideas—and besides, she surrounded herself with other ideas and people during that period when she gave so much to Strauss: The future George Eliot lived one mile from the center of Coventry where she had friends to visit; Her sister Chrissey moved in for a time with her four adorable children; She read to her father from Sir Walter Scott's novels every evening; She taught German every Saturday to the 19-year-old daughter of the Rev. John Sibree, minister of the Independent Chapel in Vicar Lane; May Anne joined the Brays on their vacations—two weeks to the Lake District and a few days to London each summer plus two weeks in Scotland; She went to Birmingham (20 miles away) to attend a performance of Shakespeare's *Julius Caesar*; and in March 1845, she had a flirtation (or love affair) with a young artist who proposed marriage. (She suffered tension headaches afterwards when doubting her decision to reject him.)

Before publication of the finished translation, a sampling was sent to Strauss for his approval, which he gave in exquisite Latin to be used as a preface. Mrs. Cara Bray wrote Sara Hennell (April 19, 1846) that Mary Anne "is delighted beyond measure with Strauss's elegant Preface. It is just what she likes. And what a nice letter too! The Latin is quite beyond me, but the letter shows how neatly he can express himself." Mary Anne wrote to Sara that the preface was "in preconceived harmony with my ideas of the appropriate."

Finally Published: June 15, 1846

The English translation was first published by Chapman Brothers, 121 Newgate Street, London. The printers were George Woodfall and Son, Angel Court,

Skinner Street, London. That first printing was a three-volume set.

Mary Anne Evans' association with John Chapman—the most important publisher of liberal books and journals—was important because it pulled her out of the provincial life she was comfortable in, and in which she might have remained for the rest of her life as old maid aunt, tutor, contributor to the local paper, and translator. Were it not for the Strauss job, she might never have met Chapman.

It was common in those days (1815 to 1890) to publish books in three parts because the owners of private circulating libraries wanted it that way. They were the means of getting books into the hands of the many up-and-coming middle class people who could not afford to buy every book they wanted to read. (Public libraries were rare in England before World War I.) With the "three-decker" method, the library owners only had to buy one-third the number of books they would have needed had each book been complete in one volume, yet they collected three check-out fees by the time the borrower read the whole book. Also, they saved advertising money by only having to promote the first volume of a new novel.

The library owners profited handsomely from George Eliot's masterpiece, *Middlemarch*, by having it issued in eight separate volumes. In that novel, fictional Edward Casaubon is thought to be one of the many D. F. Strauss imitators his *Life of Jesus* brought into being. Young Dorothea Brooke, who fell in love with the older Edward Casaubon, might be a young Mary Anne Evans intellectually stimulated by the brilliant work of Strauss or the older Dr. Brabant who flirted with her.

"Dorothea by this time had looked deep into the ungauged reservoir of Mr. Casaubon's mind, seeing reflected there in vague labyrinthine extension every quality she herself brought, had opened much of her own experience to him, and had understood from him the scope of his great work, also of attractively labyrinthine extent. For he had been as instructive as Milton's 'affable archangel,' and with something of the archangelic manner he told her how he had undertaken to show (what indeed had been attempted before, but not with that thoroughness, justice of comparison, and effectiveness of arrangement at which Mr. Casaubon aimed) that all the mythical systems or erratic mythical fragments in the world were corruptions of a tradition originally revealed. Having once mastered the true position and taken a firm footing there, the vast field of mythical constructions became intelligible, nay, luminous, with the reflected light of correspondences."

"Dorothea was altogether captivated by the wide embrace of this conception. Here was something beyond the shallows of ladies'-school literature; here was a living Bossuet, whose work would reconcile complete knowledge with devoted piety; here was a modern Augustine who united the glories of doctor and saint."
—*Middlemarch*: Book I, chapter 3

Her Early Jewish Connection

Jews were expelled from England in the year 1290 and not officially accepted again until the mid-1600s when they arrived as refugees from the Spanish and Portuguese Inquisitions.

In 1815 there were 17,000 Jews living in London, with 8,000 others living elsewhere in England—together making up only .2% (two-tenths of one percent) of the population. From being secondhand clothes dealers and peddlers of household goods, English Jews of Mary Anne Evans' time had become hat, jewelry, watch, eyeglass and umbrella makers, shopkeepers, sailors, boxers, actors and musicians. For example, Myer Leoni was a famous actor who starred in Richard Sheridan's highly successful comic opera, *Duenna*, playing at Covent Garden Theatre, which closed every Friday evening because Leoni would not perform on his Jewish Sabbath. Leoni took a gifted Jewish choirboy from London's Great Synagogue, John Braham, and trained him to be the leading English tenor and a composer (*The Death of Nelson*).

It was John Braham (1774-1856) who greatly upset a 19-year-old Mary Anne Evans in the audience of St. Michael's Church, Coventry, listening to him sing the lead in Felix Mendelssohn's oratorio, *Paul*. She thought it was blasphemous that the role of St. Paul was given to a Jew, no matter how good he could sing (Haight 1968, 22f; Roth 243f)!

Attending the same concert might have been Abraham Shute, the Jewish owner of a bookstore and pawnshop in Coventry for 58 years. Mary Anne might have exchanged greetings with him, since she patronized book sellers. Another sign of the Jewish presence close to young Mary Anne came when she was 16 years old, and the local newspaper carried the obituary notice of a 108-year-old Coventry resident: Isaac Cohen (Baker 14f).

There was a major Jewish community in Birmingham, 20 miles from Coventry, which was founded in 1730 as a base for the Jewish peddlers servicing the countryside. When the inquisitive Mary Anne visited London, she might have noticed the presence of the 17,000 Jews living there, and read their paper, *The Jewish Chronicle*, which began publishing in 1841.

During the time she was translating Strauss, Mary Anne read *Coningsby*, the new political novel by Benjamin Disraeli that had fictional Sidonia glorify "the Jewish mind . . . the living Hebrew intellect" (Book IV, chapter 15).

When she was 28 years old, Mary Anne wrote to John Sibree Jr. (February 11, 1848): "Almost all their

[Jewish] history is utterly revolting. . . . Everything specifically Jewish is of a low grade."

Hebs fascinated Brits

English people held Hebrew Scriptures in the highest esteem which coincided with a widespread Evangelical revival. The Ten Lost Tribes went to England and Jesus would soon return, it was thought. English names were unashamedly Hebrew—George Eliot had seven of her Christian characters christened "Jacob."

A respect for living Hebrews went along with the trend. Jews were the People of the Holy Book. Their independent Jewish Kingdom would be restored—once the Jews repented sufficiently, to which end the *Society for Promoting Christianity Among the Jews* was founded.

The used clothing trade that English Jews were associated with before the industrial revolution, was respected as a necessary service, for new clothing was custom-made for the wealthy, whose castoffs clothed the working people who would pass their worn-out garments to the poor, so that clothes would have several wearers in true "trickle down" fashion until the items finally fell apart, to be bought and sold again as rags. Jews were the distributors who made it happen. They bought and resold the items and walked the rural counties to clothe the whole nation.

Continental anti-Semites would condescendingly explain greater British tolerance by commenting that the English and the Jews were both nations of small tradesmen proud of their common calling (Poliakov, chapter 9).

It helps when Jewish respectability is approved at the top, and England's top helped: The story got out that when King George III reviewed the East London list of new recruits to fight Napoleon, he asked why so many had animal first names (Wolf, Lion, Bear, et al) and was told it was a Jewish custom. The Duke of Sussex—one of King George's adult sons—studied Hebrew, built a library of Jewish books and supported Jewish causes. Sussex brought his brothers, the Royal Highnesses, the Dukes of Cumberland and Cambridge, to a Friday evening Sabbath service in London's Great Synagogue in April, 1809 (Roth 243).

English literature portrayed Jews in a friendly way. Sir Walter Scott's *Ivanhoe* had a Jewish heroine, Rebecca, daughter of Isaac. Two English translations of Lessing's *Nathan the Wise* were longtime favorites, and a 35-year-old George Eliot attended an original language performance in Berlin that made her cry and change her prejudiced opinion of Jews and Judaism (letter to Charles Bray, Nov. 12, 1854). Later, she would create *Daniel Deronda* with its Jewish heroes, heroines, and plea for a national homeland—

20 years before Theodor Herzl thought to do it. The novel was published as the young scholar, James Balfour, entered Parliament.

The English looked at their neighbor's religion as being either Church of England or not, and since the "not" lumped together Catholics, Jews, Baptists and other Dissenters, then the Jews did not stick out. When the Catholic Emancipation Act of 1829 passed (Mary Anne was nine), it helped all non-Anglicans.

Future Look

1846: Strauss was translated anonymously (Mary Anne was 27).

1854: first meeting with Strauss; translates Feuerbach's *The Essence of Christianity* as "Marian Evans" and was given credit in print as the translator of Strauss.

1857: her nom de plume (pen name), "George Eliot" first used.

1858: *Scenes of a Clerical Life*, which greatly pleased Queen Victoria, in 2 volumes; second (last) meeting with Strauss.

1859: *Adam Bede* in 3 volumes (her identity was revealed).

1860: *The Mill on the Floss* (George Eliot was 41).

1861: *Silas Marner: The Weaver of Raveloe*.

1863: *Romola* in 3 volumes.

1872: *Middlemarch: A Study in Provincial Life* in 8 volumes.

1876: *Daniel Deronda* in 4 volumes.

1880: George Eliot died at 61.

Bibliography

Baker, William, *George Eliot and Judaism*, chapter 2. Salzburg Studies in English Literature. Salzburg (Austria): Univ of S. Press, 1975.

Cross, John W., arranger and editor, *George Eliot's Life as Related in her Letters and Journals*. 1885 original reprinted, NY: AMS Press, 1965.

Dodd, Valerie A., *George Eliot: An Intellectual Life*. NY: St. Martin's Press, 1990.

Haight, Gordon S., *George Eliot: A Biography*. NY: Oxford Univ Press, 1968.

Haight, Gordon S., editor, *The George Eliot Letters*, volume I. New Haven: Yale Univ Press, 1954.

Laski, Marghanita, *George Eliot*. NY: Thames and Hudson (Literary Lives Series), 1973.

Redinger, Ruby V., *George Eliot: The Emergent Self*. NY: Alfred A. Knopf, 1975.

Roberts, Neil, *George Eliot: Her Beliefs and Her Art*. Pittsburgh: Univ of P. Press, 1975.

Roth, Cecil, *A History of the Jews of England*. Oxford: O. Univ Press, 1941, 1964 (3rd edition).

Taylor, Ina, *A Woman of Contradictions: The Life of George Eliot*. NY: William Morrow, 1989.

(continued from page "j")

older; (17) seekers of truth; (18) logical thinkers; (19) happy in company of others—very sociable; (20) loved writing letters—over 2,000 from Strauss and almost 2,000 from George Eliot extant; (21) lived off inheritances and royalties; (22) questioned Christianity of childhood; (23) carefully studied Christian criticism; (24) loved music; (25) wrote poetry; (26) Lessing's *Nathan der Weise* a favorite; (27) she spent years reading and translating his book; (28) he wrote and she translated the book in small rooms with windows overlooking the countryside; (29) his Germany was her favorite foreign country; (30) brilliantly suited to be university professors, but neither were; (31) bluntly critical of what they thought wrong; (32) both were 26 years old when working on the great book.

THE LIFE OF JESUS

THE

LIFE OF JESUS

CRITICALLY EXAMINED

BY

DR. DAVID FRIEDRICH STRAUSS

Translated from the Fourth German Edition

By GEORGE ELIOT

SECOND EDITION. IN ONE VOLUME

ARDVA·QVÆ·PVLCRA

London
SWAN SONNENSCHEIN & CO.
NEW YORK: MACMILLAN & CO.
1892

BUTLER & TANNER,
THE SELWOOD PRINTING WORKS,
FROME, AND LONDON.

INTRODUCTION

TO THE PRESENT EDITION,

BY PROFESSOR OTTO PFLEIDERER, D.D.

———

THE *Leben Jesu* of David Friedrich Strauss, which was published in the year 1835, marked an epoch in the history of theology. On the one hand, this book represents the crisis in theology at which the doubts and critical objections of centuries as to the credibility of the Bible narratives had accumulated in such overwhelming volume as to break through and sweep away all the defences of orthodox apologetics. On the other hand, in the very completeness of the destructive criticism of past tradition lay the germs of a new science of constructive critical inquiry, the work of which was to bring to light the truth of history. It is quite true that the *Life of Jesus* of 1835 was far from perfect, as judged by the present standard of scientific criticism, and Biblical science has long since advanced beyond it. Nevertheless, it cannot be disputed that it takes rank amongst the standard works which are secure of a permanent place in literature for all time, for the reason that they give final expression to the spirit of their age, and represent typically one of its characteristic tendencies. The liberating and purifying influence which such works exert

on their own time, as well as the service they
render in opening out new lines of thought, lends
to them, for all coming generations, a peculiar value
as admirable weapons in the great fight for truth
and freedom.   Indeed, if our scientists are to be
believed, when they tell us that the development
of the individual is only an abbreviated repetition
of the similar but much slower phases of the
development of the species, it is hardly too much
to maintain, that in the present and in the future
every individual who determines to make his way
from the bondage of a naïve trust in authority and
tradition into the freedom and light of mature
thought must pass through precisely that stage of
thorough-going logical negative criticism which is
represented by Strauss's work in a unique manner.
As, according to Christian ethics, the formation of
a pure moral character is possible only by the death
of the old Adam, the rise of true religious convictions is by a similar *Stirb und werde*, die and
come to life.   The imaginary lights of mythological
tradition must be put out, that the eye may distinguish the false from the true in the twilight of the
Biblical origins of our religion.   The ancient struc-
tures of belief, which the childish fancy of men had
constructed of truth and poetry, *Wahrheit und
Dichtung*, must be taken down and cleared away, in
order that a new erection of more durable materials
may be raised.   To all earnest seekers after truth,
the *Leben Jesu* of Strauss may be helpful, not as
supplying the truth ready to hand, but as stripping
the bandages of prejudice from the eyes, and so
enabling them clearly to see and rightly to seek it.

For these reasons it is obvious that the publication of a new edition of the English translation of

this work needs no justification. It is only those
who consider the first appearance of the book inexcusable and unfortunate that can call in question
the desirability of its republication. But no one
can hold such an opinion who is able to follow the
course of the history of the religious thought of
Protestantism. The critical process which reached
its conclusion in Strauss's book, with its negative or
revolutionary results, was latent from the beginning
in the life-blood of Protestantism. The theologians
of the Reformed Churches of the sixteenth century
subjected the traditions of Catholic Church history
to keen historical criticism; and if they did not then
think of extending its operations to Biblical tradition, we are justified in recognising in the well-
known declarations of Luther, as to the inferior
value of certain books of the Bible, and as to the
unimportance of physical in comparison with spiritual
miracles, plain predictions of the line of development which Protestant theology was destined
ultimately to take.

It is intelligible enough that the criticism of the
Bible could not arise amongst the orthodox theologians of the sixteenth and seventeenth centuries.
They were restrained by a rigid doctrine of inspiration from an unprejudiced treatment of the Bible,
and were moreover too much absorbed in dogmatic
controversies and the defence of their confessions of
faith, to feel the need of more searching Biblical
studies. It was amongst English Free-thinkers and
Deists that the credibility of the Biblical narratives
was first seriously assailed, and with so much tem-
per as to greatly detract from the scientific value of
the result. Thomas Woolston's *Discourses on the
Miracles of our Saviour* (six in number, 1727–1729)

are specially noteworthy. They attack the literal
interpretation of the miracles as ludicrous and offensive, and advocate the allegorical interpretation of
them as figures and parables of spiritual truths.
It is possible to find in Woolston's theory an anticipation of the mythical principle of interpretation which Strauss opposes to the rationalistic one.
Reimarus, the author of the Wolfenbüttel Fragments, by the publication of which Lessing threw
German theology into a ferment, occupies the same
position as the English Deists, and indeed owed
much to their influence. But at the same time a
noteworthy difference is observable from the very
first between the way in which Lessing treated
these questions and their treatment by the earlier
Free-thinkers; and the difference is characteristic
of the two schools. German rationalism bears the
marks of its origin in the idealistic optimism of the
philosophy of Leibnitz and Wolff, and remains in
sympathy with the ethical spirit of Biblical religion;
whilst the but faintly religious naturalism of the
English Deists leads them, with their rejection of
the Biblical miracles, to attack the religion of the
Bible, and drag down into the mire its representa-
tives and heroes. With this the German Rationalists have no sympathy. They were unable to treat
the Biblical narratives of miracles as historical occurrences, but they were not prepared on that account
to regard them as deceit and delusion on the part of
Biblical heroes, or as the invention of Biblical narrators: their reverence for the Bible and its religion
kept them from both of these inferences. They
tried to get over the difficulty in two ways,—either
they looked upon the narratives of miracles, particularly those of the Old Testament, as popular reli-

gious legends, traditions, or "myths," of the same
kind as the myths to be met with in all heathen
religions ; or, on the other hand, regarding them as
containing the actual history of perfectly natural
events, they ascribed the miraculous appearance
and form which they bear simply to the mistaken
judgment of the narrators, or, in other cases, to
the erroneous view of the interpreters. The latter
method was employed especially by Dr. Paulus in
his commentary on the Gospels, in which he seeks,
with a great display of learning and ingenuity, to
explain all the miracles of the New Testament.
The theologian Schleiermacher also made frequent
use of it in his *Lectures on the Life of Jesus ;* and
traces of it are to be met with even in the commentaries of theologians of the supernaturalist school—
as, for instance, Olshausen's. The inexcusable violence which was thereby done to the Biblical narratives, by which they are forced to say something
quite different from what the unsophisticated narrators intended them to say, according to the plain
sense of their words, was not felt ; nor were these
interpreters conscious of how much the Gospels are
deprived of their choicest treasures of ideal truth
and poetic beauty by this method of treatment, and
this only for the sake of securing instead miserable
common-place stories as the final outcome of
critical examination.

The favour with which this radically false rationalistic interpretation of the Gospels was received by
very many German theologians at the beginning of
this century finds its sole explanation and excuse
in the prevailing view of the time—that our Gospels
were written very soon after the death of Jesus,
during the first generation of Christians, and two of

them by eye-witnesses—the apostles Matthew and John. On this supposition, the occurrence in the Gospels of unhistorical elements, of religious legends, such as might be without hesitation allowed in the Old Testament, could not be thought of. Or if the admissibility of this point of view was granted in the case of the birth-stories of the opening chapters of Matthew and Luke (as by De Wette), objection was felt against its application to the miracles of the public life of Jesus. Thus, on the question of the historicity of the gospel narratives, theologians held views which were confused, undecided, contradictory, and lacking thoroughness. This state of things could not last; simple faith had at every point lost its security; doubt attached to the miraculous narratives of the New no less than to those of the Old Testament. But before Strauss no one had had the courage to explain all these narratives of both Testaments alike by the logical application of one and the same principle; and mainly for the reason, that the critics were all under the bondage of the supposition of the apostolic authorship of the Gospels of Matthew and John. Yet even this supposition had received various shocks prior to Strauss. Critics had been unable to close their eyes to the fact that there are differences between these two Gospels particularly, of such a fundamental nature as to preclude the possibility of both being right, and therefore of both having been written by eye-witnesses and apostles. Under the influence of dogmatic and sentimental motives, Schleiermacher and his disciples accepted it as an *a priori* certainty that John is to be preferred to Matthew; and from this secure position, as was imagined, these theologians assailed the narrative of Matthew at all points, and undermined the tradition of its apostolic authority. But suppose the same arguments with which they assailed Matthew might be used against their favourite evangelist John? What if it could be shown that his narrative is in no respect more probable, but, on the contrary, more improbable, than that of Matthew? In that case, must not the critical verdict which those theologians had given against Matthew so triumphantly and without regard to its consequences, apply equally to John, and thereby overthrow the only remaining pillar of apostolic authority for the gospel tradition?

This logical consequence, which was at the time deemed an unheard-of innovation, notwithstanding the opinions of a few individual critics (Vogel, Bretschneider), Strauss had the courage to draw. By that act he cast off the fetters by which the examination of the Gospels had till then been bound, and secured a free field for a thorough-going criticism of them. Since the external evidence of the authorship of the Gospels is not of a kind or a date such as to compel us to consider the tradition of their apostolic origin established, and as the matter of all the Gospels alike is not free from historical improbability, there is nothing, Strauss argued, to prevent our complete abandonment of the historicity of their miraculous narratives, though the Rationalists continue to maintain it, or our treating them as religious legends or myths, similar to those which, as was admitted, the Old Testament contained. The novelty in the work of Strauss was not the application of the principle of "myth" to Biblical narratives; others had already made use of it in the case of the Old and to some extent in the case of the New Testament; the originality lay in the uncompromising

thoroughness with which the principle was applied
to every section of the gospel story ; the originality
lay in the merciless acumen and clearness with
which the discrepancies between the Gospels and
the difficulties presented to the critical understanding by their narratives were laid bare, and with
which all the subterfuges of supernaturalist apologists, as well as all the forced and artificial interpretations of semi-critical Rationalists, were exposed,
thereby cutting off all ways of escape from the final
consequences of criticism.

The merciless thoroughness and unreserved
honesty with which criticism did its negative work
in this book, by exposing the baselessness of the
supposed knowledge of the gospel history, produced a profound shock amongst theologians and
laymen. It was not merely the untaught multitude
who believed that the foundations of Christianity
must perish with the miraculous stories of the Bible;
learned theologians were distressed as the daring
critic so rudely, and without any regard to consequences, roused them from the illusions of their sentimental or speculative dogmatism and their precipi-
tate treaty of peace between faith and knowledge.
"Strauss was hated," as Baur truly said, " because the
spirit of the time was unable to look upon its own
portrait, which he held up before it in faithful, clearly
drawn lines. The spirit of this age resists with all
its power the proof of its ignorance on a matter about
which it has long thought itself certain. Instead of
acknowledging what had to be acknowledged, if any
progress was to be made, all possible attempts were
instituted to create fresh illusions as to the true state
of the case, by reviving obsolete hypotheses and by
theological charlatanism. But a higher certainty as

to the truth of the gospel history can be attained in
no other way than by acknowledging, on the basis
of Strauss's criticism, that our previous knowledge is
no knowledge at all." But here we come upon the
limits of the criticism of Strauss : it brought home to
men the fact of their want of knowledge, but it did
not conduct to the required new and positive knowledge. This Strauss was unable to do, because he
offered a critique of the gospel history only, without
a critique of the *documents* which form the *sources*
of this history.

In these words Baur has accurately described the
main defect of Strauss's book. When Strauss drew
from the discrepancies and contradictions of the
various narratives of the Gospels the conclusion that
they have all alike little credibility, the conclusion
was intelligible enough in reply to the ingenious
artifices of the traditional harmonists, who maintained that in spite of the contradictions the evangelists were all alike worthy of credit; but really
this line of procedure on the part of Strauss conformed as little as that of the harmonists to the
principles of strict historical inquiry. These principles require us to examine the relative value of
the various sources with reference to their age, to
the situation, the character, the interests, and aims
of their author; to assign accordingly to one account
a higher measure of credibility than to another ; and
so, by distinguishing between what is better and
what is not so well attested, to make out what is
probable and reach the original matter of fact. It
is true Strauss made some advance towards such
a differentiation of the relative value of the gospel
narratives ; and particularly with reference to the
inferior historical value of the Johannine in com-

parison with the Synoptic narrative, he has made
acute observations, the worth of which ought to be
estimated the higher as they boldly opposed the
then dominant preference for the Gospel of John,
and effectively prepared the way for the criticism of
Baur.   But it was not Strauss's *forte* to prepare, as
the foundation of the material critique of the gospel
history, a thorough critique of the literary sources,
nor, in the state of the general science of criticism
at the time, could this be very well expected. When
all deductions have been made, to Strauss belongs
the honour of having given, by his criticism of the
gospel narratives, the most effective impulse to a
more penetrating examination of the sources of the
gospel story, and of having prepared the way for
this to no small extent, particularly as regards the
Fourth Gospel.   Baur's classical critique of this
Gospel completed in this direction the criticism of
Strauss, and laid its foundations deeper.   As regards the Synoptic Gospels, Weisse and Ewald,
Holtzmann and Volkmar, did good work towards
clearing up the relations of the Gospels to each
other, especially in establishing the priority of
Mark, by which a firmer basis was laid for the
positive decision of the question as to the historical
foundations of the gospel tradition.   The fruit of
this critique of the sources, carried on from various
sides with painstaking industry, was the new literature dealing with the life of Jesus, which, just a
generation after the first *Leben Jesu* of Strauss,
took up again the problems it had raised, but in a
new fashion, and with improved critical apparatus.
We shall have further on to refer to Strauss's new
life of Jesus.

The same scholar, Weisse, who was the first to

point out the want in Strauss's book of a more
satisfactory critique of the sources, and who had
sought to supply this defect in his *Evangelische
Geschichte* (1838), called attention at the same time
to a defect in the mythical theory of Strauss.
Weisse was fully agreed with Strauss so far, that
we must acknowledge the presence of religious
myths in miraculous narratives of the Bible, but he
was not satisfied with the way in which Strauss had
explained their origin. According to Strauss, the
early Christians had simply transferred to Jesus as
the actual Messiah the miraculous legends of the
Old Testament, out of which the Jews were supposed to have composed the miraculous portrait of
their expected Messiah; and he was right in thinking that the miraculous stories of the Old Testament do undoubtedly supply the motives and models
of no few narratives in the New Testament, but
not, surely, of *all*. Precisely the chief miracles—
the birth of Jesus, his baptism, transfiguration,
resurrection, the change of water into wine at Cana,
the stilling of the storm, and walking on the sea—
violence must be used to explain these miracles by
reference to Old Testament types, and the Jewish
idea of the Messiah offers no lines corresponding
to these. At this point therefore, at all events, we
must look about us for another method of explanation. And Weisse was undoubtedly right in point-
ing to the spontaneous productivity of the Christian
spirit in the primitive Church as the source of the
miraculous narratives, in which it gave expression
in symbolic and allegorical forms to its ideal truth
and the new inspired life of which it was conscious.
Not that these narratives were intended by the
narrators themselves to be merely allegories, or

symbolical illustrations of spiritual truths; but the religious imagination gave birth to these illustrations after the manner of unconscious poetry, that is, without distinguishing between the poetic form and the essential truth of the idea; believing, as the religious imagination did, in the ideal content of the narratives, and being at the same time unable to give vivid and sensible expression to it in any other than the material form of outward miracles, it involuntarily came to believe also in the reality of the symbolical form of the narrative to which it had itself given rise; it conceived idea and history both together in such inseparable combination as to confer on each equal truth and certainty.

In the production of such ideal narratives the same process is observable to-day in the experience of simple religious believers: feeling the ideal truth of the content of the stories, they come to believe also in the reality of the outward history in which the idea has for them been incorporated. But the critical understanding of the historical inquirer is permitted, and indeed is bound, to distinguish clearly and definitely, as the simple-minded believer cannot do, between the spiritual idea and the outward form of its representation, and to find in the former both the productive power and the permanent kernel within the outward husk. This explanation of the miraculous legends of the Bible is not only more correct and profound than Strauss's from the point of view of historical science, but for the religious consciousness it is far less objectionable, as Weisse observes with truth; inasmuch as in this case the legends do not appear as the worthless product of the idle play of the imagination, but as the normal expression, rationally and psychologically intelligible, of a creative religious spirit, which displays its treasures of ideal truth in this legendary and mythical poetry for the benefit of the originators and the wider world. Nor should it be left unnoticed that Strauss himself had already indicated in a few cases this more profound explanation of myths by means of the religious idea. At the close of his interpretation of the story of the Transfiguration (§ 107), for instance, he says, we may see from this example very plainly how the natural system of explanation, by insisting on the historical certainty of the narratives, lets go their ideal truth, sacrificing the content to the form of the story, whereas the mythical interpretation, by resigning the historical material body of such narratives, really rescues and preserves their idea, their soul and spirit. He might, however, have unfolded the idea of the Transfiguration with greater definiteness and fulness if he had not merely alluded to the dogmatic discussion of Paul in 2 Cor. iii. 7 sq., but had recognised it as the real theme of the gospel story, and had interpreted the latter accordingly. In the same way, in the case of the story of the birth of Jesus (Luke i. and ii.), Strauss laid great emphasis on the analogies and figures of the Old Testament, which, after all, could only contribute as secondary motives in the formation of this birth-story, while its real origin is to be sought in the Pauline Messianic idea of "the Son of God, according to the spirit of holiness" (Rom. i. 4; 1 Cor. xv. 45 sq.), a fact Strauss overlooked. This defect takes a really surprising form when he comes to explain the miracles of the Fourth Gospel, which, in complete independence of any suggestion from the Old Testament, are entirely based upon the dogmatic ideas of the Alexandrian theology, and simply supply their transparent symbolic vestment. How much more truthfully and profoundly can the miracle at Cana, or the raising of Lazarus, or the cure of the man born blind, be interpreted from this point of view than from that of Strauss ! In this respect Baur's interpretation of the Fourth Gospel was an immense advance beyond Strauss, as the latter himself acknowledged subsequently.

With the above defects of Strauss's method of interpretation is connected, in the last place, the fact that the outcome of his book in reference to the decisive question,—What, then, is the historical kernel of the evangelical tradition, what the real character of Jesus and of his work ?—is meagre and unsatisfactory. In the closing essay at the end of his work, it is true, he endeavoured to restore dogmatically what he had destroyed critically, but he effected this in a way which amounted to the transformation of religious faith in Christ into a metaphysical allegory. The predications of faith with regard to Christ are to be regarded as containing predications as to the relations of the human race to the Absolute, as to the self-abasement of the Infinite to the Finite, and the return of the Infinite to itself, as to mind and its power over nature, and its dependence on it, and the like. In all this Strauss was led astray by the influence of the Hegelian philosophy, which looked for the truth of religion in logical and metaphysical categories instead of in the facts and experiences of moral feeling and volition. But as there is no essential relation between these metaphysical ideas and the person of Jesus, he is made arbitrarily, as any one else might have been, an illustration and example of absolute ideas to which he stands in no more intimate relation than the rest of the human race ; whereby the special historical importance of the originator of the Christian community, and of the first model of its religious and moral life, is not only left without explanation, but is lost altogether, a result which does violence not merely to the religious consciousness, but is unsatisfactory to historical science, which is concerned to understand Jesus as the originating source of Christianity. It is quite true that we can go with Strauss in his answer to the alternative of Ullmann whether the church created the Christ of the Gospels or he the church, by declaring the alternative false, and the two things in so far both tenable as the Christ of the Gospels is a creation of the faith of the church, but this faith an effect of the person of the historical Jesus. We find this answer to Ullmann just, but cannot free Strauss from the charge of having worked out in his book the first only of these two positions, and of having passed over the second. He has shown no more than that the church formed the mythical traditions about Jesus out of its faith in him as the Messiah. But how did the church come by the faith that Jesus of Nazareth was the Messiah ? To *this* question— which is the main question of a Life of Jesus— Strauss gave his readers no answer. Undoubtedly it can be urged in his defence that the criticism of the sources was at that time still in a condition of too great confusion and uncertainty to permit any successful answer to that problem of the historical kernel of the life of Jesus. Nevertheless the difficulty of the matter could not relieve the historian of the duty of at least making an attempt to trace from the materials left to him, as the residue of his critical analysis of the deeds and words of Jesus, the

main outlines of his character, to bring out the pecu-
liarity and originality of his religious genius, and in
this way to discover in the original personality and
reforming activity of Jesus the originating cause of
the rise of the community of his disciples and their
faith in him as the Messiah and his divine mission. If in his closing essay Strauss had presented
a religious and moral description of Jesus of this
nature, instead of a metaphysical allegory as a substitute for the shattered mythological conception of
tradition, though the objection of the church to his
work would not have been wanting, it would then
undoubtedly have taken a less passionately denun-
ciatory form than was the case, in consequence of the
purely negative character of the result, unrelieved
by any modifying conclusion.

In proportion to the strength of the feeling of
these defects, shared by readers of all parties, was
the urgency of the duty laid upon scientific theologians of preparing, by a renewed and more thorough
examination of the Gospels, the stones of a new
edifice to be reared upon the site laid bare by
Strauss's critical labours. " In the darkness which
criticism produces, by putting out all the lights
hitherto thought to be historical, the eye has first
to learn by gradual habit to again distinguish a few
single objects," as Strauss himself remarked in his
third edition. But this difficult task was not accomplished by those apologists who endeavoured to
make good the damage by the antiquated arts of
the harmonists, with their petty concessions, mysti-
fications, and evasions, but by those courageous in-
quirers who, undeterred by dogmatic considerations,
sought by a strictly historical method to set in the
true light the exact composition and the mutual re-

lations of the evangelical documents. We have
already remarked that Baur and his disciples, the
so-called Tübingen school, took a leading part in
this work, while other independent students co-
operated with them, supplementing and correcting
their labours. This, however, is not the place to
follow these inquiries in detail; but we must glance
at their result as regards the historical treatment
of the life of Jesus.

For an entire generation the examination of the
literary details of the Gospels had occupied theologians so exclusively that the interest in the
supreme problems of the evangelical history seemed
to have been almost lost sight of. But this interest
was newly awakened, and made itself felt far beyond
learned theological circles, by the nearly simul-
taneous publication of Renan's *Vie de Jésus* and
Strauss's second *Leben Jesu für das deutsche Volk*
(1864). These two works, with all their dissimi-
larity, resemble each other in this, that they were
both written by scholars of the highest eminence,
not for the learned world, but for educated people
generally, both throwing overboard, therefore, the
ballast of learned detailed criticism, and presenting the results of their inquiries in a language
intelligible to everybody, and attractive from its
literary excellence. They are alike also in this,
that both subordinate the criticism of the gospel
traditions to a positive description of the personality
of Jesus, of his essential religious tendency and
genius, of his relation to the Messianic idea of his
nation, to the law and the temple, to the hierarchy
and religious and political parties of his time, both
seeking an explanation of the reformatory success
of the commencement, and also of the tragical issue

of his labours in these factors. But inasmuch as
Strauss confines himself to what he can deem the
ascertained or probable facts, after a strict critique
of the sources, the portrait delineated by him turns
out naturally somewhat indistinct and defective in
its outlines ; the meagreness of the result answers to
the caution of his historical conscience. Renan, on
the other hand, feels no such scruples ; in his criticism of the sources he goes to work with a much
lighter heart, and claims for the biographer the
right to help himself over the *lacunæ* and obscuri-
ties or contradictions of his authorities by calling in
the aid of the creative imagination, with its powers
of combination and inference. By this means he
has succeeded in presenting a life of Jesus distinguished for its epic vividness and dramatic development, but its æsthetic charm has been purchased at
the price of its historical solidity. This novelistic
feature becomes most questionable when it wanders
into the vagaries of the naturalistic explanation of
the miracles (*e.g.* the raising of Lazarus), and in
such cases casts reflections on the moral character
of Jesus. On the other hand, for Renan must be
claimed the merit of having emphasised the social
aspects of the Messianic mission of Jesus, and of
having attempted to sketch the development of his
inner life, a change in the phases of his reformatory
labours. As to Strauss's second Life of Jesus, its
strength lies, as in the first, not so much in the first
part, which deals with the positive side of the history,
as in the second part, where it comes to treat of the
mythical side of the history. But in the second
work, in the place of the analysis of the traditions
given in the first, we get a synthetic presentation of
the rise and gradual growth and elaboration, in

more and more exalted forms, of the idea of the Christ of mythical tradition ; the successive stages of the development of the Christian consciousness are set forth by reference to the genesis of the ideas of Christ's person, power, and supernatural exaltation. Thus this genetic method of treatment, followed in the later work, supplants and confirms the result of the former one ; while the latter had shown that the miraculous narratives in the Gospels are myth and not history, the new Life shows how in these myths, after all, history is reflected, namely, the history of the religious consciousness of the Christian community. The great advance of this new treatment upon that of the previous work was the fruit of the intervening studies of Baur and his disciples, to which Renan, to the detriment of the critical and historical value of his work, had not paid sufficient attention.

The two works of Renan and Strauss were followed by a deluge of literature on the life of Jesus, the historical value of which is very various. To give an account of all these books would require more space than is at my disposal. I must confine myself to the work of Theodor Keim, an English translation of which has been published under the " Theological Translation Fund." The work is so distinguished by the richness of its learned material, and the ability with which it is handled, as to constitute it the best representation of the present condition of our knowledge of the life of Jesus. Keim's standpoint differs from that of Strauss by the warmth of religious feeling and enthusiasm which pervades his entire work, while at the same time no fetters are laid upon the critical reason ; freedom and piety join hands, in order to be just to the

double claim which the truth of history on the one
hand, and the church on the other, are justified in
presenting. The most brilliant part of Keim's work
is his delineation of the religious personality of
Jesus,—how in it were combined, in a unique degree, strength and harmony, complete openness
towards the world, with perfect inwardness towards
God, so as to become the source of a new religion,
in which self-surrender and liberty, humility and
energy, enthusiasm and lucidity, are blended, and
the chasm of previous ages between God and man
filled up. His description of the psychological
development of the Messianic consciousness of
Jesus out of inward experiences and outward impressions and impulses, is also drawn with great
delicacy of touch; at all events, it is an able and
suggestive effort to penetrate, as far as the state of
the sources admits, by means of sympathetic and
reproductive divination, to the personal experiences and mental states of the religious genius from
whom a new epoch in the world's religious history
proceeded. Still, as in the kindred efforts of Renan,
Weizsäcker, Beyschlag and Weiss, we may never
forget how much, with the poverty of the ascertained historical materials, is left to the uncontrolled
power of combination and divination; in other
words, to the imagination, which at best can do no
more than roughly and approximately arrive at the
truth, while it may no less easily go far astray. It
is certainly to be deemed an advance that in the
more recent works on the life of Jesus the subject of
main interest is not so much the external miracles
as the internal, the problems of the peculiar nature
and development of his religious consciousness and
character, his view of his vocation, his attitude towards

the Messianic idea, and the like. Yet this advance is manifestly attended by the temptation to sacrifice the caution of historical criticism to the production of a biography as rich in detail and as dramatic in movement as possible, and to represent things as the ascertained results of critical examination, which are really nothing more than subjective combinations of the writers, to which a certain degree of probability may be attached, though the possibility will always remain, that the actual facts were something quite different. The subtle examination of the question, whether Jesus himself ever declared himself to be the Messiah, or spoke of his return in celestial glory, by Martineau, in his *Seat of Authority in Religion*, is in this respect deserving of all attention, and is of great value, as at least supplying a needed lesson in caution in view of the excessive confidence with which questions such as these have been treated by Renan, Keim, and later writers. In any case, the reserve and caution of Strauss are quite justified as a corrective and counterpoise to the extravagances committed in the opposite direction.

With regard to the miraculous narratives of the Gospels, the advance of more recent criticism beyond the first book of Strauss has been in two directions. First, these questions no longer constitute the central point of historical interest, but are subordinated in importance to the problems of the religious consciousness of Jesus. Secondly, we do not now seek to interpret these narratives so exclusively and without distinction from the one motive of the transference to Jesus of the types of the Old Testament; but the great difference between the various narratives of miracles is clearly recognised, and various

clues are accordingly used in their explanation;
whilst in one narrative we observe merely symbols of
religious and dogmatic ideas, in others we discover,
behind the glorifying tendency to idealism, some
background of historical fact, for instance, in the
miracles of healing, as is now very generally acknowledged. It cannot be denied, it is true, that with
this perfectly legitimate endeavour is connected the
peril of falling back into the old abuses of rationalistic artifice. Even Keim has not quite escaped
this danger, inasmuch as he abandons the basis of
strict history in the case of the story of the resurrection of Jesus, and makes concessions to super-
naturalistic dogma; as the sequel of which the old
doctrine of miracles may be readmitted into Lives
of Jesus, as is really the case in the works of
Beyschlag and Weiss.

In this danger appears the necessity for the continued prosecution of the negative work of criticism, a duty as yet by no means supererogatory.
The inclination to sink into the slumber of dogma is
so natural to every generation that the most uncompromising critical intellect must without intermission
stand upon the watch against it. And as this task
was performed by Strauss in his first Life of Jesus
in a manner that may serve as a model for all time,
the book, like every truly classical work, must ever
retain its value. Strauss's criticism broke down the
ramparts of dogmatism, new and old, and opened
to the inquiring mind the breach through which the
conquest of historical truth might be won.

OTTO PFLEIDERER.

CERTIOR factus ex Britannia, librum meum, quem de vita Jesu XI abhinc annis composui, virorum ejusmodi studiis faventium cura in linguam Britannicam translatum, brevi illic in publicum proditurum esse, lælitia anxietate temperata commoveor.

Nam ut gratulari sibi æquum est auctorem, cujus operi contigit, patriæ terræ ac linguæ fines transgredi, ita sollicitudo eundem subeat necesse est, ne, qui domi placuit liber, foris displiceat, aut cujus inter populares vel adversariorum numero creverat auctoritas, apud exteros neglectus in obscuro maneat. Solum enim cœlumque vix minore libri quam plantæ periculo mutant. Et facilius quidem transtuleris opera in illis rebus versantia, de quibus inter diversas gentes communis quidam aut certe parum discrepans sensus obtinet : ut, quæ poetæ aut disciplinarum quas exactas dicunt periti proferunt, inter politiores hujus seculi nationes fere solent esse communia. Neque tamen vel hoc in librorum genere plane æquum Germano cum Britannis aut Gallis certamen. Peregrina enim cum facilius nostra quam illorum et lingua et indoles recipiat, longe frequentius poetæ quoque illorum in nostram quam nostri in illorum linguas transferuntur. At Germanicum opus in theologiæ et philosophiæ quasi confinio versans, si trajicere in Britanniam parat, ne illa quidem inter utramque gentem sensus et studiorum communione adjuvatur. Tam diversa enim utrimque via istæ disciplinæ processerunt, ut in theologia impii, in philosophia superstitiosi Britannis Germani iidem videamur. Cum iis, qui in Britannia ausi sunt, historias, Judæorum et Christianorum religione sacratas, examini ut ajunt critico subjicere, nihil agendum esset, nisi ut Lockii sui atque Humii principia philosophica, sicut ad reliquas omnes historias, ita ad illas etiam, quas legibus istis hucusque superstitio subtraxerat, adhiberent : in Germania ad hoc monstri res degeneraverat, ut superstitioni a theologorum potissima parte derelictæ philosophia succurreret, critico ergo non simplex sanæ philosophiæ contra theologorum superstitionem, sed duplex et contra philosophorum ex sanioribus principiis deductas ineptas conclusiones, et contra theologorum propter philosophica ista auxilia ornamentaque inflatam atque induratam superstitionem, certamen ineundum esset. Ex hoc rei statu proprie Germanico natum opus meum, nominibus insuper atque opinionibus theologorum ac philosophorum nostratium refertum, nec scholarum etiam vocabula, quibus nostræ tantum aures assuevere, satis evitans, a Britannorum usu ingenioque non posse non abhorrere, tam probe scio, ut de translato in eorum linguam, licet interpretatio, quantum quidem ejus inspicere potuerim, et accurata et perspicua sit et librum, quantum in ipsa est, popularibus commendet, num gaudendum mihi magnopere sit, mehercule nesciam.

Accedit, quod a primo libri mei ortu duo lustra, et a recentissima etiam editione unum jam lustrum intercessit. Ut tum, quum opus inchoabam, via incedebam, quam pauci ingressi, totam emensus nemo erat, ita per primum illud lustrum nullæ fere nisi adversariorum voces audiebantur, principia mea negantium et historiam in Evangeliis vel meram, vel levissima tantum erroris rumorisve adspersione tinctam contineri affirmantium, cum quibus non modo non disputandum, sed a quibus ne discendum quidem quidquam erat, quod ad rem et ad librum vere emendandum pertineret. Proximo demum lustro viri vestigia mea non refugientes neque evitantes, sed persequentes, ubi ego substiteram longius progressi, rem revera juverunt atque promoverunt. Narrationes in Evangeliis traditas, quas rerum vere gestarum esse persuadere mihi non potueram, mythorum in modum, qui inter antiquas gentes inveniuntur, aut in ore populi a minutis initiis coaluisse et eundo crevisse, aut a singulis, sed qui vere ita evenisse superstitiose in animum induxerant, fictas esse existimaveram. Quod ut sufficit explicandis plerisque eorum, quæ dubitationem moventia tribus prioribus Evangeliis continentur: ita quarti Evangelii auctorem ad tuendas et illustrandas sententias suas haud raro meras fabulas scientem confinxisse, a Baurio, theologo Tubingensi doctissimo, nuper ita demonstratum est, ut critici me judicii rigori religiosius quam verius temperasse intelligam. Dumque prima a Christo secula accuratius perscrutantur, partes partiumque certamina, quibus nova ecclesia commovebatur, in apricum proferunt, narrationum haud paucarum, quas fabulas esse ego bene quidem perspexeram, sed unde ortæ essent demonstrare non valueram, veram in illis primæ ecclesiæ motibus originem detegere theologis Tubingensibus contigit.

Imperfectum igitur opus meum, ut solent rerum initia, non ob hoc tamen, quod sententiæ deest, timerem, ne a Britannis sperneretur, nisi formæ etiam illud quod supra dixi peregrinum atque inusitatum accederet. Qui si suum Hennellium non audiverunt, de iisdem rebus cum Britannis Britannice agentem, quomodo audient, si quis Germanus surget, cujus liber cum sua lingua non potuerit cogitandi quoque disputandique morem prorsus Germanicum exuere? Sed absit omen verbis meis, atque ut pridem in Germania, ita mox in Britannia jaceat liber hic εἰς πτῶσιν καὶ ἀνάστασιν πολλῶν καὶ εἰς σημεῖον ἀντιλεγόμενον ὅπως ἂν ἀποκαλυφθῶσιν ἐκ πολλῶν καρδιῶν διαλογισμοί.

STRAUSS.

Scribebam Heilbronnæ.
Med. mens. April a. 1846.

PREFACE

TO THE FIRST GERMAN EDITION.

IT appeared to the author of the work, the first half of which is herewith submitted to the public, that it was time to substitute a new mode of considering the life of Jesus, in the place of the antiquated systems of supranaturalism and naturalism. This application of the term antiquated will in the present day be more readily admitted in relation to the latter system than to the former. For while the interest excited by the explanations of the miracles and the conjectural facts of the rationalists has long ago cooled, the commentaries now most read are those which aim to adapt the supernatural interpretation of the sacred history to modern taste. Nevertheless, in point of fact, the orthodox view of this history became superannuated earlier than the rationalistic, since it was only because the former had ceased to satisfy an advanced state of culture, that the latter was developed, while the recent attempts to recover, by the aid of a mystical philosophy, the supernatural point of view held by our forefathers, betray themselves, by the exaggerating spirit in which they are conceived, to be final, desperate efforts to render the past present, the inconceivable conceivable.

The new point of view, which must take the place of the above, is the mythical. This theory is not brought to bear on the evangelical history for the first time in the present work : it has long been applied to particular parts of that history, and is here only extended to its entire tenor. It is not by any means meant that the whole history of Jesus is to be represented as mythical, but only that every part of it is to be subjected to a critical examination, to ascertain whether it have not some admixture of the mythical. The exegesis of the ancient church set out from the double presupposition : first, that the gospels contained a history, and secondly, that this history was a supernatural one. Rationalism rejected the latter of these presuppositions, but only to cling the more tenaciously to the former, maintaining that these books present unadulterated, though only natural, history. Science cannot rest satisfied with this half-measure : the other presupposition also must ber elinquished, and the inquiry must first be made whether in fact, and to what extent, the ground on which we stand in the gospels is historical. This is the natural course of things, and thus far the appearance of a work like the present is not only justifiable, but even necessary.

It is certainly not therefore evident that the author is precisely the individual whose vocation it is to appear in this position. He has a very vivid consciousness that many others would have been able to execute such a work with incomparably superior erudition. Yet on the other hand he believes himself to be at least possessed of one qualification which especially fitted him to undertake this task. The majority of the most learned and acute theologians of the present day fail in the main requirement for such a work, a requirement without which no amount of learning will suffice to achieve anything in the domain of criticism—namely, the internal liberation of the feelings and intellect from certain religious and dogmatical presuppositions; and this the author early attained by means of philosophical studies. If theologians regard this absence of presupposition from his work, as unchristian: he regards the believing presuppositions of theirs as unscientific. Widely as in this respect the tone of the present work may be contrasted with the edifying devoutness and enthusiastic mysticism of recent books on similar subjects; still it will nowhere depart from the seriousness of science, or sink into frivolity; and it seems a just demand in return, that the judgments which are passed upon it should also confine themselves to the domain of science, and keep aloof from bigotry and fanaticism.

The author is aware that the essence of the Christian faith is perfectly independent of his criticism. The supernatural birth of Christ, his miracles, his resurrection and ascension, remain eternal truths, whatever doubts may be cast on their reality as historical facts. The certainty of this can alone give calmness and dignity to our criticism, and distinguish it from the naturalistic criticism of the last century, the design of which was, with the historical fact, to subvert also the religious truth, and which thus necessarily became frivolous. A dissertation at the close of the work will show that the dogmatic significance of the life of Jesus remains inviolate: in the meantime let the calmness and insensibility with which, in the course of it, criticism undertakes apparently dangerous operations, be explained solely by the security of the author's conviction that no injury is threatened to the Christian faith. Investigations of this kind may, however, inflict a wound on the faith of individuals. Should this be the case with theologians, they have in their science the means of healing such wounds, from which, if they would not remain behind the development of their age, they cannot possibly be exempt. For the laity the subject is certainly not adequately prepared; and for this reason the present work is so framed, that at least the unlearned among them will quickly and often perceive that the book is not destined for them. If from curiosity or excessive zeal against heresy they persist in their perusal, they will then have, as Schleiermacher says on a similar occasion, to bear the punishment in their conscience, since their feelings directly urge on them the conviction that they understand not that of which they are ambitious to speak.

A new opinion, which aims to fill the place of an older one, ought fully to adjust its position with respect to the latter. Hence the way to the mythical view is here taken in each particular point through the supranaturalistic and rationalistic opinions and their respective refutations; but, as becomes a valid refutation, with an acknowledgment of what is true in the opinions combated, and an adoption of this truth into the new theory. This method also brings with it the extrinsic advantage, that the work may now serve as a repertory of the principal opinions and treatises concerning all parts of the evangelical history. The author has not, however, aimed to give a complete bibliographical view of this department of theological literature, but, where it was possible, has adhered to the chief works in each separate class of opinions. For the rationalistic system the works of Paulus remain classical, and are therefore pre-eminently referred to ; for the orthodox opinions, the commentary of Olshausen is especially important, as the most recent and approved attempt to render the supranatural interpretation philosophical and modern ; while as a preliminary to a critical investigation of the life of Jesus, the commentaries of Fritzsche are excellently adapted, since they exhibit, together with uncommon philological learning, that freedom from prejudice and scientific indifference to results and consequences, which form the first condition of progress in this region of inquiry.

The second volume, which will open with a detailed examination of the miracles of Jesus, and which will conclude the whole work, is already prepared and will be in the press immediately on the completion of the first.

THE AUTHOR.

Tübingen, 24th May, 1835.

PREFACE

TO THE FOURTH GERMAN EDITION.

As this new edition of my critical examination of the life of Jesus appears simultaneously with the first volume of my *Dogmatik*, it will not be expected to contain any essential alterations. Indeed, even in the absence of other labours, I should scarcely have been inclined to undertake such on the present occasion. The critical researches prompted by the appearance of my work have, after the stormy reaction of the first few years, at length entered on that quiet course, which promises the most valuable assistance towards the confirmation and more precise determination of the negative results at which I have arrived. But these fruits still require some years for their maturing; and it must therefore be deferred to a future opportunity to enrich this work by the use of them. I could not persuade myself to do so, at least in the present instance, by prosecuting a polemic against opposite opinions. Already in the last edition there was more of a polemical character than accorded with the unity and calmness proper to such a work; hence I was in this respect admonished rather to abridge than to amplify. But that edition also contained too much of compliance. The intermingling voices of opponents, critics, and fellow labourers, to which I held it a duty attentively to listen, had confused the idea of the work in my mind; in the diligent comparison of divergent opinions I had lost sight of the subject itself. Hence on coming with a more collected mind to this last revision, I found alterations at which I could not but wonder, and by which I had evidently done myself injustice. In all these passages the earlier readings are now restored, and thus my labour in this new edition has chiefly consisted in whetting, as it were, my good sword, to free it from the notches made in it rather by my own grinding, than by the blows of my enemies.

THE AUTHOR.

Stuttgard, 17th October, 1840.

CONTENTS.

———◆———

INTRODUCTION.

Most important

DEVELOPMENT OF THE MYTHICAL POINT OF VIEW IN RELATION TO THE GOSPEL HISTORIES.

defines whether he means by myth and the criteria

myth does not mean Falsehood or truth
It may be eather or Both, It may be a Representation
of the truth

FIRST PART.

HISTORY OF THE BIRTH AND CHILDHOOD OF JESUS.

CHAPTER I.

ANNUNCIATION AND BIRTH OF JOHN THE BAPTIST.

CHAPTER II.

DAVIDICAL DESCENT OF JESUS, ACCORDING TO THE GENEALOGICAL TABLES OF MATTHEW
AND LUKE.

CHAPTER III.

ANNOUNCEMENT OF THE CONCEPTION OF JESUS.—ITS SUPERNATURAL CHARACTER.—
VISIT OF MARY TO ELIZABETH.

CHAPTER IV.

BIRTH AND EARLIEST EVENTS OF THE LIFE OF JESUS.

CHAPTER V.

THE FIRST VISIT TO THE TEMPLE, AND THE EDUCATION OF JESUS.

SECOND PART.

HISTORY OF THE PUBLIC LIFE OF JESUS.

CHAPTER I.

RELATIONS BETWEEN JESUS AND JOHN THE BAPTIST.

CHAPTER II.

BAPTISM AND TEMPTATION OF JESUS.

CHAPTER III.

LOCALITY AND CHRONOLOGY OF THE PUBLIC LIFE OF JESUS.

CHAPTER IV.

JESUS AS THE MESSIAH.

CHAPTER V.

THE DISCIPLES OF JESUS.

CHAPTER VI.

THE DISCOURSES OF JESUS IN THE THREE FIRST GOSPELS.

CHAPTER VII.

DISCOURSES OF JESUS IN THE FOURTH GOSPEL.

CHAPTER VIII.

EVENTS IN THE PUBLIC LIFE OF JESUS, EXCLUSIVE OF THE MIRACLES.

CHAPTER IX.

MIRACLES OF JESUS.

CHAPTER X.

THE TRANSFIGURATION OF JESUS, AND HIS LAST JOURNEY TO JERUSALEM.

THIRD PART.

HISTORY OF THE PASSION, DEATH, AND RESURRECTION OF JESUS.

CHAPTER I.

RELATION OF JESUS TO THE IDEA OF A SUFFERING AND DYING MESSIAH; HIS DISCOURSES ON HIS DEATH, RESURRECTION, AND SECOND ADVENT.

CHAPTER II.

MACHINATIONS OF THE ENEMIES OF JESUS ; TREACHERY OF JUDAS ; LAST SUPPER WITH THE DISCIPLES.

CHAPTER III.

RETIREMENT TO THE MOUNT OF OLIVES, ARREST, TRIAL, CONDEMNATION, AND CRUCIFIXION OF JESUS.

CHAPTER IV.

DEATH AND RESURRECTION OF JESUS.

CHAPTER V.

THE ASCENSION.

CONCLUDING DISSERTATION.

Most Important

THE DOGMATIC IMPORT OF THE LIFE OF JESUS.

THE LIFE OF JESUS.

INTRODUCTION.

DEVELOPMENT OF THE MYTHICAL POINT OF VIEW IN RELATION TO THE GOSPEL HISTORIES.

§ I.

INEVITABLE RISE OF DIFFERENT MODES OF EXPLAINING SACRED HISTORIES.

WHEREVER a religion, resting upon written records, prolongs and extends the sphere of its dominion, accompanying its votaries through the varied and progressive stages of mental cultivation, a discrepancy between the representations of those ancient records, referred to as sacred, and the notions of more advanced periods of mental development, will inevitably sooner or later arise. In the first instance this disagreement is felt in reference only to the unessential—the external form : the expressions and delineations are seen to be inappropriate ; but by degrees it manifests itself also in regard to that which is essential : the fundamental ideas and opinions in these early writings fail to be commensurate with a more advanced civilisation. As long as this discrepancy is either not in itself so considerable, or else is not so universally discerned and acknowledged, as to lead to a complete renunciation of these Scriptures as of sacred authority, so long will a system of reconciliation by means of interpretation be adopted and pursued by those who have a more or less distinct consciousness of the existing incongruity.

A main element in all religious records is sacred history ; a history of events in which the divine enters, without intermediation, into the human ; the ideal thus assuming an immediate embodiment. But as the progress of mental cultivation mainly consists in the gradual recognition of a chain of causes and effects connecting natural phenomena with each other ; so the mind in its development becomes ever increasingly conscious of those mediate links which are indispensable to the realization of the ideal ; [1] and hence the discrepancy between the modern culture and the ancient records, with regard to their historical portion, becomes so apparent, that the immediate intervention of the divine in human affairs loses its probability. Besides, as the humanity of these records is the humanity of an early period, consequently of an age

[1] [This passage varies slightly from the original, a subsequent amplification by Dr. Strauss being incorporated with it.—TR.]

comparatively undeveloped and necessarily rude, a sense of repulsion is likewise excited. The incongruity may be thus expressed. *The divine cannot so have happened* ; (not immediately, not in forms so rude ;) or, *that which has so happened cannot have been divine :*—and if a reconciliation be sought by means of interpretation, it will be attempted to prove, either that the divine did not manifest itself in the manner related,—which is to deny the historical validity of the ancient Scriptures ; or, that the actual occurrences were not divine—which is to explain away the absolute contents of these books. In both cases the interpretation may be partial or impartial : partial, if undertaken with a determination to close the eyes to the secretly recognised fact of the disagreement between the modern culture and the ancient records, and to see only in such interpretation the original signification of these records ; impartial, if it unequivocally acknowledges and openly avows that the matters narrated in these books must be viewed in a light altogether different from that in which they were regarded by the authors themselves. This latter method, however, by no means involves the entire rejection of the religious documents ; on the contrary, the essential may be firmly retained, whilst the unessential is unreservedly abandoned.

§ 2.

DIFFERENT EXPLANATIONS OF SACRED LEGENDS AMONG THE GREEKS.

Though the Hellenistic religion cannot be said to have rested upon written records, it became enshrined in the Greek poems, for example, in those of Homer and Hesiod ; and these, no less than its orally transmitted legends, did not fail to receive continually varying interpretations, successively adapted to the progressive intellectual culture of the Greeks. At an early period the rigid philosophy of the Greeks, and under its influence even some of the Greek poets, recognized the impossibility of ascribing to Deity manifestations so grossly human, so immediate, and so barbarous, as those exhibited and represented as divine in the wild conflicts of Hesiod's Theogony, and in the domestic occupations and trivial pursuits of the Homeric deities. Hence arose the quarrel of Plato, and prior to him of Pindar, with Homer ; [1] hence the cause which induced Anaxagoras, to whom the invention of the allegorical mode of interpretation is ascribed, to apply the Homeric delineations to virtue and to justice ; [2] hence it was that the Stoics understood the Theogony of Hesiod as relating to the action of the elements, which, according to their notions, constituted, in their highest union, the divine nature. [3] Thus did these several thinkers, each according to his own peculiar mode of thought, succeed in discovering an absolute meaning in these representations : the one finding in them a physical, the other an ethical signification, whilst, at the same time, they gave up their external form, ceasing to regard them as strictly historical.

On the other hand, the more popular and sophistical culture of another class of thinkers led them to opposite conclusions. Though, in their estimation, every semblance of the divine had evaporated from these histories ; though they were convinced that the proceedings ascribed to the gods were not godlike, still they did not abandon the historical sense of these narratives.

---

[1] Plato, de Republ. ii. p. 377. Steph. ; Pindar, Nem. vii. 31.
[2] Diog. Laërt. L. ii. c. iii. No. 7.
[3] Cic. de Nat. Deor. i. 10. 15. Comp. Athenag. Legat. 22. Tatian, c. Græc. Orat. 21. Clement. homil. 6, 1 f.

With Evemerus [4] they transformed the subjects of these histories from gods to men, to heroes and sages of antiquity, kings and tyrants, who, through deeds of might and valour, had acquired divine honours. Some indeed went still further, and, with Polybius, [5] considered the whole system of heathen theology as a fable, invented by the founders of states to awe the people into subjection.

§ 3.

ALLEGORICAL INTERPRETATIONS AMONG THE HEBREWS.—PHILO.

Whilst, on the one hand, the isolation and stability of the Hebrews served to retard the development of similar manifestations amongst this people, on the other hand, when once actually developed, they were the more marked ; because, in proportion to the high degree of authority ascribed to the sacred records, was the skill and caution required in their interpretation. Thus, even in Palestine, subsequent to the exile, and particularly after the time of the Maccabees, many ingenious attempts were made to interpret the Old Testament so as to remove offensive literalities, supply deficiencies, and introduce the notions of a later age. Examples of this system of interpretation occur in the writings of the Rabbins, and even in the New Testament ; [1] but it was at that place where the Jewish mind came into contact with Greek civilization, and under its influence was carried beyond the limits of its own national culture—namely at Alexandria—that the allegorical mode of interpretation was first consistently applied to the whole body of historical narrative in the Old Testament. Many had prepared the way, but it was Philo who first fully developed the doctrine of both a common and a deeper sense of the Holy Scriptures. He was by no means inclined to cast away the former, but generally placed the two together, side by side, and even declared himself opposed to those who, everywhere and without necessity, sacrificed the literal to the higher signification. In many cases, however, he absolutely discarded the verbal meaning and historical conception, and considered the narrative merely as the figurative representation of an idea. He did so, for example, whenever the sacred story appeared to him to present delineations unworthy of Deity, tending either to materialism or anthropomorphism, or otherwise to contain contradictions. [2]

The fact that the Jews, whilst they adopted this mode of explaining the Old Testament, (which, in order to save the purity of the intrinsic signification, often sacrificed the historical form), were never led into the opposite system of Evemerus (which preserved the historical form by divesting the history of the divine, and reducing it to a record of mere human events), is to be ascribed to the tenacity with which that people ever adhered to the supernatural point of view. The latter mode of interpretation was first brought to bear upon the Old Testament by the Christians.

§ 4.

ALLEGORICAL INTERPRETATIONS AMONG THE CHRISTIANS.—ORIGEN.

To the early Christians who, antecedent to the fixing of the christian canon, made especial use of the Old Testament as their principal sacred record, an

[4] Diodor. Sic. Bibl. Fragm. L. vi. Cic. de Nat. Deor. i. 42.
[5] Hist. vi. 56.
[1] Döpke, die Hermeneutik der neutestamentlichen Schriftsteller, s. 123. ff.
[2] Gfrörer. Dähne.

allegorical interpretation was the more indispensable, inasmuch as they had made greater advances beyond the views of the Old Testament writers than even the most enlightened of the Jews. It was no wonder therefore that this mode of explanation, already in vogue among the Jews, was almost universally adopted by the primitive christian churches. It was however again in Alexandria that it found the fullest application amongst the Christians, and that in connexion with the name of Origen. Origen attributes a threefold meaning to the Scriptures, corresponding with his distribution of the human being into three parts : the literal sense answering to the body ; the moral, to the soul ; and the mystical, to the spirit.[1] The rule with him was to retain all three meanings, though differing in worth ; in some particular cases, however, he was of opinion that the literal interpretation either gave no sense at all, or else a perverted sense, in order the more directly to impel the reader to the discovery of its mystical signification. Origen's repeated observation that it is not the purpose of the biblical narratives to transmit old tales, but to instruct in the rules of life ;[2] his assertion that the merely literal acceptation of many of the narratives would prove destructive of the christian religion ;[3] and his application of the passage " The letter killeth, but the spirit giveth life," [4] to the relative worth of the allegorical and the literal modes of biblical interpretation, may be understood as indicating only the inferiority of the literal to the deeper signification. But the literal sense is decidedly given up when it is said, " Every passage of Scripture has a spiritual element, but not every one has a corporeal element ; " [5] " A spiritual truth often exists embodied in a corporeal falsehood " ; [6] " The Scriptures contain many things which never came to pass, interwoven with the history, and he must be dull indeed who does not of his own accord observe that much which the Scriptures represent as having happened never actually occurred." [7] Among the passages which Origen regarded as admitting no other than an allegorical interpretation, besides those which too sensibly humanised the Deity,[8] he included those which attributed unworthy action to individuals who had held intimate communion with God.[9]

It was not however from the Old Testament views alone that Origen had, in consequence of his christian training, departed so widely that he felt himself compelled, if he would retain his reverence for the sacred records, to allegorize their contents, as a means of reconciling the contradiction which had arisen between them and his own mind. There was much likewise in the New Testament writings which so little accorded with his philosophical

---

[1] Homil. 5. in Levit. § 5.

[2] Homil. 2. in Exod. iii. : *Nolite putare, ut sæpe jam diximus, veterum vobis fabulas recitari, sed doceri vos per hæc, ut agnoscatis ordinem vitæ.*

[3] Homil. 5. in Levit. i. : *Hæc omnia, nisi alio sensu accipiamus quam literæ textus ostendit, obstaculum magis et subversionem Christianæ religioni, quam hortationem ædificationemque præstabunt.*

[4] Contra Cels. vi. 70.

[5] De principp. L. iv. § 20 : πᾶσα μὲν (γραφὴ) ἔχει τὸ πνευματικὸν, οὐ πᾶσα δὲ τὸ σωματικόν.

[6] Comm. in Joann., Tom. x. § 4 :—σωζομένου πολλάκις τοῦ ἀληθοῦς πνευματικοῦ ἐν τῷ σωματικῷ, ὡς ἂν εἴποι τις, ψεύδει.

[7] De principp. iv. 15 : συνύφηνεν ἡ γραφὴ τῇ ἱστορίᾳ τὸ μὴ γενόμενον, πῇ μὲν μὴ δυνατὸν γενέσθαι, πῇ δὲ δυνατὸν μὲν γενέσθαι, οὐ μὴν γεγενημένον. De principp. iv. 16 : καὶ τί δεῖ πλείω λέγειν ; τῶν μὴ πάνυ ἀμβλέων μυρία ὅσα τοιαῦτα δυναμένων συναγαγεῖν, γεγραμμένα μὲν ὡς γεγονότα, οὐ γεγενημένα δὲ κατὰ τὴν λέξιν.

[8] De principp. iv. 16.

[9] Homil. 6, in Gen. iii. : *Quæ nobis ædificatio erit, legentibus, Abraham, tantam patriarcham, non solum mentitum esse Abimelech regi, sed et pudicitiam conjugis prodidisse? Quid nos ædificat tanti patriarchæ uxor, si putetur contaminationibus exposita per conniventiam maritalem? Hæc Judæi putent et si qui cum eis sunt literæ amici, non spiritus.*

notions, that he found himself constrained to adopt a similar proceeding in reference to them. He reasoned thus :—the New Testament and the Old are the work of the same spirit, and this spirit would proceed in the same manner in the production of the one and of the other, interweaving fiction with reality, in order thereby to direct the mind to the spiritual signification.[10] In a remarkable passage of his work against Celsus, Origen classes together, and in no ambiguous language, the partially fabulous stories of profane history, and of heathen mythology, with the gospel narratives.[11] He expresses himself as follows : " In almost every history it is a difficult task, and not unfrequently an impossible one, to demonstrate the reality of the events recorded, however true they may in fact be. Let us suppose some individual to deny the reality of a Trojan war on account of the incredibilities mixed up with the history ; as, for example, the birth of Achilles from a goddess of the sea. How could we substantiate the fact, encumbered as it is with the numerous and undeniable poetical fictions which have, in some unascertainable manner, become interwoven with the generally admitted account of the war between the Greeks and the Trojans ? There is no alternative : he who would study history with understanding, and not suffer himself to be deluded, must weigh each separate detail, and consider what is worthy of credit and may be believed without further evidence ; what, on the contrary, must be regarded as merely figurative ; (τίνα δὲ τροπολογήσει) always bearing in mind the aim of the narrator— and what must be wholly mistrusted as being written with intent to please certain individuals." In conclusion Origen says, " I was desirous of making these preliminary observations in relation to the entire history of Jesus given in the Gospels, not with the view of exacting from the enlightened a blind and baseless belief, but with design to show how indispensable to the study of this history are not only judgment and diligent examination, but, so to speak, the very penetrating into the mind of the author, in order to discover the particular aim with which each narrative may have been written."

We here see Origen almost transcending the limits of his own customary point of view, and verging towards the more modern mythical view. But if his own prepossessions in favour of the supernatural, and his fear of giving offence to the orthodox church, combined to hinder him from making a wider application of the allegorical mode of interpretation to the Old Testament, the same causes operated still more powerfully in relation to the New Testament ; so that when we further inquire of which of the gospel histories in particular did Origen reject the historical meaning, in order to hold fast a truth worthy of God ? the instances will prove to be meagre in the extreme. For when he says, in illustration of the above-mentioned passage, that amongst other things, it is not to be understood literally that Satan showed to Jesus all the kingdoms of the earth from a mountain, because this is impossible to the bodily eye ; he here gives not a strictly allegorical interpretation, but merely a different turn to the literal sense, which, according to him, relates not to an external fact, but to the internal fact of a vision. Again, even where the text offers a tempting opportunity of sacrificing the literal to the spiritual meaning, as, for example, the cursing of the fig-tree,[12] Origen does not speak out freely. He is most explicit when speaking of the expulsion of the buyers and sellers from the temple ; he characterizes the conduct of Jesus,

---

[10] De principp. iv. 16 : οὐ μόνον δὲ περὶ τῶν πρὸ τῆς παρουσίας ταῦτα τὸ πνεῦμα ᾠκονόμησεν, ἀλλ', ἅτε τὸ αὐτὸ τυγχάνον καὶ ἀπὸ τοῦ ἑνὸς θεοῦ, τὸ ὅμοιον καὶ ἐπὶ τῶν εὐαγγελίων πεποίηκε καὶ ἐπὶ τῶν ἀποστόλων, οὐδὲ τούτων πάντη ἄκρατον τὴν ἱστορίαν τῶν προσυφασμένων κατὰ τὸ σωματικὸν ἐχόντων μὴ γεγενημένων.

[11] Contra Celsum, i. 40.

[12] Comm. in Matth., Tom. xvi. 26.

according to the literal interpretation, as assuming and seditious.[13]   He moreover expressly remarks that the Scriptures contain many more historical than merely scriptural truths.[14]

§ 5.

TRANSITION TO MORE MODERN TIMES.—DEISTS AND NATURALISTS OF THE 17TH AND 18TH CENTURIES.—THE WOLFENBÜTTEL FRAGMENTIST.

Thus was developed one of those forms of interpretation to which the Hebrew and Christian Scriptures, in common with all other religious records, in relation to their historical contents, became necessarily subjected; that, namely, which recognizes in them the divine, but denies it to have actually manifested itself in so immediate a manner.   The other principal mode of interpretation, which, to a certain extent, acknowledges the course of events to have been historically true, but assigns it to a human and not a divine origin, was developed amongst the enemies of Christianity by a Celsus, a Porphyry, and a Julian.   They indeed rejected much of the history as altogether fabulous ; but they admitted many of the incidents related of Moses, Jesus, and others, to be historical facts : these facts were however considered by them as originating from common motives ; and they attributed their apparently supernatural character either to gross fraud or impious sorcery.

It is worthy of observation that the circumstances attending the introduction of these several modes of interpretation into the heathen and Jewish religions, on the one hand, and into the christian religion, on the other, were different.   The religion and sacred literature of the Greeks and Hebrews had been gradually developed with the development of the nation, and it was not until the intellectual culture of the people had outgrown the religion of their fathers, and the latter was in consequence verging towards decay, that the discrepancy which is the source of these varying interpretations became apparent.   Christianity, on the contrary, came into a world of already advanced civilization ; which was, with the exception of that of Palestine, the Judaico-Hellenistic and the Greek.   Consequently a disagreement manifested itself at the very beginning ; it was not now, however, as in former times, between modern culture and an ancient religion, but between a new religion and ancient culture.   The production of allegorical interpretations among the Pagans and the Hebrews, was a sign that their religion had lost its vitality ; the allegories of Origen and the attacks of Celsus, in reference to Christianity, were evidences rather that the world had not as yet duly accommodated itself to the new religion.   As however with the christianizing of the Roman empire, and the overthrow of the chief heresies, the christian principle gained an ever-increasing supremacy ; as the schools of heathen wisdom closed ; and the uncivilized Germanic tribes lent themselves to the teaching of the church ;—the world, during the tedious centuries of the middle ages, was satisfied with Christianity, both in form and in substance.   Almost all traces of these modes of interpretation which presuppose a discrepancy between the culture of a nation, or of the world, and religion, in consequence disappeared.   The reformation effected the first breach in the solid structure of the faith of the church.   It was the first vital expression of a culture, which had now in the heart of Christendom itself, as formerly in relation to Paganism and Judaism, acquired strength and independence sufficient to create a reaction against the

[13] Comm. in Joann., Tom. x. 17.
[14] De principp. iv. 19.   After Origen, that kind of allegory only which left the historical sense unimpaired was retained in the church ; and where, subsequently, a giving up of the verbal meaning is spoken of, this refers merely to a trope or a simile.

soil of its birth, the prevailing religion.　This reaction, so long as it was directed against the dominant hierarchy, constituted the sublime, but quickly terminated, drama of the reformation.　In its later direction against the Bible, it appeared again upon the stage in the barren revolutionary efforts of deism; and many and various have been the forms it has assumed in its progress down to the present time.

The deists and naturalists of the seventeenth and eighteenth centuries renewed the polemic attacks of the pagan adversaries of Christianity in the bosom of the christian church; and gave to the public an irregular and confused mass of criticisms, impugning the authenticity and credibility of the Scriptures, and exposing to contempt the events recorded in the sacred volume. Toland,[1] Bolingbroke,[2] and others, pronounced the Bible to be a collection of unauthentic and fabulous books; whilst some spared no pains to despoil the biblical histories, and the heroes whose actions they celebrate, of every ray of divine light.　Thus, according to Morgan,[3] the law of Moses is a miserable system of superstition, blindness, and slavery; the Jewish priests are deceivers; and the Jewish prophets the originators of the distractions and civil wars of the two kingdoms of Judah and Israel.　According to Chubb,[4] the Jewish religion cannot be a revelation from God, because it debases the moral character of the Deity by attributing to him arbitrary conduct, partiality for a particular people, and above all, the cruel command to exterminate the Canaanitish nations.　Assaults were likewise made by these and other deists upon the New Testament: the Apostles were suspected of being actuated by selfish and mercenary motives;[5] the character of Jesus himself was not spared,[6] and the fact of his resurrection was denied.[7] The miracles of Jesus, wrought by an immediate exercise of divine power in human acts and concerns, were made the particular objects of attack by Woolston.[8]　This writer is also worthy of notice on account of the peculiar position taken by him between the ancient allegorists and the modern naturalists.　His whole reasoning turns upon the alternative; either to retain the historical reality of the miracles narrated in the Bible, and thus to sacrifice the divine character of the narratives, and reduce the miracles to mere artifices, miserable juggleries, or commonplace deceptions; or, in order to hold fast the divine character of these narratives, to reject them entirely as details of actual occurrences, and regard them as historical representations of certain spiritual truths.　Woolston cites the authority of the most distinguished allegorists among the fathers in support of this view.　He is wrong however in representing them as supplanting the literal by the figurative meaning.　These ancient fathers, on the contrary, were disposed to retain both the literal and the allegorical meaning.　(A few examples in Origen, it is true, are an exception to this rule.)　It may be doubted, from the language of Woolston, which alternative was adopted by himself.　If we reason from the fact, that before he appeared as the opponent of the commonly entertained views of Christianity, he occupied himself with allegorical interpretations of the Scriptures,[9] we may be led to consider the latter alternative as expressing his real conviction.　On the other hand, he enlarges with so evident a predi-

---

[1] In his Amyntor, 1698.　See Leland's View of the Deistical Writers.
[2] See Leland.
[3] In his work entitled The Moral Philosopher.
[4] Posthumous Works, 1748.
[5] Chubb, Posthumous Works, i. 102.
[6] Ibid., ii. 269.
[7] The Resurrection of Jesus Considered, by a Moral Philosopher, 1744.
[8] Six Discourses on the Miracles of our Saviour.　Published singly, from 1727–1729.
[9] Schröckh, Kirschengesch, seit der Reform. 6 Th. s. 191.

lection on the absurdities of the miracles, when literally understood, and the manner in which he treats the whole subject is so tinged with levity, that we may suspect the Deist to put forward the allegorical interpretations merely as a screen, from behind which he might inveigh the more unreservedly against the literal signification.

Similar deistical objections against the Bible, and the divine character of its history, were propagated in Germany chiefly by an anonymous author (Reimarus) whose manuscripts were discovered by Lessing in the Wolfenbüttel library. Some portions of these manuscripts, called the "Wolfenbüttel Fragments," were published by Lessing in 1774. They consist of Essays, one of which treats of the many arguments which may be urged against revealed religion in general; the others relate partly to the Old and partly to the New Testament. It is the opinion of the Fragmentist, in relation to the Old Testament, first, that the men, of whom the Scriptures narrate that they had immediate communications with God, were so unworthy, that such intercourse, admitting its reality, compromised the character of Deity; secondly, that the result of this intercourse,— the instructions and laws alleged to have been thus divinely communicated,— were so barbarous and destructive, that to ascribe them to God is impossible; and thirdly, that the accompanying miracles were at once absurd and incredible. From the whole, it appears to him clear, that the divine communications were only pretended; and that the miracles were delusions, practised with the design of giving stability and efficiency to certain laws and institutions highly advantageous to the rulers and priests. The author finds much to condemn in the conduct of the patriarchs, and their simulations of divine communications; such as the command to Abraham to sacrifice his son. But it is chiefly Moses upon whom he seeks, in a long section, to cast all the obloquy of an impostor, who did not scruple to employ the most disgraceful means in order to make himself the despotic ruler of a free people: who, to effect his purpose, feigned divine apparitions, and pretended to have received the command of God to perpetrate acts which, but for this divine sanction, would have been stigmatized as fraudulent, as highway robbery, as inhuman barbarity. For instance, the spoiling of the Egyptians, and the extirpation of the inhabitants of Canaan; atrocities which, when introduced by the words "*Jehovah hath said it,*" became instantly transformed into deeds worthy of God. The Fragmentist is as little disposed to admit the divinity of the New Testament histories. He considers the aim of Jesus to have been political; and his connexion with John the Baptist a preconcerted arrangement, by which the one party should recommend the other to the people. He views the death of Jesus as an event by no means foreseen by himself, but which frustrated all his plans; a catastrophe which his disciples knew not how else to repair than by the fraudulent pretence that Jesus was risen from the dead, and by an artful alteration of his doctrines [10].

§ 6.

NATURAL MODE OF EXPLANATION ADOPTED BY THE RATIONALISTS.—EICH-HORN.—PAULUS.

Whilst the reality of the biblical revelation, together with the divine origin and supernatural character of the Jewish and Christian histories, were tenaciously maintained in opposition to the English deists by numerous English apologists, and in opposition to the Wolfenbüttel Fragmentist by the great majority of German theologians, there arose a distinct class of theologians in

[10] Fragmente des Wolfenbüttelschen Ungenannten von G. E. Lessing herausgegeben.

Germany, who struck into a new path. The ancient pagan mythology, as understood by Evemerus, admitted of two modes of explanation, each of which was in fact adopted. The deities of the popular worship might, on the one hand, be regarded as good and benevolent men ; as wise lawgivers, and just rulers, of early times, whom the gratitude of their contemporaries and posterity had encircled with divine glory ; or they might, on the other hand, be viewed as artful impostors and cruel tyrants, who had veiled themselves in a nimbus of divinity, for the pupose of subjugating the people to their dominion. So, likewise, in the purely human explanation of the bible histories, besides the method of the deists to regard the subjects of these narratives as wicked and deceitful men, there was yet another course open ; to divest these individuals of their immediate divinity, but to accord to them an undegraded humanity ; not indeed to look upon their deeds as miraculous ;—as little on the other hand to decry them as impositions ;—but to explain their proceedings as altogether natural, yet morally irreprehensible. If the Naturalist was led by his special enmity to the Christianity of the church to the former explanation, the Rationalist, anxious, on the contrary, to remain within the pale of the church, was attracted towards the latter.

Eichhorn, in his critical examination of the Wolfenbüttel Fragments,[1] directly opposes this rationalistic view to that maintained by the Naturalist. He agrees with the Fragmentist in refusing to recognize an immediate divine agency, at all events in the narratives of early date. The mythological researches of a Heyne had so far enlarged his circle of vision as to lead Eichhorn to perceive that divine interpositions must be alike admitted, or alike denied, in the primitive histories of all people. It was the practice of all nations, of the Grecians as well as the Orientals, to refer every unexpected or inexplicable occurrence immediately to the Deity. The sages of antiquity lived in continual communion with superior intelligences. Whilst these representations (such is Eichhorn's statement of the matter) are always, in reference to the Hebrew records, understood verbally and literally, it has hitherto been customary to explain similar representations in the pagan histories, by presupposing either deception and gross falsehood, or the misinterpretation and corruption of tradition. But Eichhorn thinks justice evidently requires that Hebrew and pagan history should be treated in the same way ; so that intercourse with celestial beings during a state of infancy, must either be accorded to all nations, pagan and Hebrew, or equally denied to all. The mind hesitates to make so universal an admission : first, on account of the not unfrequent errors contained in religions claiming to have been divinely communicated ; secondly, from a sense of the difficulty of explaining the transition of the human race from a state of divine tutelage to one of self-dependence : and lastly, because in proportion as intelligence increases, and the authenticity of the records may be more and more confidently relied upon, in the same proportion do these immediate divine influences invariably disappear. If, accordingly, the notion of supernatural interposition is to be rejected with regard to the Hebrews, as well as to all other people, the view generally taken of pagan antiquity presents itself, at first sight, as that most obviously applicable to the early Hebrews ; namely, that their pretended revelations were based upon deceit and falsehood, or that their miraculous histories should be referred to the misrepresentations and corruptions of tradition. This is the view of the subject actually applied by the Fragmentist to the Old Testament ; a representation, says Eichhorn, from which the mind on a nearer contemplation recoils. Is it conceivable that the greatest men of

---

[1] Recension der übrigen, noch ungedruckten Werke des Wolfenbüttler Fragmentisten, in Eichhorns allgemeiner Bibliothek, erster Band 1tes u. 2tes Stück.

antiquity, whose influence operated so powerfully and so beneficially upon their age, should one and all have been impostors, and yet have escaped the detection of their contemporaries?

According to Eichhorn, so perverted a view could arise only in a mind that refused to interpret the ancient records in the spirit of their age. Truly, had they been composed with all the philosophical accuracy of the writers of the present day, we should have been compelled to find in them either actual divine interpositions, or a fraudulent pretence. But they are the production of an infant and unscientific age; and treat, without reserve of divine interventions, in accordance with the conceptions and phraseology of that early period. So that, in point of fact, we have neither miracles to wonder at, on the one hand, nor deceptions to unmask on the other; but simply the language of a former age to translate into that of our own day. Eichhorn observes that before the human race had gained a knowledge of the true causes of things, all occurrences were referred to supernatural agencies, or to the interposition of superhuman beings. Lofty conceptions, noble resolves, useful inventions and regulations, but more especially vivid dreams, were the operations of that Deity under whose immediate influence they believed themselves placed. Manifestations of distinguished intelligence and skill, by which some individual excited the wonder of the people, were regarded as miraculous; as signs of supernatural endowments, and of a particular intercourse with higher beings. And this was the belief, not of the people only, but also of these eminent individuals, who entertained no doubt of the fact, and who exulted in the full conviction of being in mysterious connexion with the Deity. Eichhorn is of opinion that no objection can be urged against the attempt to resolve all the Mosaic narratives into natural occurrences, and thus far he concedes to the Fragmentist his primary position; but he rejects his inference that Moses was an impostor, pronouncing the conclusion to be over-hasty and unjust. Thus Eichhorn agreed with the Naturalists in divesting the biblical narratives of all their immediately divine contents, but he differed from them in this, that he explained the supernatural lustre which adorns these histories, not as a fictitious colouring imparted with design to deceive, but as a natural and as it were spontaneous illumination reflected from antiquity itself.

In conformity with these principles Eichhorn sought to explain naturally the histories of Noah, Abraham, Moses, etc. Viewed in the light of that age, the appointment of Moses to be the leader of the Israelities was nothing more than the long cherished project of the patriot to emancipate his people, which when presented before his mind with more than usual vividness in his dreams, was believed by him to be a divine inspiration. The flame and smoke which ascended from Mount Sinai, at the giving of the law, was merely a fire which Moses kindled in order to make a deeper impression upon the imagination of the people, together with an accidental thunderstorm which arose at that particular moment. The shining of his countenance was the natural effect of being over-heated: but it was supposed to be a divine manifestation, not only by the people, but by Moses himself, he being ignorant of the true cause.

Eichhorn was more reserved in his application of this mode of interpretation to the New Testament. Indeed, it was only to a few of the narratives in the Acts of the Apostles, such as the miracle of the day of Pentecost, the conversion of the Apostle Paul, and the many apparitions of angels, that he allowed himself to apply it. Here too, he refers the supernatural to the figurative language of the Bible; in which, for example, a happy accident is called—a protecting angel; a joyous thought—the salutation of an angel; and a peaceful state of mind—a comforting angel. It is however remarkable that

Eichhorn was conscious of the inapplicability of the natural explanation to some parts of the gospel history, and with respect to many of the narratives took a more elevated view.

Many writings in a similar spirit, which partially included the New Testament within the circle of their explanations, appeared ; but it was Dr. Paulus who by his commentary on the Gospels[2] in 1800, first acquired the full reputation of a *christian Evemeru*s. In the introduction to this work he states it to be the primary requisite of the biblical critic to be able to distinguish between what is *fact*, and what is *opinion*. That which has been actually experienced, internally or externally, by the participants in an event, he calls *fact*. The interpretation of an event, the supposed causes to which it is referred either by the participants or by the narrators, he calls *opinion*. But, according to Dr. Paulus, these two elements become so easily blended and confounded in the minds both of the original sharers in an event, and of the subsequent relators and historians, that fact and opinion lose their distinction ; so that the one and the other are believed and recorded with equal confidence in their historical truth. This intermixture is particularly apparent in the historical books of the New Testament; since at the time when Jesus lived, it was still the prevailing disposition to derive every striking occurrence from an invisible and superhuman cause. It is consequently the chief task of the historian who desires to deal with matters of fact, that is to say, in reference to the New Testament, to separate these two constituent elements so closely amalgamated, and yet in themselves so distinct ; and to extricate the pure kernel of fact from the shell of opinion. In order to this, in the absence of any more genuine account which would serve as a correcting parallel, he must transplant himself in imagination upon the theatre of action, and strive to the utmost to contemplate the events by the light of the age in which they occurred. And from this point of view he must seek to supply the deficiencies of the narration, by filling in those explanatory collateral circumstances, which the relator himself is so often led by his predilection for the supernatural to leave unnoticed. It is well known in what manner Dr. Paulus applies these principles to the New Testament in his Commentary, and still more fully in his later production, " The Life of Jesus." He firmly maintains the historical truth of the gospel narratives, and he aims to weave them into one consecutive chronologically-arranged detail of facts ; but he explains away every trace of immediate divine agency, and denies all supernatural intervention. Jesus is not to him the *Son of God* in the sense of the Church, but a wise and virtuous human being ; and the effects he produced are not miracles, but acts sometimes of benevolence and friendship, sometimes of medical skill, sometimes also the results of accident and good fortune.

This view proposed by Eichhorn, and more completely developed by Paulus, necessarily presupposes the Old and New Testament writings to contain a minute and faithful narration, composed shortly after the occurrence of the events recorded, and derived, wherever this was possible, from the testimony of eye-witnesses. For it is only from an accurate and original report that the ungarbled fact can be disentangled from interwoven opinion. If the report be later and less original, what security is there that what is taken for the matter-of-fact kernel does not belong to opinion or tradition ? To avoid this objection, Eichhorn sought to assign a date to the Old Testament histories approximating as nearly as possible to the events they record : and here he, and other theologians of the same school, found no difficulty in admitting suppositions the most unnatural: for example, that the Pentateuch was written during the passage through the wilderness. However this critic admits that

---

[2] Paulus's Commentar über das neue Testament.

some portions of the Old Testament, the Book of Judges, for instance, could not have been written contemporaneously with the events ; that the historian must have contemplated his heroes through the dim mist of intervening ages, which might easily have magnified them into giant forms. No historian who had either witnessed the circumstances, or had been closely connected with them in point of time, could embellish after such fashion, except with the express aim to amuse at the expense of truth. But with regard to remote occurrences it is quite different. The imagination is no longer restricted by the fixed limits of historical reality, but is aided in its flight by the notion that in earlier times all things were better and nobler ; and the historian is tempted to speak in loftier phrase, and to use hyperbolical expressions. Least of all is it possible to avoid embellishment, when the compiler of a subsequent age derives his materials from the orally transmitted traditions of antiquity. The adventures and wondrous exploits of ancestors, handed down by father to son, and by son to grandson, in glowing and enthusiastic representations, and sung by the poet in lofty strains, are registered in the written records of the historian in similar terms of high flowing diction. Though Eichhorn took this view of a portion of the Old Testament Books, he believed he was not giving up their historical basis, but was still able, after clearing away the more or less evident legendary additions, to trace out the natural course of the history.

But in one instance at least, this master of the natural mode of interpretation in reference to the Old Testament, took a more elevated view :—namely, of the history of the creation and the fall. In his influential work on primitive history,[3] although he had from the first declared the account of the creation to be poetry, he nevertheless maintained that of the fall to be neither mythology nor allegory, but true history. The historical basis that remained after the removal of the supernatural, he stated to be this : that the human constitution had at the very beginning become impaired by the eating of a poisonous fruit. He thought it indeed very possible in itself, and confirmed by numerous examples in profane history, that purely historical narratives might be overlaid by a mythical account ; but owing to a supranaturalistic notion, he refused to allow the same possibility to the Bible, because he thought it unworthy of the Deity to admit a mythological fragment into a book, which bore such incontestable traces of its divine origin. Later, however, Eichhorn himself declared that he had changed his opinion with regard to the second and third chapters of Genesis.[4] He no longer saw in them an historical account of the effects of poison, but rather the mythical embodying of a philosophical thought ; namely, that the desire for a better condition than that in which man actually is, is the source of all the evil in the world. Thus, in this point at least, Eichhorn preferred to give up the history in order to hold fast the idea, rather than to cling to the history with the sacrifice of every more elevated conception. For the rest, he agreed with Paulus and others in considering the miraculous in the sacred history as a drapery which needs only to be drawn aside, in order to disclose the pure historic form.

§ 7.

MORAL INTERPRETATION OF KANT.

Amidst these natural explanations which the end of the eighteenth century brought forth in rich abundance, it was a remarkable interlude to see the old

[3] Eichhorn's Urgeschichte, herausgegeben von Gabler, 3 Thl. s. 98. ff.
[4] Allgem. Biblioth. 1 Bd. s. 989, and Einleitung in das A. T. 3 Thl. s. 82.

allegorical system of the christian fathers all at once called up from its grave, and revived in the form of the moral interpretation of Kant.   He, as a philosopher, did not concern himself with the history, as did the rationalist theologians, but like the fathers of the church, he sought the idea involved in the history : not however considering it as they did an absolute idea, at once theoretical as well as practical, but regarding it only on its practical side, as what he called *the moral imperative* and consequently belonging to the finite. He moreover attributed these ideas wrought into the biblical text, not to the Divine Spirit, but to its philosophical interpreters, or in a deeper sense, to the moral condition of the authors of the book themselves.   This opinion Kant [1] bases upon the fact, that in all religions old and new which are partly comprised in sacred books, intelligent and well-meaning teachers of the people have continued to explain them, until they have brought their actual contents into agreement with the universal principles of morality.   Thus did the moral philosophers amongst the Greeks and Romans with their fabulous legends ; till at last they explained the grossest polytheism as mere symbolical representations of the attributes of the one divine Being, and gave a mystical sense to the many vicious actions of their gods, and to the wildest dreams of their poets, in order to bring the popular faith, which it was not expedient to destroy, into agreement with the doctrines of morality.   The later Judaism and Christianity itself he thinks have been formed upon similar explanations, occasionally much forced, but always directed to objects undoubtedly good and necessary for all men.   Thus the Mahometans gave a spiritual meaning to the sensual descriptions of their paradise, and thus the Hindoos, or at least the more enlightened part of them, interpreted their Vedas.   In like manner, according to Kant, the Christian Scriptures of the Old and New Testament, must be interpreted throughout in a sense which agrees with the universal practical laws of a religion of pure reason : and such an explanation, even though it should, apparently or actually, do violence to the text, which is the case with many of the biblical narratives, is to be preferred to a literal one, which either contains no morality at all or is in opposition to the moral principle.   For example, the expressions breathing vengeance against enemies in many of the Psalms are made to refer to the desires and passions which we must strive by all means to bring into subjection ; and the miraculous account in the New Testament of the descent of Jesus from heaven, of his relationship to God, etc., is taken as an imaginative description of the ideal of humanity well-pleasing to God.   That such an interpretation is possible, without even always too offensive an opposition to the literal sense of these records of the popular faith, arises according to the profound observations of Kant from this : that long before the existence of these records, the disposition to a moral religion was latent in the human mind ; that its first manifestations were directed to the worship of the Deity, and on this very account gave occasion to those pretended revelations ; still, though unintentionally, imparting even to these fictions somewhat of the spiritual character of their origin.   In reply to the charge of dishonesty brought against his system of interpretation, he thinks it a sufficient defence to observe, that it does not pretend that the sense now given to the sacred books, always existed in the intention of the authors ; this question it sets aside, and only claims for itself the right to interpret them after its own fashion.

Whilst Kant in this manner sought to educe moral thoughts from the biblical writings, even in their historical part, and was even inclined to consider these

---

[1] Religion innerhalb der Grenzen der blossen Vernunft, drittes Stück. No. VI. : Der Kirchenglaube hat zu seinem höchsten Ausleger den reinen Religionsglauben.

thoughts as the fundamental object of the history : on the one hand, he derived these thoughts only from himself and the cultivation of his age, and therefore could seldom assume that they had actually been laid down by the authors of those writings ; and on the other hand, and for the same reason, he omitted to show what was the relation between these thoughts and those symbolic representations, and how it happened that the one came to be expressed by the other.

§ 8.

RISE OF THE MYTHICAL MODE OF INTERPRETING THE SACRED HISTORY, IN REFERENCE FIRST TO THE OLD TESTAMENT.

It was impossible to rest satisfied with modes of proceeding so unhistorical on the one hand, and so unphilosophical on the other. Added to which, the study of mythology, now become far more general and more prolific in its results, exerted an increasing influence on the views taken of biblical history. Eichhorn had indeed insisted that all primitive histories, whether Hebrew or Pagan, should be treated alike, but this equality gradually disappeared ; for though the mythical view became more and more developed in relation to profane history, the natural mode of explanation was still rigidly adhered to for the Hebrew records.   All could not imitate Paulus, who sought to establish consistency of treatment by extending the same natural explanation which he gave to the Bible, to such also of the Greek legends as presented any points of resemblance ; on the contrary, opinion in general took the opposite course, and began to regard many of the biblical narratives as mythi. Semler had already spoken of a kind of Jewish mythology, and had even called the histories of Samson and Esther mythi ; Eichhorn too had done much to prepare the way, now further pursued by Gabler, Schelling, and others, who established the notion of the mythus as one of universal application to ancient history, sacred as well as profane, according to the principle of Heyne : *A mythis omnis priscorum hominum cum historia tum philosophia procedit*.[1]   And Bauer in 1820 ventured so far as to publish a Hebrew mythology of the Old and New Testament.[2]   The earliest records of all nations are, in the opinion of Bauer, mythical : why should the writings of the Hebrews form a solitary exception ?—whereas in point of fact a cursory glance at their sacred books proves that they also contain mythical elements. A narrative he explains, after Gabler and Schelling, to be recognizable as mythus, first, when it proceeds from an age in which no written records existed, but in which facts were transmitted through the medium of oral tradition alone ; secondly, when it presents an historical account of events which are either absolutely or relatively beyond the reach of experience, such as occurrences connected with the spiritual world, and incidents to which, from the nature of the circumstances, no one could have been witness ; or thirdly, when it deals in the marvellous and is couched in symbolical language. Not a few narratives of this description occur in the Bible ; and an unwillingness to regard them as mythi can arise only from a false conception of the nature of a mythus, or of the character of the biblical writings. In the one case mythi are confounded with fables, premeditated fictions, and wilful falsehoods, instead of being recognised as the necessary vehicle of expression for the first efforts of the human mind ; in the other case it certainly does appear improbable, (the notion of inspiration

[1] Ad. Apollod. Athen. Biblioth. notæ, p. 3 f.
[2] Hebraische Mythologie des alten und neuen Testaments.   G. L. Bauer, 1802.

presupposed,) that God should have admitted the substitution of mythical for actual representations of facts and ideas, but a nearer examination of the scriptures shows that this very notion of inspiration, far from being any hindrance to the mythical interpretation, is itself of mythical origin.

Wegscheider ascribed this greater unwillingness to recognise mythi in the early records of the Hebrew and Christian religion than in the heathen religions, partly to the prevailing ignorance respecting the progress of historical and philosophical science ; partly to a certain timidity which dares not call things manifestly identical by the same name.   At the same time he declared it impossible to rescue the Bible from the reproaches and scoffs of its enemies except by the acknowledgment of mythi in the sacred writings, and the separation of their inherent meaning from their unhistorical form.[3]

These biblical critics gave the following general definition of the mythus. It is the representation of an event or of an idea in a form which is historical, but, at the same time characterized by the rich pictorial and imaginative mode of thought and expression of the primitive ages.   They also distinguished several kinds of mythi.[4]

1st. *Historical mythi:* narratives of real events coloured by the light of antiquity, which confounded the divine and the human, the natural and the supernatural.

2nd. *Philosophical mythi :* such as clothe in the garb of historical narrative a simple thought, a precept, or an idea of the time.

3rd. *Poetical mythi:* historical and philosophical mythi partly blended together, and partly embellished by the creations of the imagination, in which the original fact or idea is almost obscured by the veil which the fancy of the poet has woven around it.

To classify the biblical mythi according to these several distinctions is a difficult task, since the mythus which is purely symbolical wears the semblance of history equally with the mythus which represents an actual occurrence.   These critics however laid down rules by which the different mythi might be distinguished.   The first essential is, they say, to determine whether the narrative have a distinct object, and what that object is.   Where no object, for the sake of which the legend might have been invented, is discoverable, every one would pronounce the mythus to be *historical.*   But if all the principal circumstances of the narrative concur to symbolize a particular truth, this undoubtedly was the object of the narrative, and the mythus is *philosophical.*   The blending of the historical and philosophical mythus is particularly to be recognised when we can detect in the narrative an attempt to derive events from their causes.   In many instances the existence of an historical foundation is proved also by independent testimony ; sometimes certain particulars in the mythus are intimately connected with known genuine history, or bear in themselves undeniable and inherent characteristics of probability : so that the critic, while he rejects the external form, may yet retain the groundwork as historical.   The *poetical* mythus is the most difficult to distinguish, and Bauer gives only a negative criterion.   When the narrative is so wonderful on the one hand as to exclude the possibility of its being a detail of facts, and when on the other it discovers no attempt to symbolize a particular thought, it may be suspected that the entire narrative owes its birth to the imagination of the poet.   Schelling particularly remarks on the unartificial and spontaneous origin of mythi in general.   The unhistorical

[3] Institutiones Theol. Chr. Dogm. § 42.

[4] Ammon, Progr. quo inquiritur in narrationum de vitæ Jesu Christi primordiis fontes, etc., in Pott's and Ruperti's Sylloge Comm. theol. No. 5, und Gabler's n. theol. Journal, 5 Bd. s. 83 und 397.

which is interwoven with the matters of fact in the historical mythus is not, he observes, the artistical product of design and invention. It has on the contrary glided in of itself, as it were, in the lapse of time and in the course of transmission. And, speaking of philosophical mythi, he says: the sages of antiquity clothed their ideas in an historical garb, not only in order to accommodate those ideas to the apprehension of a people who must be awakened by sensible impressions, but also on their own account: deficient themselves in clear abstract ideas, and in ability to give expression to their dim conceptions, they sought to illumine what was obscure in their representations by means of sensible imagery.[5]

We have already remarked, that the natural mode of interpreting the Old Testament could be maintained only so long as the records were held to be contemporaneous, or nearly so, with the events recorded. Consequently it was precisely those theologians, Vater, De Wette and others who controverted this opinion, who contributed to establish the mythical view of the sacred histories. Vater[6] expressed the opinion that the peculiar character of the narrations in the Pentateuch could not be rightly understood, unless it were conceded that they are not the production of an eye witness, but are a series of transmitted traditions. Their traditional origin being admitted, we cease to feel surprised at the traces which they discover of a subsequent age; at numerical exaggerations, together with other inaccuracies and contradictions; at the twilight which hangs over many of the occurrences; and at representations such as, that the clothes of the Israelites waxed not old during their passage through the wilderness. Vater even contends, that unless we ascribe a great share of the marvellous contained in the Pentateuch to tradition, we do violence to the original sense of the compilers of these narratives.

The natural mode of explanation was still more decidedly opposed by De Wette than by Vater. He advocated the mythical interpretation of a large proportion of the Old Testament histories. In order to test the historical credibility of a narrative, he says,[7] we must ascertain the intention of the narrator. If that intention be not to satisfy the natural thirst for historical truth by a simple narration of facts, but rather to delight or touch the feelings, or to illustrate some philosophical or religious truth, then his narrative has no pretension to historical validity. Even when the narrator is conscious of strictly historical intentions, nevertheless his point of view may not be the historical: he may be a poetical narrator, not indeed subjectively, as a poet drawing inspiration from himself, but objectively, as enveloped by and depending on poetry external to himself. This is evidently the case when the narrator details as bonâ fide matter of fact things which are impossible and incredible, which are contrary not only to experience, but to the established laws of nature. Narrations of this description spring out of tradition. Tradition, says De Wette, is uncritical and partial; its tendency is not historical, but rather patriotic and poetical. And since the patriotic sentiment is gratified by all that flatters national pride, the more splendid, the more honourable, the more wonderful the narrative, the more acceptable it is; and where tradition has left any blanks, imagination at once steps in and fills them up. And since, he continues, a great part of the historical books of the Old Testament bear this stamp, it has hitherto been believed possible (on the part of the natural interpreters) to separate the embellishments and trans-

[5] Ueber Mythen, historische Sagen und Philosopheme der ältesten Welt. In Paulus Memorabilien, 5 stuck. 1793.

[6] Vid. die Abhandlung über Moses und die Verfasser des Pentateuchs, im 3ten. Band des Comm. über den Pent. s. 660.

[7] Kritik der Mosaischen Geschichte. Einl. s. 10. ff.

formations from the historical substance, and still to consider them available as records of facts.   This might indeed be done, had we, besides the marvellous biblical narratives, some other purely historical account of the events. But this is not the case with regard to the Old Testament history; we are solely dependent on those accounts which we cannot recognize as purely historical.   They contain no criterion by which to distinguish between the true and the false; both are promiscuously blended, and set forth as of equal dignity.   According to De Wette, the whole natural mode of explanation is set aside by the principle that the only means of acquaintance with a history is the narrative which we possess concerning it, and that beyond this narrative the historian cannot go.   In the present case, this reports to us only a supernatural course of events, which we must either receive or reject: if we reject it, we determine to know nothing at all about it, and are not justified in allowing ourselves to invent a natural course of events, of which the narrative is totally silent.   It is moreover inconsistent and arbitrary to refer the dress in which the events of the Old Testament are clothed to poetry, and to preserve the events themselves as historical; much rather do the particular details and the dress in which they appear, constitute a whole belonging to the province of poetry and mythus.   For example, if God's covenant with Abraham be denied in the form of fact, whilst at the same time it is maintained that the narrative had an historical basis,—that is to say, that though no objective divine communication took place, the occurrence had a subjective reality in Abraham's mind in a dream or in a waking vision; in other words, that a natural thought was awakened in Abraham which he, in the spirit of the age, referred to God:—of the naturalist who thus reasons, De Wette asks, how he knows that such thoughts arose in Abraham's mind? The narration refers them to God; and if we reject the narration, we know nothing about these thoughts of Abraham, and consequently cannot know that they had arisen naturally in him.   According to general experience, such hopes as are described in this covenant, that he should become the father of a mighty nation which should possess the land of Canaan, could not have sprung up naturally in Abraham's mind; but it is quite natural that the Israelites when they had become a numerous people in possession of that land, should have invented the covenant in order to render their ancestor illustrious.   Thus the natural explanation, by its own unnaturalness, ever brings us back to the mythical.

Even Eichhorn, who so extensively employed the natural explanation in reference to the Old Testament, perceived its inadmissibility in relation to the gospel histories.   Whatever in these narratives has a tendency to the supernatural, he remarks,[8] we ought not to attempt to transform into a natural occurrence, because this is impossible without violence.   If once an event has acquired a miraculous colouring, owing to the blending together of some popular notion with the occurrence, the natural fact can be disentangled only when we possess a second account which has not undergone the like transformation; as, concerning the death of Herod Agrippa, we have not only the narrative in the Acts, but also that of Josephus.[9]   But since we have no such controlling account concerning the history of Jesus, the critic who pretends to discover the natural course of things from descriptions of supernatural occurrences, will only weave a tissue of indemonstrable hypotheses:—a consideration which, as Eichhorn observes, at once annihilates many of the so-called psychological interpretations of the Gospel histories.

[8] Einleit. in das N. T. 1, s. 408. ff.
[9] Antiquit. xix. viii. 2.

It is this same difference between the natural and mythical modes of interpretation which Krug intends to point out, referring particularly to the histories of miracles, when he distinguishes the physical or material, from the genetic or formal, mode of explaining them. Following the former mode, according to him, the inquiry is : how can the wonderful event here related have possibly taken place with all its details by natural means and according to natural laws? Whereas, following the latter, the question is : whence arose the narrative of the marvellous event? The former explains the natural possibility of the thing related (the substance of the narrative); the latter traces the origin of the existing record (the form of the narrative). Krug considers attempts of the former kind to be fruitless, because they produce interpretations yet more wonderful than the fact itself; far preferable is the other mode, since it leads to results which throw light upon miraculous histories collectively. He gives the preference to the exegetist, because in his explanation of the text he is not obliged to do violence to it, but may accept it altogether literally as the author intended, even though the thing related be impossible; whereas the interpreter, who follows the material or physical explanation, is driven to ingenious subtleties which make him lose sight of the original meaning of the authors, and substitute something quite different which they neither could nor would have said.

In like manner Gabler recommended the mythical view, as the best means of escaping from the so called natural, but forced explanation, which had become the fashion. The natural interpreter, he remarks, commonly aims to make the whole narrative natural; and as this can but seldom succeed, he allows himself the most violent measures, owing to which modern exegesis has been brought into disrepute even amongst laymen. The mythical view, on the contrary, needs no such subtleties; since the greater part of a narrative frequently belongs to the mythical representation merely, while the nucleus of fact, when divested of the subsequently added miraculous envelopments, is often very small.

Neither could Horst reconcile himself to the atomistic mode of proceeding, which selected from the marvellous narratives of the Bible, as unhistorical, isolated incidents merely, and inserted natural ones in their place, instead of recognizing in the whole of each narrative a religious moral mythus in which a certain idea is embodied.

An anonymous writer in Bertholdt's Journal has expressed himself very decidedly against the natural mode of explaining the sacred history, and in favour of the mythical. The essential defect of the natural interpretation, as exhibited in its fullest development by Paulus's Commentary, is, according to that writer, its unhistorical mode of procedure. He objects : that it allows conjecture to supply the deficiencies of the record ; adopts individual speculations as a substitute for real history ; seeks by vain endeavours to represent that as natural which the narrative describes as supernatural; and lastly, evaporates all sacredness and divinity from the Scriptures, reducing them to collections of amusing tales no longer meriting the name of history. According to our author, this insufficiency of the natural mode of interpretation, whilst the supernatural also is felt to be unsatisfactory, leads the mind to the mythical view, which leaves the substance of the narrative unassailed ; and instead of venturing to explain the details, accepts the whole, not indeed as true history, but as a sacred legend. This view is supported by the analogy of all antiquity, political and religious, since the closest resemblance exists between many of the narratives of the Old and New Testament, and the mythi of profane antiquity. But the most convincing argument is this : if the mythical view be once admitted, the innumerable, and never otherwise to be harmonized, discrepancies and chronological contradictions in the gospel histories disappear, as it were, at one stroke.[10]

§ 9.

THE MYTHICAL MODE OF INTERPRETATION IN REFERENCE TO THE NEW TESTAMENT.

Thus the mythical mode of interpretation was adopted not only in relation to the Old Testament, but also to the New; not, however, without its being felt necessary to justify such a step. Gabler has objected to the Commentary of Paulus, that it concedes too little to the mythical point of view, which must be adopted for certain New Testament narratives. For many of these narratives present not only those mistaken views of things which might have been taken by eye-witnesses, and by the rectification of which a natural course of events may be made out; but frequently, also, false facts and impossible consequences which no eye-witness could have related, and which could only have been the product of tradition, and must therefore be mythically understood.[1]

The chief difficulty which opposed the transference of the mythical point of view from the Old Testament to the New, was this :—it was customary to look for mythi in the fabulous primitive ages only, in which no written records of events as yet existed; whereas, in the time of Jesus, the mythical age had long since passed away, and writing had become common among the Jews. Schelling had however conceded (at least in a note) that the term mythi, in a more extended sense, was appropriate to those narratives which, though originating in an age when it was usual to preserve documentary records, were nevertheless transmitted by the mouth of the people. Bauer[2] in like manner asserted, that though a connected series of mythi,—a history which should be altogether mythical,—was not to be sought in the New Testament, yet there might occur in it single myths, either transferred from the Old Testament to the New, or having originally sprung up in the latter. Thus he found, in the details of the infancy of Jesus, much which requires to be regarded from a mythical point of view. As after the decease of celebrated personages, numerous anecdotes are circulated concerning them, which fail not to receive many and wondrous amplifications in the legends of a wonder-loving people; so, after Jesus had become distinguished by his life, and yet more glorified by his death, his early years, which had been passed in obscurity, became adorned with miraculous embellishments. And, according to Bauer, whenever in this history of the infancy we find celestial beings, called by name and bearing the human shape, predicting future occurrences, etc., we have a right to suppose a mythus; and to conjecture as its origin, that the great actions of Jesus being referred to superhuman causes, this explanation came to be blended with the history. On the same subject, Gabler[3] remarked that the notion of ancient is relative; compared with the Mosaic religion Christianity is certainly young; but in itself it is old enough to allow us to refer the original history of its founder to ancient times. That at that time written documents on other subjects existed, proves nothing,

---

[10] Die verschiedenen Rücksichten, in welchen und für welche der Biograph Jesu arbeiten kann. In Bertholdt's krit. Journal, 5 Bd. s. 235. ff.

[1] Recens-von Paulus Commentar, im neuesten theol. Journal 7, 4, s. 395 ff. (1801).

[2] Hebräische Mythologie. 1 Thl. Einl. § 5.

[3] Ist es erlaubt, in der Bibel, und sogar im N.T., Mythen anzunehmen? Im Journal für auserlesene theol. Literatur, 2, 1, s. 49 ff.

whilst it can be shown that for a long period there was no written account of
the life of Jesus, and particularly of his infancy.   Oral narratives were alone
transmitted, and they would easily become tinged with the marvellous, mixed
with Jewish ideas, and thus grow into historical mythi.   On many other
points there was no tradition, and here the mind was left to its own surmises.
The more scanty the historical data, the greater was the scope for conjecture;
and historical guesses and inferences of this description, formed in harmony
with the Jewish-Christian tastes, may be called the philosophical, or rather,
the dogmatical mythi of the early christian Gospel.   The notion of the
mythus, concludes Gabler, being thus shown to be applicable to many of the
narratives of the New Testament, why should we not dare to call them by
their right name; why—that is to say in learned discussion—avoid an expression which can give offence only to the prejudiced or the misinformed?

As in the Old Testament Eichhorn had been brought over by the force of
internal evidence from his earlier natural explanation, to the mythical view
of the history of the fall; so in the New Testament, the same thing happened
to Usteri in relation to the history of the temptation.   In an earlier work he
had, following Schleiermacher, considered it as a parable spoken by Jesus
but misunderstood by his disciples.[4]   Soon however he perceived the difficulties of this interpretation; and since both the natural and the supernatural
views of the narrative appeared to him yet more objectionable, he had no
alternative but to adopt the mythical.   Once admit, he remarks, a state of
excitement, particularly of religious excitement, among a not unpoetical
people, and a short time is sufficient to give an appearance of the marvellous
not only to obscure and concealed, but even to public and well-known facts.
It is therefore by no means conceivable that the early Jewish Christians,
gifted with the spirit, that is, animated with religious enthusiasm, as they
were, and familiar with the Old Testament, should not have been in a
condition to invent symbolical scenes such as the temptation and other New
Testament mythi.   It is not however to be imagined that any one individual
seated himself at his table to invent them out of his own head, and write
them down, as he would a poem: on the contrary, these narratives like all
other legends were fashioned by degrees, by steps which can no longer be
traced; gradually acquired consistency, and at length received a fixed form
in our written Gospels.

We have seen that in reference to the early histories of the Old Testament,
the mythical view could be embraced by those only who doubted the composition of these Scriptures by eye-witnesses or contemporaneous writers.
This was equally the case in reference to the New.   It was not till Eichhorn [5]
became convinced that only a slender thread of that primitive Gospel believed
by the Apostles ran through the three first Gospels, and that even in Matthew
this thread was entangled in a mass of unapostolic additions, that he discarded
as unhistorical legends, the many narratives which he found perplexing, from
all share in the history of Jesus; for example, besides the Gospel of Infancy,
the details of the temptation; several of the miracles of Jesus; the rising of
the saints from their graves at his crucifixion; the guard at the sepulchre,
etc.[6]   Particularly since the opinion, that the three first Gospels originated
from oral traditions, became firmly established,[7] they have been found to

---

[4] Ueber den Täufer Johannes, die Taufe und Versuchung Christi, in Ullmann's u.
Umbreit's theol. Studien u. Kritiken, 2, 3, s. 456 ff.

[5] Beitrag zur Erklärung der Versuchungsgeschichte, in ders. Zeitschrift, 1832, 4. Heft.

[6] Einleitung in das N. T. 1, s. 422 ff. 453 ff.

[7] Besonders durch Gieseler, über die Entstehung und die frühsten Schicksale der schrift
lichen Evangelien.

contain a continually increasing number of mythi and mythical embellishments.[8]   On this account the authenticity of the Gospel of John, and consequently its historical credibility, is confidently maintained by most of the theologians of the present day : he only who, with Bretschneider,[9] questions its apostolic composition, may cede in this Gospel also a considerable place to the mythical element.

§ 10.

THE NOTION OF THE MYTHUS IN ITS APPLICATION TO SACRED HISTORIES
NOT CLEARLY APPREHENDED BY THEOLOGIANS.

Thus, indeed, did the mythical view gain application to the biblical history : still the notion of the mythus was for a long time neither clearly apprehended nor applied to a due extent.

Not clearly apprehended.   The characteristic which had been recognised as constituting the distinction between historical and philosophical mythi, however just that distinction might in itself be, was of a kind which easily betrayed the critic back again into the scarcely abandoned natural explanation.   His task, with regard to historical mythi, was still to separate the natural fact—the nucleus of historical reality—from its unhistorical and miraculous embellishments.   An essential difference indeed existed : the natural explanation attributed the embellishments to the opinion of the actors concerned, or of the narrator ; the mythical interpretation derived them from tradition ; but the mode of proceeding was left too little determined.   If the Rationalist could point out historical mythi in the Bible, without materially changing his mode of explanation ; so the Supernaturalist on his part felt himself less offended by the admission of historical mythi, which still preserved to the sacred narratives a basis of fact, than by the supposition of philosophical mythi, which seemed completely to annihilate every trace of historical foundation.   It is not surprising, therefore, that the interpreters who advocated the mythical theory spoke almost exclusively of historical mythi ; that Bauer, amongst a considerable number of mythi which he cites from the New Testament, finds but one philosophical mythus ; and that a mixed mode of interpretation, partly mythical and partly natural, (a medley far more contradictory than the pure natural explanation, from the difficulties of which these critics sought to escape,) should have been adopted. Thus Bauer[1] thought that he was explaining Jehovah's promise to Abraham as an historical mythus, when he admitted as the fundamental fact of the narrative, that Abraham's hopes of a numerous posterity were re-awakened by the contemplation of the star-sown heavens.   Another theologian[2] imagined he had seized the mythical point of view, when, having divested the announcement of the birth of the Baptist of the supernatural, he still retained the dumbness of Zachariah as the historical groundwork.   In like manner Krug,[3] immediately after assuring us that his intention is not to explain the substance of the history, (according to the natural mode,) but to explain the origin of the narrative, (according to the mythical view,) constitutes an accidental

[8] Vid. den Anhang der Schulz'schen Schrift über das Abendmahl, und die Schriften von Sieffert und Schneckenburger über den Ursprung des ersten kanonischen Evangeliums.
[9] In den Probabilien.
[1] Geschichte der hebräischen Nation, Theil. i. s. 123.
[2] In Henke's Magazin, 5ten Bdes. ites Stuck. s. 163.
[3] Versuch über die genetische oder formelle Erklärungsart de Wunder.   In Henke's Museum, i. 3. 1803.

journey of oriental merchants the basis of the narrative of the visit of the
wise men from the east.   But the contradiction is most glaring when we meet
with palpable misconceptions of the true nature of a mythus in a work on
the mythology of the New Testament, such as Bauer's ; in which for instance
he admits, in the case of the parents of John the Baptist, a marriage which
had actually been childless during many years ;—in which he explains the
angelic appearance at the birth of Jesus as a meteoric phenomenon ; supposes
the occurrence of thunder and lightning and the accidental descent of a
dove at his baptism ; constitutes a storm the groundwork of the transfiguration ; and converts the angels at the tomb of the risen Jesus into white
grave-clothes.   Kaiser also, though he complains of the unnaturalness of
many of the natural explanations, accords to a very considerable proportion
of natural explanations a place by the side of the mythical ; remarking—and
the remark is in itself just—that to attempt to explain all the miracles of the
New Testament in one and the same manner betrays a limited and partial
comprehension of the subject.   Let it be primarily admitted that the ancient
author intended to narrate a miracle, and the natural explanation is in many
instances admissible.   This may be either a physical-historical explanation,
as in the narrative of the leper whose approaching recovery Jesus doubtless
perceived ; or it may be a psychological explanation ; since, in the case of
many sick persons, the fame of Jesus and faith in him were mainly instru-
mental in effecting the cure ; sometimes indeed good fortune must be taken
into the account, as where one apparently dead revived in the presence of
Jesus, and he became regarded as the author of the sudden re-animation.
With respect to other miracles Kaiser is of opinion that the mythical interpretation is to be preferred ; he, however, grants a much larger space to
historical, than to philosophical mythi.   He considers most of the miracles
in the Old and New Testament real occurrences mythically embellished :
such as the narrative of the piece of money in the fish's mouth ; and of the
changing of water into wine : which latter history he supposes to have
originated from a friendly jest on the part of Jesus.   Few only of the miracles
are recognised by this critic as pure poetry embodying Jewish ideas ; as the
miraculous birth of Jesus, and the murder of the innocents.[4]

Gabler in particular calls attention to the error of treating philosophical
mythi as if they were historical, and of thus converting into facts things that
never happened.[5]   He is however as little disposed to admit the exclusive
existence of philosophical, as of historical mythi in the New Testament, but
adopting a middle course, he decides in each case that the mythus is of this
kind or of that according to its intrinsic character.   He maintains that it is
as necessary to guard against the arbitrary proceeding of handling as philosophical a mythus through which a fact unquestionably glimmers, as it is to
avoid the opposite tendency to explain naturally or historically that which
belongs properly to the mythical clothing.   In other words : when the derivation of a mythus from a thought is easy and natural, and when the attempt
to educe from it a matter of fact and to give the wonderful history a natural
explanation, does violence to the sense or appears ridiculous, we have, according to Gabler, certain evidence that the mythus is philosophical and not
historical.   He remarks in conclusion that the philosophical-mythical interpretation is in many cases far less offensive than the historical-mythical
explanation.[6]

Yet, notwithstanding this predilection in favour of the philosophical mythus

---

[4] Kaiser's biblische Theologie, 1 Thl.
[5] Gabler's Journal für auserlesene theol. Literatur. ii. 1. s. 46.
[6] Gabler's neuestes theolog. Journal, 7 Bd.

in relation to biblical history, one is surprised to find that Gabler himself was ignorant of the true nature both of the historical and of the philosophical mythus. Speaking of the mythological interpreters of the New Testament who had preceded him, he says that some of them, such as Dr. Paulus, discover in the history of Jesus historical mythi only; whilst others, the anonymous E. F. in Henke's Magazine for instance, find only philosophical mythi. From this we see that he confounded not only the natural explanation with the historical-mythical view, (for in Paulus's "Commentar" the former only is adopted,) but also historical with philosophical mythi; for the author E. F. is so exclusively attached to the historical-mythical view that his explanations might almost be considered as naturalistic.

De Wette has some very cogent observations directed equally against the arbitrary adoption either of the historical-mythical or of the natural explanation in relation to the Mosaic history. In reference to the New Testament an anonymous writer in Bertholdt's Critical Journal [7] is the most decided in his condemnation of every attempt to discover an historical groundwork even in the Gospel mythi. To him likewise the midway path struck out by Gabler, between the exclusive adoption of historical mythi on the one hand and of philosophical mythi on the other, appears inapplicable; for though a real occurrence may in fact constitute the basis of most of the New Testament narratives, it may still be impossible at the present time to separate the element of fact from the mythical adjuncts which have been blended with it, and to determine how much may belong to the one and how much to the other. Usteri likewise expressed the opinion that it is no longer possible to discriminate between the historical and the symbolical in the gospel mythi; no critical knife however sharp is now able to separate the one element from the other. A certain measure of *probability* respecting the preponderance of the historical in one legend, and of the symbolical in another, is the ultimate point to which criticism can now attain.

Opposed however to the onesidedness of those critics who found it so easy to disengage the historical contents from the mythical narratives of the Scriptures, is the onesidedness of other critics, who, on account of the difficulty of the proposed separation, despaired of the possibility of success, and were consequently led to handle the whole mass of gospel mythi as philosophical, at least in so far as to relinquish the endeavour to extract from them a residuum of historical fact. Now it is precisely this latter onesidedness which has been attributed to my criticism of the life of Jesus; consequently, several of the reviewers of this work have taken occasion repeatedly to call attention to the varying proportions in which the historical and the ideal in the pagan religion and primitive history, (the legitimate province of the mythus,) alternate; an interchange with the historical which in the christian primitive history, presupposing the notion of the mythus to be admitted here, must unquestionably take place in a far greater degree. Thus Ullmann distinguishes not only firstly the *philosophical*, and secondly the *historical mythus*, but makes a further distinction between the latter (that is the *historical mythus*, in which there is always a preponderance of the fictitious,) and thirdly the *mythical history*, in which the historical element, though wrought into the ideal, forms the predominating constituent; whilst fourthly in *histories of which the legend is a component element* we tread properly speaking upon historical ground, since in these histories we meet only with a few faint echoes of mythical fiction. Ullmann is moreover of opinion, and Bretschneider and others agree with him, that independently of the re-

---

[7] Bertholdt's Krit. Journal, v. s. 235.

pulsion and confusion which must inevitably be caused by the application of the term *mythus* to that which is Christian—a term originally conceived in relation to a religion of a totally different character—it were more suitable, in connexion with the primitive Christian records, to speak only of Gospel *legend*, (Sage) and the legendary element.[8]

George on the contrary has recently attempted not only more accurately to define the notions of the mythus and of the legend, but likewise to demonstrate that the gospel narratives are mythical rather than legendary. Speaking generally, we should say, that he restricts the term *mythus* to what had previously been distinguished as philosophical mythi; and that he applies the name *legend* to what had hitherto been denominated historical mythi. He handles the two notions as the antipodes of each other; and grasps them with a precision by which the notion of the mythus has unquestionably gained. According to George, *mythus* is the creation of a fact out of an idea: *legend* the seeing of an idea in a fact, or arising out of it. A people, a religious community, finds itself in a certain condition or round of institutions of which the spirit, the idea, lives and acts within it. But the mind, following a natural impulse, desires to gain a complete representation of that existing condition, and to know its origin. This origin however is buried in oblivion, or is too indistinctly discernible to satisfy present feelings and ideas. Consequently an image of that origin, coloured by the light of existing ideas, is cast upon the dark wall of the past, which image is however but a magnified reflex of existing influences.

If such be the rise of the *mythus*, the *legend*, on the contrary, proceeds from given facts: represented, indeed, sometimes in an incomplete and abridged, sometimes in an amplified form, in order to magnify the heroes of the history—but disjoined from their true connexion; the points of view from which they should be contemplated, and the ideas they originally contained, having in the course of transmission wholly disappeared. The consequence is, that new ideas, conceived in the spirit of the different ages through which the legend has passed down, become substituted in the stead of the original ideas. For example, the period of Jewish history subsequent to the time of Moses, which was in point of fact pervaded by a gradual elevation of ideas to monotheism and to a theocracy, is, in a later legend, represented in the exactly opposite light, as a state of falling away from the religious constitution of Moses. An idea so unhistorical will infallibly here and there distort facts transmitted by tradition, fill up blanks in the history, and subjoin new and significant features—and then the mythus reappears in the legend. It is the same with the mythus: propagated by tradition, it, in the process of transmission, loses its distinctive character and completeness, or becomes exaggerated in its details—as for example in the matter of numbers—and then the mythus comes under the influence of the legend. In such wise do these two formations, so essentially distinct in their origin, cross each other and mingle together. Now, if the history of the life of Jesus be of mythical formation, inasmuch as it embodies the vivid impression of the original idea which the first christian community had of their founder, this history, though unhistorical in its form, is nevertheless a faithful representation of the idea of the Christ. If instead of this, the history be legendary— if the actual external facts are given in a distorted and often magnified form —are represented in a false light and embody a false idea,—then, on the contrary, the real tenour of the life of Jesus is lost to us. So that, according to George, the recognition of the mythical element in the Gospels is far less

[8] Ullmann, Recens. meines L. J., in den Theol. Studientu. Kritiken 1836. 3.

prejudicial to the true interests of the Christian faith than the recognition of the legendary element.[9]

With respect to our own opinion, without troubling ourselves here with the dogmatic signification, we need only remark in this introduction, that we are prepared to meet with both legend and mythus in the gospel history; and when we undertake to extract the historial contents which may possibly exist in narratives recognized as mythical, we shall be equally careful neither on the one part by a rude and mechanical separation, to place ourselves on the same ground with the natural interpreter; nor on the other by a hyper-critical refusal to recognize such contents where they actually exist, to lose sight of the history.

§ 11.

THE APPLICATION OF THE NOTION OF THE MYTHUS TOO CIRCUMSCRIBED.

The notion of the mythus, when first admitted by theologians, was not only imperfectly apprehended, but also too much limited in its application to biblical history.

As Eichhorn recognized a genuine mythus only on the very threshold of the Old Testament history, and thought himself obliged to explain all that followed in a natural manner; as, some time later, other portions of the Old Testament were allowed to be mythical, whilst nothing of the kind might be suspected in the New; so, when the mythus was once admitted into the New Testament, it was here again long detained at the threshold, namely, the history of the infancy of Jesus, every farther advance being contested. Ammon,[1] the anonymous E. F. in Henke's Magazine, Usteri, and others maintained a marked distinction between the historical worth of the narratives of the public life and those of the infancy of Jesus. The records of the latter could not, they contend, have been contemporaneous; for particular attention was not at that time directed towards him; and it is equally manifest that they could not have been written during the last three years of his life, since they embody the idea of Jesus glorified, and not of Jesus in conflict and suffering. Consequently their composition must be referred to a period subsequent to his resurrection. But at this period accurate data concerning his childhood were no longer to be obtained. The apostles knew him first in manhood. Joseph was probably dead; and Mary, supposing her to be living when the first and third gospels were composed, had naturally imparted an imaginative lustre to every incident treasured in her memory, whilst her embellishments were doubtless still further magnified in accordance with the Messianic ideas of those to whom her communications were made. Much also that is narrated had no historical foundation, but originated entirely from the notions of the age, and from the Old Testament predictions—that a virgin should conceive—for example. But, say these critics, all this does not in any degree impair the credibility of what follows. The object and task of the Evangelists was merely to give an accurate account of the three last years of the life of Jesus; and here they merit implicit confidence, since they were either themselves spectators of the details they record, or else had learned them from the mouth of trustworthy eye-witnesses. This boundary line between

---

[9] George, **Mythus und Sage**; Versuch einer wissenschaftlichen Entwicklung dieser Begriffe und ihres Verhältnisses zum christlichen Glauben, s. 11. ff. 108. ff.

[1] Work cited, § 8, note 4. Hase, Leben Jesu, § 32. Tholuck, s. 208. ff. Kern, die Hauptsachen der evangelischen Geschichte, 1st Article, Tübinger Zeitschrift für Theologie, 1836, ii. s. 39.

the credibility of the history of the public life, and the fabulousness of the history of the infancy of Jesus, became yet more definitely marked, from the circumstance that many theologians were disposed to reject the two first chapters of Matthew and Luke as spurious and subsequent additions.[2]

Soon, however, some of the theologians who had conceded the commencement of the history to the province of mythi, perceived that the conclusion, the history of the ascension, must likewise be regarded as mythical.[3] Thus the two extremities were cut off by the pruning knife of criticism, whilst the essential body of the history, the period from the baptism to the resurrection, remained, as yet, unassailed : or in the words of the reviewer of Greiling's Life of Jesus :[4] the entrance to the gospel history was through the decorated portal of mythus, and the exit was similar to it, whilst the intermediate space was still traversed by the crooked and toilsome paths of natural interpretations.

In Gabler's[5] writings we meet with a somewhat more extended application of the mythical view. He distinguishes (and recently Rosenkranz[6] has agreed with him) between the miracles wrought *by* Jesus and those operated *on him* or *in relation to him*, interpreting the latter mythically, but the former naturally. Subsequently however, we find Gabler expressing himself as if with the above mentioned theologians he restricted the mythical interpretation to the miraculous narratives of the childhood of Jesus, but this restriction is in fact a limitation merely of the admitted distinction : since though all the miracles connected with the early history of Jesus were operated in relation to him and not wrought by him, many miracles of the same character occur in the history of his public life. Bauer appears to have been guided by the same rule in his Hebrew mythology. He classes as mythical the narratives of the conception and birth of Jesus, of the Baptism, the transfiguration, the angelic apparitions in Gethsemane and at the sepulchre : miracles selected from all periods of the life of Jesus, but all operated in relation to him and not by him. This enumeration, however, does not include all the miracles of this kind.

The often referred to author of the treatise " Upon the different views with which and for which a Biographer of Jesus may work," has endeavoured to show that so limited an application of the notion of the mythus to the history of the life of Jesus is insufficient and inconsequent. This confused point of view from which the gospel narrative is regarded as partly historical and partly mythical owes its origin, according to him, to those theologians who neither give up the history, nor are able to satisfy themselves with its clear results, but who think to unite both parties by this middle course—a vain endeavour which the rigid supranaturalist pronounces heretical, and the rationalist derides. The attempt of these reconcilers, remarks our author, to explain as intelligible everything which is not impossible, lays them open to all the charges so justly brought against the natural interpretation ; whilst the admission of the existence of mythi in the New Testament subjects them to the direct reproach of being inconsequent: the severest censure which can be passed upon a scholar. Besides, the proceeding of these Eclectics is most arbitrary, since they decide respecting what belongs to the history and what to the mythus almost entirely upon subjective grounds. Such distinctions

[2] Comp. Kuinöl, Prolegom. in Matthæum, § 3 ; in Lucam, § 6.
[3] e. g. Ammon, in der Diss. : Ascensus J. C. in cœlum historia biblica, in seinen Opusc. nov.
[4] In Bertholdt's Krit. Journ. v. Bd. s. 248.
[5] Gabler's neuestes theol. Journal, Bd. vii. s. 395.
[6] Encyclopädie der theol. Wissenschaften, s. 161.

are equally foreign to the evangelists, to logical reasoning, and to historical criticism. In consistency with these opinions, this writer applies the notion of the mythus to the entire history of the life of Jesus; recognizes mythi or mythical embellishments in every portion, and ranges under the category of mythus not merely the miraculous occurrences during the infancy of Jesus, but those also of his public life; not merely miracles operated on Jesus, but those wrought by him.

The most extended application of the notion of the philosophical or dogmatical mythus to the Gospel histories which has yet been made, was published in 1799 in an anonymous work concerning Revelation and Mythology. The writer contends that the whole life of Jesus, all that he should and would do, had an ideal existence in the Jewish mind long prior to his birth. Jesus as an individual was not actually such as according to Jewish anticipations he should have been. Not even that, in which all the records which recount his actions agree, is absolutely matter of fact. A popular idea of the life of Jesus grew out of various popular contributions, and from this source our written Gospels were first derived. A reviewer objects that this author appears to suppose a still smaller portion of the historical element in the gospels than actually exists. It would, he remarks, have been wiser to have been guided by a sober criticism of details, than by a sweeping scepticism.[7]

§ 12.

OPPOSITION TO THE MYTHICAL VIEW OF THE GOSPEL HISTORY.

In adopting the mythical point of view as hitherto applied to Biblical history, our theologians had again approximated to the ancient allegorical interpretation. For as both the natural explanations of the Rationalists, and the jesting expositions of the Deists, belong to that form of opinion which, whilst it sacrifices all divine meaning in the sacred record, still upholds its historical character; the mythical mode of interpretation agrees with the allegorical, in relinquishing the historical reality of the sacred narratives in order to preserve to them an absolute inherent truth. The mythical and the allegorical view (as also the moral) equally allow that the historian apparently relates that which is historical, but they suppose him, under the influence of a higher inspiration known or unknown to himself, to have made use of this historical semblance merely as the shell of an *idea*—of a religious conception. The only essential distinction therefore between these two modes of explanation is, that according to the allegorical this higher intelligence is the immediate divine agency; according to the mythical, it is the spirit of a people or a community. (According to the moral view it is generally the mind of the interpreter which suggests the interpretation.) Thus the allegorical view attributes the narrative to a supernatural source, whilst the mythical view ascribes it to that *natural* process by which legends are originated and developed. To which it should be added, that the allegorical interpreter (as well as the moral) may with the most unrestrained arbitrariness separate from the history every thought he deems to be worthy of God, as constituting its inherent meaning; whilst the mythical interpreter, on the contrary, in searching out the ideas which are embodied in the narrative, is controlled by regard to conformity with the spirit and modes of thought of the people and of the age.

This new view of the sacred Scriptures was opposed alike by the orthodox

---

[7] In Gabler's neuestem theolog. Journal, Bd. vi. 4tes Stück. s. 350.

and by the rationalistic party.   From the first, whilst the mythical interpretation was still restricted to the primitive history of the Old Testament, Hess [1]
on the orthodox side, protested against it.   The three following conclusions
may be given as comprising, however incredible this may appear, the substance of his book, a work of some compass ; upon which however it is unnecessary to remark further than that Hess was by no means the last orthodox
theologian who pretended to combat the mythical view with such weapons.
He contends, 1st, that mythi are to be understood figuratively ; now the
sacred historians intended their writings to be understood literally : consequently they do not relate mythi.   2ndly, Mythology is something heathen-
ish ; the Bible is a christian book ; consequently it contains no mythology.
The third conclusion is more complex, and, as will appear below, has more
meaning.   If, says Hess, the marvellous were confined to those earliest
biblical records of which the historical validity is less certain, and did not
appear in any subsequent writings, the miraculous might be considered as a
proof of the mythical character of the narrative ; but the marvellous is no less
redundant in the latest and undeniably historical records, than in the more
ancient ; consequently it cannot be regarded as a criterion of the mythical.   In
short the most hollow natural explanation, did it but retain the slightest vestige
of the historical—however completely it annihilated every higher meaning,—
was preferable, in the eyes of the orthodox, to the mythical interpretation.
Certainly nothing could be worse than Eichhorn's natural explanation of the
fall.   In considering the tree of knowledge as a poisonous plant, he at once
destroyed the intrinsic value and inherent meaning of the history ; of this he
afterwards became fully sensible, and in his subsequent mythical interpretation, he recognized in the narrative the incorporation of a worthy and
elevated conception.   Hess however declared himself more content with
Eichhorn's original explanation, and defended it against his later mythical
interpretation.   So true is it that supranaturalism clings with childlike fondness to the empty husk of historical semblance, though void of divine significance, and estimates it higher than the most valuable kernel divested of its
variegated covering.

Somewhat later De Wette's bold and thorough application of the mythical
view to the Mosaic writings ; his decided renunciation of the so-called *historical-mythical*, or more properly speaking of the natural mode of interpretation ;
and his strict opposition to the notion of the possibility of arriving at any
certainty respecting the residue of fact preserved in these writings, gave rise
to much controversy.   Some agreed with Steudel in totally rejecting the
mythical view in relation to the Bible, and in upholding the strictly historical
and indeed supranatural sense of the Scriptures : whilst Meyer and others
were willing to follow the guidance of De Wette, at least as far as the principles
of Vater, which permitted the attempt to extract some, if only probable,
historical data from the mythical investment.   If, says Meyer [2], the marvellousness and irrationality of many of the narratives contained in the Pentateuch,
(narratives which no one would have thought of inventing,) together with the
want of symmetry and connexion in the narration, and other considerations,
permit us not to mistake the historical groundwork of the record ; surely,
allowing the existence of an historical basis, a modest and cautious attempt
to seek out or at any rate to approximate towards a discovery of that historical

---

[1] Gränzbestimmung dessen, was in der Bibel Mythus, u. s. f., und was wirkliche
Geschichte ist.   In seiner Bibliothek der heiligen Geschichte, ii. Bd. s. 155. ff.
[2] Meyer, Apologie der geschichtlichen Auffassung der historischen Bücher des A. T.,
besonders des Pentateuchs, im Gegensatz gegen die blos mythische Deutung des letztern.
Fritzsche.   Kelle.

foundation is admissible. In the hope of preserving those who adopted the historical-mythical view from relapsing into the inconsistencies of the natural interpreters, Meyer laid down the following rules, which however serve rather to exhibit afresh the difficulty of escaping this danger. 1. To abstract every thing which is at once recognizable as mythical representation as opposed to historical fact; that is the extraordinary; the miraculous, accounts of immediate divine operation, also the religious notions of the narrators in relation to final causes. 2. To proceed from that which is simple to that which is more complicated. Let a case be supposed where we have two accounts of the same event, the one natural, the other supernatural, as, for instance, the gathering of the elders by Moses, attributed, Numbers, xi. 16., to the suggestion of Jehovah, and Exodus, xviii. 14., to the counsel of Jethro. According to this rule all divine inspiration must be subtracted from the known decisions of Noah, Abraham, Moses, and others. (Precisely the proceeding which met with the censure of De Wette quoted above.) 3. As far as possible to contemplate the fact which forms the basis of a narrative, in its simple and common character, apart from all collateral incidents. (This however, is going too far where no basis of fact exists.) For example. The story of the deluge may be reduced thus; a great inundation in Asia Minor, according to the legend, destroyed many wicked. (Here the supposed final cause is not abstracted.) Noah the father of Shem, a devout man, (*the teleological* notion again!) saved himself by swimming. The exact circumstances of this preservation, the character of the vessel, if such there were, which saved him, are left undetermined in order to avoid arbitrary explanations. Thus, in reference to the birth of Isaac, Meyer is satisfied with saying, that the wish and hope of the wealthy and pious Emir Abraham to possess an heir by his wife Sara was fulfilled unusually late, and in the eyes of others very unexpectedly. (Here again De Wette's censure is quite applicable.)

In like manner Eichhorn, in his Introduction to the New Testament, declared in yet stronger terms his opposition to the view advocated by De Wette. If the orthodox were displeased at having their historical faith disturbed by the progressive inroads of the mythical mode of interpretation, the rationalists were no less disconcerted to find the web of facts they had so ingeniously woven together torn asunder, and all the art and labour expended on the natural explanation at once declared useless. Unwillingly does Dr. Paulus admit to himself the presentiment that the reader of his Commentary may possibly exclaim: " Wherefore all this labour to give an historical explanation to such legends? how singular thus to handle mythi as history, and to attempt to render marvellous fictions intelligible according to the rules of causality!" Contrasted with the toilsomeness of his natural explanation, the mythical interpretation appears to this theologian merely as the refuge of mental indolence, which, seeking the easiest method of treating the gospel history, disposes of all that is marvellous, and all that is difficult to comprehend, under the vague term—mythus, and which, in order to escape the labour of disengaging the natural from the supernatural, fact from opinion, carries back the whole narration into the *camera-obscura* of ancient sacred legends.[3]

Still more decided was Greiling's [4] expression of disapprobation, elicited by Krug's commendation of the *genetic*—that is to say, mythical theory; but each stroke levelled by him at the mythical interpretation may be turned with far greater force against his own natural explanation. He is of opinion that among all the attempts to explain obscure passages in the New Testament,

[3] Exegetisches Handbuch, i. a. s. 1, 71.
[4] Greiling in Henke's Museum. i. 4. s. 621. ff.

scarcely any can be more injurious to the genuine historical interpretation, to the ascertaining of actual facts and their legitimate objects (that is, more prejudicial to the pretensions of the natural expounder) than the endeavour to supply, by aid of an inventive imagination, the deficiencies of the historical narrative. (The inventive imagination is that of the natural interpreter, which suggests to him collateral incidents of which there is no trace in the text. The imagination of the mythical interpreter is not inventive ; his part is merely the recognizing and detecting of the fictitious.) According to Greiling the *genetic*, or mythical mode of explaining miracles, is a needless and arbitrary invention of the imagination. (Let a groping spirit of inquiry be added, and the natural explanation is accurately depicted.) Many facts, he continues, which might be retained as such are thus consigned to the province of fable, or replaced by fictions the production of the interpreter. (But it is the *historical* mythical mode of interpretation alone which substitutes such inventions, and this only in so far as it is mixed up with the natural explanation.) Greiling thinks that the explanation of a miracle ought not to change the fact, and by means of interpretation, as by sleight of hand, substitute one thing for another ; (which is done by the natural explanation only,) for this is not to explain that which shocks the reason, but merely to deny the fact, and leave the difficulty unsolved. (It is false to say we have a fact to explain ; what immediately lies before us is a statement, respecting which we have to discover whether it embody a fact or not.) According to this learned critic the miracles wrought by Jesus should be naturally, or rather psychologically, explained ; by which means all occasion to change, clip, and amplify by invention the recorded facts, till at length they become metamorphosed into fiction, is obviated—(with how much justice this censure may be applied to the natural mode of explanation has been sufficiently demonstrated.)

Heydenreich has lately written a work expressly on the inadmissibility of the mythical interpretation of the historical portions of the New Testament. He reviews the external evidences concerning the origin of the Gospels, and finds the recognition of a mythical element in these writings quite incompatible with their substantiated derivation from the Apostles, and the disciples of the Apostles. He also examines the character of the gospel representations, and decides, in reference to their form, that narratives at once so natural and simple, so complete and exact, could be expected only from eye-witnesses, or those connected with them ; and, with respect to their contents, that those representations which are in their nature miraculous are so worthy of God, that nothing short of an abhorrence of miracles could occasion a doubt as to their historical truth. The divine operations are indeed generally mediate, but according to Heydenreich this by no means precludes the possibility of occasional intermediate exertions of the divine energy, when requisite to the accomplishment of some particular object ; and, referring to each of the divine attributes in succession, he shows that such intervention in nowise contradicts any of them ; and that each individual miracle is a peculiarly appropriate exercise of divine power.

These, and similar objections against the mythical interpretation of the gospel histories, which occur in recent commentaries and in the numerous writings in opposition to my work on the life of Jesus, will find their place and refutation in the following pages.

§ 13.

THE POSSIBILITY OF THE EXISTENCE OF MYTHI IN THE NEW TESTAMENT CONSIDERED IN REFERENCE TO THE EXTERNAL EVIDENCES.

The assertion that the Bible contains mythi is, it is true, directly opposed to the convictions of the believing christian. For if his religious view be circumscribed within the limits of his own community, he knows no reason why the things recorded in the sacred books should not literally have taken place; no doubt occurs to him, no reflection disturbs him. But, let his horizon be so far widened as to allow him to contemplate his own religion in relation to other religions, and to draw a comparison between them, the conclusion to which he then comes is that the histories related by the heathens of their deities, and by the Mussulman of his prophet, are so many fictions, whilst the accounts of God's actions, of Christ and other Godlike men contained in the Bible are, on the contrary, true. Such is the general notion expressed in the theological position: that which distinguishes Christianity from the heathen religions is this, they are mythical, it is historical.

But this position, thus stated without further definition and proof, is merely the product of the limitation of the individual to that form of belief in which he has been educated, which renders the mind incapable of embracing any but the affirmative view in relation to its own creed, any but the negative in reference to every other—a prejudice devoid of real worth, and which cannot exist in conjunction with an extensive knowledge of history. For let us transplant ourselves among other religious communities; the believing Mohammedan is of opinion that truth is contained in the Koran alone, and that the greater portion of our Bible is fabulous; the Jew of the present day, whilst admitting the truth and divine origin of the Old Testament, rejects the New; and, the same exclusive belief in the truth of their own creed and the falsity of every other was entertained by the professors of most of the heathen religions before the period of the Syncretism. But which community is right? Not all, for this is impossible, since the assertion of each excludes the others. But which particular one? Each claims for itself the true faith. The pretensions are equal; what shall decide? The origin of the several religions? Each lays claim to a divine origin. Not only does the Christian religion profess to be derived from the Son of God, and the Jewish from God himself, through Moses; the Mohammedan religion asserts itself to be founded by a prophet immediately inspired by God; in like manner the Greeks attributed the institution of their worship to the gods.

"But in no other religion" it is urged "are the vouchers of a divine origin so unequivocal as in the Jewish and the Christian. The Greek and Roman mythologies are the product of a collection of unauthenticated legends, whilst the Bible history was written by eye-witnesses; or by those whose connexion with eye-witnesses afforded them opportunities of ascertaining the truth; and whose integrity is too apparent to admit of a doubt as to the sincerity of their intentions." It would most unquestionably be an argument of decisive weight in favour of the credibility of the biblical history, could it indeed be shown that it was written by eye-witnesses, or even by persons nearly contemporaneous with the events narrated. For though errors and false representations may glide into the narrations even of an eye-witness, there is far less probability of unintentional mistake (intentional deception may easily be detected) than where the narrator is separated by a long interval from the facts he records, and is obliged to derive his materials through the medium of transmitted communications.

But this alleged ocular testimony, or proximity in point of time of the sacred historians to the events recorded, is mere assumption, an assumption originating from the titles which the biblical books bear in our Canon. Those books which describe the departure of the Israelites from Egypt, and their wanderings through the wilderness, bear the name of Moses, who being their leader would undoubtedly give a faithful history of these occurrences, unless he designed to deceive ; and who, if his intimate connexion with Deity described in these books be historically true, was likewise eminently qualified, by virtue of such connexion, to produce a credible history of the earlier periods.   In like manner, of the several accounts of the life and fate of Jesus, the superscriptions assign one to Matthew and one to John : two men who having been eye-witnesses of the public ministry of Jesus from its commencement to its close were particularly capable of giving a report of it ; and who, from their confidential intercourse with Jesus and his mother, together with that supernatural aid which, according to John, Jesus promised to his disciples to teach them and bring all things to their remembrance, were enabled to give information of the circumstances of his earlier years ; of which some details are recorded by Matthew.

But that little reliance can be placed on the headings of ancient manuscripts, and of sacred records more especially, is evident, and in reference to biblical books has long since been proved.   In the so-called books of Moses mention is made of his death and burial : but who now supposes that this was written beforehand by Moses in the form of prophecy ? Many of the Psalms bear the name of David which presuppose an acquaintance with the miseries of the exile ; and predictions are put into the mouth of Daniel, a Jew living at the time of the Babylonish captivity, which could not have been written before the reign of Antiochus Epiphanes.   It is an incontrovertible position of modern criticism that the titles of the Biblical books represent nothing more than the design of their author, or the opinion of Jewish or Christian antiquity respecting their origin ; points the first of which proves nothing ; and as to the second every thing depends upon the following considerations : 1. the date of the opinion and the authority on which it rests ; 2. the degree of harmony existing between this opinion and the internal character of the writings in question.   The first consideration includes an examination of the external, the second of the internal grounds of evidence respecting the authenticity of the biblical books.   To investigate the internal grounds of credibility in relation to each detail given in the Gospels, (for it is with them alone we are here concerned) and to test the probability or improbability of their being the production of eye-witnesses, or of competently informed writers, is the sole object of the present work.   The *external grounds* of evidence may be examined in this introduction, only so far however as is necessary in order to judge whether they yield a definite result, which may perhaps be in opposition to the internal grounds of evidence ; or whether the external evidence, insufficient of itself, leaves to the internal evidence the decision of the question.

We learn from the works of Irenæus, of Clemens Alexandrinus, and of Tertullian, that at the end of the second century after Christ our four Gospels were recognized by the orthodox church as the writings of the Apostles and the disciples of the Apostles ; and were separated from many other similar productions as authentic records of the life of Jesus.   The first Gospel according to our Canon is attributed to Matthew, who is enumerated among the twelve Apostles ; the fourth to John the beloved disciple of our Lord ;

the second to Mark the interpreter of Peter; and the third to Luke the companion of Paul.[1] We have, besides, the authority of earlier authors, both in their own works and in quotations cited by others.

It is usual, in reference to the first Gospel, to adduce the testimony of Papias, Bishop of Hierapolis, said to have been an auditor ἀκουστής of John, (probably the presbyter) and to have suffered martyrdom under Marcus Aurelius. (161–180.) Papias asserts that Matthew the Apostle wrote τὰ λόγια (τὰ κυριακὰ[2]). Schleiermacher, straining the meaning of λόγια, has latterly understood it to signify merely a collection of the sayings of Jesus. But when Papias speaks of Mark, he seems to use σύνταξιν τῶν κυριακῶν λογίων ποιεῖσθαι, and τὰ ὑπὸ τοῦ Χριστοῦ ἢ λεχθέντα ἢ πραχθέντα γράφειν as equivalent expressions. Whence it appears that the word λόγια designates a writing comprehending the acts and fate of Jesus; and the fathers of the church were justified in understanding the testimony of Papias as relating to an entire Gospel.[3] They did indeed apply this testimony decidedly to our first Gospel; but the words of the Apostolic father contain no such indication, and the manuscript, of which he speaks, cannot be absolutely identical with our Gospel; for, according to the statement given by Papias, Matthew wrote in the Hebrew language; and it is a mere assumption of the christian fathers that our Greek Matthew is a translation of the original Hebrew Gospel[4]. Precepts of Jesus, and narratives concerning him, corresponding more or less exactly with passages in our Matthew, do indeed occur in the works of other of the apostolic fathers; but then these works are not wholly genuine, and the quotations themselves are either in a form which indicates that they might have been derived from oral traditions; or where these authors refer to written sources, they do not mention them as being directly apostolic. Many citations in the writings of Justin Martyr (who died 166) agree with passages in our Matthew; but there are also, mixed up with these, other elements which are not to be found in our Gospels; and he refers to the writings from which he derives them generally as ἀπομνημονεύματα τῶν ἀποστόλων, or εὐαγγέλια, without naming any author in particular. Celsus,[5] the opponent of Christianity, (subsequent to 150) mentions that the disciples of Jesus had written his history, and he alludes to our present Gospels when he speaks of the divergence of the accounts respecting the number of angels seen at the resurrection; but we find no more precise reference to any one Evangelist in his writings, so far as we know them through Origen.

We have the testimony of the same Papias who has the notice concerning Matthew, a testimony from the mouth of John (πρεσβύτερος), that Mark, who according to him was the interpreter of Peter (ἑρμηνευτὴς Πέτρου), wrote down the discourses and actions of Jesus from his recollections of the instructions of that Apostle.[6] Ecclesiastical writers have likewise assumed that this passage from Papias refers to our second Gospel, though it does not say any thing of the kind, and is besides inapplicable to it. For our second Gospel cannot have originated from recollections of Peter's instructions, i.e., from a source peculiar to itself, since it is evidently a compilation, whether made from memory or otherwise, from the first and third Gospels.[7] As little will the remark of Papias that Mark wrote without order (οὐ τάξει) apply to our

---

[1] See the quotations given by De Wette in his "Einleitung in d. N. T." § 76.
[2] Euseb. H. E., iii. 39.
[3] Ullman, Credner, Lücke, De Wette.
[4] Hieron. de vir. illustr. 3.
[5] Contra Celsum, ii. 16. v. 56.
[6] Euseb. H. E. iii. 39.
[7] This is clearly demonstrated by Griesbach in his "Commentatio, quâ Marci Evangelium totum e Matthæi et Lucæ commentariis decerptum esse demonstratur."

Gospel.   For he cannot by this expression intend a false chronological arrangement, since he ascribes to Mark the strictest love of truth, which, united with the consciousness that he had not the means of fixing dates, must have withheld him from making the attempt.   But a total renunciation of chronological connexion, which Papias can alone have meant to attribute to him, is not to be found in the second Gospel.   This being the case, what do those echoes which our second Gospel, in like manner as our first, seems to find in the most ancient ecclesiastical writers, prove?

That Luke, the companion of Paul, wrote a Gospel, is not attested by any authority of corresponding weight or antiquity with that of Papias in relation to Matthew and to Mark.   The third Gospel however possesses a testimony of a particular kind in the " Acts of the Apostles ;" not indeed authenticating it as the composition of Luke, but attributing it to an occasional companion of the Apostle Paul.   According to the proëm to the Acts and that to the Gospel of Luke, these two books proceeded from the same author or compiler : an origin which these writings do not, in other respects, contradict. In several chapters in the second half of the Book of the Acts the author, speaking of himself together with Paul, makes use of the first person plural,[8] and thus identifies himself with the companion of that apostle.   The fact is, however, that many of the details concerning Paul, contained in other parts of the book of the Acts, are so indefinite and marvellous, and are moreover so completely at variance with Paul's genuine epistles, that it is extremely difficult to reconcile them with the notion that they were written by a companion of that apostle.   It is also not a little remarkable that the author, neither in the introduction to the Acts, nor in that to the Gospel, alludes to his connexion with one of the most distinguished of the Apostles, so that it is impossible not to suspect that the passages in which the writer speaks of himself as an actor in the scenes described, belong to a distinct memorial by another hand, which the author of the Acts has merely incorporated into his history.   But leaving this conjecture out of the question, it is indeed possible that the companion of Paul may have composed his two works at a time, and under circumstances, when he was no longer protected by Apostolic influence against the tide of tradition ; and that he saw no reason why, because he had not heard them previously from this Apostle, he should therefore reject the instructive, and (according to his notions, which certainly would not lead him to shun the marvellous,) credible narratives derived from that source.   Now, it is asserted that because the Book of the Acts terminates with the two years' imprisonment of Paul at Rome, therefore this second work of the disciple of that apostle, must have been written during that time, (63–65, A.D.) before the decision of Paul's trial, and that consequently, the Gospel of Luke, the earlier work of the same author, could not have been of later date.   But, the breaking off of the Acts at that particular point might have been the result of many other causes ; at all events such testimony, standing alone, is wholly insufficient to decide the historical worth of the Gospel.

It were to be wished that Polycarp, (he died 167) who both heard and saw the Apostle John,[9] had left us a testimony respecting him similar to that of Papias concerning Matthew.   Still his silence on this subject, in the one short epistle which has come down to us, is no evidence against the authenticity of that Gospel, any more than the more or less ambiguous allusions in several of the Apostolic fathers to the *Epistles* of John are proofs in its favour. But it is matter of surprise that Irenæus the disciple of Polycarp, who was

[8] Chap. xvi. 10–17 ; xx. 5–15 ; xxi. 1–17 ; xxvii. 1–28 ; xxviii. 10–16.
[9] Euseb. H. E. v. 20, 24.

called upon to defend this Gospel from the attacks of those who denied its composition by John, should neither on this occasion, nor once in his diffuse work, have brought forward the weighty authority of his Apostolic master, as to this fact. Whether or not the fourth Gospel originally bore the name of John remains uncertain. We meet with it first among the Valentinians and the Montanists, about the middle of the second century. Its Apostolic origin was however (immediately after) denied by the so-called Alogi, who ascribed it to Cerinthus ; partly because the Montanists derived from it their idea of the Paraclete ; partly also because it did not harmonize with the other Gospels.[10] The earliest quotation expressly stated to be from the Gospel of John is found in Theophilus of Antioch, about the year 172.[11] How little reason the numerous theologians of the present day have to boast of the evidences in favour of the fourth Gospel, whilst they deny the not less well attested Apocalypse, has been well remarked by Tholuck. Lastly, that there were two Johns, the Apostle and the Presbyter, living contemporaneously at Ephesus, is a circumstance which has not received sufficient attention in connexion with the most ancient testimonies in favour of the derivation from John, of the Apocalypse on the one hand, and of the Gospels and Epistles on the other.

Thus these most ancient testimonies tell us, firstly, that an apostle, or some other person who had been acquainted with an apostle, wrote a Gospel history ; but not whether it was identical with that which afterwards came to be circulated in the church under his name ; secondly, that writings similar to our Gospels were in existence ; but not that they were ascribed with certainty to any one individual apostle or companion of an apostle. Such is the uncertainty of these accounts, which after all do not reach further back than the third or fourth decade of the second century. According to all the rules of probability, the Apostles were all dead before the close of the first century ; not excepting John, who is said to have lived till A.D. 100 ; concerning whose age and death, however, many fables were early invented. What an ample scope for attributing to the Apostles manuscripts they never wrote ! The Apostles, dispersed abroad, had died in the latter half of the first century ; the Gospel became more widely preached throughout the Roman empire, and by degrees acquired a fixed form in accordance with a particular type. It was doubtless from this orally circulated Gospel that the many passages agreeing accurately with passages in our Gospels, which occur without any indication of their source in the earliest ecclesiastical writers, were actually derived. Before long this oral traditionary Gospel became deposited in different manuscripts : this person or that, possibly an apostle, furnishing the principal features of the history. But these manuscripts were not at first compiled according to a particular form and order, and consequently had to undergo many revisions and re-arrangements, of which we have an example in the Gospel of the Hebrews and the citations of Justin. It appears that these manuscripts did not originally bear the names of their compilers, but either that of the community by whom they were first read, as the Gospel of Hebrews ; or that of the Apostle or disciple after whose oral discourses or notes some other person had composed a connected history. The latter seems to have been the original meaning attached to the word κατὰ ; as in the title to our first Gospel.[12] Nothing however was more natural than the supposition which arose among the early christians, that the histories concerning Jesus which were circulated and used by the churches had been

---

[10] De Wette, Gieseler.
[11] Ad. Autol. ii., 22.
[12] See Schleiermacher.

written by his immediate disciples.   Hence the ascription of the gospel writings generally to the apostles by Justin and by Celsus ; and also of particular gospels to those particular apostles and disciples, whose oral discourses or written notes might possibly have formed the groundwork of a gospel manuscript, or who had perhaps been particularly connected with some certain district, or had been held in especial esteem by some particular community.   The Gospel of the Hebrews successively received all three kinds of appellations ; being first called εὐαγγέλιον καθ' Ἑβραίους, after the community by which it was read ; somewhat later, *Evangelium juxta duodecim apostolos ;* and finally, *secundum Matthæum.*

Admitting however that we do not possess the immediate record of an eye-witness in any one of the four Gospels, it is still very incomprehensible, replies the objector, how in Palestine itself, and at a time when so many eye-witnesses yet lived, unhistorical legends and even collections of them should have been formed.   But, in the first place, the fact that many such compilations of narratives concerning the life of Jesus were already in general circulation during the lifetime of the Apostles, and more especially that any one of our gospels was known to an Apostle and acknowledged by him, can never be proved.   With respect to isolated anecdotes, it is only necessary to form an accurate conception of Palestine and of the real position of the eye-witnesses referred to, in order to understand that the origination of legends, even at so early a period, is by no means incomprehensible.   Who informs us that they must necessarily have taken root in that particular district of Palestine where Jesus tarried longest, and where his actual history was well known ?   And with respect to eye-witnesses, if by these we are to understand the Apostles, it is to ascribe to them absolute ubiquity, to represent them as present here and there, weeding out all the unhistorical legends concerning Jesus in whatever places they had chanced to spring up and flourish.   Eye-witnesses in the more extended sense, who had only seen Jesus occasionally and not been his constant companions, must, on the contrary, have been strongly tempted to fill up their imperfect knowledge of his history with mythical representations.

But it is inconceivable, they say, that such a mass of mythi should have originated in an age so historical as that of the first Roman emperors.   We must not however be misled by too comprehensive a notion of an historical age.   The sun is not visible at the same instant to every place on the same meridian at the same time of year ; it gleams upon the mountain summits and the high plains before it penetrates the lower valleys and the deep ravines.   No less true is it that the historic age dawns not upon all people at the same period.   The people of highly civilized Greece, and of Rome the capital of the world, stood on an eminence which had not been reached in Galilee and Judæa.   Much rather may we apply to this age an expression become trite among historians, but which seems in the present instance willingly forgotten : namely, that incredulity and superstition, scepticism and fanaticism go hand in hand.

But the Jews, it is said, had long been accustomed to keep written records ; nay, the most flourishing period of their literature was already past, they were no longer a progressing and consequently a productive people, they were a nation verging to decay.   But the fact is, the pure historic idea was never developed among the Hebrews during the whole of their political existence ; their latest historical works, such as the Books of the Maccabees, and even the writings of Josephus, are not free from marvellous and extravagant tales. Indeed no just notion of the true nature of history is possible, without a perception of the inviolability of the chain of finite causes, and of the impossibility of miracles.   This perception which is wanting to so many minds of our own day was still more deficient in Palestine, and indeed throughout the Roman empire.   And to a mind still open to the reception of the marvellous, if it be once carried away by the tide of religious enthusiasm, all things will appear credible, and should this enthusiasm lay hold of a yet wider circle, it will awaken a new creative vigour, even in a decayed people.   To account for such an enthusiasm it is by no means necessary to presuppose the gospel miracles as the existing cause.   This may be found in the known religious dearth of that period, a dearth so great that the cravings of the mind after some religious belief excited a relish for the most extravagant forms of worship ; secondly in the deep religious satisfaction which was afforded by the belief in the resurrection of the deceased Messiah, and by the essential principles of the doctrine of Jesus.

§ 14.

THE POSSIBILITY OF MYTHI IN THE NEW TESTAMENT CONSIDERED ON
INTERNAL GROUNDS.

Seeing from what has already been said that the external testimony respecting the composition of our Gospels, far from forcing upon us the conclusion that they proceeded from eye-witnesses or well-informed contemporaries, leaves the decision to be determined wholly by internal grounds of evidence, that is, by the nature of the Gospel narratives themselves : we might immediately proceed from this introduction to the peculiar object of the present work, which is an examination of those narratives in detail.   It may however appear useful, before entering upon this special inquiry, to consider the general question, how far it is consistent with the character of the Christian religion that mythi should be found in it, and how far the general construction of the Gospel narratives authorizes us to treat them as mythi.   Although, indeed, if the following critical examination of the details be successful in proving the actual existence of mythi in the New Testament, this preliminary demonstration of their possibility becomes superfluous.

If with this view we compare the acknowledged mythical religions of antiquity with the Hebrew and Christian, it is true that we are struck by many differences between the sacred histories existing in these religious forms and those in the former.   Above all, it is commonly alleged that the sacred histories of the Bible are distinguished from the legends of the Indians, Greeks, Romans, etc., by their moral character and excellence.   " In the latter, the stories of the battles of the gods, the loves of Krishna, Jupiter, etc., contain much which was offensive to the moral feeling even of enlightened heathens, and which is revolting to ours : whilst in the former, the whole course of the narration, offers only what is worthy of God, instructive, and ennobling."   To this it may be answered with regard to the heathens, that the appearance of immorality in many of their narratives is merely the consequence of a subsequent misconception of their original meaning : and with regard to the Old Testament, that the perfect moral purity of its history has been contested.   Often indeed, it has been contested without good grounds, because a due distinction is not made between that which is ascribed to individual men, (who, as they are represented, are by no means spotless examples of purity,) and that which is ascribed to God :[1] nevertheless it is

[1] This same want of distinction has led the Alexandrians to allegorize, the Deists to scoff,

true that we have commands called divine, which, like that to the Israelites on their departure out of Egypt to purloin vessels of gold, are scarcely less revolting to an enlightened moral feeling, than the thefts of the Grecian Hermes.   But even admitting this difference in the morality of the religions to its full extent (and it must be admitted at least with regard to the New Testament), still it furnishes no proof of the historical character of the Bible ; for though every story relating to God which is immoral is necessarily fictitious, even the most moral is not necessarily true.

"But that which is incredible and inconceivable forms the staple of the heathen fables ; whilst in the biblical history, if we only presuppose the immediate intervention of the Deity, there is nothing of the kind."   Exactly, if this be presupposed.   Otherwise, we might very likely find the miracles in the life of Moses, Elias, or Jesus, the Theophany and Angelophany of the Old and New Testament, just as incredible as the fables of Jupiter, Hercules, or Bacchus : presuppose the divinity or divine descent of these individuals, and their actions and fate become as credible as those of the biblical person-ages with the like presupposition.   Yet not quite so, it may be returned. Vishnu appearing in his three first avatars as a fish, a tortoise, and a boar ; Saturn devouring his children ; Jupiter turning himself into a bull, a swan, etc.—these are incredibilities of quite another kind from Jehovah appearing to Abraham in a human form under the terebinth tree, or to Moses in the burning bush.   This extravagant love of the marvellous is the character of the heathen mythology.   A similar accusation might indeed be brought against many parts of the Bible, such as the tales of Balaam, Joshua, and Samson ; but still it is here less glaring, and does not form as in the Indian religion and in certain parts of the Grecian, the prevailing character.   What however does this prove?   Only that the biblical history *might* be true, sooner than the Indian or Grecian fables ; not in the least that on this account it *must* be true, and can contain nothing fictitious.

" But the subjects of the heathen mythology are for the most part such, as to convince us beforehand that they are mere inventions : those of the Bible such as at once to establish their own reality.   A Brahma, an Ormusd, a Jupiter, without doubt never existed; but there still is a God, a Christ, and there have been an Adam, a Noah, an Abraham, a Moses."   Whether an Adam or a Noah, however, were such as they are represented, has already been doubted, and may still be doubted.   Just so, on the other side, there may have been something historical about Hercules, Theseus, Achilles, and other heroes of Grecian story.   Here, again, we come to the decision that the biblical history *might* be true sooner than the heathen mythology, but is not necessarily so.   This decision however, together with the two distinctions already made, brings us to an important observation.   How do the Grecian divinities approve themselves immediately to us as non-existing beings, if not because things are ascribed to them which we cannot reconcile with our idea of the divine? whilst the God of the Bible is a reality to us just in so far as he corresponds with the idea we have formed of him in our own minds. Besides the contradiction to our notion of the divine involved in the plurality of heathen gods, and the intimate description of their motives and actions, we are at once revolted to find that the gods themselves have a history ; that they are born, grow up, marry, have children, work out their purposes, suffer difficulties and weariness, conquer and are conquered.   It is irreconcileable with our idea of the Absolute to suppose it subjected to time and change, to

and the Supernaturalists to strain the meaning of words ; as was done lately by Hoffmann in describing David's behaviour to the conquered Ammonites. (Christoterpe auf 1838, s. 184.)

opposition and suffering ; and therefore where we meet with a narrative in which these are attributed to a divine being, by this test we recognize it as unhistorical or mythical.

It is in this sense that the Bible, and even the Old Testament, is said to contain no mythi. The story of the creation with its succession of each day's labour ending in a rest after the completion of the task ; the expression often recurring in the farther course of the narrative, God repented of having done so and so ;—these and similar representations cannot indeed be entirely vindicated from the charge of making finite the nature of the Deity, and this is the ground which has been taken by mythical interpreters of the history of the creation. And in every other instance where God is said to reveal himself exclusively at any definite place or time, by celestial apparition, or by miracle wrought immediately by himself, it is to be presumed that the Deity has become finite and descended to human modes of operation. It may however be said in general, that in the Old Testament the divine nature does not appear to be essentially affected by the temporal character of its operation, but that the temporal shows itself rather as a mere form, an unavoidable appearance, arising out of the necessary limitation of human, and especially of uncultivated powers of representation. It is obvious to every one, that there is something quite different in the Old Testament declarations, that God made an alliance with Noah, and Abraham, led his people out of Egypt, gave them laws, brought them into the promised land, raised up for them judges, kings, and prophets, and punished them at last for their disobedience by exile ;—from the tales concerning Jupiter, that he was born of Rhea in Crete, and hidden from his father Saturn in a cave ; that afterwards he made war upon his father, freed the Uranides, and with their help and that of the lightning with which they furnished him, overcame the rebellious Titans, and at last divided the world amongst his brothers and children. The essential difference between the two representations is, that in the latter, the Deity himself is the subject of progression, becomes another being at the end of the process from what he was at the beginning, something being effected in himself and for his own sake : whilst in the former, change takes place only on the side of the world ; God remains fixed in his own identity as the I AM, and the temporal is only a superficial reflection cast back upon his acting energy by that course of mundane events which he both originated and guides. In the heathen mythology the gods have a history : in the Old Testament, God himself has none, but only his people : and if the proper meaning of mythology be the history of gods, then the Hebrew religion has no mythology.

From the Hebrew religion, this recognition of the divine unity and immutability was transmitted to the Christian. The birth, growth, miracles, sufferings, death, and resurrection of Christ, are circumstances belonging to the destiny of the Messiah, above which God remains unaffected in his own changeless identity. The New Testament therefore knows nothing of mythology in the above sense. The state of the question is however somewhat changed from that which it assumed in the Old Testament : for Jesus is called the Son of God, not merely in the same sense as kings under the theocracy were so called, but as actually begotten by the divine spirit, or from the incarnation in his person of the divine λόγος. Inasmuch as he is one with the Father, and in him the whole fullness of the godhead dwells bodily, he is more than Moses. The actions and sufferings of such a being are not external to the Deity : though we are not allowed to suppose a *theopaschitic* union with the divine nature, yet still, even in the New Testament, and more in the later doctrine of the Church, it is a divine being that here lives and suffers, and what befals him has an absolute worth and significance.

Thus according to the above accepted notion of the mythus, the New Testament has more of a mythical character than the Old.   But to call the history of Jesus mythical in this sense, is as unimportant with regard to the historical question as it is unexceptionable ; for the idea of God is in no way opposed to such an intervention in human affairs as does not affect his own immutability ; so that as far as regards this point, the gospel history, notwithstanding its mythical designation, might be at the same time throughout historically true.

Admitting that the biblical history does not equally with the heathen mythology offend our idea of Deity, and that consequently it is not in like manner characterized by this mark of the unhistorical, however far it be from bearing any guarantee of being historical,—we are met by the further question whether it be not less accordant with our idea of the world, and whether such discordancy may not furnish a test of its unhistorical nature.

In the ancient world, that is, in the east, the religious tendency was so preponderating, and the knowledge of nature so limited, that the law of connexion between earthly finite beings was very loosely regarded.   At every link there was a disposition to spring into the Infinite, and to see God as the immediate cause of every change in nature or the human mind.   In this mental condition the biblical history was written.   Not that God is here represented as doing all and every thing himself :—a notion which, from the manifold direct evidence of the fundamental connexion between finite things, would be impossible to any reasonable mind :—but there prevails in the biblical writers a ready disposition to derive all things down to the minutest details, as soon as they appear particularly important, immediately from God. He it is who gives the rain and sunshine ; he sends the east wind and the storm ; he dispenses war, famine, pestilence ; he hardens hearts and softens them, suggests thoughts and resolutions.   And this is particularly the case with regard to his chosen instruments and beloved people.   In the history of the Israelites we find traces of his immediate agency at every step : through Moses, Elias, Jesus, he performs things which never would have happened in the ordinary course of nature.

Our modern world, on the contrary, after many centuries of tedious research, has attained a conviction, that all things are linked together by a chain of causes and effects, which suffers no interruption.   It is true that single facts and groups of facts, with their conditions and processes of change, are not so circumscribed as to be unsusceptible of external influence ; for the action of one existence or kingdom in nature intrenches on that of another : human freedom controls natural development, and material laws react on human freedom.   Nevertheless the totality of finite things forms a vast circle, which, except that it owes its existence and laws to a superior power, suffers no intrusion from without.   This conviction is so much a habit of thought with the modern world, that in actual life, the belief in a supernatural manifestation, an immediate divine agency, is at once attributed to ignorance or imposture.   It has been carried to the extreme in that modern explanation, which, in a spirit exactly opposed to that of the Bible, has either totally removed the divine causation, or has so far restricted it that it is immediate in the act of creation alone, but mediate from that point onwards ;—i.e., God operates on the world only in so far as he gave to it this fixed direction at the creation.   From this point of view, at which nature and history appear as a compact tissue of finite causes and effects, it was impossible to regard the narratives of the Bible, in which this tissue is broken by innumerable instances of divine interference, as historical.

It must be confessed on nearer investigation, that this modern explanation, although it does not exactly deny the existence of God, yet puts aside the idea of him, as the ancient view did the idea of the world. For this is, as it has been often and well remarked, no longer a God and Creator, but a mere finite Artist, who acts immediately upon his work only during its first production, and then leaves it to itself; who becomes excluded with his full energy from one particular sphere of existence. It has therefore been attempted to unite the two views so as to maintain for the world its law of sequence, and for God his unlimited action, and by this means to preserve the truth of the biblical history. According to this view, the world is supposed to move in obedience to the law of consecutive causes and effects bound up with its constitution, and God to act upon it only mediately : but in single instances, where he finds it necessary for particular objects, he is not held to be restricted from entering into the course of human changes immediately. This is the view of modern Supranaturalism [2]; evidently a vain attempt to reconcile two opposite views, since it contains the faults of both, and adds a new one in the contradiction between the two ill-assorted principles. For here the consecutiveness of nature and history is broken through as in the ancient biblical view ; and the action of God limited as in the contrary system. The proposition that God works sometimes mediately, sometimes immediately, upon the world, introduces a changeableness, and therefore a temporal element, into the nature of his action, which brings it under the same condemnation as both the other systems ; that, namely, of distinguishing the maintaining power, in the one case from individual instances of the divine agency, and in the other from the act of creation.[3]

Since then our idea of God requires an immediate, and our idea of the world a mediate divine operation ; and since the idea of combination of the two species of action is inadmissible :—nothing remains for us but to regard them both as so permanently and immoveably united, that the operation of God on the world continues for ever and every where twofold, both immediate and mediate ; which comes just to this, that it is neither of the two, or this distinction loses its value. To explain more closely : if we proceed from the idea of God, from which arose the demand for his immediate operation, then the world is to be regarded in relation to him as a Whole : on the contrary, if we proceed from the idea of the finite, the world is a congeries of separate parts, and hence has arisen the demand for a merely mediate agency of God :—so that we must say—God acts upon the world as a Whole immediately, but on each part only by means of his action on every other part, that is to say, by the laws of nature.[4]

This view brings us to the same conclusion with regard to the historical value of the Bible as the one above considered. The miracles which God wrought for and by Moses and Jesus, do not proceed from his immediate

---

[2] Heydenreich, über die Unzulässigkeit, u. s. f. 1 stück. Compare Storr, doctr. christ. § 35, ff.

[3] If the Supranatural view contains a theological contradiction, so the new evangelical theology, which esteems itself raised so far above the old supranatural view, contains a logical contradiction. To say that God acts only mediately upon the world as the general rule, but sometimes, by way of exception, immediately,—has some meaning, though perhaps not a wise one. But to say that God acts always immediately on the world, but in some cases more particularly immediately,—is a flat contradiction in itself. On the principle of the immanence or immediate agency of God in the world, to which the new evangelical theology lays claim, the idea of the miraculous is impossible. Comp. my Streitschriften, i. 3, s. 46 f.

[4] In this view essentially coincide Wegscheider, instit. theol. dogm. § 12 ; De Wette, bibl. Dogm., Vorbereitung ; Schleiermacher, Glaubensl. § 46 f.; Marheineke, Dogm. § 269 ff. Comp. George, s. 78 f.

operation on the Whole, but presuppose an immediate action in particular cases, which is a contradiction to the type of the divine agency we have just given. The supranaturalists indeed claim an exception from this type on behalf of the biblical history; a presupposition which is inadmissible from our point of view[5], according to which the same laws, although varied by various circumstances, are supreme in every sphere of being and action, and therefore every narrative which offends against these laws, is to be recognized as so far unhistorical.

The result, then, however surprising, of a general examination of the biblical history, is that the Hebrew and Christian religions, like all others, have their mythi. And this result is confirmed, if we consider the inherent nature of religion, what essentially belongs to it and therefore must be common to all religions, and what on the other hand is peculiar and may differ in each. If religion be defined as the perception of truth, not in the form of an idea, which is the philosophic perception, but invested with imagery; it is easy to see that the mythical element can be wanting only when religion either falls short of, or goes beyond, its peculiar province, and that in the proper religious sphere it must necessarily exist.

It is only amongst the lowest and most barbarous people, such as the Esquimaux, that we find religion not yet fashioned into an objective form, but still confined to a subjective feeling. They know nothing of gods, of superior spirits and powers, and their whole piety consists in an undefined sentiment excited by the hurricane, the eclipse, or the magician. As it progresses however, the religious principle loses more and more of this indefiniteness, and ceasing to be subjective, becomes objective. In the sun, moon, mountains, animals, and other objects of the sensible world, higher powers are discovered and revered; and in proportion as the significance given to these objects is remote from their actual nature, a new world of mere imagination is created a sphere of divine existences whose relations to one another, actions, and influences, can be represented only after human analogy, and therefore as temporal and historical. Even when the mind has raised itself to the conception of the Divine unity, still the energy and activity of God are considered only under the form of a series of acts: and on the other hand, natural events and human actions can be raised to a religious significance only by the admission of divine interpositions and miracles. It is only from the philosophic point of view that the world of imagination is seen again to coincide with the actual, because the thought of God is comprehended to be his essence, and in the regular course itself of nature and of history, the revelation of the divine idea is acknowledged.

It is certainly difficult to conceive, how narratives which thus speak of imagination as reality can have been formed without intentional deceit, and believed without unexampled credulity; and this difficulty has been held an invincible objection to the mythical interpretation of many of the narratives of the Old and New Testament. If this were the case, it would apply equally to the Heathen legends; and on the other hand, if profane Mythology have

[5] To a freedom from this presupposition we lay claim in the following work; in the same sense as a state might be called free from presupposition where the privileges of station, etc., were of no account. Such a state indeed has one presupposition, that of the natural equality of its citizens; and similarly do we take for granted the equal amenability to law of all events; but this is merely an affirmative form of expression for our former negation. But to claim for the biblical history especial laws of its own, is an affirmative proposition, which, according to the established rule, is that which requires proof, and not our denial of it, which is merely negative. And if the proof cannot be given, or be found insufficient, it is the former and not the latter, which is to be considered a presupposition. See my Streitschriften i. 3. s. 36 ff.

steered clear of the difficulty, neither will that of the Bible founder upon it. I shall here quote at length the words of an experienced inquirer into Grecian mythology and primitive history, Otfried Müller, since it is evident that this preliminary knowledge of the subject which must be derived from general mythology, and which is necessary for the understanding of the following examination of the evangelic mythus, is not yet familiar to all theologians. " How," says Müller [6], " shall we reconcile this combination of the true and the false, the real and ideal, in mythi, with the fact of their being believed and received as truth ? The ideal, it may be said, is nothing else than poetry and fiction clothed in the form of a narration. But a fiction of this kind cannot be invented at the same time by many different persons without a miracle, requiring, as it does, a peculiar coincidence of intention, imagination, and expression. It is therefore the work of one person :—but how did he convince all the others that his fiction had an actual truth ? Shall we suppose him to have been one who contrived to delude by all kinds of trickery and deception, and perhaps allied himself with similar deceivers, whose part it was to afford attestation to the people of his inventions as having been witnessed by themselves ? Or shall we think of him as a man of higher endowments than others, who believed him upon his word ; and received the mythical tales under whose veil he sought to impart wholesome truths, as a sacred revelation ? But it is impossible to prove that such a caste of deceivers existed in ancient Greece (or Palestine) ; on the contrary, this skilful system of deception, be it gross or refined, selfish or philanthropic, if we are not misled by the impression we have received from the earliest productions of the Grecian (or Christian) mind, is little suited to the noble simplicity of those times. Hence an inventer of the mythus in the proper sense of the word is inconceivable. This reasoning brings us to the conclusion, that the idea of a deliberate and intentional fabrication, in which the author clothes that which he knows to be false in the appearance of truth, must be entirely set aside as insufficient to account for the origin of the mythus. Or in other words, that there is a certain necessity in this connexion between the ideal and the real, which constitutes the mythus ; that the mythical images were formed by the influence of sentiments common to all mankind ; and that the different elements grew together without the author's being himself conscious of their incongruity. It is this notion of a certain necessity and unconsciousness in the formation of the ancient mythi, on which we insist. If this be once understood, it will also be perceived that the contention whether the mythus proceed from one person or many, from the poet or the people, though it may be started on other grounds, does not go to the root of the matter. For if the one who invents the mythus is only obeying the impulse which acts also upon the minds of his hearers, he is but the mouth through which all speak, the skilful interpreter who has the address first to give form and expression to the thoughts of all. It is however very possible that this notion of necessity and unconsciousness, might appear itself obscure and mystical to our antiquarians (and theologians), from no other reason than that this mythicising tendency has no analogy in the present mode of thinking. But is not history to acknowledge even what is strange, when led to it by unprejudiced research ? "

As an example to show that even very complicated mythi, in the formation of which many apparently remote circumstances must have combined, may

[6] Prolegomena zu einer wissenschaftlichen Mythologie, s. 110 ff. With this Ullmann, and J. Müller in their reviews of this work, Hoffmann, s. 113 f., and others are agreed as far as relates to the heathen mythi. Especially compare George, Mythus and Sage, s. 15 ff. 103.

yet have arisen in this unconscious manner, Müller then refers to the Grecian mythus of Apollo and Marsyas. "It was customary to celebrate the festivals of Apollo with playing on the lyre, and it was necessary to piety, that the god himself should be regarded as its author. In Phrygia, on the contrary, the national music was the flute, which was similarly derived from a demon of their own, named Marsyas. The ancient Grecians perceived that the tones of these two instruments were essentially opposed : the harsh shrill piping of the flute must be hateful to Apollo, and therefore Marsyas his enemy. This was not enough : in order that the lyre-playing Grecian might flatter himself that the invention of his god was the more excellent instrument, Apollo must triumph over Marsyas. But why was it necessary in particular that the un-lucky Phrygian should be flayed? Here is the simple origin of the mythus. Near the castle of Celœne in Phrygia, in a cavern whence flowed a stream or torrent named Marsyas, was suspended a skin flask, called by the Phrygians, the bottle of Marsyas ; for Marsyas was, like the Grecian Silenus, a demi-god symbolizing the exuberance of the juices of nature. Now where a Grecian, or a Phrygian with Grecian prepossessions, looked on the bottle, he plainly saw the catastrophe of Marsyas ; here was still suspended his skin, which had been torn off and made into a bottle :—Apollo had flayed him. In all this there is no arbitrary invention : the same ideas might have occurred to many, and if one first gave expression to them, he knew well that his auditors, imbued with the same prepossessions, would not for an instant doubt his accuracy."

"The chief reason of the complicated character of mythi in general, is their having been formed for the most part, not at once, but successively and by degrees, under the influence of very different circumstances and events both external and internal. The popular traditions, being orally transmitted and not restricted by any written document, were open to receive every new addition, and thus grew in the course of long centuries to the form in which we now find them. (How far this applies to a great part of the New Testament mythi, will be shown hereafter.) This is an important and luminous fact, which however is very frequently overlooked in the explanation of mythi ; for they are regarded as allegories invented by one person, at one stroke, with the definite purpose of investing a thought in the form of a narration."

The view thus expressed by Müller, that the mythus is founded not upon any individual conception, but upon the more elevated and general conception of a whole people (or religious community), is said by a competent judge of Müller's work to be the necessary condition for a right understanding of the ancient mythus, the admission or rejection of which henceforth ranges the opinions on mythology into two opposite divisions.[7]

It is not however easy to draw a line of distinction between intentional and unintentional fiction. In the case where a fact lay at the foundation, which, being the subject of popular conversation and admiration, in the course of time formed itself into a mythus, we readily dismiss all notion of wilful fraud, at least in its origin. For a mythus of this kind is not the work of one man, but of a whole body of men, and of succeeding generations ; the narrative passing from mouth to mouth, and like a snowball growing by the involuntary addition of one exaggerating feature from this, and another from that narrator. In time however these legends are sure to fall into the way of some gifted minds, which will be stimulated by them to the exercise of their own poetical, religious, or didactic powers. Most of the mythical narratives which have come down to us from antiquity, such as the Trojan, and the Mosaic series of legends, are presented to us in this elaborated form. Here then it would

[7] The words of Baur in his review of Müller's Prolegomena, in Jahn's Jahrbüchern f. Philol. u. Pädag. 1828, 1 Heft, s. 7.

appear there must have been intentional deception : this however is only the result of an erroneous assumption. It is almost impossible, in a critical and enlightened age like our own, to carry ourselves back to a period of civilization in which the imagination worked so powerfully, that its illusions were believed as realities by the very minds that created them. Yet the very same miracles which are wrought in less civilized circles by the imagination, are produced in the more cultivated by the understanding. Let us take one of the best didactic historians of ancient or modern times, Livy, as an example. "Numa," he says, "gave to the Romans a number of religious ceremonies, *ne luxuriarentur otio animi,* and because he regarded religion as the best means of bridling *multitudinem imperitam et illis seculis rudem. Idem,*" he continues, "*nefastos dies fastosque fecit, quia aliquando nihil cum populo agi utile futurum erat.*"[8] How did Livy know that these were the motives of Numa? In point of fact they certainly were not. But Livy believed them to be so. The inference of his own understanding appeared to him so necessary, that he treated it with full conviction as an actual fact. The popular legend, or some ancient poet, had explained this fertility of religious invention in Numa otherwise; namely, that it arose from his communication with the nymph Egeria, who revealed to him the forms of worship that would be most acceptable to the gods. It is obvious, that the case is pretty nearly the same with regard to both representations. If the latter had an individual author, it was his opinion that the historical statement could be accounted for only upon the supposition of a communication with a superior being; as it was that of Livy, that its explanation must lie in political views. The one mistook the production of his imagination, the other the inference of his understanding, for reality.

Perhaps it may be admitted that there is a possibility of unconscious fiction, even when an individual author is assigned to it, provided that the mythical consists only in the filling up and adorning some historical event with imaginary circumstances : but that where the whole story is invented, and not any historical nucleus is to be found, this unconscious fiction is impossible. Whatever view may be taken of the heathen mythology, it is easy to show with regard to the New Testament, that there was the greatest antecedent probability of this very kind of fiction having arisen respecting Jesus without any fraudulent intention. The expectation of a Messiah had grown up amongst the Israelitish people long before the time of Jesus, and just then had ripened to full maturity. And from its beginning this expectation was not indefinite, but determined, and characterized by many important particulars. Moses was said to have promised his people a prophet like unto himself (Deut. xviii. 15), and this passage was in the time of Jesus applied to the Messiah (Acts iii. 22 ; vii. 37). Hence the rabbinical principle : as the first redeemer (*Goël*), so shall be the second; which principle was carried out into many particulars to be expected in the Messiah after his prototype Moses.[9] Again, the Messiah was to come of the race of David, and as a second David take possession of his throne (Matt. xxii. 42 ;

---

[8] I. 19.
[9] Midrasch Koheleth f. 73, 3 (in Schöttgen, *horæ hebraicæ et talmudicæ,* 2, S. 251 f.). *R. Berechias nomine R. Isaaci dixit: Quemadmodum Goël primus* (Moses), *sic etiam postremus* (Messias) *comparatus est. De Goële primo quidnam scriptura dicit?* Exod. iv. 20 : *et sumsit Moses uxorem et filios, eosque asino imposuit. Sic Goël postremus,* Zachar. ix. 9 : *pauper et insidens asino. Quidnam de Goële primo nosti? Is descendere fecit Man, q. d.* Exod. xvi. 14 : *ecce ego pluere faciam vobis panem de cælo. Sic etiam Goël postremus Manna descendere faciet, q. d.* Ps. lxxii. 16 : *erit multitudo frumenti in terra. Quomodo Goël primus comparatus fuit? Is ascendere fecit puteum : sic quoque Goël postremus ascendere faciet aquas, q. d.* Joel iv. 18 : *et fons e domo Domini egredietur, et torrentem Sittim irrigabit.*

Luke i. 32; Acts ii. 30): and therefore in the time of Jesus it was expected that he, like David, should be born in the little village of Bethlehem (John vii. 42; Matt. ii. 5 f.). In the above passage Moses describes the supposed Messiah as a prophet; so in his own idea, Jesus was the greatest and last of the prophetic race. But in the old national legends the prophets were made illustrious by the most wonderful actions and destiny. How could less be expected of the Messiah? Was it not necessary beforehand, that his life should be adorned with that which was most glorious and important in the lives of the prophets? Must not the popular expectation give him a share in the bright portion of their history, as subsequently the sufferings of himself and his disciples were attributed by Jesus, when he appeared as the Messiah, to a participation in the dark side of the fate of the prophets (Matt. xxiii. 29 ff.; Luke xiii. 33 ff.; comp. Matt. v. 12)? Believing that Moses and all the prophets had prophesied of the Messiah (John v. 46; Luke iv. 21; xxiv. 27), it was as natural for the Jews, with their allegorizing tendency, to consider their actions and destiny as types of the Messiah, as to take their sayings for predictions. In general the whole Messianic era was expected to be full of signs and wonders. The eyes of the blind should be opened, the ears of the deaf should be unclosed, the lame should leap, and the tongue of the dumb praise God (Isa. xxxv. 5 f.; xlii. 7; comp. xxxii. 3, 4). These merely figurative expressions soon came to be understood literally (Matt. xi. 5; Luke vii. 21 f.), and thus the idea of the Messiah was continually filled up with new details, even before the appearance of Jesus.[10] Thus many of the legends respecting him had not to be newly invented; they already existed in the popular hope of the Messiah, having been mostly derived with various modifications[11] from the Old Testament, and had merely to be transferred to Jesus,[12] and accommodated to his character and doctrines. In no case could it be easier for the person who first added any new feature to the description of Jesus, to believe himself its genuineness, since his argument would be: Such and such things must have happened to the Messiah; Jesus was the Messiah; therefore such and such things happened to him.[13]

Truly it may be said that the middle term of this argument, namely, that Jesus was the Messiah, would have failed in proof to his contemporaries all the more on account of the common expectation of miraculous events, if that expectation had not been fulfilled by him. But the following critique

---

[10] Tanchuma f. 54, 4. (in Schöttgen, p. 74): *R. Acha nomine R. Samuelis bar Nachmani dixit: Quæcumque Deus S. B. facturus est* לבא לעתיד *(tempore Messiano) ea jam ante fecit per manus justorum* בעולם הזה *(seculo ante Messiam elapso). Deus S. B. suscitabit mortuos, id quod jam ante fecit per Eliam, Elisam et Ezechielem. Mare exsiccabit, prout per Mosen factum est. Oculos cæcorum aperiet, id quod per Elisam fecit. Deus S. B. futuro tempore visitabit steriles, quemadmodum in Abrahamo et Sarâ fecit.*

[11] The Old Testament legends have undergone many changes and amplifications, even without any reference to the Messiah, so that the partial discrepancy between the narratives concerning Jesus with those relating to Moses and the prophets, is not a decisive proof that the former were not derived from the latter. Compare Acts vii. 22, 53, and the corresponding part of Josephus Antiq. ii. & iii. with the account of Moses given in Exodus. Also the biblical account of Abraham with Antiq. i. 8, 2; of Jacob with i. 19, 6; of Joseph with ii. 5, 4.

[12] George, s. 125: If we consider the firm conviction of the disciples, that all which had been prophesied in the Old Testament of the Messiah must necessarily have been fulfilled in the person of their master; and moreover that there were many blank spaces in the history of Christ; we shall see that it was impossible to have happened otherwise than that these ideas should have embodied themselves, and thus the mythi have arisen which we find. Even if a more correct representation of the life of Jesus had been possible by means of tradition, this conviction of the disciples must have been strong enough to triumph over it.

[13] Compare O. Müller, Prolegomena, s. 7, on a similar conclusion of Grecian poets.

on the Life of Jesus does not divest it of all those features to which the character of miraculous has been appropriated : and besides we must take into account the overwhelming impression which was made upon those around him by the personal character and discourse of Jesus, as long as he was living amongst them, which did not permit them deliberately to scrutinize and compare him with their previous standard. The belief in him as the Messiah extended to wider circles only by slow degrees; and even during his lifetime the people may have reported many wonderful stories of him (comp. Matt. xiv. 2). After his death, however, the belief in his resurrection, however that belief may have arisen, afforded a more than sufficient proof of his Messiahship ; so that all the other miracles in his history need not be considered as the foundation of the faith in this, but may rather be adduced as the consequence of it.

It is however by no means necessary to attribute this same freedom from all conscious intention of fiction, to the authors of all those narratives in the Old and New Testament which must be considered as unhistorical. In every series of legends, especially if any patriotic or religious party interest is associated with them, as soon as they become the subject of free poetry or any other literary composition, some kind of fiction will be intentionally mixed up with them. The authors of the Homeric songs could not have believed that every particular which they related of their gods and heroes had really happened ; and just as little could the writer of the Chronicles have been ignorant that in his deviation from the books of Samuel and of the Kings, he was introducing many events of later occurrence into an earlier period ; or the author of the book of Daniel [14] that he was modelling his history upon that of Joseph, and accommodating prophecies to events already past ; and exactly as little may this be said of all the unhistorical narratives of the Gospels, as for example, of the first chapter of the third, and many parts of the fourth Gospel. But a fiction, although not undesigned, may still be without evil design. It is true, the case is not the same with the supposed authors of many fictions in the Bible, as with poets properly so called, since the latter write without any expectation that their poems will be received as history : but still it is to be considered that in ancient times, and especially amongst the Hebrews, and yet more when this people was stirred up by religious excitement, the line of distinction between history and fiction, prose and poetry, was not drawn so clearly as with us. It is a fact also deserving attention that amongst the Jews and early Christians, the most reputable authors published their works with the substitution of venerated names, without an idea that they were guilty of any falsehood or deception by so doing.

[14] The comparison of the first chapter of this book with the history of Joseph in Genesis, gives an instructive view of the tendency of the later Hebrew legend and poetry to form new relations upon the pattern of the old. As Joseph was carried captive to Egypt, so was Daniel to Babylon (i. 2); like Joseph he must change his name (7). God makes the שַׂר הַסָּרִיסִים favourable to him, as the סָרִים שַׂר הַטַבָּחִים to Joseph (9) ; he abstains from polluting himself with partaking of the king's meats and drinks, which are pressed upon him (8) ; a self-denial held as meritorious in the time of Antiochus Epiphanes, as that of Joseph with regard to Potiphar's wife ; like Joseph he gains eminence by the interpretation of a dream of the king, which his חַרְטֻמִּים were unable to explain to him (ii.) ; whilst the additional circumstance that Daniel is enabled to give not only the interpretation, but the dream itself, which had escaped the memory of the king, appears to be a romantic exaggeration of that which was attributed to Joseph. In the account of Josephus, the history of Daniel has reacted in a singular manner upon that of Joseph ; for as Nebuchadnezzar forgets his dream, and the interpretation according to Josephus revealed to him at the same time, so does he make Pharaoh forget the interpretation shown to him with the dream. Antiq. ii. 5, 4.

The only question that can arise here is whether to such fictions, the work of an individual, we can give the name of mythi? If we regard only their own intrinsic nature, the name is not appropriate ; but it is so when these fictions, having met with faith, come to be received amongst the legends of a people or religious party, for this is always a proof that they were the fruit, not of any individual conception, but of an accordance with the sentiments of a multitude.[15]

A frequently raised objection remains, for the refutation of which the remarks above made, upon the date of the origin of many of the gospel mythi, are mainly important : the objection, namely, that the space of about thirty years, from the death of Jesus to the destruction of Jerusalem, during which the greater part of the narratives must have been formed ; or even the interval extending to the beginning of the second century, the most distant period which can be allowed for the origin of even the latest of these gospel narratives, and for the written composition of our gospels ;—is much too short to admit of the rise of so rich a collection of mythi. But, as we have shown, the greater part of these mythi did not arise during that period, for their first foundation was laid in the legends of the Old Testament, before and after the Babylonish exile ; and the transference of these legends with suitable modifications to the expected Messiah, was made in the course of the centuries which elapsed between that exile and the time of Jesus. So that for the period between the formation of the first Christian community and the writing of the Gospels, there remains to be effected only the transference of Messianic legends, almost all ready formed, to Jesus, with some alterations to adapt them to christian opinions, and to the individual character and circumstances of Jesus : only a very small proportion of mythi having to be formed entirely new.

§ 15.

DEFINITION OF THE EVANGELICAL MYTHUS AND ITS DISTINCTIVE CHARACTERISTICS.

The precise sense in which we use the expression *mythus,* applied to certain parts of the gospel history, is evident from all that has already been said ; at the same time the different kinds and gradations of the mythi which we shall meet with in this history may here by way of anticipation be pointed out.

We distinguish by the name *evangelical mythus* a narrative relating directly or indirectly to Jesus, which may be considered not as the expression of a fact, but as the product of an idea of his earliest followers : such a narrative being mythical in proportion as it exhibits this character. The mythus in this sense of the term meets us, in the Gospel as elsewhere, sometimes in its pure form, constituting the substance of the narrative, and sometimes as an accidental adjunct to the actual history.

The pure mythus in the Gospel will be found to have two sources, which in most cases contributed simultaneously, though in different proportions, to form the mythus. The one source is, as already stated, the Messianic ideas and expectations existing according to their several forms in the Jewish mind before Jesus, and independently of him ; the other is that particular impression which was left by the personal character, actions, and fate of Jesus, and which served to modify the Messianic idea in the minds of his people. The account of the Transfiguration, for example, is derived almost

[15] Thus J. Müller, theol. Studien u. Kritiken, 1836, iii. s. 839 ff.

exclusively from the former source; the only amplification taken from the latter source being—that they who appeared with Jesus on the Mount spake of his decease.   On the other hand, the narrative of the rending of the veil of the temple at the death of Jesus seems to have had its origin in the hostile position which Jesus, and his church after him, sustained in relation to the Jewish temple worship.   Here already we have something historical, though consisting merely of certain general features of character, position, etc.; we are thus at once brought upon the ground of the historical mythus.

The historical mythus has for its groundwork a definite individual fact which has been seized upon by religious enthusiasm, and twined around with mythical conceptions culled from the idea of the Christ.   This fact is perhaps a saying of Jesus such as that concerning "fishers of men" or the barren fig-tree, which now appear in the Gospels transmuted into marvellous histories: or, it is perhaps a real transaction or event taken from his life; for instance, the mythical traits in the account of the baptism were built upon such a reality.   Certain of the miraculous histories may likewise have had some foundation in natural occurrences, which the narrative has either exhibited in a supernatural light, or enriched with miraculous incidents.

All the species of imagery here enumerated may justly be designated as mythi, even according to the modern and precise definition of George, inasmuch as the unhistorical which they embody—whether formed gradually by tradition, or created by an individual author—is in each case the product of an *idea*.   But for those parts of the history which are characterized by indefiniteness and want of connexion, by misconstruction and transformation, by strange combinations and confusion,—the natural results of a long course of oral transmission; or which, on the contrary, are distinguished by highly coloured and pictorial representations, which also seem to point to a traditionary origin;—for these parts the term *legendary* is certainly the more appropriate.

Lastly.   It is requisite to distinguish equally from the mythus and the legend, that which, as it serves not to clothe an idea on the one hand, and admits not of being referred to tradition on the other, must be regarded as *the addition of the author*, as purely individual, and designed merely to give clearness, connexion, and climax, to the representation.

It is to the various forms of the unhistorical in the Gospels that this enumeration exclusively refers: it does not involve the renunciation of the *historical* which they may likewise contain.

§ 16.

CRITERIA BY WHICH TO DISTINGUISH THE UNHISTORICAL IN THE GOSPEL NARRATIVE.

Having shown the possible existence of the mythical and the legendary in the Gospels, both on extrinsic and intrinsic grounds, and defined their distinctive characteristics, it remains in conclusion to inquire how their actual presence may be recognised in individual cases?

The mythus presents two phases: in the first place it is not history; in the second it is fiction, the product of the particular mental tendency of a certain community.   These two phases afford the one a negative, the other a positive criterion, by which the mythus is to be recognised.

I. *Negative.*   That an account is not historical—that the matter related could not have taken place in the manner described is evident,

First. When the narration is irreconcilable with the known and universal laws which govern the course of events. Now according to these laws, agreeing with all just philosophical conceptions and all credible experience, the absolute cause never disturbs the chain of secondary causes by single arbitrary acts of interposition, but rather manifests itself in the production of the aggregate of finite casualities, and of their reciprocal action. When therefore we meet with an account of certain phenomena or events of which it is either expressly stated or implied that they were produced immediately by God himself (divine apparitions—voices from heaven and the like), or by human beings possessed of supernatural powers (miracles, prophecies), such an account is *in so far* to be considered as not historical. And inasmuch as, in general, the intermingling of the spiritual world with the human is found only in unauthentic records, and is irreconcilable with all just conceptions ; so narratives of angels and of devils, of their appearing in human shape and interfering with human concerns, cannot possibly be received as historical.

Another law which controls the course of events is the law of succession, in accordance with which all occurrences, not excepting the most violent convulsions and the most rapid changes, follow in a certain order of sequence of increase and decrease. If therefore we are told of a celebrated individual that he attracted already at his birth and during his childhood that attention which he excited in his manhood ; that his followers at a single glance recognized him as being all that he actually was ; if the transition from the deepest despondency to the most ardent enthusiasm after his death is represented as the work of a single hour ; we must feel more than doubtful whether it is a real history which lies before us. Lastly, all those psychological laws, which render it improbable that a human being should feel, think, and act in a manner directly opposed to his own habitual mode and that of men in general, must be taken into consideration. As for example, when the Jewish Sanhedrim are represented as believing the declaration of the watch at the grave that Jesus was risen, and instead of accusing them of having suffered the body to be stolen away whilst they were asleep, bribing them to give currency to such a report. By the same rule it is contrary to all the laws belonging to the human faculty of memory, that long discourses, such as those of Jesus given in the fourth Gospel, could have been faithfully recollected and reproduced.

It is however true that effects are often far more rapidly produced, particularly in men of genius and by their agency, than might be expected ; and that human beings frequently act inconsequently, and in opposition to their general modes and habits ; the two last mentioned tests of the mythical character must therefore be cautiously applied, and in conjunction only with other tests.

Secondly. An account which shall be regarded as historically valid, must neither be inconsistent with itself, nor in contradiction with other accounts.

The most decided case falling under this rule, amounting to a positive contradiction, is when one account affirms what another denies. Thus, one gospel represents the first appearance of Jesus in Galilee as subsequent to the imprisonment of John the Baptist, whilst another Gospel remarks, long after Jesus had preached both in Galilee and in Judea, that "John was not yet cast into prison."

When on the contrary, the second account, without absolutely contradicting the first, differs from it, the disagreement may be merely between the incidental particulars of the narrative ; such as *time*, (the clearing of the Temple,) *place*, (the original residence of the parents of Jesus ;) *number*, (the Gadarenes, the angels at the sepulchre ;) *names*, (Matthew and Levi ;) or it may concern the essential substance of the history. In the latter case, sometimes the character and circumstances in one account differ altogether from those in another. Thus, according to one narrator, the Baptist recognizes Jesus as the Messiah destined to suffer; according to the other, John takes offence at his suffering condition. Sometimes an occurrence is represented in two or more ways, of which one only can be consistent with the reality; as when in one account Jesus calls his first disciples from their nets whilst fishing on the sea of Galilee, and in the other meets them in Judea on his way to Galilee. We may class under the same head instances where events or discourses are represented as having occurred on two distinct occasions, whilst they are so similar that it is impossible to resist the conclusion that both the narratives refer to the same event or discourse.

It may here be asked: is it to be regarded as a contradiction if one account is wholly silent respecting a circumstance mentioned by another? In itself, apart from all other considerations, the argumentum ex silentio is of no weight; but it is certainly to be accounted of moment when, at the same time, it may be shown that had the author known the circumstance he could not have failed to mention it, and also that he must have known it had it actually occurred.

II. *Positive.* The positive characters of legend and fiction are to be recognized sometimes in the form, sometimes in the substance of a narrative.

If the form be poetical, if the actors converse in hymns, and in a more diffuse and elevated strain than might be expected from their training and situations, such discourses, at all events, are not to be regarded as historical. The absence of these marks of the unhistorical do not however prove the historical validity of the narration, since the mythus often wears the most simple and apparently historical form: in which case the proof lies in the substance.

If the contents of a narrative strikingly accords with certain ideas existing and prevailing within the circle from which the narrative proceeded, which ideas themselves seem to be the product of preconceived opinions rather than of practical experience, it is more or less probable, according to circumstances, that such a narrative is of mythical origin. The knowledge of the fact, that the Jews were fond of representing their great men as the children of parents who had long been childless, cannot but make us doubtful of the historical truth of the statement that this was the case with John the Baptist; knowing also that the Jews saw predictions everywhere in the writings of their prophets and poets, and discovered types of the Messiah in all the lives of holy men recorded in their Scriptures; when we find details in the life of Jesus evidently sketched after the pattern of these prophecies and prototypes, we cannot but suspect that they are rather mythical than historical.

The more simple characteristics of the legend, and of additions by the author, after the observations of the former section, need no further elucidation.

Yet each of these tests, on the one hand, and each narrative on the other, considered apart, will rarely prove more than the possible or probable unhistorical character of the record. The concurrence of several such indications, is necessary to bring about a more definite result. The accounts of the visit of the Magi, and of the murder of the innocents at Bethlehem, harmonize remarkably with the Jewish Messianic notion, built upon the prophecy of Balaam, respecting the star which should come out of Jacob; and with the history of the sanguinary command of Pharaoh. Still this would not alone suffice to stamp the narratives as mythical. But we have also the corroborative facts that the described appearance of the star is contrary to the physical, the alleged conduct of Herod to the psychological laws; that Josephus, who gives in other respects so circumstantial an account of Herod, agrees with all other historical authorities in being silent concerning the Bethlehem massacre; and that the visit of the Magi together with the flight into Egypt related in the one Gospel, and the presentation in the temple related in another Gospel, mutually exclude one another. Wherever, as in this instance, the several criteria of the mythical character concur, the result is certain, and certain in proportion to the accumulation of such grounds of evidence.

It may be that a narrative, standing alone, would discover but slight indications, or perhaps, might present no one distinct feature of the mythus; but it is connected with others, or proceeds from the author of other narratives which exhibit unquestionable marks of a mythical or legendary character; and consequently suspicion is reflected back from the latter, on the former. Every narrative, however miraculous, contains some details which might in themselves be historical, but which, in consequence of their connexion with the other supernatural incidents, necessarily become equally doubtful.

In these last remarks we are, to a certain extent, anticipating the question which is, in conclusion, to be considered: viz., whether the mythical character is restricted to those features of the narrative, upon which such character is actually stamped; and whether a contradiction between two accounts invalidate one account only, or both? That is to say, what is the precise boundary line between the historical and the unhistorical?—the most difficult question in the whole province of criticism.

In the first place, when two narratives mutually exclude one another, one only is thereby proved to be unhistorical. If one be true the other must be false, but though the one be false the other may be true. Thus, in reference to the original residence of the parents of Jesus, we are justified in adopting the account of Luke which places it at Nazareth, to the exclusion of that of Matthew, which plainly supposes it to have been at Bethlehem; and, generally speaking, when we have to choose between two irreconcilable accounts, in selecting as historical that which is the least opposed to the laws of nature, and has the least correspondence with certain national or party opinions. But upon a more particular consideration it will appear that, since one account is false, it is possible that the other may be so likewise: the existence of a mythus respecting some certain point, shows that the imagination has been active in reference to that particular subject; (we need only refer to the genealogies;) and the historical accuracy of either of two such accounts cannot be relied upon, unless substantiated by its agreement with some other well authenticated testimony.

Concerning the different parts of one and the same narrative: it might be thought for example, that though the appearance of an angel, and his announcement to Mary that she should be the Mother of the Messiah, must certainly be regarded as unhistorical, still, that Mary should have indulged this hope before the birth of the child, is not in itself incredible. But what should have excited this hope in Mary's mind? It is at once apparent that that which is credible in itself is nevertheless unhistorical when it is so intimately connected with what is incredible that, if you discard the latter, you at the same time remove the basis on which the former rests. Again, any action of Jesus represented as a miracle, when divested of the marvellous, might be thought to exhibit a perfectly natural occurrence; with respect to some of the miraculous histories, the expulsion of devils for instance, this might with some limitation, be possible. But for this reason alone: in these instances, a cure, so instantaneous, and effected by a few words merely, as it is described in the Gospels, is not psychologically incredible; so that, the essential in these

narratives remains untouched.   It is different in the case of the healing of a
man born blind.   A natural cure could not have been effected otherwise than
by a gradual process ; the narrative states the cure to have been immediate ;
if therefore the history be understood to record a natural occurrence, the most
essential particular is incorrectly represented, and consequently all security for
the truth of the otherwise natural remainder is gone, and the real fact cannot
be discovered without the aid of arbitrary conjecture.

The following examples will serve to illustrate the mode of deciding in such
cases.   According to the narrative, as Mary entered the house and saluted
her cousin Elizabeth, who was then pregnant, the babe leaped in her womb,
she was filled with the Holy Ghost, and she immediately addressed Mary as
the mother of the Messiah.   This account bears indubitable marks of an unhistorical character.   Yet, it is not, in itself, impossible that Mary should have
paid a visit to her cousin, during which everything went on quite naturally.
The fact is however that there are psychological difficulties connected with
this journey of the betrothed ; and that the visit, and even the relationship of
the two women, seem to have originated entirely in the wish to exhibit a
connexion between the mother of John the Baptist, and the mother of
the Messiah.   Or when in the history of the transfiguration it is stated, that the
men who appeared with Jesus on the Mount were Moses and Elias : and that
the brilliancy which illuminated Jesus was supernatural ; it might seem here
also that, after deducting the marvellous, the presence of two men and a
bright morning beam might be retained as the historical facts.   But the legend
was predisposed, by virtue of the current idea concerning the relation of the
Messiah to these two prophets, not merely to make any two men (whose persons, object and conduct, if they were not what the narrative represents them,
remain in the highest degree mysterious) into Moses and Elias, but to create
the whole occurrence ; and in like manner not merely to conceive of some
certain illumination as a supernatural effulgence (which, if a natural one, is
much exaggerated and misrepresented), but to create it at once after the
pattern of the brightness which illumined the face of Moses on Mount Sinai.

Hence is derived the following rule.   Where not merely the particular nature
and manner of an occurrence is critically suspicious, its external circumstances
represented as miraculous and the like ; but where likewise the essential substance and groundwork is either inconceivable in itself, or is in striking harmony with some Messianic idea of the Jews of that age, then not the particular
alleged course and mode of the transaction only, but the entire occurrence
must be regarded as unhistorical.   Where on the contrary, the form only, and
not the general contents of the narration, exhibits the characteristics of the
unhistorical, it is at least possible to suppose a kernel of historical fact ;
although we can never confidently decide whether this kernel of fact actually
exists, or in what it consists ; unless, indeed, it be discoverable from other
sources.   In legendary narratives, or narratives embellished by the writer, it is
less difficult,—by divesting them of all that betrays itself as fictitious imagery,
exaggeration, etc.—by endeavouring to abstract from them every extraneous
adjunct and to fill up every hiatus—to succeed, proximately at least, in separat-
ing the historical groundwork.

The boundary line, however, between the historical and the unhistorical, in
records, in which as in our Gospels this latter element is incorporated, will
ever remain fluctuating and unsusceptible of precise attainment.   Least of all
can it be expected that the first comprehensive attempt to treat these records
from a critical point of view should be successful in drawing a sharply defined
line of demarcation.   In the obscurity which criticism has produced, by the
extinction of all lights hitherto held historical, the eye must accustom itself

by degrees to discriminate objects with precision ; and at all events the author of this work, wishes especially to guard himself in those places where he declares he knows not what happened, from the imputation of asserting that he knows that nothing happened.

FIRST PART.

HISTORY OF THE BIRTH AND CHILDHOOD OF JESUS.

CHAPTER I.

ANNUNCIATION AND BIRTH OF JOHN THE BAPTIST.

-----

§ 17.

ACCOUNT GIVEN BY LUKE.* IMMEDIATE, SUPERNATURAL CHARACTER OF THE REPRESENTATION.

EACH of the four Evangelists represents the public ministry of Jesus as preceded by that of John the Baptist; but it is peculiar to Luke to make the Baptist the precursor of the Messiah in reference also to the event of his birth. This account finds a legitimate place in a work devoted exclusively to the consideration of the life of Jesus: firstly, on account of the intimate connexion which it exhibits as subsisting from the very commencement between the life of John and the life of Jesus; and secondly, because it constitutes a valuable contribution, aiding essentially towards the formation of a correct estimate of the general character of the gospel narratives. The opinion that the two first chapters of Luke, of which this particular history forms a portion, are a subsequent and unauthentic addition, is the uncritical assumption of a class of theologians who felt that the history of the childhood of Jesus seemed to require a mythical interpretation, but yet demurred to apply the comparatively modern mythical view to the remainder of the Gospel.[1]

A pious sacerdotal pair had lived and grown old in the cherished, but unrealized hope, of becoming parents, when, on a certain day, as the priest is offering incense in the sanctuary, the angel Gabriel appears to him, and promises him a son, who shall live consecrated to God, and who shall be the harbinger of the Messiah, to prepare his way when he shall visit and redeem his people. Zacharias, however, is incredulous, and doubts the prediction on account of his own advanced age and that of his wife; whereupon the angel, both as a sign and as a punishment, strikes him dumb until the time of its accomplishment; an infliction which endures until the day of the circumcision of the actually born son, when the father, being called upon to assign to the child the name predetermined by the angel, suddenly recovers his speech, and with the regained powers of utterance, breaks forth in a hymn of praise. (Luke i. 5-25, 57-80.)

It is evidently the object of this gospel account to represent a series of external and miraculous occurrences. The announcement of the birth of the

-----

* It may here be observed, once for all, that whenever in the following inquiry the names "Matthew," "Luke," etc., are used, it is the author of the several Gospels who is thus briefly indicated, quite irrespective of the question whether either of the Gospels was written by an apostle or disciple of that name, or by a later unknown author.

[1] See Kuinöl Comm. in Luc., Proleg., p. 247

forerunner of the Messiah is divinely communicated by the apparition of a
celestial spirit; the conception takes place under the particular and preter-
natural blessing of God; and the infliction and removal of dumbness are
effected by extraordinary means.   But it is quite another question, whether
we can accede to the view of the author, or can feel convinced that the birth
of the Baptist was in fact preceded by such a series of miraculous events.

The first offence against our modern notions in this narrative is the appearance of the angel : the event contemplated in itself, as well as the peculiar
circumstances of the apparition.   With respect to the latter, the angel
announces himself to be *Gabriel that stands in the presence of God.*   Now it is
inconceivable that the constitution of the celestial hierarchy should actually
correspond with the notions entertained by the Jews subsequent to the exile ;
and that the names given to the angels should be in the language of this
people.[2]   Here the supranaturalist finds himself in a dilemma, even upon his
own ground.   Had the belief in celestial beings, occupying a particular station
in the court of heaven, and distinguished by particular names, originated from
the revealed religion of the Hebrews,—had such a belief been established by
Moses, or some later prophet,—then, according to the views of the supranaturalist, they might, nay they must, be admitted to be correct.   But it is in
the Maccabæan Daniel[3] and in the apocryphal Tobit,[4] that this doctrine of
angels, in its more precise form, first appears ; and it is evidently a product of
the influence of the Zend religion of the Persians on the Jewish mind.   We
have the testimony of the Jews themselves, that they brought the names of
the angels with them from Babylon.[5]   Hence arises a series of questions
extremely perplexing to the supranaturalist.   Was the doctrine false so long
as it continued to be the exclusive possession of the heathens, but true as
soon as it became adopted by the Jews? or was it at all times equally
true, and was an important truth discovered by an idolatrous nation sooner
than by the people of God?   If nations shut out from a particular and divine
revelation, arrived at truth by the light of reason alone, sooner than the Jews
who were guided by that revelation, then either the revelation was superfluous,
or its influence was merely negative : that is, it operated as a check to the
premature acquisition of knowledge.   If, in order to escape this consequence,
it be contended that truths were revealed by the divine influence to other
people besides the Israelites, the supranaturalistic point of view is annihilated;
and, since all things contained in religions which contradict each other cannot
have been revealed, we are compelled to exercise a critical discrimination.
Thus, we find it to be by no means in harmony with an elevated conception
of God to represent him as an earthly monarch, surrounded by his court :
and when an appeal is made, in behalf of the reality of angels standing round
the throne, to the reasonable belief in a graduated scale of created intelligences,[6] the Jewish representation is not thereby justified, but merely a
modern conception substituted for it.   We should, thus, be driven to the

---

[2] Paulus, exeget. Handbuch, 1 a. s. 78 f. 96.   Bauer, hebr. Mythol., 2 Bd. s. 218 f.

[3] Here Michael is called *one of the chief princes.*

[4] Here Raphael is represented as *one of the seven angels which go in and out before the glory of the holy One ;* (Tobit, xii. 15), almost the same as Gabriel in Luke i. 19, excepting the mention of the number.   This number is in imitation of the Persian Amschaspands.   Vid. De Wette, bibl. Dogmatik, § 171 b.

[5] Hieros. rosch haschanah f. lvi. 4. (Lightfoot, horæ hebr. et talmud. in IV. Evangg., p. 723) : *R. Simeon ben Lachisch dicit : nomina angelorum ascenderunt in manu Israëlis ex Babylone.   Nam antea dictum est : advolavit ad me unus* τῶν *Seraphim, Seraphim steterunt ante eum,* Jes. vi. ; *at post : vir Gabriel,* Dan. ix. 21, *Michaël princeps vester,* Dan. x. 21.

[6] Olshausen, biblischer Commentar zum N.T., 1 Thl. s. 29 (2te Auflage).   Comp. Hoffmann, s. 124 f.

expedient of supposing an accommodation on the part of God : that he sent a celestial spirit with the command to simulate a rank and title which did not belong to him, in order that, by this conformity to Jewish notions, he might insure the belief of the father of the Baptist. Since however it appears that Zacharias did not believe the angel, but was first convinced by the result, the accommodation proved fruitless, and consequently could not have been a divine arrangement. With regard to the name of the angel, and the improbability that a celestial being should bear a Hebrew name, it has been remarked that the word Gabriel, taken appellatively in the sense of *Man of God*, very appropriately designates the nature of the heavenly visitant ; and since it may be rendered with this signification into every different language, the name cannot be said to be restricted to the Hebrew.[7] This explanation however leaves the difficulty quite unsolved, since it converts into a simple appellative a name evidently employed as a proper name. In this case likewise an accommodation must be supposed, namely, that the angel, in order to indicate his real nature, appropriated a name which he did not actually bear : an accommodation already judged in the foregoing remarks.

But it is not only the name and the alleged station of the angel which shock our modern ideas, we also feel his discourse and his conduct to be unworthy. Paulus indeed suggests that none but a levitical priest, and not an angel of Jehovah, could have conceived it necessary that the boy should live in nazarite abstemiousness,[8] but to this it may be answered that the angel also might have known that under this form John would obtain greater influence with the people. But there is a more important difficulty. When Zacharias, overcome by surprise, doubts the promise and asks for a sign, this natural incredulity is regarded by the angel as a crime, and immediately punished with dumbness. Though some may not coincide with Paulus that a real angel would have lauded the spirit of inquiry evinced by the priest, yet all will agree in the remark, that conduct so imperious is less in character with a truly celestial being than with the notions the Jews of that time entertained of such. Moreover we do not find in the whole province of supranaturalism a parallel severity.

The instance, cited by Paulus, of Jehovah's far milder treatment of Abraham, who asks precisely the same question unreproved, Gen xv. 8, is refuted by Olshausen, because he considers the words of Abraham, chap. v. 6, an evidence of his faith ; but this observation does not apply to chap. xviii. 12, where the greater incredulity of Sarah, in a similar case, remains unpunished ; nor to chap. xvii. 17, where Abraham himself is not even blamed, though the divine promise appears to him so incredible as to excite laughter. The example of Mary is yet closer, who (Luke i. 34) in regard to a still greater improbability, but one which was similarly declared by a special divine messenger to be no impossibility, puts exactly the same question as Zacharias ; so that we must agree with Paulus that such inconsistency certainly cannot belong to the conduct of God or of a celestial being, but merely to the Jewish representation of them. Feeling the objectionableness of the representation in its existing form, orthodox theologians have invented various motives to justify this infliction of dumbness. Hess has attempted to screen it from the reproach of an arbitrary procedure by regarding it as the only means of keeping secret, even against the will of the priest, an event, the premature proclamation of which might have been followed by disastrous consequences, similar to those which attended the announcement by the wise men of the birth of

---

[7] Olshausen, ut sup. Hoffmann, s. 135.
[8] Ut sup. s. 77.

the child Jesus.[9] But, in the first place, the angel says nothing of such an object, he inflicts the dumbness but as a sign and punishment ; secondly, the loss of speech did not hinder Zacharias from communicating, at any rate to his wife, the main features of the apparition, since we see that she was acquainted with the destined name of the child before appeal was made to the father.   Thirdly, what end did it serve thus to render difficult the communication of the miraculous annunciation of the unborn babe, since no sooner was it born than it was at once exposed to all the dreaded dangers ?—for the father's sudden recovery of speech, and the extraordinary scene at the circumcision excited attention and became noised abroad in all the country. Olshausen's view of the thing is more admissible.   He regards the whole proceeding, and especially the dumbness, as a moral training destined to teach Zacharias to know and conquer his want of faith.[10]   But of this too we have no mention in the text ; besides, the unexpected accomplishment of the prediction would have made Zacharias sufficiently ashamed of his unbelief, if instead of inflicting dumbness the angel had merely remonstrated with him.

But however worthy of God we might grant the conduct of his messenger to have been, still many of the present day will find an angelic apparition, as such, incredible.   Bauer insists that wherever angels appear, both in the New Testament and in the Old, the narrative is mythical.[11]   Even admitting the existence of angels, we cannot suppose them capable of manifesting themselves to human beings, since they belong to the invisible world, and spiritual existences are not cognizable by the organs of sense ; so that it is always advisable to refer their pretended apparitions to the imagination.[12]   It is not probable, it is added, that God should make use of them according to the popular notion, for these apparitions have no apparent adequate object, they serve generally only to gratify curiosity, or to encourage man's disposition passively to leave his affairs in higher hands.[13]   It is also remarkable that in the old world these celestial beings show themselves active upon the smallest occasions, whilst in modern times they remain idle even during the most important occurrences.[14]   But to deny their appearance and agency among men is to call in question their very being, because it is precisely this occupation which is a main object of their existence (Heb. i. 14).   According to Schleiermacher [15] we cannot indeed actually disprove the existence of angels, yet the conception is one which could not have originated in our time, but belongs wholly to the ancient ideas of the world.   The belief in angels has a twofold root or source : the one the natural desire of the mind to presuppose a larger amount of intelligence in the universe than is realized in the human race.   We who live in these days find this desire satisfied in the conviction that other worlds exist besides our own, and are peopled by intelligent beings ; and thus the first source of the belief in angels is destroyed.   The other source, namely, the representation of God as an earthly monarch surrounded by his court, contradicts all enlightened conceptions of Deity ; and further, the phenomena in the natural world and the transitions in human life, which were formerly thought to be wrought by God himself through ministering angels, we are now able to explain by natural causes ; so that the belief in

---

[9] Geschichte der drei letzten Lebensjahre Jesu, sammt dessen Jugendgeschichte. Tübingen 1779. 1 Bd. s. 12.

[10] Bibl. Comm. I, s. 115.

[11] Hebr. Mythol. ii. s. 218.

[12] Bauer, ut sup. i. s. 129.   Paulus, exeget. Handbuch, i. a. 74.

[13] Paulus, Commentar, i. s. 12.

[14] Bauer, ut sup.

[15] Glaubenslehre, 1 Thl. § 42 und 43 (2te Ausgabe).

angels is without a link by which it can attach itself to rightly apprehended modern ideas; and it exists only as a lifeless tradition. The result is the same if, with one of the latest writers on the doctrine of angels,[16] we consider as the origin of this representation, man's desire to separate the two sides of his moral nature, and to contemplate, as beings existing external to himself, angels and devils. For, the origin of both representations remains merely subjective, the angel being simply the ideal of created perfection : which, as it was formed from the subordinate point of view of a fanciful imagination, disappears from the higher and more comprehensive observation of the intellect.[17]

Olshausen, on the other hand, seeks to deduce a positive argument in favour of the reality of the apparition in question, from those very reasonings of the present day which, in fact, negative the existence of angels; and he does so by viewing the subject on its speculative side. He is of opinion that the gospel narrative does not contradict just views of the world, since God is immanent in the universe and moves it by his breath.[18] But if it be true that God is immanent in the world, precisely on that account is the intervention of angels superfluous. It is only a Deity who dwells apart, throned in heaven, who requires to send down his angels to fulfil his purposes on earth. It would excite surprise to find Olshausen arguing thus, did we not perceive from the manner in which this interpreter constantly treats of angelology and demo-nology, that he does not consider angels to be independent personal entities ; but regards them rather as divine powers, transitory emanations and fulgura-tions of the Divine Being. Thus Olshausen's conception of angels, in their relation to God, seems to correspond with the Sabellian doctrine of the Trinity; but as his is not the representation of the Bible, as also the arguments in favour of the former prove nothing in relation to the latter, it is useless to enter into further explanation. The reasoning of this same theologian, that we must not require the ordinariness of every-day life for the most pregnant epochs in the life of the human race ; that the incarnation of the eternal word was accompanied by extraordinary manifestations from the world of spirits, uncalled for in times less rich in momentous results,[19] rests upon a misapprehension. For the ordinary course of every-day life is interrupted in such moments, by the very fact that exalted beings like the Baptist are born into the world, and it would be puerile to designate as ordinary those times and circumstances which gave birth and maturity to a John, because they were unembellished by angelic apparitions. That which the spiritual world does for ours at such periods is to send extraordinary human intelligences, not to cause angels to ascend and descend.

Finally, if, in vindication of this narrative, it be stated that such an exhibi-tion by the angel, of the plan of education for the unborn child, was necessary in order to make him the man he should become [20], the assumption includes too much ; namely, that all great men, in order by their education to become such, must have been introduced into the world in like manner, or cause must be shown why that which was unnecessary in the case of great men of other ages and countries was indispensable for the Baptist. Again, the assumption attaches too much importance to external training, too little to the internal development of the mind. But in conclusion, many of the circumstances in the life of the Baptist, instead of serving to confirm a belief

16 Binder, Studien der evang. Geistlichkeit Würtembergs, ix. 2, 5. 11 ff.
17 Compare my Dogmatik, i. § 49.
18 Bibl. Comm., 1. Thl. s. 119.
19 Ut sup. s. 92.
20 Hess, Geschichte der drei letzten Lebensjahre Jesu u. s. w., 1. Thl. s. 13, 33.

in the truth of the miraculous history, are on the contrary, as has been justly maintained, altogether irreconcilable with the supposition, that his birth was attended by these wonderful occurrences. If it were indeed true, that John was from the first distinctly and miraculously announced as the forerunner of the Messiah, it is inconceivable that he should have had no acquaintance with Jesus prior to his baptism; and that, even subsequent to that event, he should have felt perplexed concerning his Messiahship (John i. 30; Matt. xi. 2).[21]

Consequently the *negative* conclusion of the rationalistic criticism and controversy must, we think, be admitted, namely, that the birth of the Baptist could not have been preceded and attended by these supernatural occurrences. The question now arises, what *positive* view of the matter is to replace the rejected literal orthodox explanation?

§ 18.

NATURAL EXPLANATION OF THE NARRATIVE.

In treating the narrative before us according to the rationalistic method, which requires the separation of the pure fact from the opinion of interested persons, the simplest alteration is this: to retain the two leading facts, the apparition and the dumbness, as actual external occurrences; but to account for them in a natural manner. This were possible with respect to the apparition, by supposing that a man, mistaken by Zacharias for a divine messenger, really appeared to him, and addressed to him the words he believed he heard. But this explanation, viewed in connexion with the attendant circumstances, being too improbable, it became necessary to go a step further, and to transform the event from an external to an internal one; to remove the occurrence out of the physical into the psychological world. To this view the opinion of Bahrdt, that a flash of lightning was perhaps mistaken by Zacharias for an angel,[1] forms a transition; since he attributes the greater part of the scene to Zacharias's imagination. But that any man, in an ordinary state of mind, could have created so long and consecutive a dialogue out of a flash of lightning is incredible. A peculiar mental state must be supposed; whether it be a swoon, the effect of fright occasioned by the lightning,[2] but of this there is no trace in the text (no falling down as in Acts ix. 4); or, abandoning the notion of the lightning, a dream, which, however, could scarcely occur whilst burning incense in the temple. Hence, it has been found necessary, with Paulus, to call to mind that there are waking visions or ecstasies, in which the imagination confounds internal images with external occurrences.[3] Such ecstasies, it is true, are not common; but, says Paulus, in Zacharias's case many circumstances combined to produce so unusual a state of mind. The exciting causes were, firstly, the long-cherished desire to have a posterity; secondly, the exalted vocation of administering in the Holy of Holies, offering up with the incense the prayers of the people to the throne of Jehovah, which seemed to Zacharias to foretoken the acceptance of his own prayer; and thirdly, perhaps an exhortation from his wife as he left his house, similar to that of Rachel to Jacob. Gen. xxx. 1 (!) In

---

[21] Horst in Henke's Museum, i. 4. s. 733 f.   Gabler in seinem neuest. theol. Journal, vii. 1. s. 403.

[1] Briefe über die Bibel im Volkstone (Ausg. Frankfurt und Leipzig, 1800), ites Bändchen, 6ter Brief, s. 51 f.

[2] Bahrdt, ut sup. s. 52.

[3] Exeget. Handb. 1, a. s. 74 ff.

this highly excited state of mind, as he prays in the dimly-lighted sanctuary, he thinks of his most ardent wish, and expecting that now or never his prayer shall be heard, he is prepared to discern a sign of its acceptance in the slightest occurrence. As the glimmer of the lamps falls upon the ascending cloud of incense, and shapes it into varying forms, the priest imagines he perceives the figure of an angel. The apparition at first alarms him; but he soon regards it as an assurance from God that his prayer is heard. No sooner does a transient doubt cross his mind, than the sensitively pious priest looks upon himself as sinful, believes himself reproved by the angel, and—here two explanations are possible—either an apoplectic seizure actually deprives him of speech, which he receives as the just punishment of his incredulity, till the excessive joy he experiences at the circumcision of his son restores the power of utterance: so that the dumbness is retained as an external, physical, though not miraculous, occurrence;[4] or the proceeding is psychologically understood, namely, that Zacharias, in accordance with a Jewish superstition, for a time denied himself the use of the offending member.[5] Re animated in other respects by the extraordinary event, the priest returns home to his wife, and she becomes a second Sarah.

With regard to this account of the angelic apparition given by Paulus,— and the other explanations are either of essentially similar character, or are so manifestly untenable, as not to need refutation—it may be observed that the object so laboriously striven after is not attained. Paulus fails to free the narrative of the marvellous; for by his own admission, the majority of men have no experience of the kind of vision here supposed.[6] If such a state of ecstasy occur in particular cases, it must result either from a predisposition in the individual, of which we find no sign in Zacharias, and which his advanced age must have rendered highly improbable; or it must have been induced by some peculiar circumstances, which totally fail in the present instance.[7] A hope which has been long indulged is inadequate to the production of ecstatic vehemence, and the act of burning incense is insufficient to cause so extraordinary an excitement, in a priest who has grown old in the service of the temple. Thus Paulus has in fact substituted a miracle of chance for a miracle of God. Should it be said that to God nothing is impossible, or to chance nothing is impossible, both explanations are equally precarious and unscientific.

Indeed, the dumbness of Zacharias as explained from this point of view is very unsatisfactory. For had it been, as according to one explanation, the result of apoplexy; admitting Paulus's reference to Lev. xxi. 16, to be set aside by the contrary remark of Lightfoot,[8] still, we must join with Schleiermacher in wondering how Zacharias, nothwithstanding this apoplectic seizure, returned home in other respects healthy and vigorous;[9] and that in spite of partial paralysis his general strength was unimpaired, and his long-cherished hope fulfilled. It must also be regarded as a strange coincidence, that the father's tongue should have been loosed exactly at the time of the circumcision; for if the recovery of speech is to be considered as the effect of joy,[10] surely the father must have been far more elated at the birth of the

[4] Bahrdt, ut sup. 7ter Brief, s. 60.—E. F. über die beiden ersten Kapitel des Matthäus und Lukas, in Henke's Magazin, v. 1. s. 163. Bauer, hebr. Mythol. 2, s. 220.

[5] Exeget. Handb. 1, a. s. 77–80.

[6] Ut sup. s. 73.

[7] Comp. Schleiermacher über die Schriften des Lukas, s. 25.

[8] Horæ hebr. et talmud., ed. Carpzov. p. 722.

[9] Ut sup. s. 26.

[10] Examples borrowed from Aulus Gellius, v. 9, and from Valerius Maximus, i. 8, are cited.

earnestly-desired son, than at the circumcision ; for by that time he would have become accustomed to the possession of his child.

The other explanation : that Zacharias's silence was not from any physical impediment, but from a notion, to be psychologically explained, that he ought not to speak, is in direct contradiction to the words of Luke. What do all the passages, collected by Paulus to show that οὐ δύναμαι may signify not only a positive *non posse*, but likewise a mere *non sustinere*,[11] prove against the clear meaning of the passage and its context? If perhaps the narrative phrase (v. 22), οὐκ ἠδύνατο λαλῆσαι αὐτοῖς might be forced to bear this sense, yet certainly in the supposed vision of Zacharias, had the angel only forbidden him to speak, instead of depriving him of the power of speech, he would not have said : καὶ ἔσῃ σιωπῶν, μὴ δυνάμενος λαλῆσαι, but ἴσθι σιωπῶν, μηδ᾽ ἐπιχειρήσῃς λαλῆσαι. The words διέμενε κωφὸς (v. 21) also most naturally mean actual dumbness. This view assumes, and indeed necessarily so, that the gospel history is a correct report of the account given by Zacharias himself ; if then it be denied that the dumbness was actual, as Zacharias affirms that actual dumbness was announced to him by the angel, it must be admitted that, though perfectly able to speak, he believed himself to be dumb ; which leads to the conclusion that he was mad : an imputation not to be laid upon the father of the Baptist without compulsory evidence in the text.

Again, the natural explanation makes too light of the incredibly accurate fulfilment of a prediction originating, as it supposes, in an unnatural, over-excited state of mind. In no other province of inquiry would the realization of a prediction which owed its birth to a vision be found credible, even by the Rationalist. If Dr. Paulus were to read that a somnambulist, in a state of ecstasy, had foretold the birth of a child, under circumstances in the highest degree improbable ; and not only of a child, but of a boy ; and had moreover, with accurate minuteness, predicted his future mode of life, character, and position in history ; and that each particular had been exactly verified by the result : would he find such a coincidence credible? Most assuredly to no human being, under any conditions whatsoever, would he concede the power thus to penetrate the most mysterious workings of nature ; on the contrary he would complain of the outrage on human free-will, which is annihilated by the admission that a man's entire intellectual and moral development may be predetermined like the movements of a clock. And he would on this very ground complain of the inaccuracy of observation, and untrustworthiness of the report which represented, as matters of fact, things in their very nature impossible. Why does he not follow the same rule with respect to the New Testament narrative? Why admit in the one case what he rejects in the other? Is biblical history to be judged by one set of laws, and profane history by another?—An assumption which the Rationalist is compelled to make, if he admits as credible in the Gospels that which he rejects as unworthy of credit in every other history—which is in fact to fall back on the supranaturalistic point of view, since the assumption, that the natural laws which govern in every other province are not applicable to sacred history, is the very essential of supranaturalism.

No other rescue from this self-annihilation remains to the anti-supernatural mode of explanation, than to question the verbal accuracy of the history. This is the simplest expedient, felt to be such by Paulus himself, who remarks, that his efforts may be deemed superfluous to give a natural explanation of a narrative, which is nothing more than one of those stories invented either after the death or even during the lifetime of every distinguished man to em-

---

[11] Ut sup. s. 26.

bellish his early history.   Paulus, however, after an impartial examination, is
of opinion that the analogy, in the present instance, is not applicable.   The
principal ground for this opinion is the too short interval between the birth
of the Baptist, and the composition of the Gospel of Luke.[12]   We, on the
contrary, in harmony with the observations in the introduction, would reverse
the question and inquire of this interpreter, how he would render it credible,
that the history of the birth of a man so famed as the Baptist should have
been transmitted, in an age of great excitement, through a period of more
than sixty years, in all its primitive accuracy of detail?   Paulus's answer
is ready : an answer approved by others (Heidenreich, Olshausen) :—the
passage inserted by Luke (i. 5 ; ii. 39) was possibly a family record, which
circulated among the relatives of the Baptist and of Jesus ; and of which
Zacharias was probably the author.[13]

K. Ch. L. Schmidt controverts this hypothesis with the remark, that it is
impossible that a narrative so disfigured (we should rather say, so embellished)
could have been a family record ; and that, if it does not belong altogether
to the class of legends, its historical basis, if such there be, is no longer to be
distinguished.[14]   It is further maintained, that the narrative presents certain
features which no poet would have conceived, and which prove it to be a
direct impression of facts ; for instance, the Messianic expectations expressed
by the different personages introduced by Luke (chap. i. and ii.) correspond
exactly with the situation and relation of each individual.[15]   But these distinctions are by no means so striking as Paulus represents ; they are only the
characteristics of a history which goes into details, making a transition from
generalities to particulars, which is natural alike to the poet and to the popular legend ; besides, the peculiar Judaical phraseology in which the Messianic
expectations are expressed, and which it is contended confirm the opinion
that this narrative was written, or received its fixed form, before the death of
Jesus, continued to be used after that event (Acts i. 6[16]).   Moreover we
must agree with Schleiermacher when he says :[17] least of all is it possible to
regard these utterances as strictly historical ; or to maintain that Zacharias,
in the moment that he recovered his speech, employed it in a song of praise,
uninterrupted by the exultation and wonder of the company, sentiments
which the narrator interrupts himself to indulge.   It must, at all events, be
admitted, that the author has made additions of his own, and has enriched
the history by the lyric effusions of his muse.   Kuinöl supposes that Zacharias
composed and wrote down the canticle subsequent to the occasion ; but this
strange surmise contradicts the text.   There are some other features which,
it is contended, belong not to the creations of the poet ; such as, the signs
made to the father, the debate in the family, the position of the angel on the
right hand of the altar.[18]   But this criticism is merely a proof that these
interpreters have, or determine to have, no just conception of poetry or
popular legend ; for the genuine characteristic of poetry and mythus is
natural and pictorial representation of details.[19]

[12] Ut sup. s. 72 f.
[13] Ut sup. s. 69.
[14] In Schmidt's Bibliothek für Kritik und Exegese, iii. 1, s. 119.
[15] Paulus, ut sup.
[16] Comp. De Wette, exeg. Handb., i. 2, s. 9.
[17] Über die Schriften des Lukas, s. 23.
[18] Paulus und Olshausen z. d. St., Heydenreich a. a. O. 1, s. 87.
[19] Comp. Horst, in Henke's Museum, i. 4, s. 705 ; Vater, Commentar zum Pentateuch,
3, s. 597 ff. ; Hase L. J., § 35 ; auch George, s. 33 f. 91.

§ 19.

MYTHICAL VIEW OF THE NARRATIVE IN ITS DIFFERENT STAGES.

The above exposition of the necessity, and lastly, of the possibility of doubting the historical fidelity of the gospel narrative, has led many theologians to
explain the account of the birth of the Baptist as a poetical composition ;
suggested by the importance attributed by the Christians to the forerunner of
Jesus, and by the recollection of some of the Old Testament histories, in
which the births of Ishmael, Isaac, Samuel, and especially of Samson, are
related to have been similarly announced.   Still the matter was not allowed
to be altogether invented.   It may have been historically true that Zacharias
and Elizabeth lived long without offspring ; that, on one occasion whilst in
the temple, the old man's tongue was suddenly paralyzed ; but that soon afterwards his aged wife bore him a son, and he, in his joy at the event, recovered
the power of speech.   At that time, but still more when John became a remarkable man, the history excited attention, and out of it the existing legend
grew.[1]

It is surprising to find an explanation almost identical with the natural one
we have criticised above, again brought forward under a new title ; so that the
admission of the possibility of an admixture of subsequent legends in the narrative has little influence on the view of the matter itself.   As the mode of
explanation we are now advocating denies all confidence in the historical
authenticity of the record, all the details must be in themselves equally prob-
lematic ; and whether historical validity can be retained for this or that particular incident, can be determined only by its being either less improbable
than the rest, or else less in harmony with the spirit, interest, and design of
the poetic legend, so as to make it probable that it had a distinct origin.   The
barrenness of Elizabeth and the sudden dumbness of Zacharias are here retained as incidents of this character : so that only the appearing and prediction of the angel are given up.   But by taking away the angelic apparition,
the sudden infliction and as sudden removal of the dumbness loses its only
adequate supernatural cause, so that all difficulties which beset the natural interpretation remain in full force : a dilemma into which these theologians are,
most unnecessarily, brought by their own inconsequence ; for the moment we
enter upon mythical ground, all obligation to hold fast the assumed historical
fidelity of the account ceases to exist.   Besides, that which they propose to
retain as historical fact, namely, the long barrenness of the parents of the
Baptist, is so strictly in harmony with the spirit and character of Hebrew
legendary poetry, that of this incident the mythical origin is least to be mistaken.   How confused has this misapprehension made, for example, the
reasoning of Bauer !   It was a prevailing opinion, says he, consonant with
Jewish ideas, that all children born of aged parents, who had previously been
childless, became distinguished personages.   John was the child of aged
parents, and became a notable preacher of repentance ; consequently it was
thought justifiable to infer that his birth was predicted by an angel.   What an
illogical conclusion ! for which he has no other ground than the assumption
that John was the son of aged parents.   Let this be made a settled point,
and the conclusion follows without difficulty.   It was readily believed, he proceeds, of remarkable men that they were born of aged parents, and that their
birth, no longer in the ordinary course of nature to be expected, was an-

---

[1] E. F. über die zwei ersten Kapitel u. s. w. in Henke's Magazin, v. 1, s. 162 ff., und
Bauer hebr. Mythol., ii. 220 f.

nounced by a heavenly messenger[2]; John was a great man and a prophet; consequently, the legend represented him to have been born of an aged couple, and his birth to have been proclaimed by an angel.

Seeing that this explanation of the narrative before us, as a half (so called historical) mythus, is encumbered with all the difficulties of a half measure, Gabler has treated it as a pure philosophical, or dogmatical mythus.[3] Horst likewise considers it, and indeed the entire two first chapters of Luke, of which it forms a part, as an ingenious fiction, in which the birth of the Messiah, together with that of his precursor, and the predictions concerning the character and ministry of the latter, framed after the event, are set forth; it being precisely the loquacious circumstantiality of the narration which betrays the poet.[4] Schleiermacher likewise explains the first chapter as a little poem, similar in character to many of the Jewish poems which we meet with in their apocrypha. He does not however consider it altogether a fabrication. It might have had a foundation in fact, and in a widespread tradition; but the poet has allowed himself so full a license in arranging, and combining, in moulding and embodying the vague and fluctuating representations of tradition, that the attempt to detect the purely historical in such narratives, must prove a fruitless and useless effort.[5] Horst goes so far as to suppose the author of the piece to have been a Judaising Christian; whilst Schleiermacher imagines it to have been composed by a Christian of the famed Jewish school, at a period when it comprised some who still continued strict disciples of John; and whom it was the object of the narrative to bring over to Christianity, by exhibiting the relationship of John to the Christ as his peculiar and highest destiny; and also by holding out the expectation of a state of temporal greatness for the Jewish people at the reappearance of Christ.

An attentive consideration of the Old Testament histories, to which, as most interpreters admit, the narrative of the annunciation and birth of the Baptist bears a striking affinity, will render it abundantly evident that this is the only just view of the passage in question. But it must not here be imagined, as is now so readily affirmed in the confutation of the mythical view of this passage, that the author of our narrative first made a collection from the Old Testament of its individual traits; much rather had the scattered traits respecting the late birth of different distinguished men, as recorded in the Old Testament, blended themselves into a compound image in the mind of their reader, whence he selected the features most appropriate to his present subject. Of the children born of aged parents, Isaac is the most ancient prototype. As it is said of Zacharias and Elizabeth, "they both were advanced in their days" (v. 7) προβεβηκότες ἐν ταῖς ἡμέραις αὐτῶν, so Abraham and Sarah "were advanced in their days" בָּאִים בַּיָּמִים (Gen. xviii. 11; LXX: προβεβηκότες ἡμερῶν), when they were promised a son. It is likewise from this history that the incredulity of the father, on account of the advanced age of both

---

[2] The adoption of this opinion is best explained by a passage—with respect to this matter classical—in the Evangelium de nativitate Mariæ, in Fabricius codex apocryphus N. Ti. 1, p. 22 f., and in Thilo 1, p. 322, " *Deus* "—it is here said,—*cum alicujus uterum claudit, ad hoc facit, ut mirabilius denuo aperiat*, et non libidinis esse, quod nascitur, sed divini muneris cognoscatur. *Prima enim gentis vestræ Sara mater nonne usque ad octogesimum annum infecunda fuit? et tamen in ultimâ senectutis ætate genuit Isaac, cui repromissa erat benedictio omnium gentium. Rachel quoque, tantum Domino grata tantumque a sancto Jacob amata diu sterilis fuit, et tamen Joseph genuit, non solum dominum Ægypti, sed plurimarum gentium fame periturarum liberatorem. Quis in ducibus vel fortior Sampsone, vel sanctior Samuele? et tamen hi ambo steriles matres habuere.—ergo—crede—dilatos diu conceptus et steriles partus mirabiliores esse solere.*

[3] Neuestes theol. Journal, vii. 1, s. 402 f.

[4] In Henke's Museum, i. 4, s. 702 ff.

[5] Hase in his Leben Jesu makes the same admission; compare § 52 with § 32.

parents, and the demand of a sign, are borrowed in our narrative. As Abraham, when Jehovah promises him he shall have a son and a numerous posterity who shall inherit the land of Canaan, doubtingly inquires, "Whereby shall I know that I shall inherit it?" κατὰ τί γνώσομαι, ὅτι κληρονομήσω αὐτήν; (sc. τὴν γῆν. Gen. xv. 8. LXX): so Zacharias—"Whereby shall I know this?" κατὰ τί γνώσομαι τοῦτο; (v. 18.)   The incredulity of Sarah is not made use of for Elizabeth; but she is said to be of the daughters of Aaron, and the name Elizabeth may perhaps have been suggested by that of Aaron's wife (Exod. vi. 23. LXX.).   The incident of the angel announcing the birth of the Baptist is taken from the history of another late-born child, Samson. In our narrative indeed, the angel appears first to the father in the temple, whereas in the history of Samson he shows himself first to the mother, and afterwards to the father in the field.   This, however, is an alteration arising naturally out of the different situations of the respective parents (Judges xiii.). According to popular Jewish notions, it was no unusual occurrence for the priest to be visited by angels and divine apparitions whilst offering incense in the temple.[6]   The command which before his birth predestined the Baptist —whose later ascetic mode of life was known—to be a Nazarite, is taken from the same source. As, to Samson's mother during her pregnancy, wine, strong drink, and unclean food, were forbidden, so a similar diet is prescribed for her son,[7] adding, as in the case of John, that the child shall be consecrated to God from the womb.[8]   The blessings which it is predicted that these two men shall realize for the people of Israel are similar (comp. Luke i. 16, 17, with Judges xiii. 5), and each narrative concludes with the same expression respecting the hopeful growth of the child.[9]   It may be too bold to derive the Levitical descent of the Baptist from a third Old Testament history of a late-born son—from the history of Samuel (compare 1 Sam. i. 1; Chron. vii. 27); but the lyric effusions in the first chapter of Luke are imitations of this history. As Samuel's mother, when consigning him to the care of the high priest, breaks forth into a hymn (1 Sam. ii. 1), so the father of John does the same at the circumcision; though the particular expressions in the Canticle uttered by Mary—of which we shall have to speak hereafter—have a closer resemblance to Hannah's song of praise than that of Zacharias.   The significant appellation *John* (יְהוֹחָנָן=Θεόχαρις), predetermined by the angel, had its precedent in the announcements of the names of Ishmael and Isaac [10]; but the ground of its selection was the apparently providential coincidence between the signification of the name and the historical destination of the man.   The

---

[6] Wetstein zu Luke i. 11, s. 647 f. adduces passages from Josephus and from the Rabbins recording apparitions seen by the high priests.   How readily it was presumed that the same thing happened to ordinary priests is apparent from the narrative before us.

[7] Judges xiii. 14 (LXX.) :

καὶ οἶνον καὶ σίκερα (al. μέθυσμα, hebr. שֵׁכָר)
μὴ πιέτω.

Luc. i. 15.

καὶ οἶνον καὶ σίκερα οὐ μὴ πίῃ.

[8] Judg. xiii. 5 :

ὅτι ἡγιασμένον ἔσται τῷ θεῷ (al. Ναζὶρ θεοῦ ἔσται) τὸ παιδάριον οὐκ τῆς γαστρός (al. ἀπὸ τῆς κοιλίας).

Luc. i. 15 :

καὶ πνεύματος ἁγίου πλησθήσεται ἔτι ἐκ κοιλίας μητρός αὐτοῦ.

[9] Judg. xiii. 24 f. :

καὶ ηὐλόγησεν αὐτὸν Κύριος, καὶ η'ξήθη (al. ἡδρύνθη) τὸ παιδάριον· καὶ ἤρξατο πνεῦμα Κυρίου συμπορεύεσθαι αὐτῷ ἐν παρεμβολῇ Δὰν, ἀναμέσον Σαρὰ καὶ ἀναμέσον Ἐσθαόλ.

Comp. Gen. xxi. 20.

Luc. i. 80 :

τὸ δὲ παιδίον ηὔξανε καὶ ἐκραταιοῦτο πνεύματι, καὶ ἦν ἐν ταῖς ἐρήμοις, ἕως ἡμέρας ἀναδείξεως αὐτοῦ πρὸς τὸν Ἰσραήλ.

[10] Gen. xvi. 11. (LXX.) :

καὶ καλέσεις τὸ ὄνομα αὐτοῦ Ἰσμαήλ.
xvii. 19 : — — Ἰσαάκ.

Luc. i. 13 :

καὶ καλέσεις τὸ ὄνομα αὐτοῦ Ἰωάννην.

remark, that the name of John was not in the family (v. 61), only brought its celestial origin more fully into view. The tablet (πινακίδιον) upon which the father wrote the name (v. 63), was necessary on account of his incapacity to speak ; but it also had its type in the Old Testament. Isaiah was commanded to write the significant names of the child Maher-shalal-hash-baz upon a tablet (Isaiah viii. 1 ff.). The only supernatural incident of the narrative, of which the Old Testament may seem to offer no precise analogy, is the dumbness ; and this is the point fixed upon by those who contest the mythical view.[11] But if it be borne in mind that the asking and receiving a sign from heaven in confirmation of a promise or prophecy was usual among the Hebrews (comp. Isaiah vii. 11 ff.) ; that the temporary loss of one of the senses was the peculiar punishment inflicted after a heavenly vision (Acts ix. 8, 17 ff.) ; that Daniel became dumb whilst the angel was talking with him, and did not recover his speech till the angel had touched his lips and opened his mouth (Dan. x. 15 f.) : the origin of this incident also will be found in the legend, and not in historical fact. Of two ordinary and subordinate features of the narrative, the one, the righteousness of the parents of the Baptist (v. 6), is merely a conclusion founded upon the belief that to a pious couple alone would the blessing of such a son be vouchsafed, and consequently is void of all historical worth ; the other, the statement that John was born in the reign of Herod (the Great) (v. 5), is without doubt a correct calculation.

So that we stand here upon purely mythical-poetical ground ; the only historical reality which we can hold fast as positive matter of fact being this : —the impression made by John the Baptist, by virtue of his ministry and his relation to Jesus, was so powerful as to lead to the subsequent glorification of his birth in connection with the birth of the Messiah in the Christian legend.[12]

[11] Olshausen, bibl. Commentar, I. s. 116. Hoffmann, s. 146.
[12] With this view of the passage compare De Wette, Exeg. Handbuch zum N. T., i. 2, s. 12.

CHAPTER II.

DAVIDICAL DESCENT OF JESUS, ACCORDING TO THE GENEALOGICAL TABLES OF MATTHEW AND LUKE.

----

§ 20.

THE TWO GENEALOGIES OF JESUS CONSIDERED SEPARATELY AND IRRESPECTIVELY OF ONE ANOTHER.

IN the history of the birth of the Baptist, we had the single account of Luke ; but regarding the genealogical descent of Jesus we have also that of Matthew ; so that in this case the mutual control of two narrators in some respects multiplies, whilst in others it lightens, our critical labour. It is indeed true that the authenticity of the two first chapters of Matthew, which contain the history of the birth and childhood of Jesus, as well as that of the parallel section of Luke, has been questioned : but as in both cases the question has originated merely in a prejudiced view of the subject, the doubt has been silenced by a decisive refutation.[1]

Each of these two Gospels contains a genealogical table designed to exhibit the Davidical descent of Jesus, the Messiah. That of Matthew (i. 1–17) precedes, that of Luke (iii. 23–38) follows, the history of the announcement and birth of Jesus. These two tables, considered each in itself, or both compared together, afford so important a key to the character of the evangelic records in this section, as to render a close examination of them imperative. We shall first consider each separately, and then each, but particularly that of Matthew, in comparison with the passages in the Old Testament to which it is parallel.

In the Genealogy given by the author of the first Gospel, there is a comparison of the account with itself which is important, as it gives a result, a sum at its conclusion, whose correctness may be proved by comparing it with the previous statements. In the summing up it is said, that from Abraham to Christ there are three divisions of fourteen generations each, the first from Abraham to David, the second from David to the Babylonish exile, the third from the exile to Christ. Now if we compute the number of names for ourselves, we find the first fourteen from Abraham to David, both included, complete (2–5) ; also that from Solomon to Jechonias, after whom the Babylonish exile is mentioned (6–11) ; but from Jechonias to Jesus, even reckoning the latter as one, we can discover only thirteen (12–16). How shall we explain this discrepancy ? The supposition that one of the names has escaped from the third division by an error of a transcriber,[2] is in the highest degree improb-

----

[1] Kuinöl, Comm. in Matth. Proleg., p. xxvii. f.
[2] Paulus, p. 292.

able, since the deficiency is mentioned so early as by Porphyry.[3]   The insertion, in some manuscripts and versions, of the name *Jehoiakim*[4] between Josias and Jechonias, does not supply the deficiency of the third division; it only adds a superfluous generation to the second division, which was already complete.   As also there is no doubt that this deficiency originated with the author of the genealogy, the question arises: in what manner did he reckon so as to count fourteen generations for his third series?   Truly it is possible to count in various ways, if an arbitrary inclusion and exclusion of the first and last members of the several series be permitted.   It might indeed have been presupposed, that a generation already included in one division was necessarily excluded from another: but the compiler of the genealogy may perhaps have thought otherwise; and since David is twice mentioned in the table, it is possible that the author counted him twice: namely, at the end of the first series, and again at the beginning of the second.   This would not indeed, any more than the insertion of Jehoiakim, fill up the deficiency in the third division, but give too many to the second; so that we must, with some commentators,[5] conclude the second series not with Jechonias, as is usually done, but with his predecessor Josias: and now, by means of the double enumeration of David, Jechonias, who was superfluous in the second division, being available for the third, the last series, including Jesus, has its fourteen members complete.   But it seems very arbitrary to reckon the concluding member of the first series twice, and not also that of the second: to avoid which inconsistency some interpreters have proposed to count Josias twice, as well as David, and thus complete the fourteen members of the third series without Jesus.   But whilst this computation escapes one blunder, it falls into another; namely, that whereas the expression ἀπὸ Ἀβραὰμ ἕως Δαβὶδ κ. τ. λ. (v. 17) is supposed to include the latter, in ἀπὸ μετοικεσίας Βαβυλῶνος ἕως τοῦ Χριστοῦ, the latter is excluded.   This difficulty may be avoided by counting Jechonias twice instead of Josias, which gives us fourteen names for the third division, including Jesus; but then, in order not to have too many in the second, we must drop the double enumeration of David, and thus be liable to the same charge of inconsistency as in the former case, since the double enumeration is made between the second and third divisions, and not between the first and second.   Perhaps De Wette has found the right clue when he remarks, that in v. 17, in both transitions some member of the series is mentioned twice, but in the first case only that member is a *person* (David), and therefore to be twice reckoned.   In the second case it is the *Babylonish captivity* occurring between Josias and Jechonias, which latter, since he had reigned only three months in Jerusalem (the greater part of his life having passed after the carrying away to Babylon), was mentioned indeed at the conclusion of the second series for the sake of connexion, but was to be reckoned only at the beginning of the third.[6]

If we now compare the genealogy of Matthew (still without reference to that of Luke) with the corresponding passages of the Old Testament, we shall also find discrepancy, and in this case of a nature exactly the reverse of the preceding: for as the table considered in itself required the duplication of one member in order to complete its scheme, so when compared with the Old Testament, we find that many of the names there recorded have been omitted, in order that the number fourteen might not be exceeded.   That is to say, the Old Testament affords data for comparison with this genealogical

[3] Hieron. in Daniel. init.
[4] See Wetstein.
[5] *e.g.* Frische, Comm. in Matth., p. 13.
[6] Exegt. Handbuch, i. 1, s. 12 f.

table as the famed pedigree of the royal race of David, from Abraham to
Zorobabel and his sons ; after whom the Davidical line begins to retire into
obscurity, and from the silence of the Old Testament the genealogy of Matthew ceases to be under any control. The series of generations from Abraham
to Judah, Pharez, and Hezron, is sufficiently well known from Genesis; from
Pharez to David we find it in the conclusion of the book of Ruth, and in the
2nd chapter of the 1st Chronicles ; that from David to Zerubbabel in the 3rd
chapter of the same book ; besides passages that are parallel with separate
portions of the series.

To complete the comparison : we find the line from Abraham to David,
that is, the whole first division of fourteen in our genealogy, in exact accordance with the names of men given in the Old Testament : leaving out
however the names of some women, one of which makes a difficulty. It is
said v. 5 that Rahab was the mother of Boaz. Not only is this without confirmation in the Old Testament, but even if she be made the great-grandmother
of Jesse, the father of David, there are too few generations between her time
and that of David (from about 1450 to 1050 B.C.), that is, counting either
Rahab or David as one, four for 400 years. Yet this error falls back upon
the Old Testament genealogy itself, in so far as Jesse's great-grandfather
Salmon, whom Matthew calls the husband of Rahab, is said Ruth iv. 20, as
well as by Matthew, to be the son of a Nahshon, who, according to Numbers
i. 7, lived in the time of the march through the wilderness[7] : from which circumstance the idea was naturally suggested, to marry his son with that Rahab
who saved the Israelitish spies, and thus to introduce a woman for whom the
Israelites had an especial regard (compare James ii. 25, Heb. xi. 31) into the
lineage of David and the Messiah.

Many discrepancies are found in the second division from David to Zorobabel and his son, as well as in the beginning of the third. Firstly, it is said
v. 8 *Joram begat Ozias;* whereas we know from 1 Chron. iii. 11, 12, that
Uzziah was not the son, but the grandson of the son of Joram, and that three
kings occur between them, namely, Ahaziah, Joash, and Amaziah, after whom
comes Uzziah (2 Chron. xxvi. 1, or as he is called 1 Chron. iii. 12, and 2
Kings xiv. 21, Azariah). Secondly : our genealogy says v. 11, *Josias begat
Jechonias and his brethren.* But we find from 1 Chron. iii. 16, that the son
and successor of Josiah was called Jehoiakim, after whom came his son and
successor Jechoniah or Jehoiachin. Moreover *brethren* are ascribed to
Jechoniah, whereas the Old Testament mentions none. Jehoiakim, however,
had brothers : so that the mention of the *brethren of Jechonias* in Matthew
appears to have originated in an exchange of these two persons.—A third
discrepancy relates to Zorobabel. He is here called, v. 12, a son of Salathiel ;
whilst in 1 Chron. iii. 19, he is descended from Jechoniah, not through
Shealtiel, but through his brother Pedaiah. In Ezra v. 2, and Haggai i. 1,
however, Zerubbabel is designated, as here, the son of Shealtiel.—In the last
place, Abiud, who is here called the son of Zorobabel, is not to be found
amongst the children of Zerubbabel mentioned 1 Chron. iii. 19 f. : perhaps
because Abiud was only a surname derived from a son of one of those there
mentioned.[8]

The second and third of these discrepancies may have crept in without evil
intention, and without any great degree of carelessness, for the omission of
Jehoiakim may have arisen from the similar sound of the names (יְהוֹיָקִים and

---

[7] The expedient of Kuinöl, Comm. in Matth. p. 3, to distinguish the Rahab here mentioned from the celebrated one, becomes hence superfluous, besides that it is perfectly
arbitrary.

[8] Hoffmann, s. 154, according to Hug, Einl., ii. s. 271.

יְהוֹיָכִין), which accounts also for the transposition of the brothers of Jechoniah; whilst respecting Zorobabel the reference to the Old Testament is partly adverse, partly favourable.   But the first discrepancy we have adduced, namely, the omission of three known kings, is not so easily to be set aside. It has indeed been held that the similarity of names may here also have led the author to pass unintentionally from Joram to Ozias, instead of to the similar sounding Ahaziah (in the LXX. Ochozias).   But this omission falls in so happily with the author's design of the threefold fourteen (admitting the double enumeration of David), that we cannot avoid believing, with Jerome, that the oversight was made on purpose with a view to it.[9]   From Abraham to David, where the first division presented itself, having found fourteen members, he seems to have wished that those of the following divisions should correspond in number.   In the whole remaining series the Babylonish exile offered itself as the natural point of separation.   But as the second division from David to the exile gave him four supernumerary members, therefore he omitted four of the names.   For what reason these particular four were chosen would be difficult to determine, at least for the three last mentioned.

The cause of the compiler's laying so much stress on the threefold equal numbers, may have been simply, that by this adoption of the Oriental custom of division into equal sections, the genealogy might be more easily committed to memory[10]: but with this motive a mystical idea was probably combined. The question arises whether this is to be sought in the number which is thrice repeated, or whether it consists in the threefold repetition ?   Fourteen is the double of the sacred number seven ; but it is improbable that it was selected for this reason,[11] because otherwise the seven would scarcely have been so completely lost sight of in the fourteen.   Still more improbable is the conjecture of Olshausen, that the number fourteen was specially chosen as being the numeric value of the name of David[12] ; for puerilities of this kind, appropriate to the rabbinical gematria, are to be found in no other part of the Gospels.   It is more likely that the object of the genealogists consisted merely in the repetition of an equal number by retaining the fourteen which had first accidentally presented itself: since it was a notion of the Jews that signal divine visitations, whether of prosperity or adversity, recurred at regular periodical intervals.   Thus, as fourteen generations had intervened between Abraham, the founder of the holy people, and David the king after God's own heart, so fourteen generations must intervene between the re-establishment of the kingdom and the coming of the son of David, the Messiah.[13] The most ancient genealogies in Genesis exhibit the very same uniformity. As according to the βίβλος γενέσεως ἀνθρώπων, cap. v., from Adam the first, to Noah the second, father of men, were ten generations: so from Noah, or rather from his son, the tenth is Abraham the father of the faithful.[14]

[9] Compare Fritsche, Comm. in Matth., p. 19 ; Paulus, exeget. Handbuch, i. s. 289 ; De Wette, exeg. Handb. in loco.

[10] Fritsche in Matth., p. 11.

[11] Paulus, s. 292.

[12] Bibl. Comm., p. 46, note.

[13] See Schneckenburger, Beiträge zur Einleitung in das N. T., s. 41 f., and the passage cited from Josephus, B. j. vi. 8.   Also may be compared the passage cited by Schöttgen, horæ hebr. et talm. zu Matth. i. from Synopsis Sohar, p. 132, n. 18.   *Ab Abrahamo usque ad Salomonem XV. sunt generationes ; atque tunc luna fuit in plenilunio. A Salomone usque ad Zedekiam iterum sunt XV. generationes, et tunc luna defecit, et Zedekiæ effossi sunt oculi.*

[14] De Wette has already called attention to the analogy between these Old Testament genealogies and those of the Gospels, with regard to the intentional equality of numbers. Kritik der mos. Geschichte, s 69.   Comp. s. 48.

This *à priori* treatment of his subject, this Procrustes-bed upon which the author of our genealogy now stretches, now curtails it, almost like a philosopher constructing a system,—can excite no predisposition in his favour. It is in vain to appeal to the custom of Oriental genealogists to indulge themselves in similar licence ; for when an author presents us with a pedigree expressly declaring that *all the generations* during a space of time were fourteen, whereas, through accident or intention, many members are wanting,—he betrays an arbitrariness and want of critical accuracy, which must shake our confidence in the certainty of his whole genealogy.

The genealogy of Luke, considered separately, does not present so many defects as that of Matthew. It has no concluding statement of the number of generations comprised in the genealogy, to act as a check upon itself, neither can it be tested, to much extent, by a comparison with the Old Testament. For, from David to Nathan, the line traced by Luke has no correspondence with any Old Testament genealogy, excepting in two of its members, Salathiel and Zorobabel ; and even with respect to these two, there is a contradiction between the statement of Luke and that of 1 Chron. iii. 17. 19 f. : for the former calls Salathiel a son of Neri, whilst, according to the latter, he was the son of Jechoniah. Luke also mentions one Resa as the son of Zorobabel, a name which does not appear amongst the children of Zerubbabel in 1 Chron. iii. 17, 19. Also, in the series before Abraham, Luke inserts a Cainan, who is not to be found in the Hebrew text, Gen. x. 24 ; xi. 12 ff., but who was however already inserted by the LXX. In fact, the original text has this name in its first series as the third from Adam, and thence the translation appears to have transplanted him to the corresponding place in the second series as the third from Noah.

§ 21.

COMPARISON OF THE TWO GENEALOGIES—ATTEMPT TO RECONCILE THEIR CONTRADICTIONS.

If we compare the genealogies of Matthew and Luke together, we become aware of still more striking discrepancies. Some of these differences indeed are unimportant, as the opposite direction of the two tables, the line of Matthew descending from Abraham to Jesus, that of Luke ascending from Jesus to his ancestors. Also the greater extent of the line of Luke ; Matthew deriving it no farther than from Abraham, while Luke (perhaps lengthening some existing document in order to make it more consonant with the universalism of the doctrines of Paul [1] ;) carries it back to Adam and to God himself. More important is the considerable difference in the number of generations for equal periods, Luke having 41 between David and Jesus, whilst Matthew has only 26. The main difficulty, however, lies in this : that in some parts of the genealogy, in Luke totally different individuals are made the ancestors of Jesus from those in Matthew. It is true, both writers agree in deriving the lineage of Jesus through Joseph from David and Abraham, and that the names of the individual members of the series correspond from Abraham to David, as well as two of the names in the subsequent portion : those of Salathiel and Zorobabel. But the difficulty becomes desperate when we find that, with these two exceptions about midway, the whole of the names from David to the foster-father of Jesus are totally different in Matthew and

---

[1] See Chrysostom and Luther, in Credner, Einleitung in d. N. T., 1, s. 143 f. Winer, bibl. Realwörterbuch, 1. s. 659.

in Luke.   In Matthew, the father of Joseph is called Jacob; in Luke, Heli. In Matthew, the son of David through whom Joseph descended from that king is Solomon ; in Luke, Nathan : and so on, the line descends, in Matthew, through the race of known kings ; in Luke, through an unknown collateral branch, coinciding only with respect to Salathiel and Zorobabel, whilst they still differ in the names of the father of Salathiel and the son of Zorobabel.   Since this difference appears to offer a complete contradiction, the most industrious efforts have been made at all times to reconcile the two. Passing in silence explanations evidently unsatisfactory, such as a mystical signification, [2] or an arbitrary change of names,[3] we shall consider two pairs of hypotheses which have been most conspicuous, and are mutually supported, or at least bear affinity to one another.

The first pair is formed upon the presupposition of Augustine, that Joseph was an adopted son, and that one evangelist gave the name of his real, the other that of his adopted, father [4]; and the opinion of the old chronologist Julius Africanus, that a Levirate marriage had taken place between the parents of Joseph, and that the one genealogy belonged to the natural, the other to the legal, father of Joseph, by the one of whom he was descended from David through Solomon, by the other through Nathan.[5]   The farther question : to which father do the respective genealogies belong ? is open to two species of criticism, the one founded upon literal expressions, the other upon the spirit and character of each gospel : and which lead to opposite conclusions.   Augustine as well as Africanus, has observed, that Matthew makes use of an expression in describing the relationship between Joseph and his so-called father, which more definitely points out the natural filial relationship than that of Luke : for the former says Ἰακὼβ ἐγέννησε τὸν Ἰωσήφ : whilst the expression of the latter, Ἰωσὴφ τοῦ Ἡλὶ, appears equally applicable to a son by adoption, or by virtue of a Levirate marriage.   But since the very object of a Levirate marriage was to maintain the name and race of a deceased childless brother, it was the Jewish custom to inscribe the first-born son of such a marriage, not on the family register of his natural father, as Matthew has done here, but on that of his legal father, as Luke has done on the above supposition.   Now that a person so entirely imbued with Jewish opinions as the author of the first Gospel, should have made a mistake of this kind, cannot be held probable.   Accordingly, Schleiermacher and others conceive themselves bound by the spirit of the two Gospels to admit that Matthew, in spite of his ἐγέννησε, must have given the lineage of the legal father, according to Jewish custom : whilst Luke, who perhaps was not born a Jew, and was less familiar with Jewish habits, might have fallen upon the genealogy of the younger brothers of Joseph, who were not, like the firstborn, inscribed amongst the family of the deceased legal father, but with that of their natural father, and might have taken this for the genealogical table of the first-born Joseph, whilst it really belonged to him only by natural descent, to which Jewish genealogists paid no regard.[6]   But, besides the fact, which we shall show hereafter, that the genealogy of Luke can with difficulty be proved to be the work of the author of that Gospel :—in which case the little acquaintance of Luke with

---

[2] Orig. homil. in Lucam 28.
[3] Luther, Werke, Bd. 14.   Walch. Ausg. s. 8 ff.
[4] De consensu Evangelistarum, ii. 3, u. c. Faust., iii. 3 ; amongst the moderns, for example, E. F. in Henke's Magazin 5, 1, 180 f.   After Augustine had subsequently become acquainted with the writing of Africanus, he gave up his own opinion for that of the latter. Retract. ii. 7.
[5] Eusebius, H. E. i. 7, and lately *e.g.* Schleiermacher on Luke, p. 53.
[6] S. 53.   Comp. Winer, bibl. Realwörterbuch, 1 Bd. s. 660.

H

Jewish customs ceases to afford any clue to the meaning of this genealogy;—it is also to be objected, that the genealogist of the first Gospel could not have written his ἐγέννησε thus without any addition, if he was thinking of a mere legal paternity. Wherefore these two views of the genealogical relationship are equally difficult.

However, this hypothesis, which we have hitherto considered only in general, requires a more detailed examination in order to judge of its admissibility. In considering the proposition of a Levirate marriage, the argument is essentially the same if, with Augustine and Africanus, we ascribe the naming of the natural father to Matthew, or with Schleiermacher, to Luke. As an example we shall adopt the former statement: the rather because Eusebius, according to Africanus, has left us a minute account of it. According to this representation, then, the mother of Joseph was first married to that person whom Luke calls the father of Joseph, namely Heli. But since Heli died without children, by virtue of the Levirate law, his brother, called by Matthew Jacob the father of Joseph, married the widow, and by her begot Joseph, who was legally regarded as the son of the deceased Heli, and so described by Luke, whilst naturally he was the son of his brother Jacob, and thus described by Matthew.

But, merely thus far, the hypothesis is by no means adequate. For if the two fathers of Joseph were real brothers, sons of the same father, they had one and the same lineage, and the two genealogies would have differed only in the father of Joseph, all the preceding portion being in agreement. In order to explain how the discordancy extends so far back as to David, we must have recourse to the second proposition of Africanus, that the fathers of Joseph were only half-brothers, having the same mother, but not the same father. We must also suppose that this mother of the two fathers of Joseph, had twice married; once with the Matthan of Matthew, who was descended from David through Solomon and the line of kings, and to whom she bore Jacob; and also, either before or after, with the Matthat of Luke, the offspring of which marriage was Heli: which Heli, having married and died childless, his half-brother Jacob married his widow, and begot for the deceased his legal child Joseph.

This hypothesis of so complicated a marriage in two successive generations, to which we are forced by the discrepancy of the two genealogies, must be acknowledged to be in no way impossible, but still highly improbable: and the difficulty is doubled by the untoward agreement already noticed, which occurs midway in the discordant series, in the two members Salathiel and Zorobabel. For to explain how Neri in Luke, and Jechonias in Matthew, are both called the father of Salathiel, who was the father of Zorobabel;—not only must the supposition of the Levirate marriage be repeated, but also that the two brothers who successively married the same wife, were brothers only on the mother's side. The difficulty is not diminished by the remark, that any nearest blood-relation, not only a brother, might succeed in a Levirate marriage,—that is to say, though not obligatory, it was at least open to his choice (Ruth iii. 12. f. iv. 4 f.[7]). For since even in the case of two cousins, the concurrence of the two branches must take place much earlier than here for Jacob and Eli, and for Jechonias and Neri, we are still obliged to have recourse to the hypothesis of half-brothers; the only amelioration in this hypothesis over the other being, that these two very peculiar marriages do not take place in immediately consecutive generations. Now that this extraordinary double incident should not only have been twice repeated, but that

---

[7] Comp. Michaelis, Mos. Recht. ii. s. 200. Winer, bibl. Realwörterb. ii. s. 22 f.

the genealogists should twice have made the same selection in their statements respecting the natural and the legal father, and without any explanation,—is so improbable, that even the hypothesis of an adoption, which is burdened with only one-half of these difficulties, has still more than it can bear. For in the case of adoption, since no fraternal or other relationship is required, between the natural and adopting fathers, the recurrence to a twice-repeated half-brotherhood is dispensed with ; leaving only the necessity for twice supposing a relationship by adoption, and twice the peculiar circumstance, that the one genealogist from want of acquaintance with Jewish customs was ignorant of the fact, and the other, although he took account of it, was silent respecting it.

It has been thought by later critics that the knot may be loosed in a much easier way, by supposing that in one Gospel we have the genealogy of Joseph, in the other that of Mary, in which case there would be no contradiction in the disagreement :[8] to which they are pleased to add the assumption that Mary was an heiress.[9] The opinion that Mary was of the race of David as well as Joseph has been long held. Following indeed the idea, that the Messiah, as a second Melchizedec, ought to unite in his person the priestly with the kingly dignity,[10] and guided by the relationship of Mary with Elizabeth, who was a daughter of Aaron (Luke i. 36) ; already in early times it was not only held by many that the races of Judah and Levi were blended in the family of Joseph ;[11] but also the opinion was not rare that Jesus, deriving his royal lineage from Joseph, descended also from the priestly race through Mary.[12] The opinion of Mary's descent from David, soon however became the more prevailing. Many apocryphal writers clearly state this opinion,[13] as well as Justin Martyr, whose expression, that the virgin was of the race of David, Jacob, Isaac, and Abraham, may be considered an indication that he applied to Mary one of our genealogies, which are both traced back to Abraham through David.[14]

On inquiring which of these two genealogies is to be held that of Mary? we are stopped by an apparently insurmountable obstacle, since each is distinctly announced as the genealogy of Joseph ; the one in the words Ἰακὼβ ἐγέννησε τὸν Ἰωσήφ, the other by the phrase υἱὸς Ἰωσὴφ τοῦ Ἡλί. Here also, however, the ἐγέννησε of Matthew is more definite than the τοῦ of Luke, which according to those interpreters may mean just as well a son-in-law or grandson ; so that the genitive of Luke in iii. 23 was either intended to express that Jesus was in common estimation a son of Joseph, who was the son-in-law of Heli, the father of Mary[15] :—or else, that Jesus was, as was believed, a son of Joseph, and through Mary a grandson of Heli.[16] As it may here be objected, that the Jews in their genealogies were accustomed to take no account of the

8 Thus *e.g.* Spanheim, dubia evang. p. 1. s. 13 ff. Lightfoot, Michaelis, Paulus, Kuinöl, Olshausen, lately Hoffmann and others.

9 Epiphanius, Grotius. Olshausen, s. 43.

10 Testament XII. Patriarch., Test. Simeon c. 71. In Fabric. Codex pseudepigr. V. T. p. 542 : ἐξ αὐτῶν (the races of Levi and Juda) ἀνατελεῖ ὑμῖν τὸ σωτήριον τοῦ θεοῦ. Ἀναστήσει γὰρ Κύριος ἐκ τοῦ Λευΐ ὡς ἀρχιερέα, καὶ ἐκ τοῦ Ἰουδα ὡς βασιλέα κ. τ. λ.

11 Comp. Thilo, cod. apocr. N.T. 1, s. 374 ff.

12 Thus *e.g.* the Manichæan Faustus in Augustin. contra Faust. L. xxiii. 4.

13 Protevangel. Jacobi c. 1 f. u. 10. and evangel. de nativitate Mariæ c. 1. Joachim and Anna, of the race of David, are here mentioned as the parents of Mary. Faustus on the contrary, in the above cited passage, gives Joachim the title of *Sacerdos*.

14 Dial. c. Tryph. 43. 100. (Paris, 1742.)

15 Paulus. The Jews also in their representation of a Mary, the daughter of Heli, tormented in the lower world (see Lightfoot), appear to have taken the genealogy of Luke, which sets out from Heli, for that of Mary.

16 *e.g.* Lightfoot, horæ, p. 750 ; Osiander, s. 86.

female line,[17] a farther hypothesis is had recourse to, namely, that Mary was an heiress, *i.e.* the daughter of a father without sons : and that in this case, according to Numbers xxxvi. 6, and Nehemiah vii. 63, Jewish custom required that the person who married her should not only be of the same race with herself, but that he should henceforth sink his own family in hers, and take her ancestors as his own.   But the first point only is proved by the reference to Numbers; and the passage in Nehemiah, compared with several similar ones (Ezra ii. 61 ; Numbers xxxii. 41 ; comp. with 1 Chron. ii. 21 f.), shows only that sometimes, by way of exception, a man took the name of his maternal ancestors.   This difficulty with regard to Jewish customs, however, is cast into shade by one much more important.   Although undeniably the genitive case used by Luke, expressing simply derivation in a general sense, may signify any degree of relationship, and consequently that of son-in-law or grandson; yet this interpretation destroys the consistency of the whole passage.   In the thirty-four preceding members, which are well known to us from the Old Testament, this genitive demonstrably indicates throughout the precise relationship of a son ; likewise when it occurs between Salathiel and Zorobabel: how could it be intended in the one instance of Joseph to indicate that of son-in-law ? or, according to the other interpretation, supposing the nominative υἱὸς to govern the whole series, how can we suppose it to change its signification from son to grandson, great-grandson, and so on to the end? If it be said the phrase Ἀδὰμ τοῦ θεοῦ is a proof that the genitive does not necessarily indicate a son in the proper sense of the word, we may reply that it bears a signification with regard to the immediate Author of existence equally inapplicable to either father-in-law or grandfather.

A further difficulty is encountered by this explanation of the two genealogies in common with the former one, in the concurrence of the two names of Salathiel and Zorobabel.   The supposition of a Levirate marriage is as applicable to this explanation as the other, but the interpreters we are now examining prefer for the most part to suppose, that these similar names in the different genealogies belong to different persons.   When Luke however, in the twenty-first and twenty-second generations from David, gives the very same names that Matthew (including the four omitted generations), gives in the nineteenth and twentieth, one of these names being of great notoriety, it is certainly impossible to doubt that they refer to the same persons.

Moreover, in no other part of the New Testament is there any trace to be found of the Davidical descent of Mary : on the contrary, some passages are directly opposed to it.   In Luke i. 27, the expression ἐξ οἴκου Δαβίδ refers only to the immediately preceding ἀνδρὶ ᾧ ὄνομα Ἰωσὴφ, not to the more remote παρθένον μεμνηστευμένην.   And more pointed still is the turn of the sentence Luke ii. 4, ἀνέβη δὲ καὶ Ἰωσὴφ—διὰ τὸ εἶναι αὐτὸν ἐξ οἴκου καὶ πατριᾶς Δαβὶδ, ἀπο-γράψασθαι σὺν Μαρίᾳ κ. τ. λ., where αὐτοὺς might so easily have been written instead of αὐτὸν, if the author had any thought of including Mary in the descent from David.   These expressions fill to overflowing the measure of proof already adduced, that it is impossible to apply the genealogy of the third Evangelist to Mary.

---

[17] Juchasin f. 55, 2. in Lightfoot s. 183, and Bava bathra, f. 110, 2. in Wetstein s. 230 f. Comp. Joseph. Vita, 1.

§ 22.

THE GENEALOGIES UNHISTORICAL.

A consideration of the insurmountable difficulties, which unavoidably embarrass every attempt to bring these two genealogies into harmony with one another, will lead us to despair of reconciling them, and will incline us to acknowledge, with the more free-thinking class of critics, that they are mutually contradictory.[1] Consequently they cannot both be true : if, therefore, one is to be preferred before the other, several circumstances would seem to decide in favour of the genealogy of Luke, rather than that of Matthew. It does not exhibit an arbitrary adherence to a fixed form and to equal periods : and whilst the ascribing of twenty generations to the space of time from David to Jechonias or Neri, in Luke, is at least not more offensive to probability, than the omission of four generations in Matthew to historical truth ; Luke's allotment of twenty-two generations for the period from Jechonias (born 617 B.C.) to Jesus, *i.e.* about 600 years, forming an average of twenty-seven years and a half to each generation, is more consonant with natural events, particularly amongst eastern nations, than the thirteen generations of Matthew, which make an average of forty-two years for each. Besides the genealogy of Luke is less liable than that of Matthew to the suspicion of having been written with a design to glorify Jesus, since it contents itself with ascribing to Jesus a descent from David, without tracing that descent through the royal line. On the other hand, however, it is more improbable that the genealogy of the comparatively insignificant family of Nathan should have been preserved, than that of the royal branch. Added to which, the frequent recurrence of the same names is, as justly remarked by Hoffmann, an indication that the genealogy of Luke is fictitious.

In fact then neither table has any advantage over the other. If the one is unhistorical, so also is the other, since it is very improbable that the genealogy of an obscure family like that of Joseph, extending through so long a series of generations, should have been preserved during all the confusion of the exile, and the disturbed period that followed. Yet, it may be said, although we recognise in both, so far as they are not copied from the Old Testament, an unrestrained play of the imagination, or arbitrary applications of other genealogies to Jesus,—we may still retain as an historical basis that Jesus was descended from David, and that only the intermediate members of the line of descent were variously filled up by different writers. But the one event on which this historical basis is mainly supported, namely, the journey of the parents of Jesus to Bethlehem in order to be taxed, so far from sufficing to prove them to be of the house and lineage of David, is itself, as we shall presently show, by no means established as matter of history. Of more weight is the other ground, namely, that Jesus is universally represented in the New Testament, without any contradiction from his adversaries, as the descendant of David. Yet even the phrase υἱὸς Δαβὶδ is a predicate that may naturally have been applied to Jesus, not on historical, but on dogmatical grounds. According to the prophecies, the Messiah could only spring from David. When therefore a Galilean, whose lineage was utterly unknown, and of whom consequently no one could prove that he was not descended from David, had acquired the

---

[1] Thus Eichhorn, Einl. in das N. T. 1 Bd. s. 425. Kaiser, bibl. Theol. 1, s. 232. Wegscheider, Institut. § 123, not. d. de Wette, bibl. Dogm. § 279, and exeget. Handbuch 1, 2, s. 32. Winer, bibl. Realwörterb. 1, s. 660 f. Hase, Leben Jesu, § 33. Fritzsche, Comm. in Matt. p. 35. Ammon, Fortbildung des Christenthums zur Weltreligion, 1, s. 196 ff.

reputation of being the Messiah ; what more natural than that tradition should under different forms have early ascribed to him a Davidical descent, and that genealogical tables, corresponding with this tradition, should have been formed? which, however, as they were constructed upon no certain data, would necessarily exhibit such differences and contradictions as we find actually existing between the genealogies in Matthew and in Luke.[2]

If, in conclusion, it be asked, what historical result is to be deduced from these genealogies? we reply: a conviction (arrived at also from other sources), that Jesus, either in his own person or through his disciples, acting upon minds strongly imbued with Jewish notions and expectations, left among his followers so firm a conviction of his Messiahship, that they did not hesitate to attribute to him the prophetical characteristic of Davidical descent, and more than one pen was put in action, in order, by means of a genealogy which should authenticate that descent, to justify his recognition as the Messiah.[3]

[2] See De Wette, bibl. Dogm. and exeg. Handb. 1, 1, s. 14 ; Hase, L. J. Eusebius gives a not improbable explanation of this disagreement (ad. Steph. quæst. iii., pointed out by Credner, 1, p. 68 f.) that besides the notion amongst the Jews, that the Messiah must spring from the royal line of David, another had arisen, that this line having become polluted and declared unworthy of continuing on the throne of David (Jerem. xxii. 30), by the wickedness of its later reigning members, a line more pure though less famed was to be preferred to it.

[3] The farther considerations on the origin and import of these genealogies, which arise from their connexion with the account of the miraculous birth of Jesus, must be reserved till after the examination of the latter point.

CHAPTER III.

ANNOUNCEMENT OF THE CONCEPTION OF JESUS.—ITS SUPERNATURAL
CHARACTER.—VISIT OF MARY TO ELIZABETH.

---

§ 23.

SKETCH OF THE DIFFERENT CANONICAL AND APOCRYPHAL ACCOUNTS.

THERE is a striking gradation in the different representations of the conception and birth of Jesus given in the canonical and in the apocryphal Gospels.
They exhibit the various steps, from a simple statement of a natural occurrence, to a minute and miraculously embellished history, in which the event
is traced back to its very earliest date. Mark and John presuppose the fact
of the birth of Jesus, and content themselves with the incidental mention of
Mary as the mother (Mark vi. 3), and of Joseph as the father of Jesus (John
i. 46). Matthew and Luke go further back, since they state the particular
circumstances attending the conception as well as the birth of the Messiah.
But of these two evangelists Luke mounts a step higher than Matthew.
According to the latter Mary, the betrothed of Joseph, being *found with
child*, Joseph is offended, and determines to put her away ; but the angel of
the Lord visits him in a dream, and assures him of the divine origin and exalted destiny of Mary's offspring ; the result of which is that Joseph takes
unto him his wife : but knows her not till she has brought forth her first-born
son. (Matt. i. 18–25.) Here the pregnancy is discovered in the first place,
and then afterwards justified by the angel ; but in Luke the pregnancy is pre-
faced and announced by a celestial apparition. The same Gabriel, who had
predicted the birth of John to Zacharias, appears to Mary, the betrothed of
Joseph, and tells her that she shall conceive by the power of the Holy
Ghost ; whereupon the destined mother of the Messiah pays a visit full of
holy import to the already pregnant mother of his forerunner ; upon which
occasion both Mary and Elizabeth pour forth their emotions to one another
in the form of a hymn (Luke i. 26–56). Matthew and Luke are content to
presuppose the connexion between Mary and Joseph ; but the apocryphal
Gospels, the *Protevangelium Jacobi*, and the *Evangelium de Nativitate Mariae*,[1]
(books with the contents of which the Fathers partially agree,) seek to represent the origin of this connexion ; indeed they go back to the birth of Mary,
and describe it to have been preceded, equally with that of the Messiah and
the Baptist, by a divine annunciation. As the description of the birth of
John in Luke is principally borrowed from the Old Testament accounts of
Samuel and of Samson, so this history of the birth of Mary is an imitation
of the history in Luke, and of the Old Testament histories.

Joachim, so says the apocryphal narrative, and Anna (the name of Samuel's

---

[1] Fabricius, Codex apocryphus N. T. 1, p. 19 ff. 66 ff. ; Thilo, 1, p. 161 ff. 319 ff.

mother [2]) are unhappy on account of their long childless marriage (as were the parents of the Baptist) ; when an angel appears to them both (so in the history of Samson) at different places, and promises them a child, who shall be the mother of God, and commands that this child shall live the life of a Nazarite (like the Baptist). In early childhood Mary is brought by her parents to the temple (like Samuel); where she continues till her twelfth year, visited and fed by angels and honoured by divine visions. Arrived at womanhood she is to quit the temple, her future provision and destiny being revealed by the oracle to the high priest. In conformity with the prophecy of Isaiah xi. 1 f.: *egredietur virga de radice Jesse, et flos de radice ejus ascendet, et requiescet super eum spiritus Domini*; this oracle commanded, according to one Gospel,[3] that all the unmarried men of the house of David,—according to the other,[4] that all the widowers among the people,—should bring their rods, and that he on whose rod a sign should appear (like the rod of Aaron, Numb. xvii.), namely the sign predicted in the prophecy, should take Mary unto himself. This sign was manifested upon Joseph's rod ; for, in exact accordance with the oracle, it put forth a blossom and a dove lighted upon it.[5] The apocryphal Gospels and the Fathers agree in representing Joseph as an old man ;[6] but the narrative is somewhat differently told in the two apocryphal Gospels. According to the *Evang. de nativ. Mariae*, notwithstanding Mary's alleged vow of chastity, and the refusal of Joseph on account of his great age, betrothment took place at the command of the priest, and subsequently a marriage—(which marriage, however, the author evidently means to represents also as chaste). According to the *Protevang. Jacobi*, on the contrary, neither betrothment nor marriage are mentioned, but Joseph is regarded merely as the chosen protector of the young virgin,[7] and Joseph on the journey to Bethlehem doubts whether he shall describe his charge as his wife or as his daughter ; fearing to bring ridicule upon himself, on account of his age, if he called her his wife. Again, where in Matthew Mary is called ἡ γυνὴ of Joseph, the apocryphal Gospel carefully designates her merely as ἡ παῖς, and even avoids using the term παραλαβεῖν or substitutes διαφυλάξαι, with which many of the Fathers concur.[8] In the *Protevangelium* it is further related that Mary, having been received into Joseph's house, was charged, together with other young women, with the fabrication of the veil for the temple, and that it fell to her lot to spin the true purple.—But whilst Joseph was absent on business Mary was visited by an angel, and Joseph on his return found her with child and called her to account, not as a husband, but as the guardian of her honour. Mary, however, had forgotten the words of the angel and protested her ignorance of the cause of her pregnancy. Joseph was perplexed and determined to remove her secretly from under his protection ; but an angel appeared to him in a dream and reassured him by his explanation. The matter was then brought before the priest, and both

---

[2] Gregory of Nyssa or his interpolator is reminded of this mother of Samuel by the apocryphal Anna when he says of her : Μιμεῖται τοίνυν καὶ αὕτη τὰ περὶ τῆς μητρὸς τοῦ Σαμουὴλ διηγήματα κ.τ.λ. Fabricius, 1, p. 6.

[3] Evang. de nativ. Mar. c. 7 : *cunctos de domo et familia David nuptui habiles, non conjugatos.*

[4] Protev. Jac. c. 8 : τοὺς χηρεύοντας τοῦ λαοῦ.

[5] It is thus in the Evang. de nativ. Mariae vii. and viii. ; but rather different in the Protev. Jac. c. ix.

[6] Protev. c. 9 : πρεσβύτης. Evang. de nativ. Mar. 8. : grandaevus. Epiphan. adv. haeres. 78, 8 : λαμβάνει τὴν Μαρίαν χῆρος, κατάγων ἡλικίαν περί που ὀγδοήκοντα ἐτῶν καὶ πρόσω ὁ ἀνήρ.

[7] Παράλαβε αὐτὴν εἰς τήρησιν σεαυτῷ. c. ix. Compare with Evang. de nativ. Mar. viii. and x.

[8] See the variations in *Thilo*, p. 227, and the quotations from the Fathers at p. 365 not.

Joseph and Mary being charged with incontinence were condemned to drink the "bitter water,"[9] ὕδωρ τῆς ἐλέγξεως, but as they remained uninjured by it, they were declared innocent. Then follows the account of the taxing and of the birth of Jesus.[10]

Since these apocryphal narratives were for a long period held as historical by the church, and were explained, equally with those of the canonical accounts, from the supranaturalistic point of view as miraculous, they were entitled in modern times to share with the New Testament histories the benefit of the natural explanation. If, on the one hand, the belief in the marvellous was so superabundantly strong in the ancient church, that it reached beyond the limits of the New Testament even to the embracing of the apocryphal narratives, blinding the eye to the perception of their manifestly unhistorical character; so, on the other hand, the positive rationalism of some of the heralds of the modern modes of explanation was so overstrong that they believed it adequate to explain even the apocryphal miracles. Of this we have an example in the author of the natural history of the great prophet of Nazareth;[11] who does not hesitate to include the stories of the lineage and early years of Mary within the circle of his representations, and to give them a natural explanation. If we in our day, with a perception of the fabulous character of such narratives, look down alike upon the Fathers of the church and upon these naturalistic interpreters, we are certainly so far in the right, as it is only by gross ignorance that this character of the apocryphal accounts is here to be mistaken; more closely considered, however, the difference between the apocryphal and the canonical narratives concerning the early history of the Baptist and of Jesus, is seen to be merely a difference of form: they have sprung, as we shall hereafter find, from the same root, though the one is a fresh and healthy sprout, and the other an artificially nurtured and weak aftergrowth. Still, the Fathers of the church and these naturalistic interpreters had this superiority over most of the theologians of our own time; that they did not allow themselves to be deceived respecting the inherent similarity by the difference of form, but interpreted the kindred narratives by the same method; treating both as miraculous or both as natural; and not, as is now usual, the one as fiction and the other as history.

§ 24.

DISAGREEMENTS OF THE CANONICAL GOSPELS IN RELATION TO THE FORM OF THE ANNUNCIATION.

After the foregoing general sketch, we now proceed to examine the external circumstances which, according to our Gospels, attended the first communication of the future birth of Jesus to Mary and Joseph. Leaving out of sight, for the present, the special import of the annunciation, namely, that Jesus should be supernaturally begotten of the Holy Ghost, we shall, in the first place, consider merely the form of the announcement; by whom, when, and in what manner it was made.

As the birth of the Baptist was previously announced by an angel, so the conception of Jesus was, according to the gospel histories, proclaimed after the same fashion. But whilst, in the one case, we have but one history of the apparition, that of Luke; in the other we have two accounts, accounts however which do not correspond, and which we must now compare. Apart from

---

[9] Numb. v. 18.
[10] Protev. Jac. x.–xvi. The account in the Evang. de nativ. Mar. is less characteristic.
[11] "Die natürliche Geschichte des grossen Propheten von Nazaret," 1ter Band, s. 119 ff.

the essential signification the two accounts exhibit the following differences. 1. The individual who appears is called in Matthew by the indefinite appellation, *angel of the Lord*, ἄγγελος Κυρίου : in Luke by name, *the angel Gabriel*, ὁ ἄγγελος Γαβριὴλ. 2. The person to whom the angel appears is, according to Matthew, Joseph, according to Luke, Mary. 3. In Matthew the apparition is seen in a dream, in Luke whilst awake. 4. There is a disagreement in relation to the time at which the apparition took place : according to Matthew, Joseph receives the heavenly communication after Mary was already pregnant : according to Luke it is made to Mary prior to her pregnancy. 5. Lastly, both the purpose of the apparition and the effect produced are different ; it was designed, according to Matthew, to comfort Joseph, who was troubled on account of the pregnancy of his betrothed : according to Luke to prevent, by a previous announcement, all possibility of offence.

Where the discrepancies are so great and so essential, it may, at first sight, appear altogether superfluous to inquire whether the two Evangelists record one and the same occurrence, though with considerable disagreement ; or whether they record distinct occurrences, so that the two accounts can be blended together, and the one be made to amplify the other ? The first supposition cannot be admitted without impeaching the historical validity of the narrative ; for which reason most of our theologians, indeed all who see in the narrative a true history, whether miraculous or natural, have decided in favour of the second supposition. Maintaining, and justly, that the silence of one Evangelist concerning an event which is narrated by the other, is not a negation of the event,[1] they blend the two accounts together in the following manner: 1, First, the angel makes known to Mary her approaching pregnancy (Luke) ; 2, she then journeys to Elizabeth (the same Gospel) ; 3, after her return her situation being discovered, Joseph takes offence (Matthew) ; whereupon, 4, he likewise is visited by an angelic apparition (the same Gospel [2]).

But this arrangement of the incidents is, as Schleiermacher has already remarked, full of difficulty[3] ; and it seems that what is related by one Evangelist is not only not presupposed, but excluded, by the other. For, in the first place, the conduct of the angel who appears to Joseph is not easily explained, if the same or another angel had previously appeared to Mary. The angel (in Matthew) speaks altogether as if his communication were the first in this affair : he neither refers to the message previously received by Mary, nor reproaches Joseph because he had not believed it ; but more than all, the informing Joseph of the name of the expected child, and the giving him a full detail of the reasons why he should be so called, (Matt. i. 21,) would have been wholly superfluous had the angel (according to Luke i. 34) already indicated this name to Mary.

Still more incomprehensible is the conduct of the betrothed parties according to this arrangement of events. Had Mary been visited by an angel, who had made known to her an approaching supernatural pregnancy, would not the first impulse of a delicate woman have been, to hasten to impart to her betrothed the import of the divine message, and by this means to anticipate the humiliating discovery of her situation, and an injurious suspicion on the part of her affianced husband. But exactly this discovery Mary allows Joseph to make from others, and thus excites suspicions ; for it is evident that the expression εὑρέθη ἐν γαστρὶ ἔχουσα (Matt. i. 18) signifies a discovery

[1] Augustin, *de consens. evangelist.* ii. 5.
[2] Paulus, Olshausen, Fritzsche, Comm. in Matth. p. 56.
[3] Comp. de Wette's exeg. Handbuch, i. 1, s. 18. Schleiermacher, Ueber die Schriften des Lukas, s. 42 ff.

made independent of any communication on Mary's part, and it is equally clear that in this manner only does Joseph obtain the knowledge of her situation, since his conduct is represented as the result of that discovery (εὑρίσκεσθαι). The apocryphal *Protevangelium Jacobi* felt how enigmatical Mary's conduct must appear, and sought to solve the difficulty in a manner which, contemplated from the supranaturalistic point of view, is perhaps the most consistent. Had Mary retained a recollection of the import of the heavenly message—upon this point the whole ingenious representation of the apocryphal Gospel rests—she ought to have imparted it to Joseph ; but since it is obvious from Joseph's demeanour that she did not acquaint him with it, the only remaining alternative is, to admit that the mysterious communication made to Mary had, owing to her excited state of mind, escaped her memory, and that she was herself ignorant of the true cause of her pregnancy.[4] In fact, nothing is left to supranaturalism in the present case but to seek refuge in the miraculous and the incomprehensible. The attempts which the modern theologians of this class have made to explain Mary's silence, and even to find in it an admirable trait in her character, are so many rash and abortive efforts to make a virtue of necessity. According to Hess [5] it must have cost Mary much self-denial to have concealed the communication of the angel from Joseph ; and this reserve, in a matter known only to herself and to God, must be regarded as a proof of her firm trust in God. Without doubt Mary communed thus with herself : It is not without a purpose that this apparition has been made to me alone ; had it been intended that Joseph should have participated in the communication, the angel would have appeared to him also (if each individual favoured with a divine revelation were of this opinion, how many special revelations would it not require ?) ; besides it is an affair of God alone, consequently it becomes me to leave it with him to convince Joseph (the argument of indolence). Olshausen concurs, and adds his favourite general remark, that in relation to events so extraordinary the measure of the ordinary occurrences of the world is not applicable : a category under which, in this instance, the highly essential considerations of delicacy and propriety are included.

More in accordance with the views of the natural interpreters, the *Evangelium de nativitate Mariae*,[6] and subsequently some later writers, for example, the author of the Natural History of the Great Prophet of Nazareth, have sought to explain Mary's silence, by supposing Joseph to have been at a distance from the abode of his affianced bride at the time of the heavenly communication. According to them Mary was of Nazareth, Joseph of Bethlehem ; to which latter place Joseph departed after the betrothing, and did not return to Mary until the expiration of three months, when he discovered the pregnancy which had taken place in the interim. But since the assumption that Mary and Joseph resided in different localities has no foundation, as will presently be seen, in the canonical Gospels, the whole explanation falls to the ground. Without such an assumption, Mary's silence towards Joseph might, perhaps, have been accounted for from the point of view of the naturalistic interpreters, by imagining her to have been held back through modesty from confessing a situation so liable to excite suspicion. But one who, like Mary, was so fully convinced of the divine agency in the matter, and had shown so ready a

---

[4] Protev. Jac. c. 12 : Μαριὰμ δέ ἐπελάθετο τῶν μυστηρίων ὧν εἶπε πρὸς αὐτὴν Γαβριήλ. When questioned by Joseph she assures him with tears : οὐ γινώσκω, πόθεν ἐστὶ τοῦτο τὸ ἐν τῇ γαστρί μου. c. 13.

[5] Geschichte der drei letzten Lebensjahre Jesu u. s. w. 1. Thl. s. 36. Comp. Hoffmann, s. 176 f.

[6] Ch. viii.–x.

comprehension of her mysterious destination (Luke i. 38), could not possibly have been tongue-tied by petty considerations of false shame.

Consequently, in order to rescue Mary's character, without bringing reproach upon Joseph's, and at the same time to render his unbelief intelligible, interpreters have been compelled to assume that a communication, though a tardy one, was actually made by Mary to Joseph. Like the last-named apocryphal Gospel, they introduce a journey, not of Joseph, but of Mary—the visit to Elizabeth mentioned in Luke—to account for the postponement of the communication. It is probable, says Paulus, that Mary did not open her heart to Joseph before this journey, because she wished first to consult with her older friend as to the mode of making the disclosure to him, and whether she, as the mother of the Messiah, ought to marry.

It was not till after her return, and then most likely through the medium of others, that she made Joseph acquainted with her situation, and with the promises she had received. But Joseph's mind was not properly attuned and prepared for such a disclosure; he became haunted by all kinds of thoughts; and vacillated between suspicion and hope till at length a dream decided him.[7] But in the first place a motive is here given to Mary's journey which is foreign to the account in Luke. Mary sets off to Elizabeth, not to take counsel of her, but to assure herself regarding the sign appointed by the angel. No uneasiness which the friend is to dissipate, but a proud joy, unalloyed by the smallest anxiety, is expressed in her salutation to the future mother of the Baptist. But besides, a confession so tardily made can in nowise justify Mary. What behaviour on the part of an affianced bride—after having received a divine communication, so nearly concerning her future husband, and in a matter so delicate—to travel miles away, to absent herself for three months, and then to permit her betrothed to learn through third persons that which could no longer be concealed!

Those, therefore, who do not impute to Mary a line of conduct which certainly our Evangelists do not impute to her, must allow that she imparted the message of the angel to her future husband as soon as it had been revealed to her; but that he did not believe her.[8] But now let us see how Joseph's character is to be dealt with! Even Hess is of opinion that, since Joseph was acquainted with Mary, he had no cause to doubt her word, when she told him of the apparition she had had. This scepticism presupposes a mistrust of his betrothed which is incompatible with his character as a *just man* (Matt. i. 19), and an incredulity respecting the marvellous which is difficult to reconcile with a readiness on other occasions to believe in angelic apparitions; nor, in any case, would this want of faith have escaped the censure of the angel who subsequently appeared to himself.

Since then, to suppose that the two accounts are parallel, and complete one another, leads unavoidably to results inconsistent with the sense of the Gospels, in so far as they evidently meant to represent the characters of Joseph and Mary as free from blemish; the supposition cannot be admitted, but the accounts mutually exclude each other. An angel did not appear, first to Mary, and also afterwards to Joseph; he can only have appeared either to the one or to the other. Consequently, it is only the one or the other relation which can be regarded as historical. And here different considerations would conduct to opposite decisions. The history in Matthew might appear the more probable from the rationalistic point of view, because it is more easy to interpret naturally an apparition in a dream; whilst that in

[7] Paulus, exeg. Handb. 1 a, s. 121. 145.
[8] To this opinion Neander inclines, L. J. Ch. s. 18.

Luke might be preferred by the supranaturalist, because the manner in which the suspicion cast upon the holy virgin is refuted is more worthy of God. But in fact, a nearer examination proves, that neither has any essential claim to be advanced before the other. Both contain an angelic apparition, and both are therefore encumbered with all the difficulties which, as was stated above in relation to the annunciation of the birth of the Baptist, oppose the belief in angels and apparitions. Again, in both narrations the import of the angelic message is, as we shall presently see, an impossibility. Thus every criterion which might determine the adoption of the one, and the rejection of the other, disappears; and we find ourselves, in reference to both accounts, driven back by necessity to the mythical view.

From this point of view, all the various explanations, which the Rationalists have attempted to give of the two apparitions, vanish of themselves. Paulus explains the apparition in Matthew as a natural dream, occasioned by Mary's previous communication of the announcement which had been made to her; and with which Joseph must have been acquainted, because this alone can account for his having heard the same words in his dream, which the angel had beforehand addressed to Mary: but much rather, is it precisely this similarity in the language of the presumed second angel to that of the first, with the absence of all reference by the latter to the former, which proves that the words of the first angel were not presupposed by the second. Besides, the natural explanation is annihilated the moment the narratives are shown to be mythical. The same remark applies to the explanation, expressed guardedly indeed by Paulus, but openly by the author of the Natural History of the Great Prophet of Nazareth, namely, that the angel who visited Mary (in Luke) was a human being; of which we must speak hereafter.

According to all that has been said, the following is the only judgment we can form of the origin of the two narratives of the angelic apparitions. The conception of Jesus through the power of the Holy Ghost ought not to be grounded upon a mere uncertain suspicion; it must have been clearly and positively asserted; and to this end a messenger from heaven was required, since theocratic decorum seemed to demand it far more in relation to the birth of the Messiah, than of a Samson or a John. Also the words which the angels use, correspond in part with the Old Testament annunciations of extraordinary children.[9] The appearing of the angel in the one narrative beforehand to Mary, but in the other at a later period to Joseph, is to be regarded as a variation in the legend or in the composition, which finds an explanatory counterpart in the history of the annunciation of Isaac. Jehovah (Gen. xvii. 15) promises Abraham a son by Sarah, upon which the Patriarch cannot refrain from laughing; but he receives a repetition of the assurance; Jehovah (Gen. xviii. 1 ff.) makes this promise under the Terebinth tree at Mamre, and Sarah laughs as if it were something altogether novel and unheard of by her; lastly, according to Genesis xxi. 5 ff. it is first after Isaac's birth that

[9] Gen. xvii. 19; LXX. (Annunciation of Isaac):

ἰδοὺ Σάρρα ἡ γυνή σου τέξεται σοι υἱόν, καὶ καλέσεις τὸ ὄνομα αὐτοῦ Ἰσαάκ.

Judg. xiii. 5. (Annunciation of Samson):

καὶ αὐτὸς ἄρξεται σῶσαι τὸν Ἰσραὴλ ἐκ χειρὸς Φυλιστιίμ.

Gen. xvi. 11 ff. (Annunciation of Ishmael):

καὶ εἶπεν αὐτῇ ὁ ἄγγελος Κυρίου· ἰδοὺ σὺ ἐν γαστρὶ ἔχεις, καὶ τέξῃ υἱὸν καὶ καλέσεις τὸ ὄνομα αὐτοῦ Ἰσμαήλ. Οὗτος ἔσται——.

Matt. i. 21.

(μὴ φοβηθῇς παραλαβεῖν Μαριὰμ τὴν γυναῖκα σου—) τέξεται δὲ υἱόν, καὶ καλέσεις τὸ ὄνομα αὐτοῦ Ἰησοῦν· αὐτὸς γὰρ σώσει τὸν λαὸν αὐτοῦ ἀπὸ τῶν ἁμαρτιῶν αὐτῶν.

Luke i. 30 ff.

καὶ εἶπεν ὁ ἄγγελος αὐτῇ—ἰδοὺ συλλήψῃ ἐν γαστρί, καὶ τέξῃ υἱόν, καὶ καλέσεις τὸ ὄνομα αὐτοῦ Ἰησοῦν. Οὗτος ἔσται——.

Sarah mentions the laughing of the people, which is said to have been the occasion of his name ; whereby it appears that this last history does not presuppose the existence of the two other accounts of the annunciation of the birth of Isaac.[10]   As in relation to the birth of Isaac, different legends or poems were formed without reference to one another, some simpler, some more embellished : so we have two discordant narratives concerning the birth of Jesus.   Of these the narrative in Matthew [11] is the simpler and ruder style of composition, since it does not avoid, though it be but by a transient suspicion on the part of Joseph, the throwing a shade over the character of Mary which is only subsequently removed ; that in Luke, on the contrary, is a more refined and artistical representation, exhibiting Mary from the first in the pure light of a bride of heaven.[12]

§ 25.

IMPORT OF THE ANGEL'S MESSAGE.—FULFILMENT OF THE PROPHECY OF ISAIAH.

According to Luke, the angel who appears to Mary, in the first place informs her only that she shall become pregnant, without specifying after what manner : that she shall bring forth a son and call his name Jesus ; He shall be great, and shall be called the Son of the Highest ($\upsilon\iota\grave{o}\varsigma$ $\upsilon\psi\acute{\iota}\sigma\tau\upsilon$) ; and God shall give unto him the throne of his father David, and he shall reign over the house of Jacob for ever.   The subject, the Messiah is here treated precisely in the language common to the Jews, and even the term *Son of the Highest*, if nothing further followed, must be taken in the same sense ; as according to 2 Sam. vii. 14, Ps. ii. 7 an ordinary king of Israel might be so named ; still more, therefore, the greatest of these kings, the Messiah, even considered merely as a man.   This Jewish language reflects in addition a new light upon the question of the historic validity of the angelic apparition ; for we must agree with Schleiermacher that the real angel Gabriel would hardly have proclaimed the advent of the Messiah in a phraseology so strictly Jewish :[1] for which reason we are inclined to coincide with this theologian, and to ascribe this particular portion of the history, as also that which precedes and relates to the Baptist, to one and the same Jewish-christian author.   It is not till Mary opposes the fact of her virginity to the promises of a son, that the angel defines the nature of the conception : that it shall be by the Holy Ghost, by the power of the Highest ; after which the appellation $\upsilon\iota\grave{o}\varsigma$ $\theta\epsilon\upsilon\hat{}$ receives a more precise metaphysical sense.   As a confirmatory sign that a matter of this kind is nowise impossible to God, Mary is

[10] Comp. de Wette, Kritik der mos. Geschichte, s. 86 ff.

[11] The vision which, according to Matthew, Joseph had in his sleep, had besides a kind of type in the vision by which, according to the Jewish tradition related by Josephus, the father of Moses was comforted under similar circumstances, when suffering anxiety concerning the pregnancy of his wife, although for a different reason.   Joseph. Antiq. II. ix. 3. "A man whose name was Amram, one of the nobler sort of Hebrews, was afraid for his whole nation, lest it should fail, by the want of young men to be brought up hereafter, and was very uneasy at it, his wife being then with child, and he knew not what to do.   Hereupon he betook himself to prayer to God. . . . Accordingly God had mercy on him, and was moved by his supplication.   He stood by him in his sleep, and exhorted him not to despair of his future favours. . . . For this child of thine shall deliver the Hebrew nation from the distress they are under from the Egyptians.   His memory shall be famous while the world lasts."

[12] Comp. Ammon, Fortbildung des Christenthums, i. s. 208 f.

[1] Ueber die Schriften des Lukas, s. 23.

referred to that which had occurred to her relative Elizabeth; whereupon she resigns herself in faith to the divine determination respecting her.

In Matthew, where the main point is to dissipate Joseph's anxiety, the angel begins at once with the communication, that the child conceived by Mary is (as the Evangelist had already stated of his own accord, chap. i. 18), of the *Holy Ghost* (πνεῦμα ἅγιον); and hereupon the Messianic destination of Jesus is first pointed out by the expression, *He shall save his people from their sins.* This language may seem to sound less Jewish than that by which the Messianic station of the child who should be born, is set forth in Luke; it is however to be observed, that under the term *sins* (ἁμαρτίαις) is comprehended *the punishment* of those sins, namely, the subjection of the people to a foreign yoke; so that here also the Jewish element is not wanting; as neither in Luke, on the other hand, is the higher destination of the Messiah left wholly out of sight, since under the term *to reign*, βασιλεύειν, the rule over an obedient and regenerated people is included. Next is subjoined by the angel, or more probably by the narrator, an oracle from the Old Testament, introduced by the often recurring phrase, *all this was done, that it might be fulfilled which was spoken of the Lord by the prophet* [v. 22]. It is the prophecy from Isaiah (chap. vii. 14) which the conception of Jesus after this manner should accomplish: namely, *a virgin shall be with child, and shall bring forth a son, and they shall call His name Emmanuel*—God-with-us.

The original sense of this passage in Isaiah is, according to modern research,[2] this. The prophet is desirous of giving Ahaz, who, through fear of the kings of Syria and Israel, was disposed to make a treaty with Assyria, a lively assurance of the speedy destruction of his much dreaded enemies; and he therefore says to him: suppose that an unmarried woman now on the point of becoming a wife[3] shall conceive; or categorically: a certain young woman is, or is about to be with child (perhaps the prophet's own wife); now, before this child is born, the political aspect of affairs shall be so much improved, that a name of good omen shall be given to the child; and before he shall be old enough to use his reason, the power of these enemies shall be completely annihilated. That is to say, prosaically expressed: before nine months shall have passed away, the condition of the kingdom shall be amended, and within about three years the danger shall have disappeared. Thus much, at all events, is demonstrated by modern criticism, that, under the circumstances stated by Isaiah in the introduction to the oracle, it is only a sign having reference to the actual moment and the near future, which could have any meaning. How ill chosen, according to Hengstenberg's[4] interpretation, is the prophet's language: As certainly as the day shall arrive when, in fulfilment of the covenant, the Messiah shall be born, so impossible is it that the people among whom he shall arise, or the family whence he shall spring, shall pass away. How ill-judged, on the part of the prophet, to endeavour to make the improbability of a speedy deliverance appear less improbable, by an appeal to a yet greater improbability in the far distant future!—And then the given limit of a few years! The overthrow of the two kingdoms, such is Hengstenberg's explanation, shall take place—not in the immediately succeeding years, before the child specified shall have acquired the use of

---

[2] Compare Gesenius and Hitzig. Commentaren zum Jesaia; Umbreit, Ueber die Geburt des Immanuel durch eine Jungfrau, in den theol. Studien u. Krit., 1830, 3. Heft, s. 541 ff.

[3] This explanation does away with the importance of the controversy respecting the word עַלְמָה. Moreover it ought to be decided by the fact that the word does not signify an immaculate, but a marriageable young woman (see *Gesenius*). So early as the time of Justin the Jews maintained that the word עַלְמָה ought not to be rendered by παρθένος, but by νεᾶνις. *Dial c. Tryph.* no. 43. p. 130 E. Comp. *Iren. adv. haer.* iii. 21.

[4] Christologie des A. T. s. 1, b, s. 47.

his reason, but—within such a space of time, as in the far future will elapse between the birth of the Messiah and the first development of his mental powers; therefore in about three years. What a monstrous confounding of times! A child is to be born in the distant future, and that which shall happen before this child shall know how to use his reason, is to take place in the nearest present time.

Thus Paulus and his party are decidedly right in opposing to Hengstenberg and his party, that the prophecy of Isaiah has relation, in its original local signification, to the then existing circumstances, and not to the future Messiah, still less to Jesus. Hengstenberg, on the other hand, is equally in the right, when in opposition to Paulus he maintains, that the passage from Isaiah is adopted by Matthew as a prophecy of the birth of Jesus of a virgin. Whilst the orthodox commentators explain the often recurring *that it might be fulfilled* (ἵνα πληρωθῇ), and similar expressions as signifying: this happened by divine arrangement, in order that the Old Testament prophecy, which in its very origin had reference to the New Testament occurrence, might be fulfilled;—the rationalistic interpreters, on the contrary, understand merely: this took place after such a manner, that it was so constituted, that the Old Testament words, which, originally indeed, had relation to something different, should admit of being so applied; and in such application alone do they receive their full verification. In the first explanation, the relation between the Old Testament passage and the New Testament occurrence is objective, arranged by God himself: in the last it is only subjective, a relation perceived by the later author; according to the former it is a relationship at once precise and essential: according to the latter both inexact and adventitious. But opposed to this latter interpretation of New Testament passages, which point out an Old Testament prophecy as fulfilled, is the language, and equally so the spirit of the New Testament writers. The language: for neither can πληροῦσθαι signify in such connexion anything than *ratum fieri, eventu comprobari*, nor ἵνα ὅπως anything than *eo consilio ut*, whilst the extensive adoption of ἵνα ἐκβατικὸν has arisen only from dogmatic perplexity.[5] But such an interpretation is altogether at variance with the Judaical spirit of the authors of the Gospels. Paulus maintains that the Orientalist does not seriously believe that the ancient prophecy was designedly spoken, or was accomplished by God, precisely in order that it should prefigure a modern event, and vice versâ; but this is to carry over our sober European modes of thought into the imaginative life of the Orientals. When however Paulus adds: much rather did the coincidence of a later event with an earlier prophecy assume only the *form* of a designed coincidence in the mind of the Oriental: he thus, at once, annuls his previous assertion; for this is to admit, that, what in our view is mere coincidence, appeared to the oriental mind the result of design; and we must acknowledge this to be the meaning of an oriental representation, if we would interpret it according to its original signification. It is well known that the later Jews found prophecies, of the time being and of the future, everywhere in the Old Testament; and that they constructed a complete image of the future Messiah, out of various, and in part falsely interpreted Old Testament passages.[6] And the Jew believed he saw in the application he gave to the Scripture, however perverted it might be, an actual fulfilment of the prophecy. In the words of Olshausen: it is a mere dogmatic prejudice to attribute to this formula, when used by the New Testament writers, an altogether different sense from that

---

[5] See Winer, Grammatik des neutest. Sprachidioms, 3te Aufl. s. 382 ff. Fritzsche, Comm. in Matth. p 49. 317 und Excurs. 1, p. 836 ff.

[6] See the Introduction, § 14.

which it habitually bears among their countrymen ; and this solely with the view to acquit them of the sin of falsely interpreting the Scripture.

Many theologians of the present day are sufficiently impartial to admit, with regard to the Old Testament, in opposition to the ancient orthodox interpretation, that many of the prophecies originally referred to near events ; but they are not sufficiently rash, with regard to the New Testament, to side with the rationalistic commentators, and to deny the decidedly Messianic application which the New Testament writers make of these prophecies ; they are still too prejudiced to allow, that here and there the New Testament has falsely interpreted the Old. Consequently, they have recourse to the expedient of distinguishing a double sense in the prophecy ; the one relating to a near and minor occurrence, the other to a future and more important event ; and thus they neither offend against the plain grammatical and historical sense of the Old Testament passage on the one hand, nor distort or deny the signification of the New Testament passage on the other.[7] Thus, in the prophecy of Isaiah under consideration, the spirit of prophecy, they contend, had a double intention : to announce a near occurrence, the delivery of the affianced bride of the prophet, and also a distinct event in the far distant future, namely the birth of the Messiah of a virgin. But a double sense so monstrous owes its origin to dogmatic perplexity alone. It has been adopted, as Olshausen himself remarks, in order to avoid the offensive admission that the New Testament writers, and Jesus himself, did not interpret the Old Testament rightly, or, more properly speaking, according to modern principles of exegesis, but explained it after the manner of their own age, which was not the most correct. But so little does this offence exist for the unprejudiced, that the reverse would be the greater difficulty, that is, if, contrary to all the laws of historical and national development, the New Testament writers had elevated themselves completely above the modes of interpretation common to their age and nation. Consequently, with regard to the prophecies brought forward in the New Testament, we may admit, according to circumstances, without further argument, that they are frequently interpreted and applied by the evangelists, in a sense which is totally different from that they originally bore.

We have here in fact a complete table of all the four possible views on this point : two extreme and two conciliatory ; one false and one, it is to be hoped, correct.

1. *Orthodox view* (Hengstenberg and others) : Such Old Testament passages had in their very origin an exclusive prophetic reference to Christ, for the New Testament writers so understand them ; and they must be in the right even should human reason be confounded.

2. *Rationalistic view* (Paulus and others) : The New Testament writers do not assign a strictly Messianic sense to the Old Testament prophecies, for this reference to Christ is foreign to the original signification of these prophecies viewed by the light of reason ; and the New Testament writings must accord with reason, whatever ancient beliefs may say to the contrary.

3. *Mystical conciliatory view* (Olshausen and others) : The Old Testament passages originally embody both the deeper signification ascribed to them by the New Testament writers, and that more proximate meaning which common sense obliges us to recognize : thus sound reason and the ancient faith are reconcilable.

4. *Decision of criticism :* Very many of the Old Testament prophecies had, originally, only an immediate reference to events belonging to the time : but they came to be regarded by the men of the New Testament as actual

[7] See Bleek in den theol. Studien u. Kritiken, 1835, 2, s. 441 ff.

I

predictions of Jesus as the Messiah, because the intelligence of these men was limited by the manner of thinking of their nation, a fact recognized neither by Rationalism nor the ancient faith.[8]

Accordingly we shall not hesitate for a moment to allow, in relation to the prophecy in question, that the reference to Jesus is obtruded upon it by the Evangelists. Whether the actual birth of Jesus of a virgin gave rise to this application of the prophecy, or whether this prophecy, interpreted beforehand as referring to the Messiah, originated the belief that Jesus was born of a virgin, remains to be determined.

§ 26.

JESUS BEGOTTEN OF THE HOLY GHOST. CRITICISM OF THE ORTHODOX OPINION.

The statement of Matthew and of Luke concerning the mode of Jesus's conception has, in every age, received the following interpretation by the church; that Jesus was conceived in Mary not by a human father, but by the Holy Ghost. And truly the gospel expressions seem, at first sight, to justify this interpretation; since the words πρὶν ἢ συνελθεῖν αὐτούς (Matt. i. 18) and ἐπεὶ ἄδνρα οὐ γινώσκω (Luke i. 34) preclude the participation of Joseph or any other man in the conception of the child in question. Nevertheless the terms πνεῦμα ἅγιον and δύναμις ὑψίστου do not represent the Holy Ghost in the sense of the church, as the third person in the Godhead, but rather the רוּחַ אֱלֹהִים, Spiritus Dei as used in the Old Testament: God in his agency upon the world, and especially upon man. In short the words ἐν γαστρὶ ἔχουσα ἐκ πνεύματος ἁγίου in Matthew, and πνεῦμα ἅγιον ἐπελεύσεται ἐπὶ σὲ κ. τ. λ. in Luke, express with sufficient clearness that the absence of human agency was supplied—not physically after the manner of heathen representations—but by the divine creative energy.

Though this seems to be the representation intended by the evangelists in the passages referred to concerning the origin of the life of Jesus, still it cannot be completed without considerable difficulties. We may separate what we may term the *physico-theological* from the *historical-exegetical* difficulties.

The physiological difficulties amount to this, that such a conception would be a most remarkable deviation from all natural laws. However obscure the physiology of the fact, it is proved by an exceptionless experience that only by the concurrence of the two sexes is a new human being generated; on which account Plutarch's remark, "παιδίον οὐδεμία ποτὲ γυνὴ λέγεται ποιῆσαι δίχα κοινωνίας ἀνδρὸς,"[1] and Cerinthus's "*impossible*" become applicable.[2] It is

[8] The whole rationalistic interpretation of Scripture rests upon a sufficiently palpable paralogism, by which it stands or falls :

The New Testament authors are not to be interpreted as if they said something irrational (certainly not something contrary to *their own* modes of thinking).

Now according to a particular interpretation their assertions are irrational (that is contrary to *our* modes of thinking).

Consequently the interpretation cannot give the original sense, and a different interpretation must be given.

Who does not here perceive the *quaternio terminorum* and the fatal inconsequence, when Rationalism takes its stand upon the same ground with supernaturalism ; that, namely, whilst with regard to all other men the first point to be examined is whether they speak or write what is just and true, to the New Testament writers the prerogative is granted of this being, in their case, already presupposed ?

[1] Conjugial. præcept. Opp. ed. Hutton, Vol. 7. s. 428.

[2] Irenäus, adv. haer. I, 26 : Cerinthus, Jesum subjecit non ex virgine natum, impossibile enim hoc ei visum est.

only among the lowest species of the animal kingdom that generation takes place without the union of sexes ; [3] so that, regarding the matter purely physiologically, what Origen says, in the supranaturalistic sense, would indeed be true of a man of the like origin ; namely, that the words in Psalm xxii. 7, *I am a worm and no man* is a prophecy of Jesus in the above respect.[4]   But to the merely physical consideration a theological one is subjoined by the angel (Luke i. 37), when he appeals to the divine omnipotence to which nothing is impossible.   But since the divine omnipotence, by virtue of its unity with divine wisdom, is never exerted in the absence of an adequate motive, the existence of such, in the present instance, must be demonstrated.   But nothing less than an object worthy of the Deity, and at the same time necessarily unattainable except by a deviation from the ordinary course of nature, could constitute a sufficient cause for the suspension by God of a natural law which he had established.   Only here, it is said, the end, the redemption of mankind, required impeccability on the part of Jesus ; and in order to render him exempt from sin, a divinely wrought conception, which excluded the participation of a sinful father, and severed Jesus from all connexion with original sin, was necessary.[5]   To which it has been answered by others,[6] (and Schleiermacher has recently most decisively argued this side of the question,[7]) that the exclusion of the paternal participation is insufficient, unless, indeed, the inheritance of original sin, on the maternal side, be obviated by the adoption of the Valentinian assertion, that Jesus only passed through the body of Mary.   But that the gospel histories represent an actual maternal participation is undeniable ; consequently a divine intervention which should sanctify the participation of the sinful human mother in the conception of Jesus must be supposed in order to maintain his assumed necessary impeccability.   But if God determined on such a purification of the maternal participation, it had been easier to do the same with respect to that of the father, than by his total exclusion, to violate the natural law in so unprecedented a manner ; and consequently, a fatherless conception cannot be insisted upon as the necessary means of compassing the impeccability of Jesus.

Even he who thinks to escape the difficulties already specified, by enveloping himself in a supranaturalism, inaccessible to arguments based on reason or the laws of nature, must nevertheless admit the force of the *exegetical-historical* difficulties meeting him upon his own ground, which likewise beset the view of the supernatural conception of Jesus.   Nowhere in the New Testament is such an origin ascribed to Jesus, or even distinctly alluded to, except in these two accounts of his infancy in Matthew and in Luke.[8]   The history of the conception is omitted not only by Mark, but also by John, the supposed author of the fourth Gospel and an alleged inmate with the mother of Jesus subsequent to his death, who therefore would have been the most accurately informed concerning these occurrences.   It is said that John sought rather to record the heavenly than the earthly origin of Jesus ; but the question arises, whether the doctrine which he sets forth in his prologue, of a divine

---

[3] In Henke's neuem Magazin, iii. 3, s. 369.

[4] Homil. in Lucam xiv.   Comp. my Streitschriften, i. 2, s. 72 f.

[5] Olshausen, Bibl. Comm. s. 49.   Neander, L. J. Ch. s. 16 f.

[6] *e. g.* by Eichhorn, Einleitung in das N. T. 1. Bd. s. 407.

[7] Glaubenslehre, 2 Thl. § 97. s. 73 f. der zweiten Auflage.

[8] This side is particularly considered in der Skiagraphie des Dogma's von Jesu übernatürlicher Geburt, in Schmidt's Bibliothek, i. 3, s. 400 ff. ; in den Bemerkungen über den Glaubenspunkt : Christus ist empfangen vom heil. Geist, in Henke's neuem Magazin, iii. 3, 365 ff. ; in Kaiser's bibl. Theol. I, s. 231 f. ; De Wette's bibl. Dogmatik, § 281 ; Schleiermacher's Glaubenslehre, 2 Thl. § 97.

hypostasis actually becoming flesh and remaining immanent in Jesus, is reconcilable with the view given in the passages before us, of a simple divine operation determining the conception of Jesus ; whether therefore John could have presupposed the history of the conception contained in Matthew and Luke? This objection, however, loses its conclusive force if in the progress of our investigation the apostolic origin of the fourth Gospel is not established. The most important consideration therefore is, that no retrospective allusion to this mode of conception occurs throughout the four Gospels ; not only neither in John nor in Mark, but also neither in Matthew nor in Luke. Not only does Mary herself designate Joseph simply as the father of Jesus (Luke ii. 48), and the Evangelist speak of both as his parents, γονεῖς (Luke ii. 41),—an appellation which could only have been used in an ulterior sense by one who had just related the miraculous conception,—but all his contemporaries in general, according to our Evangelists, regarded him as a son of Joseph, a fact which was not unfrequently alluded to contemptuously and by way of reproach in his presence (Matt. xiii. 55 ; Luke iv. 22 ; John vi. 42), thus affording him an opportunity of making a decisive appeal to his miraculous conception, of which, however, he says not a single word. Should it be answered, that he did not desire to convince respecting the divinity of his person by this external evidence, and that he could have no hope of making an impression by such means on those who were in heart his opponents,—it must also be remembered, that, according to the testimony of the fourth Gospel, his own disciples, though they admitted him to be the son of God, still regarded him as the actual son of Joseph. Philip introduces Jesus to Nathanael *as the son of Joseph,* Ἰησοῦν τὸν υἱὸν Ἰωσὴφ (John i. 46), manifestly in the same sense of real paternity which the Jews attached to the designation ; and nowhere is this represented as an erroneous or imperfect notion which these Apostles had subsequently to relinquish ; much rather does the whole sense of the narrative, which is not to be mistaken, exhibit the Apostles as having a right belief on this point. The enigmatical presupposition, with which, at the marriage in Cana, Mary addressed herself to Jesus,[9] is far too vague to prove a recollection of his miraculous conception on the part of the mother ; at all events this feature is counterbalanced by the opposing one that the family of Jesus, and, as appears from Matt. xii. 46 ff. compared with Mark iii. 21 ff., his mother also were, at a later time, in error respecting his aims ; which is scarcely explicable, even of his brothers, supposing them to have had such recollections.

Just as little as in the Gospels, is anything in confirmation of the view of the supernatural conception of Jesus, to be found in the remaining New Testament writings. For when the Apostle Paul speaks of Jesus as *made of a woman,* γενόμενον ἐκ γυναικὸς (Gal. iv. 4), this expression is not to be understood as an exclusion of paternal participation ; since the addition *made under the law,* γενόμενον ὑπὸ νόμον, clearly shows that he would here indicate (in the form which is frequent in the Old and New Testament, for example Job xiv. 1 ; Matt. xi. 11) human nature with all its conditions. When Paul (Rom. i. 3, 4 compared with ix. 5) makes Christ *according to the flesh,* κατὰ σάρκα, descend from David, but declares him to be the son of God *according to the Spirit of Holiness,* κατὰ πνεῦμα ἁγιωσύνης ; no one will here identify the antithesis *flesh* and *spirit* with the maternal human participation, and the divine energy superseding the paternal participation in the conception of Jesus. Finally when in the Epistle to the Hebrews (vii. 3) Melchisedec is compared with *the son of God,* υἱὸς τοῦ θεοῦ, because *without father,* ἀπάτωρ, the application of the literally interpreted ἀπάτωρ to Jesus, as he

---

[9] Brought to bear upon this point by Neander, L. J. Ch. s. 12.

appeared upon earth, is forbidden by the addition *without mother,* ἀμήτωρ, which agrees as little with him as the immediately following *without descent,* ἀγενεαλόγητος.

§ 27.

RETROSPECT OF THE GENEALOGIES.

The most conclusive exegetical ground of decision against the supernatural conception of Jesus, which bears more closely on the point than all the hitherto adduced passages, is found in the two genealogies previously considered. Even the Manichæan Faustus asserted that it is impossible without contradiction to trace the descent of Jesus from David through Joseph, as is done by our two genealogists, and yet assume that Joseph was not the father of Jesus; and Augustine had nothing convincing to answer when he remarked that it was necessary, on account of the superior dignity of the masculine gender, to carry the genealogy of Jesus through Joseph, who was Mary's husband if not by a natural by a spiritual alliance.[1] In modern times also the construction of the genealogical tables in Matthew and in Luke has led many theologians to observe, that these authors considered Jesus as the actual son of Joseph.[2] The very design of these tables is to prove Jesus to be of the lineage of David through Joseph; but what do they prove, if indeed Joseph was not the father of Jesus? The assertion that Jesus was the son of David, υἱὸς Δαβὶδ, which in Matthew (i. 1) prefaces the genealogy and announces its object, is altogether annulled by the subsequent denial of his conception by means of the Davidical Joseph. It is impossible, therefore, to think it probable that the genealogy and the history of the birth of Jesus emanate from the same author[3]; and we must concur with the theologians previously cited, that the genealogies are taken from a different source. Scarcely could it satisfy to oppose the remark, that as Joseph doubtlessly adopted Jesus, the genealogical table of the former became fully valid for the latter. For adoption might indeed suffice to secure to the adopted son the reversion of certain external family rights and inheritances; but such a relationship could in no wise lend a claim to the Messianic dignity, which was attached to the true blood and lineage of David. He, therefore, who had regarded Joseph as nothing more than the adopted father of Jesus, would hardly have given himself the trouble to seek out the Davidical descent of Joseph; but if indeed, besides the established belief that Jesus was the son of God, it still remained important to represent him as the son of David, the pedigree of Mary would have been preferred for this purpose; for, however contrary to custom, the maternal genealogy must have been admitted in a case where a human father did not exist. Least of all is it to be believed, that several authors would have engaged in the compilation of a genealogical table for Jesus which traced his descent through Joseph, so that two different genealogies of this kind are still preserved to us, if a closer relationship between Jesus and Joseph had not been admitted at the time of their composition.

Consequently, the decision of the learned theologians who agree that these genealogies were composed in the belief that Jesus was the actual son of Joseph and Mary, can hardly be disputed; but the authors or compilers of our Gospels, notwithstanding their own conviction of the divine origin of

---

[1] Augustinus contra Faustum Manichaeum, L. 23. 3. 4. 8.
[2] See Schmidt, Schleiermacher, and Wegscheider, Instit. § 123 (not. ᵈ).
[3] Eichhorn thinks this probable, Einl. in das N. T. i. s. 425, De Wette possible, exeg. Handb. i. 1, s. 7.

Jesus, received them among their materials; only that Matthew (i. 16) changed the original *Joseph begat Jesus of Mary*—Ἰωσὴφ δὲ ἐγέννησε τὸν Ἰησοῦν ἐκ τῆς Μαρίας (comp. verses 3. 5. 6) according to his own view; and so likewise Luke (iii. 23) instead of commencing his genealogy simply with, *Jesus— the son of Joseph*—Ἰησοῦς υἱὸς Ἰωσὴφ, inserts *being as was supposed*, ὢν, ὡς ἐνομίζετο κ. τ. λ.

Let it not be objected that the view for which we contend, namely, that the genealogies could not have been composed under the notion that Joseph was not the father of Jesus, leaves no conceivable motive for incorporating them into our present Gospels. The original construction of a genealogy of Jesus, even though in the case before us it consisted simply in the adapting of foreign already existing genealogical tables to Jesus, required a powerful and direct inducement; this was the hope thereby to gain—the corporeal descent of Jesus from Joseph being presupposed—a main support to the belief in his Messiahship; whilst, on the other hand, a less powerful inducement was sufficient to incite to the admission of the previously constructed genealogies: the expectation that, notwithstanding the non-existence of any real relationship between Joseph and Jesus, they might nevertheless serve to link Jesus to David. Thus we find, that in the histories of the birth both in Matthew and in Luke, though they each decidedly exclude Joseph from the conception, great stress is laid upon the Davidical descent of Joseph (Matt. i. 20, Luke i. 27, ii. 4); that which in fact had no real significance, except in connexion with the earlier opinion, is retained even after the point of view is changed.

Since, in this way, we discover both the genealogies to be memorials belonging to the time and circle of the primitive church, in which Jesus was still regarded as a naturally begotten man, the sect of the Ebionites cannot fail to occur to us; as we are told concerning them, that they held this view of the person of Christ at this early period.[4] We should therefore have expected, more especially, to have found these genealogies in the old Ebionitish Gospels, of which we have still knowledge, and are not a little surprised to learn that precisely in these Gospels the genealogies were wanting. It is true Epiphanius states that the Gospel of the Ebionites commenced with the public appearance of the Baptist[5]; accordingly, by the genealogies, γενεαλογίαις, which they are said to have cut away, might have been meant, those histories of the birth and infancy comprised in the two first chapters of Matthew; which they could not have adopted in their present form, since they contained the fatherless conception of Jesus, which was denied by the Ebionites: and it might also have been conjectured that this section which was in opposition to their system had alone perhaps been wanting in their Gospel; and that the genealogy which was in harmony with their view might nevertheless have been somewhere inserted. But this supposition vanishes as soon as we find that Epiphanius, in reference to the Nazarenes, defines the genealogies, (of which he is ignorant whether they possessed them or not,) as *reaching from Abraham to Christ*, τὰς ἀπὸ τοῦ Ἀβραὰμ ἕως Χριστοῦ[6]; consequently, by the genealogies which were wanting to some heretics, he evidently understood the genealogical tables, though, in relation to the Ebionites, he might likewise have included under this expression the history of the birth.

How is the strange phenomenon, that these genealogies are not found among that very sect of Christians who retained the particular opinion upon which they were constructed, to be explained? A modern investigator has

[4] Justin Mart. Dial. cum Tryphone, 48; Origines contra Celsum, L. 5, 61. Euseb. H. E. 3, 27.
[5] Epiphan. haeres. 30, 14.
[6] Haeres. 29, 9.

advanced the supposition, that the Jewish-christians omitted the genealogical tables from prudential motives, in order not to facilitate or augment the persecution which, under Domitian, and perhaps even earlier, threatened the family of David.[7]   But explanations, having no inherent connexion with the subject, derived from circumstances in themselves of doubtful historical validity, are admissible only as a last refuge, when no possible solution of the questionable phenomenon is to be found in the thing itself, as here in the principles of the Ebionitish system.

But in this case the matter is by no means so difficult.   It is known that the Fathers speak of two classes of Ebionites, of which the one, besides strenuously maintaining the obligation of the Mosaic law, held Jesus to be the naturally begotten Son of Joseph and Mary ; the other, from that time called also Nazarenes, admitted with the orthodox church the conception by the Holy Ghost.[8]   But besides this distinction there existed yet another. The most ancient ecclesiastic writers, Justin Martyr and Irenæus for example, are acquainted with those Ebionites only, who regarded Jesus as a naturally born man first endowed with divine powers at his baptism.[9]   In Epiphanius and the Clementine Homilies, on the other hand, we meet with Ebionites who had imbibed an element of speculative Gnosticism.   This tendency, which according to Epiphanius is to be dated from one Elxai, has been ascribed to Essenic influence,[10] and traces of the same have been discovered in the heresies referred to in the Epistle to the Colossians ; whereas the first class of Ebionites evidently proceeded from common Judaism.   Which form of opinion was the earlier and which the later developed is not so easily determined ; with reference to the last detailed difference, it might seem, since the speculative Ebionites are mentioned first by the Clementines and Epiphanius, whilst Ebionites holding a simpler view are spoken of by Justin and by Irenæus, that the latter were the earlier ; nevertheless as Tertullian already notices in his time the Gnosticising tendency of the opinions of the Ebionites respecting Christ[11], and as the germ of such views existed among the Essenes in the time of Jesus, the more probable assumption is, that both opinions arose side by side about the same period.[12]   As little can it be proved with regard to the other difference, that the views concerning Christ held by the Nazarenes became first, at a later period, lowered to those of the Ebionites[13] ; since the notices, partly confused and partly of late date, of the ecclesiastical writers, may be naturally explained as arising out of what may be called an optical delusion of the church, which,—whilst she in fact made continual advances in the glorification of Christ, but a part of the Jewish Christians remained stationary,—made it appear to her as if she herself remained stationary, whilst the others fell back into heresy.

By thus distinguishing the simple and the speculative Ebionites, so much is gained, that the failure of the genealogies among the latter class, mentioned by Epiphanius, does not prove them to have been also wanting among the

---

[7] Credner, in den Beiträgen zur Einleitung in das N. T. 1, s. 443. Anm.

[8] Orig. ut sup.

[9] See Neander, K. G. 1, 2, s. 615 f.

[10] Credner, über Essener, und einen theilweisen Zusammenhang beider, in Winer's Zeitschrift f. wissenschaftliche Theologie, 1. Bd. 2tes and 3tes Heft ; see Baur, *Progr. de Ebionitarum origine et doctrinâ ab Essenis repetendâ*, und christl. Gnosis, s. 403.

[11] De carne Christi, c. 14 : *Poterit haec opinio Hebioni convenire, qui nudum hominem, et tantum ex semine David, i.e. non et Dei filium, constituit Jesum, ut in illo angelum fuisse edicat.*

[12] Neander and Schneckenburger are of the latter, Gieseler and Credner of the former opinion.

[13] I here refer to the account of Hegesippus in Eusebius, H. E. iv. 22.

former.   And the less if we should be able to make it appear probable, that the grounds of their aversion to the genealogical table, and the grounds of distinction between them and the other class of Ebionites, were identical. One of these grounds was evidently the unfavourable opinion, which the Ebionites of Epiphanius and of the Clementine Homilies had of David, from whom the genealogy traces the descent of Jesus.   It is well known that they distinguished in the Old Testament a twofold prophecy, male and female, pure and impure, of which the former only promised things heavenly and true, the latter things earthly and delusive ; that proceeding from Adam and Abel, this from Eve and Cain ; and both constituted an under current through the whole history of the revelation.[14]   It was only the pious men from Adam to Joshua whom they acknowledged as true prophets : the later prophets and men of God, among whom David and Solomon are named, were not only not recognized, but abhorred.[15]   We even find positive indications that David was an object of their particular aversion.   There were many things which created in them a detestation of David (and Solomon).   David was a bloody warrior ; but to shed blood was, according to the doctrines of these Ebionites, one of the greatest of sins ; David was known to have committed adultery, (Solomon to have been a voluptuary); and adultery was even more detested by this sect than murder.   David was a performer on stringed instruments ; this art, the invention of the Canaanites (Gen. iv. 21), was held by these Ebionites to be a sign of false prophecy ; finally, the prophecies announced by David and those connected with him, (and Solomon,) had reference to the kingdoms of this world, of which the Gnosticising Ebionites desired to know nothing [16]   Now the Ebionites who had sprung from common Judaism could not have shared this ground of aversion to the genealogies ; since to the orthodox Jew David was an object of the highest veneration.

Concerning a second point the notices are not so lucid and accordant as they should be ; namely, whether it was a further development of the general Ebionitish doctrine concerning the person of the Christ, which led these Ebionites to reject the genealogies.   According to Epiphanius, they fully recognized the Gnostic distinction between Jesus the son of Joseph and Mary, and the Christ who descended upon him [17] ; and consequently might have been withheld from referring the genealogy to Jesus only perhaps by their abhorrence of David.   On the other hand, from the whole tenor of the Clementines, and from one passage in particular,[18] it has recently been inferred, and not without apparent reason, that the author of these writings had himself abandoned the view of a natural conception, and even birth of Jesus [19] ; whereby it is yet more manifest that the ground of the rejection of the genealogies by this sect was peculiar to it, and not common to the other Ebionites.

Moreover positive indications, that the Ebionites who proceeded from Judaism possessed the genealogies, do not entirely fail.   Whilst the Ebionites

[14] Homil. 3, 23–27.

[15] Epiphan. haeres. 30, 18. comp. 15.

[16] That these were the traits in David's character which displeased the Christian sect in question, is sufficiently evident from a passage in the Clementine Homilies, though the name is not given : Homil. 3, 25 ; ἔτι μὴν καὶ οἱ ἀπὸ τῆς τούτου (τοῦ Καῒν) διαδοχῆς προεληλυθότες πρῶτοι μοιχοὶ ἐγένοντο, καὶ ψαλτήρια, καὶ κιθάραι, καὶ χαλκεῖς ὅπλων πολεμικῶν ἐγένοντο.   Δὶ δ καὶ ἡ τῶν ἐγγόνων προφητεία, μοιχῶν καὶ ψαλτηρίων γέμουσα, λανθανόντως διὰ τῶν ἡδυπαθειῶν ὡς τοὺς πολέμους ἐγείρει.

[17] Epiphan. haer. 30, 14. 16. 34.

[18] Homil. 3, 17.

[19] Schneckenburger, über das Evang. der Aegypter, s. 7 ;   Baur, christl. Gnosis, s. 760 ff. See on the other side Credner and Hoffmann.

of Epiphanius and of the Clementines called Jesus only Son of God, but rejected the appellation Son of David, as belonging to the common opinion of the Jews [20]; other Ebionites were censured by the Fathers for recognizing Jesus only as the Son of David, to whom he is traced in the genealogies, and not likewise as the Son of God.[21] Further, Epiphanius relates of the earliest Judaising Gnostics, Cerinthus and Carpocrates, that they used a Gospel the same in other respects indeed as the Ebionites, but that they adduced the genealogies, which they therefore read in the same, in attestation of the human conception of Jesus by Joseph.[22] Also the ἀπομνημονεύματα cited by Justin, and which originated upon Judæo-christian ground, appear to have contained a genealogy similar to that in our Matthew; since Justin as well as Matthew speaks, in relation to Jesus, of a γένος τοῦ Δαβὶδ καὶ Ἀβραάμ, of a σπέρμα ἐξ Ἰακὼβ, διὰ Ἰούδα, καὶ Φαρὲς καὶ Ἰεσσαὶ καὶ Δαβὶδ κατερχόμενον [23]; only that at the time, and in the circle of Justin, the opinion of a supernatural conception of Jesus had already suggested the reference of the genealogy to Mary, instead of to Joseph.

Hence it appears that we have in the genealogies a memorial, agreeing with indications from other sources, of the fact that in the very earliest Christian age, in Palestine, a body of Christians, numerous enough to establish upon distinct fundamental opinions two different Messianic tables of descent, considered Jesus to have been a naturally conceived human being. And no proof is furnished to us in the apostolic writings, that the Apostles would have declared this doctrine to be unchristian; it appeared so first from the point of view adopted by the authors of the histories of the birth in the first and third Gospels: notwithstanding which, however, it is treated with surprising lenity by the Fathers of the church.

§ 28.

NATURAL EXPLANATION OF THE HISTORY OF THE CONCEPTION.

If, as appears from the foregoing statements, so many weighty difficulties, philosophical as well as exegetical, beset the supranaturalistic explanation, it is well worth while to examine whether it be not possible to give an interpretation of the gospel history which shall obviate these objections. Recourse has been had to the natural explanation, and the two narratives singly and conjointly have been successively subjected to the rationalistic mode of interpretation.

In the first place, the account in Matthew seemed susceptible of such an interpretation. Numerous rabbinical passages were cited to demonstrate, that it was consonant with Jewish notions to consider a son of pious parents to be conceived by the divine co-operation, and that he should be called the son of the Holy Spirit, without its being ever imagined that paternal participation was thereby excluded. It was consequently contended, that the section in

[20] Orig. Comm. in Matth. T. 16, 12. Tertullian, De carne Christi, 14, s. Anm. 13 (a passage in which indeed the speculative and ordinary Ebionites are mingled together).
[21] Clement. homil. 18, 13. They referred the words of Matth. xi. 27 : οὐδεὶς ἔγνω τὸν πατέρα, εἰ μὴ ὁ υἱὸς κ. τ. λ. to τοὺς πατέρα νομίζοντας χριστοῦ τὸν Δαβὶδ, καὶ αὐτὸν δὲ τὸν χριστὸν υἱὸν ὄντα, καὶ υἱὸν θεοῦ μὴ ἐγνωκότας, and complained that αἰτὶ τοῦ θεοῦ τὸν Δαβὶδ πάντες ἔλεγον.
[22] Haeres. 30, 14 : ὁ μὲν γὰρ Κήρινθος καὶ Κάρποκρας τῷ αὐτῷ χρώμενοι παρ’ αὐτοῖς (τοῖς Ἐβιωναίοις) εὐαγγελίῳ, ἀπὸ τῆς ἀρχις τοῦ κατὰ Ματθαῖον εὐαγγελίου διὰ τῆς γενεαλογίας βούλονται παριστᾶν ἐκ σπέρματος Ἰωσὴφ καὶ Μαρίας εἶναι τὸν χριστόν.
[23] Dial. c. Tryph. 100. 120.

Matthew represented merely the intention of the angel to inform Joseph, not indeed that Mary had become pregnant in the absence of all human intercourse, but that notwithstanding her pregnancy she was to be regarded as pure, not as one fallen from virtue. It was maintained that the exclusion of paternal participation—which is an embellishment of the original representation—occurs first in Luke in the words ἄνδρα οὐ γινώσκω (i. 34).[1] When however this view was justly opposed by the remark, that the expression πρὶν ἢ συνελθεῖν αὐτοὺς in Matthew (i. 18) decidedly excludes the participation of the only individual in question, namely Joseph; it was then thought possible to prove that even in Luke the paternal exclusion was not so positive : but truly this could be done only by an unexegetical subversion of the clear sense of the words, or else by uncritically throwing suspicion on a part of a well-connected narrative. The first expedient is to interpret Mary's inquiry of the angel i. 34, thus : Can I who am already betrothed and married give birth to the Messiah, for as the mother of the Messiah I must have no husband? whereupon the angel replies, that God, through his power, could make something distinguished even of the child conceived of her and Joseph.[2] The other proceeding is no less arbitrary. Mary's inquiry of the angel is explained as an unnatural interruption of his communication, which being abstracted, the passage is found to contain no decided intimation of the supernatural conception.[3]

If consequently, the difficulty of the natural explanation of the two accounts be equally great, still, with respect to both it must be alike attempted or rejected; and for the consistent Rationalist, a Paulus for example, the latter is the only course. This commentator considers the participation of Joseph indeed excluded by Matt. i. 18, but by no means that of every other man; neither can he find a supernatural divine intervention in the expression of Luke i. 35. The *Holy Ghost*—πνεῦμα ἅγιον—is not with him objective, an external influence operating upon Mary, but her own pious imagination. The *power of the Highest*—δύναμις ὑψίστου—is not the immediate divine omnipotence, but every natural power employed in a manner pleasing to God may be so called. Consequently, according to Paulus, the meaning of the angelic announcement is simply this : prior to her union with Joseph, Mary, under the influence of a pure enthusiasm in sacred things on the one hand, and by an human co-operation pleasing to God on the other, became the mother of a child who on account of this holy origin was to be called a son of God.

Let us examine rather more accurately the view which this representative of rationalistic interpretation takes of the particulars of the conception of Jesus. He begins with Elizabeth, the patriotic and wise daughter of Aaron, as he styles her. She, having conceived the hope that she might give birth to one of God's prophets, naturally desired moreover that he might be the first of prophets, the forerunner of the Messiah; and that the latter also might speedily be born. Now there was among her own kinsfolk a person suited in every respect for the mother of the Messiah, Mary, a young virgin, a descendant of David; nothing more was needful than to inspire her likewise with such a special hope. Whilst these intimations prepare us to anticipate a cleverly concerted plan on the part of Elizabeth in reference to her young relative, in the which we hope to become initiated; Paulus here suddenly lets

---

[1] Br . . . , die Nachricht, dass Jesus durch den heil. Geist und von einer Jungfrau geboren sei, aus Zeitbegriffen erläutert. In Schmidt's Bibl. 1, 1. s. 101 ff.—Horst, in Henke's Museum 1, 4, 497 ff., über die beiden ersten Kapitel in Evang. Lukas.

[2] Bemerkungen über den Glaubenspunkt : Christus ist empfangen vom heil. Geist. In Henke's neuem Magazin, 3, 3. 399.

[3] Schleiermacher, über den Lukas, s. 26 f.

fall the curtain, and remarks, that the exact manner in which Mary was convinced that she should become the mother of the Messiah must be left historically undetermined; thus much only is certain, that Mary remained pure, for she could not with a clear conscience have stationed herself, as she afterwards did, under the Cross of her Son, had she felt that a reproach rested on her concerning the origin of the hopes she had entertained of him. The following is the only hint subsequently given of the particular view held by Paulus. It is probable, he thinks, that the angelic messenger visited Mary in the evening or even at night; indeed according to the correct reading of Luke i. 28, which has not the word angel, καὶ εἰσελθὼν πρὸς αὐτὴν εἶπε, without ὁ ἄγγελος, the evangelist here speaks only of some one who had come in. (As if in this case, the participle εἰσελθὼν must not necessarily be accompanied by τὶς ; or, in the absence of the pronoun be referred to the subject, the angel Gabriel—ὁ ἄγγελος Γαβριὴλ, v. 26 !) Paulus adds: that this visitant was the angel Gabriel was the subsequent suggestion of Mary's own mind, after she had heard of the vision of Zacharias.

Gabler, in a review of Paulus's Commentary [4] has fully exposed, with commensurate plainness of speech, the transaction which lies concealed under this explanation. It is impossible, says he, to imagine any other interpretation of Paulus's view than that some one passed himself off for the angel Gabriel, and as the pretended Messenger of God remained with Mary in order that she might become the mother of the Messiah. What! asks Gabler, is Mary, at the very time she is betrothed, to become pregnant by another, and is this to be called an innocent holy action, pleasing to God and irreproachable? Mary is here pourtrayed as a pious visionary, and the pretended messenger of heaven as a deceiver, or he too is a gross fanatic. The reviewer most justly considers such an assertion as revolting, if contemplated from the christian point of view; if from the scientific, as at variance both with the principles of interpretation and of criticism.

The author of the Natural History of the Great Prophet of Nazareth is, in this instance, to be considered as the most worthy interpreter of Paulus; for though the former could not, in this part of his work, have made use of Paulus's Commentary, yet, in exactly the same spirit, he unreservedly avows what the latter carefully veils. He brings into comparison a story in Josephus,[5] according to which, in the very time of Jesus, a Roman knight won the chaste wife of a Roman noble to his wishes, by causing her to be invited by a priest of Isis into the temple of the goddess, under the pretext that the god Anubis desired to embrace her. In innocence and faith, the woman resigned herself, and would perhaps afterwards have believed she had given birth to the child of a god, had not the intriguer, with bitter scorn, soon after discovered to her the true state of the case. It is the opinion of the author that Mary, the betrothed bride of the aged Joseph, was in like manner deceived by some amorous and fanatic young man (in the sequel to the history he represents him to be Joseph of Arimathea), and that she on her part, in perfect innocence, continued to deceive others.[6] It is evident that this interpretation does not differ from the ancient Jewish blasphemy, which we find in Celsus and in the Talmud; that Jesus falsely represented himself as born of a pure virgin, whereas, in fact, he was the offspring of the adultery of Mary with a certain Panthera.[7]

---

[4] Im neuesten theol. Journal, 7. Bd. 4. Stück, s. 407 f.

[5] Antiq. xviii. 3, 4.

[6] 1ter Theil, s. 140 ff.

[7] The legend has undergone various modifications, but the name of *Panthera* or *Pandira* has been uniformly retained. Vid. Origenes c. Cels. 1, 28. 32. Schöttgen, Horæ 2, 693 ff.

This whole view, of which the culminating point is in the calumny of the Jews, cannot be better judged than in the words of Origen. If, says this author, they wished to substitute something else in the place of the history of the supernatural conception of Jesus, they should at any rate have made it happen in a more probable manner; they ought not, as it were against their will, to admit that Mary knew not Joseph, but they might have denied this feature, and yet have allowed Jesus to have been born of an ordinary human marriage; whereas the forced and extravagant character of their hypothesis betrays its falsehood.[8] Is not this as much as to say, that if once some particular features of a marvellous narrative are doubted, it is inconsequent to allow others to remain unquestioned? each part of such an account ought to be subjected to critical examination. The correct view of the narrative before us is to be found, that is indirectly, in Origen. For when at one time he places together, as of the same kind, the miraculous conception of Jesus and the story of Plato's conception by Apollo (though here, indeed, the meaning is that only ill-disposed persons could doubt such things [9]), and when at another time he says of the story concerning Plato, that it belongs to those mythi by which it was sought to exhibit the distinguished wisdom and power of great men (but here he does not include the narrative of Jesus's conception), he in fact states the two premises, namely, the similarity of the two narratives and the mythical character of the one [10]; from which the inference of the merely mythical worth of the narrative of the conception of Jesus follows; a conclusion which can never indeed have occurred to his own mind.

§ 29.

HISTORY OF THE CONCEPTION OF JESUS VIEWED AS A MYTHUS.

If, says Gabler in his review of the Commentary of Paulus, we must relinquish the supernatural origin of Jesus, in order to escape the ridicule of our contemporaries, and if, on the other hand, the natural explanation leads to conclusions not only extravagant, but revolting; the adoption of the mythus, by which all these difficulties are obviated, is to be preferred. In the world of mythology many great men had extraordinary births, and were sons of the gods. Jesus himself spoke of his heavenly origin, and called God his father; besides, his title as Messiah was—Son of God. From Matthew i. 22, it is further evident that the passage of Isaiah, vii. 14, was referred to Jesus by the early Christian Church. In conformity with this passage the belief prevailed that Jesus, as the Messiah, should be born of a virgin by means of divine agency; it was therefore taken for granted that what was to be actually did occur; and thus originated a philosophical (dogmatical) mythus concerning the birth of Jesus. But according to historical truth, Jesus was the offspring of an ordinary marriage, between Joseph and Mary; an explanation which, it has been justly remarked, maintains at once the dignity of Jesus and the respect due to his mother.[1]

aus Tract. Sanhedrin u. A.; Eisenmenger, entdecktes Judenthum, 1, s. 105 ff. aus der Schmähschrift: Toledoth Jeschu; Thilo, cod. apocr. s. 528. Comp. my Abhandlung über die Namen Panther, Pantheras, Pandera, in jüdischen und patristischen Erzählungen von der Abstammung Jesu. Athenäum, Febr. 1839, s. 15 ff.

[8] Orig. c. Celsus i. 32.
[9] Ibid. vi. 8.
[10] Ibid. i. 37.
[1] Gabler, in seinem neuesten theol. Journal, 7, 4. s. 408 f; Eichhorn, Einleitung in das N. T. 1, s. 428 f.; Bauer, hebr. Mythol. 1, 192 e ff.; Kaiser, bibl. Theologie, 1, s. 231 f.;

The proneness of the ancient world to represent the great men and bene-factors of their race as the sons of the gods, has therefore been referred to, in order to explain the origin of such a mythus. Our theologians have accumulated examples from the Greco-Roman mythology and history. They have cited Hercules, and the Dioscuri; Romulus, and Alexander; but above all Pythagoras,[2] and Plato. Of the latter philosopher Jerome speaks in a manner quite applicable to Jesus: sapientiæ principem non aliter arbitrantur, nisi de partu virginis editum.[3]

From these examples it might have been inferred that the narratives of the supernatural conception had possibly originated in a similar tendency, and had no foundation in history. Here however the orthodox and the rationalists are unanimous in denying, though indeed upon different grounds, the validity of the analogy. Origen, from a perception of the identical character of the two classes of narratives, is not far from regarding the heathen legends of the sons of the gods as true supernatural histories. Paulus on his side is more decided, and is so logical as to explain both classes of narratives in the same manner, as natural, but still as true histories. At least he says of the narrative concerning Plato: it cannot be affirmed that the groundwork of the history was a subsequent creation; it is far more probable that Perictione believed herself to be pregnant by one of her gods. The fact that her son became a Plato might indeed have served to confirm that belief, but not to have originated it. Tholuck invites attention to the important distinction that the mythi concerning Romulus and others were formed many centuries after the lifetime of these men: the mythi concerning Jesus, on the contrary, must have existed shortly after his death.[4] He cleverly fails to remember the narrative of Plato's birth, since he is well aware that precisely in that particular, it is a dangerous point. Osiander however approaches the subject with much pathos, and affirms that Plato's apotheosis as son of Apollo did not exist till several centuries after him[5]; whereas in fact Plato's sister's son speaks of it as a prevailing legend in Athens.[6] Olshausen, with whom Neander coincides, refuses to draw any detrimental inference from this analogy of the mythical sons of the gods; remarking that though these narratives are un-historical, they evince a general anticipation and desire of such a fact, and therefore guarantee its reality, at least in one historical manifestation. Certainly, a general anticipation and representation must have truth for its basis; but the truth does not consist in any one individual fact, presenting an accurate correspondence with that notion, but in *an idea* which realizes itself in a series of facts, which often bear no resemblance to the general notion. The widely spread notion of a golden age does not prove the existence of a golden age: so the notion of divine conceptions does not prove that some one individual was thus produced. The truth which is the basis of this notion is something quite different.

A more essential objection[7] to the analogy is, that the representations of

Wegscheider, Instit. § 123; De Wette, bibl. Dogmat. § 281, und exeg. Handb. 1, 1, s. 18 f., Ammon, Fortbildung des Christenth. s. 201 ff.; Hase, L. J. § 33; Fritzsche, Comment. in Matth. s. 56. The latter justly remarks in the title to the first chapter: *non minus ille (Jesus) ut ferunt doctorum Judaicorum de Messiâ sententiæ, patrem habet spiritum divinum, matrem virginem.*

[2] Jamblich. vita Pythagoræ, cap. 2, ed. Kiessling.

[3] Adv. Jovin. 1, 26. Diog. Laërt., 3, 1, 2.

[4] Glaubwürdigkeit, s. 64.

[5] Apologie des L. J. s. 92.

[6] Diog. Laërt. a. a. O.: Σπεύσιππος (*Sororis Platonis filius*, Hieron.) δ' ἐν τῷ ἐπιγραφομένῳ Πλάτωνος περδείπνῳ καὶ Κλέαρχος ἐν τῷ Πλάτωνος ἐγκωμίῳ καὶ Ἀναξιλίδης ἐν τῷ δευτέρῳ περὶ φιλοσόφων, φασίν, Ἀθήνησιν ἦν λόγος, κ. τ. λ.

[7] Neander, L. J. Ch. s. 10.

the heathen world prove nothing with respect to the isolated Jews; and that the idea of sons of the gods, belonging to polytheism, could not have exerted an influence on the rigidly monotheistic notion of the Messiah.   At all events such an inference must not be too hastily drawn from the expression "sons of God," found likewise among the Jews, which as applied in the Old Testament to magistrates, (Ps. lxxxii. 6, or to theocratic kings, 2 Sam. vii. 14, Ps. ii. 7,) indicates only a theocratic, and not a physical or metaphysical relation.   Still less is importance to be attached to the language of flattery used by a Roman, in Josephus, who calls beautiful children of the Jewish princes children of God.[8]   It was, however, a notion among the Jews, as was remarked in a former section, that the Holy Spirit co-operated in the conception of pious individuals; moreover, that God's choicest instruments were conceived by divine assistance of parents, who could not have had a child according to the natural course of things.   And if, according to the believed representation, the extinct capability on both sides was renewed by divine intervention (Rom. iv. 19), it was only one step further to the belief that in the case of the conception of the most distinguished of all God's agents, the Messiah, the total absence of participation on the one side was compensated by a more complete superadded capability on the other.   The latter is scarcely a degree more marvellous than the former.   And thus must it have appeared to the author of Luke i., since he dissipates Mary's doubts by the same reply with which Jehovah repelled Sara's incredulity.[9]   Neither the Jewish reverence for marriage, nor the prevalent representation of the Messiah as a human being, could prevent the advance to this climax; to which, on the other hand, the ascetic estimation of celibacy, and the idea, derived from Daniel, of the Christ as a superhuman being, contributed.   But decided impulse to the development of the representations embodied in our histories of the birth, consisted partly in the title, *Son of God*, at one time usually given to the Messiah.   For it is the nature of such originally figurative expressions, after a while to come to be interpreted according to their more precise and literal signification; and it was a daily occurrence, especially among the later Jews, to attach a sensible signification to that which originally had merely a spiritual or figurative meaning.   This natural disposition to understand the Messianic title *Son of God* more and more literally, was fostered by the expression in the Psalms (ii. 7), interpreted of the Messiah : *Thou art my Son; this day have I begotten thee :* words which can scarcely fail to suggest a physical relation; it was also nurtured by the prophecy of Isaiah respecting the virgin who should be with child, which it appears was applied to the Messiah; as were so many other prophecies of which the immediate signification had become obscure.   This application may be seen in the Greek word chosen by the Septuagint, παρθένος, a pure unspotted virgin, whereas by Aquila and other Greek translators the word νεᾶνις is used.[10]   Thus did the notions of a *son of God* and a *son of a virgin* complete one another, till at last the divine agency was substituted for human paternal participation.   Wetstein indeed affirms that no Jew ever applied the prophecy of Isaiah to the Messiah; and it was with extreme labour that Schoettgen collected traces of the notion that the Messiah should be the son of a virgin from the Rabbinical writings.   This however, considering the paucity of records of the Messianic ideas of that age,[11] proves nothing in opposition to the presumption that a

---

[8] Antiq. 15. 2. 6.
[9] Gen. xviii., 14 Sept.   Luke i. 37.
   μὴ ἀδυνατήσει παρὰ τῷ θεῷ ῥῆμα ;   ὅτι οὐκ ἀδυνατήσει παρὰ τῷ θεῷ πᾶν ῥῆμα.
[10] De Wette, Exeg. Handb. I, I, s. 17.
[11] They are to be found however in the more modern Rabbins, s. Matthæi, Religionsgl. der Apostel 2, a. s. 555 ff.

notion then prevailed, of which we have the groundwork in the Old Testament, and an inference hardly to be mistaken in the New.

One objection yet remains, which I can no longer designate as peculiar to Olshausen, since other theologians have shown themselves solicitous of sharing the fame. The objection is, that the mythical interpretation of the gospel narrative is especially dangerous, it being only too well fitted to engender, obscurely indeed, profane and blasphemous notions concerning the origin of Jesus ; since it cannot fail to favour an opinion destructive of the belief in a Redeemer, namely, that Jesus came into being through unholy means ; since, in fact, at the time of her pregnancy Mary was not married.[12] In Olshausen's first edition of his work, he adds that he willingly allows that these interpreters know not what they do : it is therefore but just to give him the advantage of the same concession, since he certainly appears not to know what mythical interpretation means. How otherwise would he say, that the mythical interpretation is fitted only to favour a blasphemous opinion ; therefore that all who understand the narrative mythically, are disposed to commit the absurdity with which Origen reproaches the Jewish calumniators ; the retaining one solitary incident, namely, that Mary was not married, whilst the remainder of the narrative is held to be unhistorical ; a particular incident which evidently serves only as a support to the other, that Jesus was conceived without human paternal participation, and with it, therefore, stands or falls. No one among the interpreters who, in this narrative, recognise a mythus, in the full signification of that term, has been thus blind and inconsequent ; all have supposed a legitimate marriage between Joseph and Mary ; and Olshausen merely paints the mythical mode of interpretation in caricature, in order the more easily to set it aside ; for he confesses that in relation to this portion of the Gospel in particular, it has much that is dazzling.

§ 30.

RELATION OF JOSEPH TO MARY—BROTHERS OF JESUS.

Our Gospels, in the true spirit of the ancient legend, find it unbecoming to allow the mother of Jesus, so long as she bore the heavenly germ, to be approached or profaned by an earthly husband. Consequently Luke (ii. 5) represents the connexion between Joseph and Mary, prior to the birth of Jesus, as a betrothment merely. And, as it is stated respecting the father of Plato, after his wife had become pregnant by Apollo : ὅθεν καθαρὰν γάμου φυλάξαι ἕως τῆς ἀποκυήσεως,[1] so likewise it is remarked of Joseph in Matthew (i. 25) : καὶ οὐκ ἐγίνωσκεν αὐτὴν (τὴν γυναῖκα αὐτοῦ) ἕως οὗ ἔτεκε τὸν υἱὸν αὐτῆς τὸν πρωτότοκον. In each of these kindred passages the Greek word ἕως (till) must evidently receive the same interpretation. Now in the first quotation the meaning is incontestably this :—that till the time of Plato's birth his father abstained from intercourse with his wife, but subsequently assumed his conjugal rights, since we hear of Plato's brothers. In reference, therefore, to the parents of Jesus, the ἕως cannot have a different signification ; in each case it indicates precisely the same limitation. So again the expression πρωτότοκος (firstborn) used in reference to Jesus in both the Gospels (Matt. i. 25, Luke ii. 7) supposes that Mary had other children, for as Lucian says : εἰ μὲν πρῶτος, οὐ μόνος· εἰ δὲ μόνος, οὐ πρῶτος.[2] Even in the same Gospels (Matt. xiii. 55,

---

[12] Bibl. Comm. I, s. 47. Also Daub. 2 a. s. 311 f ; Theile, § 14. Neander, s. 9.
[1] Diog. Laërt. a. a. O. See Origenes c. Cels. I, 37.
[2] Demonax, 29.

Luke viii. 19) mention is made of ἀδελφοῖς Ἰησοῦ (*the brothers of Jesus*). In the words of Fritzsche : *Lubentissime post Jesu natales Mariam concessit Matthæus* (Luke does the same) *uxorem Josepho, in hoc uno occupatus, ne quis ante Jesu primordia mutuâ venere usos suspicaretur.* But this did not continue to satisfy the orthodox ; as the veneration for Mary rose even higher, she who had once become fruitful by divine agency was not subsequently to be profaned by the common relations of life.[3] The opinion that Mary after the birth of Jesus became the wife of Joseph, was early ranked among the heresies,[4] and the orthodox Fathers sought every means to escape from it and to combat it. They contended that according to the exegetical interpretation of ἕως οὗ, it sometimes affirmed or denied a thing, not merely up to a certain limit, but beyond that limitation and for ever ; and that the words of Matthew οὐκ ἐγίνωσκεν αὐτὴν ἕως οὗ ἔτεκε κ. τ. λ. excluded a matrimonial connexion between Joseph and Mary for all time.[5] In like manner it was asserted of the term πρωτότοκος, that it did not necessarily include the subsequent birth of other children, but that it merely excluded any previous birth.[6] But in order to banish the thought of a matrimonial connexion between Mary and Joseph, not only grammatically but physiologically, they represented Joseph as a very old man, under whom Mary was placed for control and protection only ; and the brothers of Jesus mentioned in the New Testament they regarded as the children of Joseph by a former marriage.[7] But this was not all ; soon it was insisted not only that Mary never became the wife of Joseph, but that in giving birth to Jesus she did not lose her virginity.[8] But even the conservation of Mary's virginity did not long continue to satisfy : perpetual virginity was likewise required on the part of Joseph. It was not enough that he had no connexion with Mary ; it was also necessary that his entire life should be one of celibacy. Accordingly, though Epiphanius allows that Joseph had sons by a former marriage, Jerome rejects the supposition as an impious and audacious invention ; and from that time the brothers of Jesus were degraded to the rank of cousins.[9]

Some modern theologians agree with the Fathers of the Church in maintaining that no matrimonial connexion subsisted at any time between Joseph and Mary, and believe themselves able to explain the gospel expressions which appear to assert the contrary. In reference to the term *firstborn*, Olshausen contends that it signifies an only son: no less than the eldest of several. Paulus allows that here he is right, and Clemen [10] and Fritzsche seek in vain to demonstrate the impossibility of this signification. For when it is said in Ex. xiii. 2, קַדֶּשׁ־לִי כָל־בְּכוֹר פֶּטֶר כָּל־רֶחֶם (πρωτότοκον πρωτογενὲς LXX.) it was not merely a firstborn followed by others subsequently born, who was sanctified to Jehovah, but the fruit of the body of that mother of whom no

---

[3] S. Origenes in Matthæum, Opp. ed. de la Rue, Vol. 3. s. 463.

[4] The Arian Eunomius according to Photius taught τὸν Ἰωσὴφ μετὰ τὴν ἄφραστον κυοφορίαν συνάπτεσθαι τῇ παρθένῳ. This was also, according to Epiphanius, the doctrine of those called by him Dimaerites and Antidicomarianites, and in the time of Jerome, of Helvidius and his followers. Compare on this point the Sammlung von Suicer, im Thesaurus ii., s. v. Μαρία, fol. 305 f.

[5] Comp. Hieron. adv. Helv. 6, 7, Theophylact and Suidas in Suicer, 1, s. v. ἕως, fol. 1294 f.

[6] Hieron. z. d. St.

[7] See Orig. in Matth. Tom. 10, 17 ; Epiphan. haeres. 78, 7 ; Historia Josephi, c. 2 ; Protev. Jac. 9. 18.

[8] Chrysostomus, hom. 142, in Suicer, s. v. Μαρία, most repulsively described in the Protev. Jac. xix. and xx.

[9] Hieron. ad Matth. 12, und advers. Helvid. 19.

[10] Die Brüder Jesu. In Winer's Zeitschrift für wissenschaftliche Theologie, 1, 3. s. 364 f.

other child had previously been born. Therefore the term πρωτότοκος must of necessity bear also this signification. Truly however we must confess with Winer [11] and others, on the other side, that if a narrator who was acquainted with the whole sequel of the history used that expression, we should be tempted to understand it in its primitive sense ; since had the author intended to exclude other children, he would rather have employed the word μονογενής, or would have connected it with πρωτότοκος. If this be not quite decisive, the reasoning of Fritzsche in reference to the ἕως οὗ, κ. τ. λ., is more convincing. He rejects the citations adduced in support of the interpretation of the Fathers of the Church, proving that this expression according to its primitive signification affirms only to a given limit, and beyond that limit supposes the logical opposite of the affirmation to take place ; a signification which it loses only when the context shows clearly that the opposite is impossible in the nature of things. [12] For example, when it is said οὐκ ἐγίνωσκεν αὐτὴν, ἕως οὗ ἀπέθανεν, it is self-evident that the negation, during the time elapsed till death—cannot be transformed after death into an affirmation ; but when it is said, as in Matthew, οὐκ ἐ. ἀ. ἕως οὗ ἔτεκεν, the giving birth to the divine fruit opposes no impossibility to the establishment of the conjugal relations ; on the contrary it renders it possible, i.e. suitable [13] for them now to take place.

Olshausen, impelled by the same doctrinal motives which influenced the Fathers, is led in this instance to contradict both the evidence of grammar and of logic. He thinks that Joseph, without wishing to impair the sanctity of marriage, must have concluded after the experiences he had had (?) that his marriage with Mary had another object than the production of children ; besides it was but natural (?) in the last descendant of the house of David, and of that particular branch from which the Messiah should come forth, to terminate her race in this last and eternal offshoot.

A curious ladder may be formed of these different beliefs and superstitions in relation to the connexion between Mary and Joseph.

1. Contemporaries of Jesus and composers of the genealogies : Joseph and Mary man and wife—Jesus the offspring of their marriage.

2. The age and authors of our histories of the birth of Jesus : Mary and Joseph betrothed only ; Joseph having no participation in the conception of the child, and previous to his birth no conjugal connexion with Mary.

3. Olshausen and others : subsequent to the birth of Jesus, Joseph, though then the husband of Mary, relinquishes his matrimonial rights.

4. Epiphanius, Protevangelium Jacobi and others : Joseph a decrepit old man, no longer to be thought of as a husband : the children attributed to him are of a former marriage. More especially it is not as a bride and wife that he receives Mary ; he takes her merely under his guardianship.

5. Protevang., Chrysostom and others : Mary's virginity was not only not destroyed by any subsequent births of children by Joseph, it was not in the slightest degree impaired by the birth of Jesus.

6. Jerome : not Mary only but Joseph also observed an absolute virginity, and the pretended brothers of Jesus were not his sons but merely cousins to Jesus.

[11] Biblisches Realwörterbuch, 1 Bd. s. 664, Anm. De Wette, z. d. St. Neander L. J. Ch., s. 34.

[12] Comment. in Matth. s. 53 ff., vgl. auch s. 835.

[13] Olshausen is exceedingly unhappy in the example chosen by him in support of his interpretation of ἕως οὗ. For when it is said, *we waited till midnight but no one came*, certainly this by no means implies that after midnight some one did come, but it does imply that after midnight we waited no longer ; so that here the expression *till* retains its signification of exclusion.

The opinion that the ἀδελφοὶ (brothers) and ἀδελφαὶ Ἰησοῦ (sisters of Jesus) mentioned in the New Testament, were merely half brothers or indeed cousins, appears in its origin, as shown above, together with the notion that no matrimonial connexion ever subsisted between Joseph and Mary, as the mere invention of superstition, a circumstance highly prejudicial to such an opinion. It is however no less true that purely exegetical grounds exist, in virtue of which theologians who were free from prejudice have decided, that the opinion that Jesus actually had brothers is untenable.[14]   Had we merely the following passages—Matt. xiii. 55, Mark vi. 3, where the people of Nazareth, astonished at the wisdom of their countryman, in order to mark his well known origin, immediately after having spoken of τέκτων (the carpenter) his father, and his mother Mary, mention by name his ἀδελφοὺς (brothers) James, Joses, Simon, and Judas, together with his sisters whose names are not given [15]; again Matt. xii. 46, Luke viii. 19, when his mother and his brethren come to Jesus ; John ii. 12, where Jesus journeys with his mother and his brethren to Capernaum ; Acts i. 14, where they are mentioned in immediate connexion with his mother —if we had these passages only, we could not for a moment hesitate to recognize here real brothers of Jesus at least on the mother's side, children of Joseph and Mary ; not only on account of the proper signification of the word ἀδελφὸς, but also in consequence of its continual conjunction with Mary and Joseph. Even the passages—John vii. 5, in which it is remarked that his brethren did not believe on Jesus, and Mark iii. 21, compared with 31, where, according to the most probable explanation, the brothers of Jesus with his mother went out to lay hold of him as one beside himself—furnish no adequate grounds for relinquishing the proper signification of ἀδελφὸς.   Many theologians have interpreted ἀδελφοὺς Ἰησοῦ in the last cited passage *half brothers, sons of Joseph by a former marriage*, alleging that the real brothers of Jesus must have believed on him, but this is a mere assumption.   The difficulty seems greater when we read in John xix. 26 f. that Jesus, on the cross, enjoined John to be a son to his mother ; an injunction it is not easy to regard as suitable under the supposition that Mary had other children, except indeed these were half-brothers and unfriendly to Jesus.   Nevertheless we can imagine the existence both of external circumstances and of individual feelings which might have influenced Jesus to confide his mother to John rather than to his brothers. That these brothers appeared in company with his apostles after the ascension (Acts i. 14) is no proof that they must have believed on Jesus at the time of his death.

The real perplexity in the matter, however, originates in this : that besides the James and Joses spoken of as the brothers of Jesus, two men of the same name are mentioned as the sons of another Mary (Mark xv. 40, 47, xvi. 1, Matt. xxvii. 56), without doubt that Mary who is designated, John xix. 25, as the sister of the mother of Jesus, and the wife of Cleophas ; so that we have a James and a Joses not only among the children of Mary the mother of Jesus, but again among her sister's children.   We meet with several others among those immediately connected with Jesus, whose names are identical.   In the lists of the apostles (Matt. x. 2 ff., Luke vi. 14 ff.) we have two more of the name of James : that is four, the brother and cousin of Jesus included ; two more of the name of Judas : that is three, the brother of Jesus included ; two of the name of Simon, also making three with the brother of Jesus of the

[14] On this subject compare in particular Clemen, die Brüder Jesu, in Winer's Zeitschrift für wiss. Theol. 1, 3, s. 329 ff. ; Paulus, Exeg. Handbuch, 1 Bd. s. 557 ff. ; Fritzsche, a. a. O. s. 480 ff. ; Winer, bibl. Realwörterbuch, in den A. A. ; Jesus, Jacobus, Apostel.
[15] See the different names assigned them in the legend in Thilo, Codex apocryphus N. T., 1, s. 360 note.

same name. The question naturally arises, whether the same individual is not here taken as distinct persons? The suspicion is almost unavoidable in reference to James. As James the son of Alpheus is, in the list of the apostles, introduced after the son of Zebedee, as the second, perhaps the younger ; and as James the cousin of Jesus is called ὁ μικρὸς ("the less") Mark xv. 40 ; and since by comparing John xix. 25, we find that the latter is called the son of Cleophas, it is possible that the name Κλωπᾶς (Cleophas) given to the husband of Mary's sister, and the name Ἀλφαῖος (Alpheus) given to the father of the apostle, may be only different forms of the Hebrew חלפי. Thus would the second James enumerated among the apostles and the cousin of Jesus of that name be identical, and there would remain besides him only the son of Zebedee and the brother of Jesus. Now in the Acts (xv. 13) a James appears who takes a prominent part in the so-called apostolic council, and as, according to Acts xii. 2, the son of Zebedee had previously been put to death, and as in the foregoing portion of the book of the Acts no mention is made of any other James besides the son of Alpheus (i. 13), so this James, of whom (Acts xv. 13) no more precise description is given, can be no other than the son of Alpheus. But Paul speaks of a James (Gal. i. 19) *the Lord's brother*, whom he saw at Jerusalem, and it is doubtless he of whom he speaks in connexion with Cephas and John as the στύλοι (pillars) of the church—for this is precisely in character with the (Apostle) James as he appeared at the apostolic council—so that this James may be considered as identical with the Lord's brother, and the rather as the expression ἕτερον δὲ τῶν ἀποστόλων οὐκ εἶδον, εἰ μὴ Ἰάκωβον τὸν ἀδελφὸν τοῦ Κυρίου (*but other of the apostles saw I none, save James the Lord's brother.* Gal. i. 19), makes it appear as if the Lord's brother were reckoned among the apostles ; with which also the ancient tradition which represents James the Just, a brother of Jesus, as the first head of the church at Jerusalem, agrees.[16] But admitting the James of the Acts to be identical with the distinguished apostle of that name, then is he the son of Alpheus, and not the son of Joseph ; consequently if he be at the same time ἀδελφὸς τοῦ Κυρίου, then ἀδελφὸς cannot signify a brother. Now if Alpheus and Cleophas are admitted to be the same individual, the husband of the sister of Mary the mother of Jesus, it is obvious that ἀδελφὸς, used to denote the relationship of his son to Jesus, must be taken in the signification, cousin. If, after this manner, James the Apostle the son of Alpheus be identified with the cousin, and the cousin be identified with the brother of Jesus of the same name, it is obvious that Ἰούδας Ἰακώβου in the catalogue of the Apostles in Luke (Luke vi. 16, Acts i. 13), must be translated *brother of James* (son of Alpheus) ; and this Apostle Jude must be held as identical with the Jude ἀδελφὸς Ἰησοῦ, that is, with the cousin of the Lord and son of Mary Cleophas (though the name of Jude is never mentioned in connexion with this Mary). If the Epistle of Jude in our canon be authentic, it is confirmatory of the above deduction, that the author (verse 1) designates himself as the ἀδελφὸς Ἰακώβου (*brother of James*). Some moreover have identified the Apostle Simon ὁ ζηλωτὴς or Κανανίτης (*Zelotes, or the Canaanite*) with the Simon enumerated among the brothers of Jesus (Mark vi. 3), and who according to a tradition of the church succeeded James as head of the church at Jerusalem [17] ; so that Joses alone appears without further designation or appellative.

If, accordingly, those spoken of as ἀδελφοὶ Ἰησοῦ were merely cousins, and three of these were apostles, it must excite surprise that not only in the Acts (i. 14), after an enumeration of the apostles, the brothers of Jesus are separ-

---

[16] Euseb. H. E. 2, 1.
[17] Euseb. H. E. 3, 11.

ately particularized, but that also (1 Cor. ix. 5) they appear to be a class distinct from the apostles. Perhaps, also, the passage Gal. i. 19 ought to be understood as indicating that James, the Lord's brother, was not an apostle.[18] If, therefore, the ἀδελφοὶ Ἰησοῦ seem thus to be extruded from the number of the apostles, it is yet more difficult to regard them merely as the cousins of Jesus, since they appear in so many places immediately associated with the mother of Jesus, and in two or three passages only are two men bearing the same names mentioned in connexion with the other Mary, who accordingly would be their real mother. The Greek word ἀδελφὸς may indeed signify, in language which pretends not to precision, as well as the Hebrew אח, a more distant relative; but as it is repeatedly used to express the relationship of these persons to Jesus, and is in no instance replaced by ἀνεψιὸς—a word which is not foreign to the New Testament language when the relationship of cousin is to be denoted (Col. iv. 10), it cannot well be taken in any other than its proper signification. Further, it need only be pointed out that the highest degree of uncertainty exists respecting not only the identity of the names Alpheus and Cleophas, upon which the identity of James the cousin of Jesus and of the Apostle James the Less rests, but also regarding the translation of Ἰούδας Ἰακώβου by the *brother of James*; and likewise respecting the assumed identity of the author of the last Catholic Epistle with the Apostle Jude.

Thus the web of this identification gives way at all points, and we are forced back to the position whence we set out; so that we have again real brothers of Jesus, also two cousins distinct from these brothers, though bearing the same names with two of them, besides some apostles of the same names with both brothers and cousins. To find two pairs of sons of the same names in a family is, indeed, not so uncommon as to become a source of objection. It is, however, remarkable that the same James who in the Epistle to the Galatians is designated ἀδελφὸς Κυρίου (*the Lord's brother*), must unquestionably, according to the Acts of the Apostles, be regarded as the son of Alpheus; which he could not be if this expression signified a brother. So that there is perplexity on every side, which can be solved only (and then, indeed, but negatively and without historical result) by admitting the existence of obscurity and error on this point in the New Testament writers, and even in the very earliest Christian traditions; error which, in matters of involved relationships and family names, is far more easily fallen into than avoided.[19]

We have consequently no ground for denying that the mother of Jesus bore her husband several other children besides Jesus, younger, and perhaps also older; the latter, because the representation in the New Testament that Jesus was the first-born may belong no less to the mythus than the representation of the Fathers that he was an only son.

§ 31.

VISIT OF MARY TO ELIZABETH.

The angel who announced to Mary her own approaching pregnancy, at the same time informed her (Luke i. 36) of that of her relative Elizabeth, with whom it was already the sixth month. Hereupon Mary immediately set out on a journey to her cousin, a visit which was attended by extraordinary occurrences; for when Elizabeth heard the salutation of Mary, the babe leaped in her womb for joy; she also became inspired, and in her exultation poured

[18] Fritzsche, Comm. in Matth. p. 482.
[19] Theile, Biographie Jesu, § 18.

forth an address to Mary as the future mother of the Messiah, to which Mary responded by a hymn of praise (Luke i. 39–56).

The rationalistic interpreter believes it to be an easy matter to give a natural explanation of this narrative of the Gospel of Luke. He is of opinion [1] that the unknown individual who excited such peculiar anticipations in Mary, had at the same time acquainted her with the similar situation of her cousin Elizabeth. This it was which impelled Mary the more strongly to confer on the subject with her older relative. Arrived at her cousin's dwelling, she first of all made known what had happened to herself; but upon this the narrator is silent, not wishing to repeat what he had just before described. And here the Rationalist not only supposes the address of Elizabeth to have been preceded by some communication from Mary, but imagines Mary to have related her history piecemeal, so as to allow Elizabeth to throw in sentences during the intervals. The excitement of Elizabeth—such is the continuation of the rationalistic explanation—communicated itself, according to natural laws, to the child, who, as is usual with an embryo of six months, made a movement, which was first regarded by the mother as significant, and as the consequence of the salutation, after Mary's farther communications. Just as natural does it appear to the Rationalist that Mary should have given utterance to her Messianic expectations, confirmed as they were by Elizabeth, in a kind of psalmodic recitative, composed of reminiscences borrowed from various parts of the Old Testament.

But there is much in this explanation which positively contradicts the text. In the first place, that Elizabeth should have learned the heavenly message imparted to Mary from Mary herself. There is no trace in the narrative either of any communication preceding Elizabeth's address, or of interruptions occasioned by farther explanations on the part of Mary. On the contrary, as it is a supernatural revelation which acquaints Mary with the pregnancy of Elizabeth, so also it is to a revelation that Elizabeth's immediate recognition of Mary, as the chosen mother of the Messiah, is attributed.[2] As little will the other feature of this narrative—that the entrance of the mother of the Messiah occasioned a responsive movement in his mother's womb on the part of his forerunner—bear a natural explanation. In modern times, indeed, even orthodox interpreters have inclined to this explanation, but with the modification, that Elizabeth in the first place received a revelation, in which however the child, owing to the mother's excitement, a matter to be physiologically explained, likewise took part.[3] But the record does not represent the thing as if the excitement of the mother were the determining cause of the movement of the child; on the contrary (v. 41), the emotion of the mother follows the movement of the child, and Elizabeth's own account states, that it was the salutation of Mary (v. 44), not indeed from its particular signification, but merely as the voice of the mother of the Messiah, which produced the movement of the unborn babe : undeniably assuming something supernatural. And indeed the supranaturalistic view of this miracle is not free from objection, even on its own ground ; and hence the anxiety of the above-mentioned modern orthodox interpreters to evade it. It may be possible to conceive the human mind immediately acted upon by the divine mind, to which it is related, but how solve the difficulty of an immediate communication of the divine mind to an unintelligent embryo? And if we inquire the object of so strange a miracle, none which is worthy presents itself. Should

[1] Paulus, exeg. Handb. 1. a, s. 120 ff.
[2] S. Olshausen und de Wette, z. d. St.
[3] Hess, Geschichte Jesu, 1, s. 26 ; Olshausen, bibl. Comm. z. d. St. ; Hoffmann, s. 226 ; Lange, s. 76 ff.

it be referred to the necessity that the Baptist should receive the earliest possible intimation of the work to which he was destined ; still we know not how such an impression could have been made upon an embryo. Should the purpose be supposed to centre in the other individuals, in Mary or Elizabeth ; they had been the recipients of far higher revelations, and were consequently already possessed of an adequate measure of insight and faith.

No fewer difficulties oppose the rationalistic than the supranaturalistic explanation of the hymn pronounced by Mary. For though it is not, like the Canticle of Zacharias (v. 67) and the address of Elizabeth (v. 41), introduced by the formula ἐπλήσθη πνεύματος ἁγίου, *she was filled with the Holy Ghost*, still the similarity of these utterances is so great, that the omission cannot be adduced as a proof that the narrator did not intend to represent this, equally with the other two, as the operation of the πνεῦμα (spirit). But apart from the intention of the narrator, can it be thought natural that two friends visiting one another should, even in the midst of the most extraordinary occurrences, break forth into long hymns, and that their conversation should entirely lose the character of dialogue, the natural form on such occasions ? By a supernatural influence alone could the minds of the two friends be attuned to a state of elevation, so foreign to their every-day life. But if, indeed, Mary's hymn is to be understood as the work of the Holy Spirit, it is surprising that a speech emanating immediately from the divine source of inspiration should not be more striking for its originality, but should be so interlarded with reminiscences from the Old Testament, borrowed from the song of praise spoken by the mother of Samuel (1 Sam. ii.) under analogous circumstances.[4] Accordingly we must admit that the compilation of this hymn, consisting of recollections from the Old Testament, was put together in a natural way ; but allowing its composition to have been perfectly natural, it cannot be ascribed to the artless Mary, but to him who poetically wrought out the tradition in circulation respecting the scene in question.

Since then we find all the principal incidents of this visit inconceivable according to the supernatural interpretation ; also that they will not bear a natural explanation ; we are led to seek a mythical exposition of this as well as the preceding portions of the gospel history. This path has already been entered upon by others. The view of this narrative given by the anonymous E. F. in Henke's Magazine [5] is, that it does not pourtray events as they actually did occur, but as they might have occurred ; that much which the sequel taught of the destiny of their sons was carried back into the speeches of these women, which were also enriched by other features gleaned from tradition ; that a true fact however lies at the bottom, namely an actual visit of Mary to Elizabeth, a joyous conversation, and the expression of gratitude to God ; all which might have happened solely in virtue of the high importance attached by Orientals to the joys of maternity, even though the two mothers had been at that time ignorant of the destination of their children. This author is of opinion that Mary, when pondering over at a later period the remarkable life of her son, may often have related the happy meeting with her cousin and

[4] Compare   Luke i. 47 with 1 Sam. ii. 1.
                     i. 49   ii. 2.
                     i. 51   ii. 3, 4.
                     i. 52   ii. 8.
                     i. 53   ii. 5.
Particularly Luke i. 48 with 1 Sam. i. 11.
Compare   Luke i. 50   Deut. vii. 9.
                     i. 52   Ecclesiasticus x. 14.
                     i. 54   Ps. xcviii. 3.
[5] 5 Band, 1. Stück, s. 161. f.

their mutual expressions of thankfulness to God, and that thus the history gained currency. Horst also, who has a just conception of the fictitious nature of this section in Luke, and ably refutes the natural mode of explanation, yet himself slides unawares half-way back into it. He thinks it not improbable that Mary during her pregnancy, which was in many respects a painful one, should have visited her older and more experienced cousin, and that Elizabeth should during this visit have felt the first movement of her child: an occurrence which as it was afterwards regarded as ominous, was preserved by the oral tradition.[6]

These are farther examples of the uncritical proceeding which pretends to disengage the mythical and poetical from the narrative, by plucking away a few twigs and blossoms of that growth, whilst it leaves the very root of the mythus undisturbed as purely historical. In our narrative the principal mythical feature (the remainder forms only its adjuncts) is precisely that which the above-mentioned authors, in their pretended mythical explanations, retain as historical: namely, the visit of Mary to the pregnant Elizabeth. For, as we have already seen, the main tendency of the first chapter of Luke is to magnify Jesus by connecting the Baptist with him from the earliest possible point in a relation of inferiority. Now this object could not be better attained than by bringing about a meeting, not in the first instance of the sons, but of the mothers in reference to their sons, during their pregnancy, at which meeting some occurrence which should prefigure the future relative positions of these two men should take place. Now the more apparent the existence of a dogmatical motive as the origin of this visit, the less probability is there that it had an historical foundation. With this principal feature the other details are connected in the following order:—The visit of the two women must be represented as possible and probable by the feature of family relationship between Mary and Elizabeth (v. 36), which would also give a greater suitability to the subsequent connexion of the sons. Further, a visit, so full of import, made precisely at that time, must have taken place by special divine appointment; therefore it is an angel who refers Mary to her cousin. At the visit the subservient position of the Baptist to Jesus is to be particularly exhibited;—this could have been effected by the mother, as indeed it is, in her address to Mary, but it were better if possible that the future Baptist himself should give a sign. The mutual relation of Esau and Jacob had been prefigured by their struggles and position in their mother's womb (Gen. xxv. 22 ff.). But, without too violent an offence against the laws of probability, an ominous movement would not be attributed to the child prior to that period of her pregnancy at which the motion of the fœtus is felt; hence the necessity that Elizabeth should be in the sixth month of her pregnancy when Mary, in consequence of the communication of the angel, set out to visit her cousin (v. 36). Thus, as Schleiermacher remarks,[7] the whole arrangement of times had reference to the particular circumstance the author desired to contrive—the joyous responsive movement of the child in his mother's womb at the moment of Mary's entrance. To this end only must Mary's visit be delayed till after the fifth month; and the angel not appear to her before that period.

Thus not only does the visit of Mary to Elizabeth with all the attendant circumstances disappear from the page of history, but the historical validity of the further details—that John was only half a year older than Jesus; that the two mothers were related; that an intimacy subsisted between the families;—cannot be affirmed on the testimony of Luke, unsupported by other authorities: indeed, the contrary rather will be found substantiated in the course of our critical investigations.

[6] In Henke's Museum, 1, 4, s. 725.   [7] Ueber den Lukas, s. 23 f.

CHAPTER IV.

BIRTH AND EARLIEST EVENTS OF THE LIFE OF JESUS.

---

§ 32.

THE CENSUS.

WITH respect to the birth of Jesus, Matthew and Luke agree in representing it as taking place at Bethlehem; but whilst the latter enters into a minute detail of all the attendant circumstances, the former merely mentions the event as it were incidentally, referring to it once in an appended sentence as the sequel to what had gone before (i. 25), and again as a presupposed occurrence (ii. 1). The one Evangelist seems to assume that Bethlehem was the habitual residence of the parents; but according to the other they are led thither by very particular circumstances. This point of difference between the Evangelists however can only be discussed after we shall have collected more data; we will therefore leave it for the present, and turn our attention to an error into which Luke, when compared with himself and with dates otherwise ascertained, seems to have fallen. This is the statement, that the census, decreed by Augustus at the time when Cyrenius (Quirinus) was governor of Syria, was the occasion of the journey of the parents of Jesus, who usually resided at Nazareth, to Bethlehem where Jesus was born (Luke ii. 1 ff.).

The first difficulty is that the ἀπογραφὴ (namely, the inscription of the name and amount of property in order to facilitate the taxation) commanded by Augustus, is extended to *all the world*, πᾶσαν τὴν οἰκουμένην. This expression, in its common acceptation at that time, would denote the *orbis Romanus*. But ancient authors mention no such general census decreed by Augustus; they speak only of the assessment of single provinces decreed at different times. Consequently, it was said Luke meant to indicate by οἰκουμένη merely the land of Judea, and not the Roman world according to its ordinary signification. Examples were forthwith collected in proof of the possibility of such an interpretation,[1] but they in fact prove nothing. For supposing it could not be shown that in all these citations from the Septuagint, Josephus, and the New Testament, the expression really does signify, in the extravagant sense of these writers, the whole known world; still in the instance in question, where the subject is a decree of the Roman emperor, πᾶσα ἡ οἰκουμένη must necessarily be understood of the regions which he governed, and therefore of the *orbis Romanus*. This is the reason that latterly the opposite side has been taken up, and it has been maintained, upon the authority of Savigny, that in the time of Augustus a census of the

---

[1] Olshausen, Paulus, Kuinöl.

whole empire was actually undertaken.[2] This is positively affirmed by late
Christian writers [3] : but the statement is rendered suspicious by the absence
of all more ancient testimony [4]; and it is even contradicted by the fact, that
for a considerable lapse of time an equal assessment throughout the empire
was not effected. Finally, the very expressions of these writers show that
their testimony rests upon that of Luke.[5] But, it is said, Augustus at all
events attempted an equal assessment of the empire by means of an universal census ; and he began the carrying out his project by an assessment of
individual provinces, but he left the further execution and completion to his
successors.[6] Admit that the gospel term δόγμα (decree) may be interpreted
as a mere design, or, as Hoffmann thinks, an undetermined project expressed
in an imperial decree ; still the fulfilment of this project in Judea at the time
of the birth of Jesus was impossible.

Matthew places the birth of Jesus shortly before the death of Herod the
Great, whom he represents (ii. 19) as dying during the abode of Jesus in
Egypt. Luke says the same indirectly, for when speaking of the announcement of the birth of the Baptist, he refers it to the days of Herod the Great,
and he places the birth of Jesus precisely six months later ; so that according
to Luke, also, Jesus was born, if not, like John, previous to the death of
Herod I., shortly after that event. Now, after the death of Herod the
country of Judea fell to his son Archelaus (Matt. ii. 22), who, after a reign
of something less than ten years, was deposed and banished by Augustus,[7]
at which time Judea was first constituted a Roman province, and began to
be ruled by Roman functionaries.[8] Thus the Roman census in question must
have been made either under Herod the Great, or at the commencement of
the reign of Archelaus. This is in the highest degree improbable, for in those
countries which were not reduced in formam provinciæ, but were governed by
regibus sociis, the taxes were levied by these princes, who paid a tribute to the
Romans [9]; and this was the state of things in Judea prior to the deposition
of Archelaus. It has been the object of much research to make it appear
probable that Augustus decreed a census, as an extraordinary measure, in
Palestine under Herod. Attention has been directed to the circumstance
that the breviarium imperii, which Augustus left behind him, contained the
financial state of the whole empire, and it has been suggested that, in order
to ascertain the financial condition of Palestine, he caused a statement to be
prepared by Herod.[10] Reference has been made first to the record of
Josephus, that on account of some disturbance of the relations between Herod

[2] Tholuck, s. 194 ff. Neander, s. 19.
[3] Cassiodor. Variarum, 3, 52. Isidor. Orig. 5, 36.
[4] To refer here to the Monumentum Ancyranum, which is said to record a census of the
whole empire in the year of Rome 746 (Osiander, p. 95), is proof of the greatest carelessness.
For he who examines this inscription will find mention only of three assessments census
civium Romanorum, which Suetonius designates census populi, and of which Dio Cassius
speaks, at least of one of them, as ἀπογραφὴ τῶν ἐν τῇ Ἰταλίᾳ κατοικούντων. See Ideler,
Chronol. 2, s. 339.
[5] In the authoritative citations in Suidas are the words taken from Luke, αὕτη ἡ ἀπογραφὴ
πρώτη ἐγένετο.
[6] Hoffmann, s. 231.
[7] Joseph. Antiq. 17, 13, 2. B. j. 2, 7, 3.
[8] Antiq. 17, 13, 5. 18, 1, 1. B. j. 2, 8, 1.
[9] Paulus, exeg. Handb. I, a, s. 171. Winer, bibl. Realwörterbuch.
[10] Tacit. Annal. I, 11. Sueton. Octav. 191. But if in this document opes publicæ con-
tinebantur : quantum civium sociorumque in armis ; quot classes, regna, provinciæ, tributa
aut vectigalia, et necessitates ac largitiones : the number of troops and the sum which the
Jewish prince had to furnish, might have been given without a Roman tax being levied in
their land. For Judea in particular Augustus had before him the subsequent census made
by Quirinus.

and Augustus, the latter threatened for the future to make him feel his subjection [11]; secondly, also to the oath of allegiance to Augustus which, according to Josephus, the Jews were forced to take even during the lifetime of Herod.[12] From which it is inferred that Augustus, since he had it in contemplation after the death of Herod to restrict the power of his sons, was very likely to have commanded a census in the last years of that prince.[13]   But it seems more probable that it took place shortly after the death of Herod, from the circumstance that Archelaus went to Rome concerning the matter of succession, and that during his absence the Roman procurator Sabinus occupied Jerusalem, and oppressed the Jews by every possible means.[14]

The Evangelist relieves us from a farther inquiry into this more or less historical or arbitrary combination by adding, that this taxing was first made when Cyrenius (Quirinus) *was governor of Syria*, ἡγεμονεύοντος τῆς Συρίας Κυρηνίου; for it is an authenticated point that the assessment of Quirinus did not take place either under Herod or early in the reign of Archelaus, the period at which, according to Luke, Jesus was born.   Quirinus was not at that time governor of Syria, a situation held during the last years of Herod by Sentius Saturninus, and after him by Quintilius Varus; and it was not till long after the death of Herod that Quirinus was appointed governor of Syria. That Quirinus undertook a census of Judea we know certainly from Josephus,[15] who, however, remarks that he was sent to execute this measure, τῆς Ἀρχελάου χώρας εἰς ἐπαρχίαν περιγραφείσης, or, ὑποτελοῦς προσνεμηθείσης τῇ Σύρων [16]; thus about ten years after the time at which, according to Matthew and Luke, Jesus must have been born.

Yet commentators have supposed it possible to reconcile this apparently undeniable contradiction between Luke and history.   The most dauntless explain the whole of the second verse as a gloss, which was early incorporated into the text.[17]   Some change the reading of the verse; either of the *nomen proprium*, by substituting the name of Saturninus or Quintilius,[18] according to the example of Tertullian, who ascribed the census to the former [19]; or of the other words, by various additions and modifications.   Paulus's alteration is the most simple.   He reads, instead of αὕτη, αὐτὴ, and concludes, from the reasons stated above, that Augustus actually gave orders for a census during the reign of Herod I., and that the order was so far carried out as to occasion the journey of Joseph and Mary to Bethlehem; but that Augustus being afterwards conciliated, the measure was abandoned, and αὐτὴ ἡ ἀπογραφὴ was only carried into effect a considerable time later, by Quirinus.   Trifling as this alteration, which leaves the letters unchanged, may appear, in order to render it admissible it must be supported by the context.   The reverse, however, is the fact.   For if one sentence narrates a command issued by a prince, and

---

[11] Ὅτι, πάλαι χρώμενος αὐτῷ φίλῳ, νῦν ὑπηκόῳ χρήσεται.   Joseph. Antiq. 16, 9, 3.   But the difference was adjusted long before the death of Herod.   Antiq. 16, 10, 9.

[12] Joseph. Ant. 17, 2, 4.   παντὸς τοῦ Ἰουδαϊκοῦ βεβαιώσαντος δι' ὅρκων ἦ μὴν εὐνοῆσαι Καίσαρι καὶ τοῖς βασιλέως πράγμασι.   That this oath, far from being a humiliating measure for Herod, coincided with his interest, is proved by the zeal with which he punished the Pharisees who refused to take it.

[13] Tholuck, s. 192 f.   But the insurrection which the ἀπογραφὴ after the depositions of Archelaus actually occasioned—a fact which outweighs all Tholuck's surmises—proves it to have been the first Roman measure of the kind in Judea.

[14] Antiq. 17, 9, 10, 1 ff.   B. j. 2. 2. 2.   His oppressions however had reference only to the fortresses and the treasures of Herod.

[15] Antiq. 18, 1, 1.

[16] Bell. jud. 2, 8, 1. 9, 1.   Antiq. 17, 13, 5.

[17] Kuinöl, Comm. in Luc. p. 320.

[18] Winer.

[19] Adv. Marcion. 4, 19.

the very next sentence its execution, it is not probable that a space of ten years intervened. But chiefly, according to this view the Evangelist speaks, verse 1, of the decree of the emperor; verse 2, of the census made ten years later; but verse 3, without any remark, again of a journey performed at the time the command was issued; which, in a rational narrative, is impossible. Opposed to such arbitrary conjectures, and always to be ranked above them, are the attempts to solve a difficulty by legitimate methods of interpretation. Truly, however, to take πρώτη in this connexion for προτέρα, and ἡγεμονεύοντος K. not for a genitive absolute, but for a genitive governed by a comparative, and thus to understand an enrolment *before* that of Quirinus,[20] is to do violence to grammatical construction; and to insert πρὸ τῆς after πρώτη [21] is is no less uncritical. As little is it to be admitted that some preliminary measure, in which Quirinus was not employed, perhaps the already mentioned oath of allegiance, took place during the lifetime of Herod, in reference to the census subsequently made by Quirinus; and that this preliminary step and the census were afterwards comprised under the same name. In order in some degree to account for this appellation, Quirinus is said to have been sent into Judea, in Herod's time, as an extraordinary tax-commissioner [22]; but this interpretation of the word ἡγεμονεύοντος is rendered impossible by the addition of the word Συρίας, in combination with which the expression can denote only the *Præses Syriæ*.

Thus at the time at which Jesus, according to Matt. ii. 1, and Luke i. 5, 26, was born, the census of which Luke ii. 1 f. speaks could not have taken place; so that if the former statements are correct, the latter must be false. But may not the reverse be the fact, and Jesus have been born after the banishment of Archelaus, and at the time of the census of Quirinus? Apart from the difficulties in which this hypothesis would involve us in relation to the chronology of the future life of Jesus, a Roman census, subsequent to the banishment of Archelaus, would not have taken the parents of Jesus from Nazareth in Galilee to Bethlehem in Judea. For Judea only, and what otherwise belonged to the portion of Archelaus, became a Roman province and subjected to the census. In Galilee Herod Antipas continued to reign as an allied prince, and none of his subjects dwelling at Nazareth could have been called to Bethlehem by the census. The Evangelist therefore, in order to get a census, must have conceived the condition of things such as they were after the deposition of Archelaus; but in order to get a census extending to Galilee, he must have imagined the kingdom to have continued undivided, as in the time of Herod the Great. Thus he deals in manifest contradictions; or rather he has an exceedingly sorry acquaintance with the political relations of that period; for he extends the census not only to the whole of Palestine, but also (which we must not forget) to the whole Roman world.

Still these chronological incongruities do not exhaust the difficulties which beset this statement of Luke. His representation of the manner in which the census was made is subject to objection. In the first place, it is said, the taxing took Joseph to Bethlehem, *because he was of the house and lineage of David*, διὰ τὸ εἶναι αὐτὸν ἐξ οἴκου καὶ πατριᾶς Δαβὶδ, and likewise every one into his own city, εἰς τὴν ἰδίαν πόλιν, *i.e.* according to the context, to the place whence his family had originally sprung. Now, that every individual should be registered in his own city was required in all Jewish inscriptions, because among the Jews the organization of families and tribes constituted the very basis of the state. The Romans, on the contrary, were in the habit of taking

[20] Storr, opusc. acad. 3, s. 126 f. Süskind, vermischte Aufsätze, s. 63. Tholuck, s. 182 f.
[21] Michaelis, Anm. z. d. St. und Einl. in d. N.T. 1, 71.
[22] Münter, Stern der Weisen. s. 88.

the census at the residences, and at the principal cities in the district. [23] They conformed to the usages of the conquered countries only in so far as they did not interfere with their own objects.   In the present instance it would have been directly contrary to their design, had they removed individuals—Joseph for example—to a great distance, where the amount of their property was not known, and their statement concerning it could not be checked.[24]   The view of Schleiermacher is the more admissible, that the real occasion which took the parents to Bethlehem was a sacerdotal inscription, which the Evangelist confounded with the better known census of Quirinus.   But this concession does not obviate the contradiction in this dubious statement of Luke.   He allows Mary to be inscribed with Joseph, but according to Jewish customs inscriptions had relation to men only.   Thus, at all events, it is an inaccuracy to represent Mary as undertaking the journey, in order to be inscribed with her betrothed in his own city.   Or, if with Paulus we remove this inaccuracy by a forced construction of the sentence, we can no longer perceive what inducement could have instigated Mary, in her particular situation, to make so long a journey, since, unless we adopt the airy hypothesis of Olshausen and others, that Mary was the heiress of property in Bethlehem, she had nothing to do there.

The Evangelist, however, knew perfectly well what she had to do there; namely, to fulfil the prophecy of Micah (v. 1), by giving birth, in the city of David, to the Messiah.   Now as he set out with the supposition that the habitual abode of the parents of Jesus was Nazareth, so he sought after a lever which should set them in motion towards Bethlehem, at the time of the birth of Jesus.   Far and wide nothing presented itself but the celebrated census ; he seized it the more unhesitatingly because the obscurity of his own view of the historical relations of that time, veiled from him the many difficulties connected with such a combination.   If this be the true history of the statement in Luke, we must agree with K. Ch. L. Schmidt when he says, that to attempt to reconcile the statement of Luke concerning the ἀπογραφὴ with chronology, would be to do the narrator too much honour ; he wished to place Mary in Bethlehem, and therefore times and circumstances were to accommodate themselves to his pleasure.[25]

Thus we have here neither a fixed point for the date of the birth of Jesus, nor an explanation of the occasion which led to his being born precisely at Bethlehem.   If then—it may justly be said—no other reason why Jesus should have been born at Bethlehem can be adduced than that given by Luke, we have absolutely no guarantee that Bethlehem was his birth-place.

§ 33.

PARTICULAR CIRCUMSTANCES OF THE BIRTH OF JESUS.   THE CIRCUMCISION.

The basis of the narrative, the arrival of Joseph and Mary as strangers in Bethlehem on account of the census, being once chosen by Luke, the farther details are consistently built upon it.   In consequence of the influx of strangers brought to Bethlehem by the census, there is no room for the travellers in the inn, and they are compelled to put up with the accommodation of a stable where Mary is forthwith delivered of her first-born.   But the child, who upon

[23] Paulus.   Wetstein.
[24] Credner.
[25] In Schmidt's Bibliothek für Kritik und Exegese, 3, 1. s. 124.   See Kaiser, bibl. Theol. 1, s. 230 ; Ammon, Fortbildung, 1, s. 196 ; Credner, Einleitung, in d. N.T. 1, s. 155 ; De Wette, exeget. Handbuch.

earth comes into being in so humble an abode, is highly regarded in heaven. A celestial messenger announces the birth of the Messiah to shepherds who are guarding their flocks in the fields by night, and directs them to the child in the manger. A choir of the heavenly host singing hymns of praise next appears to them, after which they seek and find the child. (Luke ii. 6–20.)

The apocryphal gospels and the traditions of the Fathers still further embellished the birth of Jesus. According to the *Protevangelium Jacobi*,[1] Joseph conducts Mary on an ass to Bethlehem to be taxed. As they approach the city she begins to make now mournful, now joyous gestures, and upon inquiry explains that—(as once in Rebecca's womb the two hostile nations struggled, Gen. xxv. 23)—she sees two people before her, the one weeping, the other laughing : *i.e.* according to one explanation, the two portions of Israel, to one of whom the advent of Jesus *was set* (Luke ii. 34) εἰς πτῶσιν, *for the fall*, to the other εἰς ἀνάστασιν, *for the rising again*. According to another interpretation, the two people were the Jews who should reject Jesus, and the heathens who should accept him.[2] Soon, however, whilst still without the city—as appears from the context and the reading of several MSS.—Mary is seized with the pains of child-bearing, and Joseph brings her into a cave situated by the road side, where, veiled by a cloud of light, all nature pausing in celebration of the event, she brings her child into the world, and after her delivery is found, by women called to her assistance, still a virgin.[3] The legend of the birth of Jesus in a cave was known to Justin[4] and to Origen,[5] who, in order to reconcile it with the account in Luke that he was laid in a manger, suppose a manger situated within the cave. Many modern commentators agree with them[6]; whilst others prefer to consider the cave itself as φάτνη, in the sense of foddering-stall.[7] For the birth of Jesus in a cave, Justin appeals to the prophecy in Isaiah xxviii. 16 : οὗτος (the righteous) οἰκήσει ἐν ὑψηλῷ σπηλαίῳ πέτρας ἰσχυρᾶς. In like manner, for the statement that on the third day the child Jesus, when brought from the cave into the stable, was worshipped by the oxen and the asses, the *Historia de Nativitate Mariae*,[8] etc. refers to Isaiah i. 3 : *cognovit bos possessorem suum, et asinus praesepe domini sui.* In several apocryphas, between the Magi and the women who assist at the birth, the shepherds are forgotten ; but they are mentioned in the *Evangelium infantiae arabicum*,[9] where it says, that when they arrived at the cave, and had kindled a fire of rejoicing, the heavenly host appeared to them.

If we take the circumstances attending the birth of Jesus, narrated by Luke, in a supranaturalistic sense, many difficulties occur. First, it may reasonably be asked, to what end the angelic apparition ? The most obvious answer is, to make known the birth of Jesus ; but so little did it make it known that, in the neighbouring city of Jerusalem, it is the Magi who give the first information of the new-born king of the Jews; and in the future history of Jesus, no trace of any such occurrence at his birth is to be found. Consequently, the object of that extraordinary phenomenon was not to give a wide-spreading intimation of the fact ; for if so, God failed in his object. Must we then agree with Schleiermacher, that the aim was limited to an immediate opera-

[1] Chap. 17. Compare Historia de nativ. Mariae et de infantiâ Servatoris, c. 13.
[2] Fabricius, im Codex Apocryph. N.T. I, s. 105, not. y.
[3] Ambrosius and Jerome. See Gieseler, K. G. I, s. 516.
[4] Dial. c. Tryph. 78.
[5] C. Cels. I, 51.
[6] Hess, Olshausen, Paulus.
[7] Paulus.
[8] Chap. 14.
[9] Chap. 4 in Thilo, s. 69.

tion upon the shepherds? Then we must also suppose with him, that the shepherds, equally with Simeon, were filled with Messianic expectations, and that God designed by this apparition to reward and confirm their pious belief. The narrative however says nothing of this heavenly frame of mind, neither does it mention any abiding effects produced upon these men. According to the whole tenor of the representation, the apparition seems to have had reference, not to the shepherds, but exclusively to the glorification and the proclaiming of the birth of Jesus, as the Messiah. But as before observed, the latter aim was not accomplished, and the former, by itself, like every mere empty display, is an object unworthy of God. So that this circumstance in itself presents no inconsiderable obstacle to the supranaturalistic conception of the history. If, to the above considerations, we add those already stated which oppose the belief in apparitions and the existence of angels in general, it is easy to understand that with respect to this narrative also refuge has been sought in a natural explanation.

The results of the first attempts at a natural explanation were certainly sufficiently rude. Thus Eck regarded the angel as a messenger from Bethlehem, who carried a light which caught the eye of the shepherds, and the song of the heavenly host as the merry tones of a party accompanying the messenger.[10] Paulus has woven together a more refined and matter of fact explanation. Mary, who had met with a hospitable reception in a herdsman's family, and who was naturally elated with the hope of giving birth to the Messiah, told her expectations to the members of this family; to whom as inhabitants of a city of David the communication could not have been indifferent. These shepherds therefore on perceiving, whilst in the fields by night, a luminous appearance in the air—a phenomenon which travellers say is not uncommon in those regions—they interpret it as a divine intimation that the stranger in their foddering-stall is delivered of the Messiah; and as the meteoric light extends and moves to and fro, they take it for a choir of angels chaunting hymns of praise. Returning home they find their anticipations confirmed by the event, and that which at first they merely conjectured to be the sense and interpretation of the phenomenon, they now, after the manner of the East, represent as words actually spoken.[11]

This explanation rests altogether on the assumption, that the shepherds were previously acquainted with Mary's expectation that she should give birth to the Messiah. How otherwise should they have been led to consider the sign as referring particularly to the birth of the Messiah in their manger? Yet this very assumption is the most direct contradiction of the gospel account. For, in the first place, the Evangelist evidently does not suppose the manger to belong to the shepherds: since after he has narrated the delivery of Mary in the manger, he then goes on to speak of the shepherds as a new and distinct subject, not at all connected with the manger. His words are: *and there were in the same country shepherds*, καὶ ποιμένες ἦσαν ἐν τῇ χώρᾳ τῇ αὐτῇ. If this explanation were correct he would, at all events, have said, *the shepherds etc.* οἱ δὲ ποιμένες κ. τ. λ.; besides he would not have been wholly silent respecting the comings and goings of these shepherds during the day, and their departure to guard the flock at the approach of night. But, grant these presupposed circumstances, is it consistent in Paulus to represent Mary, at first so reserved concerning her pregnancy as to conceal it even from Joseph, and then so communicative that, just arrived among strangers, she

---

[10] In seinem Versuch über die Wundergeschichten des N. T. See Gabler's Neuestes theol. Journal, 7, 4, s. 411.

[11] Exeg. Handb. s. 180 ff. As Paulus supposes an external natural phenomenon so Matthæi imagines a mental vision of angels. Synopse der vier Evangelien, s. 3.

parades the whole history of her expectations? Again the sequel of the narrative contradicts the assumption that the shepherds were informed of the matter by Mary herself, before her delivery. For, according to the gospel history, the shepherds receive the first intelligence of the birth of the Saviour σωτήρ from the angel who appears to them, and who tells them, as a sign of the truth of his communication, that they shall find the babe lying in a manger. Had they already heard from Mary of the approaching birth of the Messiah, the meteoric appearance would have been a confirmation to them of Mary's words, and not the finding of the child a proof of the truth of the apparition. Finally, may we so far confide in the investigations already made as to inquire, whence, if neither a miraculous announcement nor a supernatural conception actually occurred, could Mary have derived the confident anticipation that she should give birth to the Messiah?

In opposition to this natural explanation, so full of difficulties on every side, Bauer announced his adoption of the mythical view [12]; in fact, however, he did not advance one step beyond the interpretation of the Rationalists, but actually repeated Paulus's exposition point for point. To this mixed mythical explanation Gabler justly objected that it, equally with the natural interpretation, multiplies improbabilities: by the adoption of the pure, dogmatic mythus, everything appears simpler; thereby, at the same time, greater harmony is introduced into the early christian history, all the preceding narratives of which ought equally to be interpreted as pure mythi.[13] Gabler, accordingly, explained the narrative as the product of the ideas of the age, which demanded the assistance of angels at the birth of the Messiah. Now had it been known that Mary was delivered in a dwelling belonging to shepherds, it would also have been concluded that angels must have brought the tidings to these good shepherds that the Messiah was born in their manger; and the angels who cease not praising God, must have sung a hymn of praise on the occasion. Gabler thinks it impossible, that a Jewish christian who should have known some of the data of the birth of Jesus, could have thought of it otherwise than as here depicted.[14]

This explanation of Gabler shows, in a remarkable manner, how difficult it is entirely to extricate oneself from the natural explanation, and to rise completely to the mythical; for whilst this theologian believes he treads on pure mythical ground, he still stands with one foot upon that of the natural interpretation. He selects from the account of Luke one incident as historical which, by its connexion with other unhistorical statements and its conformity to the spirit of the primitive christian legend, is proved to be merely mythical; namely, that Jesus was really born in a shepherd's dwelling. He also borrows an assumption from the natural explanation, which the mythical needs not to obtrude on the text: that the shepherds, to whom it is alleged the angels appeared, were the possessors of the manger in which Mary was delivered. The first detail, upon which the second is built, belongs to the same machinery by which Luke, with the help of the census, transported the parents of Jesus from Nazareth to Bethlehem. Now we know what is the fact respecting the census; it crumbles away inevitably before criticism, and with it the datum built entirely upon it, that Jesus was born in a manger. For had not the parents of Jesus been strangers, and had they not come to Bethlehem in company with so large a concourse of strangers as the census might have occasioned, the cause which obliged Mary to accept a stable for her place of

[12] Hebräische Mythologie, 2. Thl. s. 223 ff.
[13] Recension von Bauer's hebr. Mythologie in Gabler's Journal für auserlesene theol. Literatur, 2, 1, s. 58 f.
[14] Neuestes theol. Journal, 7, 4, s. 412 f.

delivery would no longer have existed. But, on the other hand, the incident, that Jesus was born in a stable and saluted in the first instance by
shepherds, is so completely in accordance with the spirit of the ancient
legend, that it is evident the narrative may have been derived purely from
this source. Theophylact, in his time, pointed out its true character, when
he says : the angels did not appear to the scribes and pharisees of Jerusalem
who were full of all malice, but to the shepherds, in the fields, on account of
their simplicity and innocence, and because they by their mode of life were
the successors of the patriarchs.[15] It was in the field by the flocks that Moses
was visited by a heavenly apparition (Exod. iii. 1 ff.) ; and God took David,
the forefather of the Messiah, from his sheepfolds (at Bethlehem), to be the shepherd of his people. Psalm lxxviii. 70 (comp. 1 Sam. xvi. 11). The mythi
of the ancient world more generally ascribed divine apparitions to countrymen[16] and shepherds[17] ; the sons of the gods, and of great men were frequently brought up among shepherds.[18] In the same spirit of the ancient
legend is the apocryphal invention that Jesus was born in a cave, and we are
at once reminded of the cave of Jupiter and of the other gods ; even though
the misunderstood passage of Isaiah xxxiii. 16 may have been the immediate
occasion of this incident.[19] Moreover the night, in which the scene is laid,
—(unless one refers here to the rabbinical representations, according to which,
the deliverance by means of the Messiah, like the deliverance from Egypt,
should take place by night[20])—forms the obscure background against which
the manifested *glory of the Lord* shone so much the more brilliantly, which, as
it is said to have glorified the birth of Moses,[21] could not have been absent
from that of the Messiah, his exalted antitype.

The mythical interpretation of this section of the gospel history has found
an opponent in Schleiermacher.[22] He thinks it improbable that this commencement of the second chapter of Luke is a continuation of the first,
written by the same author ; because the frequent opportunities of introducing
lyrical effusions—as for example, when the shepherds returned glorifying and
praising God, v. 20—are not taken advantage of as in the first chapter ; and
here indeed we can in some measure agree with him. But when he adds that
a decidedly poetical character cannot be ascribed to this narrative, since a
poetical composition would of necessity have contained more of the lyrical,
this only proves that Schleiermacher has not justly apprehended the notion
of that kind of poetry of which he here treats, namely, the poetry of the
mythus. In a word, mythical poetry is objective : the poetical exists in
the substance of the narrative, and may therefore appear in the plainest form,
free from all the adornments of lyrical effusions ; which latter are rather only
the subsequent additions of a more intelligent and artificially elaborated subjective poetry.[23] Undoubtedly this section seems to have been preserved to
us more nearly in its original legendary form, whilst the narratives of the first
chapter in Luke bear rather the stamp of having been re-wrought by some

[15] In Luc. 2. in Suicer, 2, p. 789 f.
[16] Servius ad Verg. Ecl. 10, 26.
[17] Liban. progymn. p. 138, in Wetstein, s. 662.
[18] Thus Cyrus, see Herod. 1, 110 ff.   Romulus, see Livy, 1, 4.
[19] Thilo, Codex Apocr. N. T. 1, s. 383 not.
[20] Vid. Schöttgen, 2, s. 531.
[21] Sota, 1, 48 : *Sapientes nostri perhibent, circa horam nativitatis Mosis totam domum
repletam fuisse luce* (Wetstein).
[22] Ueber den Lukas, s. 29. f.   With whom Neander and others now agree.—L. J. Ch.
s. 21 f.
[23] Comp. De Wette, Kritik der mosaischen Geschichte, s. 116 ; George, Mythus u. Sage,
s. 33 f.

poetical individual ; but historical truth is not on that account to be sought here any more than there. Consequently the obligation which Schleiermacher further imposes upon himself, to trace out the source of this narrative in the Gospel of Luke, can only be regarded as an exercise of ingenuity. He refuses to recognize that source in Mary, though a reference to her might have been found in the observation, v. 19, *she kept all these sayings in her heart;* wherein indeed he is the more right, since that observation (a fact to which Schleiermacher does not advert) is merely a phrase borrowed from the history of Jacob and his son Joseph.[24] For as the narrative in Genesis relates cf Jacob, the father of Joseph, that child of miracle, that when the latter told his significant dreams, and his brethren envied him, *his father observed the saying* : so the narrative in Luke, both here and at verse 51, relates of Mary, that she, whilst others gave utterance aloud to their admiration at the extraordinary occurrences which happened to her child, *kept all these things and pondered them in her heart.* But the above-named theologian points out the shepherds instead of Mary as the source of our narrative, alleging that all the details are given, not from Mary's point of view, but from that of the shepherds. More truly however is the point of view that of the legend which supersedes both. If Schleiermacher finds it impossible to believe that this narrative is an air-bubble conglomerated out of *nothing,* he must include under the word *nothing* the Jewish and early christian ideas—concerning Bethlehem, as the necessary birthplace of the Messiah; concerning the condition of the shepherds, as being peculiarly favoured by communications from heaven ; concerning angels, as the intermediate agents in such communications—notions we on our side cannot possibly hold in so little estimation, but we find it easy to conceive that something similar to our narrative might have formed itself out out of them. Finally, when he finds an adventitious or designed invention impossible, because the Christians of that district might easily have inquired of Mary or of the disciples concerning the truth of the matter : he speaks too nearly the language of the ancient apologists, and presupposes the ubiquity of these persons,[25] already alluded to in the Introduction, who however could not possibly have been in all places rectifying the tendency to form christian legends, wherever it manifested itself.

The notice of the circumcision of Jesus (Luke ii. 21), evidently proceeds from a narrator who had no real advice of the fact, but who assumed as a certainty that, according to Jewish custom, the ceremony took place on the eighth day, and who was desirous of commemorating this important event in the life of an Israelitish boy ;[26] in like manner as Paul (Phil. iii. 5) records his circumcision on the eighth day. The contrast however between the fulness of detail with which this point is elaborated and coloured in the life of the Baptist, and the barrenness and brevity with which it is stated in reference to Jesus, is striking, and may justify an agreement with the remark of Schleiermacher, that here, at least the author of the first chapter is no longer the originator. Such being the state of the case, this statement furnishes nothing for our object, which we might not already have known ; only we have till now had no opportunity of observing, distinctly, that the pretended appoint-

---

[24] Gen. xxxvii. 11 (LXX.) :

Ἐζήλωσαν δὲ οὐτὸν οἱ ἀδελφοὶ αὐτοῦ, ὁ δὲ πατὴρ αὐτοῦ διετήρησε τὸ ῥῆμα.—Schöttgen, horae, 1, 262.

Luc. 2, 18 f. :

καὶ πάντες οἱ ἀκούσαντες ἐθαύμασαν — — ἡ δὲ Μαριὰμ πάντα συνετήρει τὰ ῥήματα ταῦτα, συμβάλλουσα ἐν τῇ καρδίᾳ αἱτῆς. 2, 51 : καὶ ἡ μήτηρ αὐτοῦ διετήρει πάντα τὰ ῥήματα ταῦτα ἐν τῇ καρδίᾳ αὐτῆς.

[25] See Introduction.

[26] Perhaps as a precautionary measure to obviate objections on the part of the Jews. (Ammon, Fortbildung, 1, s. 217.)

ment of the name of Jesus before his birth likewise belongs merely to the mythical dress of the narrative. When it is said *his name was called Jesus, which was so named of the angel before he was conceived in the womb,* the importance attached to the circumstance is a clear sign, that a dogmatic interest lies at the bottom of this feature in the narrative ; which interest can be no other than that which gave rise to the statement—in the Old Testament concerning an Isaac and an Ishmael, and in the New Testament concerning a John—that the names of these children were, respectively, revealed to their parents prior to their birth, and on account of which interest the rabbins, in particular, expected that the same thing should occur in relation to the name of the Messiah.[27] Without doubt there were likewise other far more natural reasons which induced the parents of Jesus to give him this name (יֵשׁוּעַ an abbreviation of יְהוֹשֻׁעַ, ὁ Κύριος σωτηρία) ; a name which was very common among his countrymen ; but because this name agreed in a remarkable manner with the path of life subsequently chosen by him as Messiah and σωτήρ, it was not thought possible that this coincidence could have been accidental. Besides it seemed more appropriate that the name of the Messiah should have been determined by divine command than by human arbitration, and consequently the appointment of the name was ascribed to the same angel who had announced the conception of Jesus.

§ 34.

THE MAGI AND THEIR STAR. THE FLIGHT INTO EGYPT AND THE
MURDER OF THE CHILDREN IN BETHLEHEM. CRITICISM
OF THE SUPRANATURALISTIC VIEW.

In the Gospel of Matthew also we have a narrative of the Messiah's entrance into the world ; it differs considerably in detail from that of Luke. which we have just examined, but in the former part of the two accounts there is a general similarity (Matt. ii. 1 ff.). The object of both narratives is to describe the solemn introduction of the Messianic infant, the heralding of his birth undertaken by heaven itself, and his first reception among men.[1] In both, attention is called to the new-born Messiah by a celestial phenomenon ; according to Luke, it is an angel clothed in brightness, according to Matthew, it is a star. As the apparitions are different, so accordingly are the recipients ; the angel addresses simple shepherds ; the star is discovered by eastern magi, who are able to interpret for themselves the voiceless sign. Both parties are directed to Bethlehem ; the shepherds by the words of the angel, the magi by the instructions they obtain in Jerusalem ; and both do homage to the infant ; the poor shepherds by singing hymns of praise, the magi by costly presents from their native country. But from this point the two narratives begin to diverge widely. In Luke all proceeds happily ; the shepherds return with gladness in their hearts, the child experiences no molestation, he is presented in the temple on the appointed day, thrives and grows up in tranquillity. In Matthew, on the contrary, affairs take a tragical turn. The inquiry of the wise

[27] Pirke R. Elieser, 33 : *Sex hominum nomina dicta sunt, antequam nascerentur: Isaaci nempe, Ismaëlis, Mosis, Salomonis, Josiæ et nomen regis Messiæ.* Bereschith rabba, sect. 1, fol. 3, 3.—(Schöttgen, horae, 2, s. 436) : Sex res prævenerunt creationem mundi : quædam ex illis creatæ sunt, nempe lex et thronus gloriæ ; aliæ ascenderunt in cogitationem (Dei) ut crearentur, nimirum Patriarchæ, Israël, templum, et nomen Messiæ.
[1] Comp. Schneckenburger, über den Ursprung des ersten kanonischen Evangeliums, s. 69 ff.

men in Jerusalem concerning the new-born King of the Jews, is the occasion of a murderous decree on the part of Herod against the children of Bethlehem, a danger from which the infant Jesus is rescued only by a sudden flight into Egypt, whence he and his parents do not return to the Holy Land till after the death of Herod.

Thus we have here a double proclamation of the Messianic child: we might, however, suppose that the one by the angel, in Luke, would announce the birth of the Messiah to the immediate neighbourhood; the other, by means of the star, to distant lands. But as, according to Matthew, the birth of Jesus became known at Jerusalem, which was in the immediate vicinity, by means of the star; if this representation be historical, that of Luke, according to which the shepherds were the first to spread abroad with praises to God (v. 17, 20), that which had been communicated to them as glad tidings for all people (v. 10), cannot possibly be correct. So, on the other hand, if it be true that the birth of Jesus was made known in the neighbourhood of Bethlehem as Luke states, by an angelic communication to the shepherds, Matthew must be in error when he represents the first intelligence of the event as subsequently brought to Jerusalem (which is only from two to three hours distant from Bethlehem) by the magi. But as we have recognized many indications of the unhistorical character of the announcement by the shepherds given in Luke, the ground is left clear for that of Matthew, which must be judged of according to its inherent credibility.

Our narrative commences as if it were an admitted fact, that astrologers possessed the power of recognizing a star announcing the birth of the Messiah. That eastern magi should have knowledge of a King of the Jews to whom they owed religious homage might indeed excite our surprise; but contenting ourselves here with remarking, that seventy years later an expectation did prevail in the east that a ruler of the world would arise from among the Jewish people,[2] we pass on to a yet more weighty difficulty. According to this narrative it appears, that astrology is right when it asserts that the birth of great men and important revolutions in human affairs are indicated by astral phenomena; an opinion long since consigned to the region of superstition. It is therefore to be explained, how this deceptive science could in this solitary instance prove true, though in no other case are its inferences to be relied on. The most obvious explanation, from the orthodox point of view, is an appeal to the supernatural intervention of God; who, in this particular instance, in order to bring the distant magi unto Jesus, accommodated himself to their astrological notions, and caused the anticipated star to appear. But the adoption of this expedient involves very serious consequences. For the coincidence of the remarkable sequel with the astrological prognostic could not fail to strengthen the belief, not only of the magi and their fellow-countrymen, but also of the Jews and Christians who were acquainted with the circumstances, in the spurious science of astrology, thereby creating incalculable error and mischief. If therefore it be unadvisable to admit an extraordinary divine intervention,[3] and if the position that in the ordinary course of nature, important occurrences on this earth are attended by changes in the heavenly bodies, be abandoned, the only remaining explanation lies in

[2] Joseph. B. J. vi. vi. 4: Tacit. Histor. v. 13; Sueton. Vespas. 4. All the extant allusions to the existence of such a hope at the era of Christ's birth, relate only in an indeterminate manner to a ruler of the world. Virg. Eclog. 4; Sueton. Octav. 94.

[3] In saying that it is inadmissible to suppose a divine intervention directly tending to countenance superstition, I refer to what is called *immediate* intervention. In the doctrine of *mediate* intervention, which includes the co-operation of man, there is doubtless a mixture of truth and error. Neander confuses the two. L. J. Ch., s. 29.

the supposition of an accidental coincidence.   But to appeal to chance is in fact either to say nothing, or to renounce the supranaturalistic point of view.

But the orthodox view of this account not only sanctions the false science of astrology, but also confirms the false interpretation of a passage in the prophets.   For as the magi, following their star, proceed in the right direction, so the chief priests and scribes of Jerusalem whom Herod, on learning the arrival and object of the magi, summons before him and questions concerning the birth-place of the King of the Jews, interpret the passage in Micah v. 1 as signifying that the Messiah should be born in Bethlehem ; and to this signification the event corresponds.   Now such an application of the above passage can only be made by forcing the words from their true meaning and from all relation with the context, according to the well-known practice of the rabbins. For independently of the question whether or not under the word מוֹשֵׁל, in the passage cited, the Messiah be intended, the entire context shows the meaning to be, not that the expected governor who was to come forth out of Bethlehem would actually be born in that city, but only that he would be a descendant of David, whose family sprang from Bethlehem.[4]   Thus allowing the magi to have been rightly directed by means of the rabbinical exegesis of the oracle, a false interpretation must have hit on the truth, either by means of divine intervention and accommodation, or by accident.   The judgment pronounced in the case of the star is applicable here also.

After receiving the above answer from the Sanhedrim, Herod summons the magi before him, and his first question concerns the time at which the star appeared (v. 7).   Why did he wish to know this[5]?   The 16th verse tells us, that he might thereby calculate the age of the Messianic child, and thus ascertain up to what age it would be necessary for him to put to death the children of Bethlehem, so as not to miss the one announced by the star.   But this plan of murdering all the children of Bethlehem up to a certain age, that he might destroy the one likely to prove fatal to the interests of his family, was not conceived by Herod until after the magi had disappointed his expectation that they would return to Jerusalem ; a deception which, if we may judge from his violent anger on account of it (v. 16), Herod had by no means anticipated.   Prior to this, according to v. 8, it had been his intention to obtain from the magi, on their return, so close a description of the child, his dwelling and circumstances, that it would be easy for him to remove his infantine rival without sacrificing any other life.   It was not until he had discovered the stratagem of the magi, that he was obliged to have recourse to the more violent measure for the execution of which it was necessary for him to know the time of the star's appearance.[6]   How fortunate for him, then, that he had ascertained this time before he had decided on the plan that made the information important ; but how inconceivable that he should make a point which was only indirectly connected with his original project, the subject of his first and most eager interrogation (v. 7) !

Herod, in the second place, commissions the magi to acquaint themselves accurately with all that concerns the royal infant, and to impart their knowledge to him on their return, that he also may go and tender his homage to the child, that is, according to his real meaning, take sure measures for putting

---

[4] Paulus and De Wette, exeg. Handb. in loc.

[5] According to Hoffmann (p. 256), that he might control the assertion of the magi by inquiring of his own astrologers, whether they had seen the star at the same time.   This is not merely unsupported by the text—it is in direct contradiction to it, for we are there told that Herod at once gave terrified credence to the magi.

[6] Fritzsche, in loc. aptly says—*comperto, quasi magos non ad se redituros statim scivisset, orti sideris tempore, etc.*

him to death (v. 8). Such a proceeding on the part of an astute monarch like Herod has long been held improbable.[7] Even if he hoped to deceive the magi, while in conference with them, by adopting this friendly mask, he must necessarily foresee that others would presently awaken them to the probability that he harboured evil designs against the child, and thus prevent them from returning according to his injunction. He might conjecture that the parents of the child on hearing of the ominous interest taken in him by the king, would seek his safety by flight, and finally, that those inhabitants of Bethlehem and its environs who cherished Messianic expectations, would not be a little confirmed in them by the arrival of the magi. On all these grounds, Herod's only prudent measure would have been either to detain the magi in Jerusalem,[8] and in the meantime by means of secret emissaries to dispatch the child to whom such peculiar hopes were attached, and who must have been easy of discovery in the little village of Bethlehem ; or to have given the magi companions who, so soon as the child was found, might at once have put an end to his existence. Even Olshausen thinks that these strictures are not groundless, and his best defence against them is the observation that the histories of all ages present unaccountable instances of forgetfulness—a proof that the course of human events is guided by a supreme hand. When the supernaturalist invokes the supreme hand in the case before us, he must suppose that God himself blinded Herod to the surest means of attaining his object, in order to save the Messianic child from a premature death. But the other side of this divine contrivance is, that instead of the one child, many others must die. There would be nothing to object against such a substitution in this particular case, if it could be proved that there was no other possible mode of rescuing Jesus from a fate inconsistent with the scheme of human redemption. But if it be once admitted, that God interposed supernaturally to blind the mind of Herod and to suggest to the magi that they should not return to Jerusalem, we are constrained to ask, why did not God in the first instance inspire the magi to shun Jerusalem and proceed directly to Bethlehem, whither Herod's attention would not then have been so immediately attracted, and thus the disastrous sequel perhaps have been altogether avoided?[9] The supranaturalist has no answer to this question but the old-fashioned argument that it was good for the infants to die, because they were thus freed by transient suffering from much misery, and more especially from the danger of sinning against Jesus with the unbelieving Jews; whereas now they had the honour of losing their lives for the sake of Jesus, and thus of ranking as martyrs, and so forth.[10]

The magi leave Jerusalem by night, the favourite time for travelling in the east. The star, which they seem to have lost sight of since their departure from home, again appears and goes before them on the road to Bethlehem, until at length it remains stationary over the house that contains the wondrous child and its parents. The way from Jerusalem to Bethlehem lies southward ; now the true path of erratic stars is either from west to east, as that of the planets and of some comets, or from east to west, as that of other comets ; the orbits of many comets do indeed tend from north to south, but the true motion of all these bodies is so greatly surpassed by their apparent motion

[7] K. Ch. L. Schmidt, exeg. Beiträge, 1, s. 150 f. Comp. Fritzsche and De Wette in loc.
[8] Hoffman thinks that Herod shunned this measure as a breach of hospitality; yet this very Herod he represents as a monster of cruelty, and that justly, for the conduct attributed to the monarch in chap. ii. of Matthew is not unworthy of his heart, against which Neander superfluously argues (p. 30 f.), but of his head.
[9] Schmidt, ut sup. p. 155 f.
[10] Stark, Synops. bibl. exeg. in N. T., p. 62.

from east to west produced by the rotation of the earth on its axis, that it is imperceptible except at considerable intervals.   Even the diurnal movement of the heavenly bodies, however, is less obvious on a short journey than the merely optical one, arising from the observer's own change of place, in consequence of which a star that he sees before him seems, as long as he moves forward, to pass on in the same direction through infinite space ; it cannot therefore stand still over a particular house and thus induce a traveller to halt there also ; on the contrary, the traveller himself must halt before the star will appear stationary.   The star of the magi could not then be an ordinary, natural star, but must have been one created by God for that particular exigency, and impressed by him with a peculiar law of motion and rest.[11] Again, this could not have been a true star, moving among the systems of our firmament, for such an one, however impelled and arrested, could never, according to optical laws, appear to pause over a particular house.   It must therefore have been something lower, hovering over the earth's surface ; hence some of the Fathers and apocryphal writers [12] supposed it to have been an angel, which, doubtless, might fly before the magi in the form of a star, and take its station at a moderate height above the house of Mary in Bethlehem ; more modern theologians have conjectured that the phenomenon was a meteor.[13]   Both these explanations are opposed to the text of Matthew: the former, because it is out of keeping with the style of our Gospels to designate anything purely supernatural, such as an angelic appearance, by an expression that implies a merely natural object, as ἀστήρ (a star) ; the latter, because a mere meteor would not last for so long a time as must have elapsed between the departure of the magi from their remote home and their arrival in Bethlehem.   Perhaps, however, it will be contended that God created one meteor for the first monition, and another for the second.

Many, even of the orthodox expositors, have found these difficulties in relation to the star so pressing, that they have striven to escape at any cost from the admission that it preceded the magi in their way towards Bethlehem, and took its station directly over a particular house.   According to Süskind, whose explanation has been much approved, the verb προῆγεν (went before) (v. 9), which is in the imperfect tense, does not signify that the star visibly led the magi on their way, but is equivalent to the pluperfect, which would imply that the star had been invisibly transferred to the destination of the magi before their arrival, so that the Evangelist intends to say : the star which the magi had seen in the east and subsequently lost sight of, suddenly made its appearance to them in Bethlehem above the house they were seeking ; it had therefore preceded them.[14]   But this is a transplantation of rationalistic artifice into the soil of orthodox exegesis.   Not only the word προῆγεν, but the less flexible expression ἕως ἐλθὼν κ. τ. λ. (till it came, etc.) denotes that the transit of the star was not an already completed phenomenon, but one brought to pass under the observation of the magi.   Expositors who persist in denying this must, to be consistent, go still farther, and reduce the entire narrative to the standard of merely natural events.   So when Olshausen admits that the position of a star could not possibly indicate a single house, that hence the magi must have inquired for the infant's dwelling, and only with child-like simplicity referred the issue as well as the commencement of their journey to a

---

[11] This was the opinion of some of the Fathers, e.g. Euseb. Demonstr. evang. 9, ap. Suicer, I, s. 559 ; Joann. Damasc. de fide orthod. ii. 7.

[12] Chrysostomus and others ap. Suicer, ut sup. and the Evang. infant. arab. c. vii.

[13] See Kuinöl, Comm. in Matth., p. 23.

[14] Vermischte Aufsätze, s. 8.

heavenly guide [15]; he deserts his own point of view for that of the rationalists, and interlines the text with explanatory particulars, an expedient which he elsewhere justly condemns in Paulus and others.

The magi then enter the house, offer their adoration to the infant, and present to him gifts, the productions of their native country. One might wonder that there is no notice of the astonishment which it must have excited in these men to find, instead of the expected prince, a child in quite ordinary, perhaps indigent circumstances.[16] It is not fair, however, to heighten the contrast by supposing, according to the common notion, that the magi discovered the child in a stable lying in the manger; for this representation is peculiar to Luke, and is altogether unknown to Matthew, who merely speaks of a *house*, οἰκία, in which the child was found. Then follows (v. 10) the warning given to the magi in a dream, concerning which, as before remarked, it were only to be wished that it had been vouchsafed earlier, so as to avert the steps of the magi from Jerusalem, and thus perchance prevent the whole subsequent massacre.

While Herod awaits the return of the magi, Joseph is admonished by an angelic apparition in a dream to flee with the Messianic child and its mother into Egypt for security (v. 13–15). Adopting the evangelist's point of view, this is not attended with any difficulty; it is otherwise, however, with the prophecy which the above event is said to fulfil, Hosea xi. 1. In this passage the prophet, speaking in the name of Jehovah, says: *When Israel was a child, then I loved him, and called my son out of Egypt.* We may venture to attribute, even to the most orthodox expositor, enough clear-sightedness to perceive that the subject of the first half of the sentence is also the object of the second, namely the people of Israel, who here, as elsewhere, (*e.g.* Exod. iv. 22, Sirach xxxvi. 14), are collectively called the Son of God, and whose past deliverance under Moses out of their Egyptian bondage is the fact referred to: that consequently, the prophet was not contemplating either the Messiah or his sojourn in Egypt. Nevertheless, as our evangelist says, v. 15, that the flight of Jesus into Egypt took place expressly that the above words of Hosea might be fulfilled, he must have understood them as a prophecy relating to Christ—must, therefore, have misunderstood them. It has been pretended that the passage has a twofold application, and, though referring primarily to the Israelitish people, is not the less a prophecy relative to Christ, because the destiny of Israel "after the flesh" was a type of the destiny of Jesus. But this convenient method of interpretation is not applicable here, for the analogy would, in the present case, be altogether external and inane, since the only parallel consists in the bare fact in both instances of a sojourn in Egypt, the circumstances under which the Israelitish people and the child Jesus sojourned there being altogether diverse.[17]

When the return of the magi has been delayed long enough for Herod to become aware that they have no intention to keep faith with him, he decrees the death of all the male children in Bethlehem and its environs up to the age of two years, that being, according to the statements of the magi as to the time of the star's appearance, the utmost interval that could have elapsed since the birth of the Messianic child (16–18). This was, beyond all question, an act of the blindest fury, for Herod might easily have informed himself whether a child who had received rare and costly presents was yet to be found in Bethlehem: but even granting it not inconsistent with the dis-

---

[15] Bibl. Comm. in loc, Hoffmann, s. 261.

[16] Schmidt, exeg. Beiträge, 1, 152 ff.

[17] This is shown in opposition to Olshausen by Steudel in Bengel's Archiv. vii. ii. 425 f. viii. iii. 487.

position of the aged tyrant to the extent that Schleiermacher supposed, it were in any case to be expected that so unprecedented and revolting a massacre would be noticed by other historians than Matthew.[18]　But neither Josephus, who is very minute in his account of Herod, nor the rabbins, who were assiduous in blackening his memory, give the slightest hint of this decree.　The latter do, indeed, connect the flight of Jesus into Egypt with a murderous scene, the author of which, however, is not Herod, but King Jannæus, and the victims not children, but rabbins.[19]　Their story is evidently founded on a confusion of the occurrence gathered from the christian history, with an earlier event; for Alexander Jannæus died 40 years before the birth of Christ.　Macrobius, who lived in the fourth century, is the only author who notices the slaughter of the infants, and he introduces it obliquely in a passage which loses all credit by confounding the execution of Antipater, who was so far from a child that he complained of his grey hairs,[20] with the murder of the infants, renowned among the Christians.[21]　Commentators have attempted to diminish our surprise at the remarkable silence in question, by reminding us that the number of children of the given age in the petty village of Bethlehem, must have been small, and by remarking that among the numerous deeds of cruelty by which the life of Herod was stained, this one would be lost sight of as a drop in the ocean.[22]　But in these observations the specific atrocity of murdering innocent children, however few, is overlooked; and it is this that must have prevented the deed, if really perpetrated, from being forgotten.[23] Here also the evangelist cites (v. 17, 18) a prophetic passage (Jerem. xxxi. 15), as having been fulfilled by the murder of the infants; whereas it originally referred to something quite different, namely the transportation of the Jews to Babylon, and had no kind of reference to an event lying in remote futurity.

While Jesus and his parents are in Egypt, Herod the Great dies, and Joseph is instructed by an angel, who appears to him in a dream, to return to his native country; but as Archelaus, Herod's successor in Judæa, was to be feared, he has more precise directions in a second oracular dream, in obedience to which he fixes his abode at Nazareth in Galilee, under the milder government of Herod Antipas (19–23).　Thus in the compass of this single chapter, we have five extraordinary interpositions of God; an anomalous star, and four visions.　For the star and the first vision, we have already remarked, one miracle might have been substituted, not only without detriment, but with advantage; either the star or the vision might from the beginning have deterred the magi from going to Jerusalem, and by this means perhaps have averted the massacre ordained by Herod.　But that the two last visions are not united in one is a mere superfluity; for the direction to Joseph to proceed to Nazareth instead of Bethlehem, which is made the object of a special vision, might just as well have been included in the first.　Such a disregard, even to prodigality, of the *lex parsimoniæ* in relation to the miraculous, one is tempted to refer to human imagination rather than to divine providence.

The false interpretations of Old Testament passages in this chapter are crowned by the last verse, where it is said that by the settlement of the

---

[18] Schmidt, ut sup. p. 156.

[19] Babylon. Sanhedr. f. cvii. 2, ap. Lightfoot, p. 207.　Comp. Schöttgen, ii. p. 533. According to Josephus Antiq. xiii. xiii. 5, xiv. 2, they were Jews of each sex and of all ages, and chiefly Pharisees.

[20] Joseph. B. J. i. xxx. 3.　Comp. Antiq. xvii. iv. 1.

[21] Macrob. Saturnal. ii. 4 : *Quum audisset* (*Augustus*) *inter pueros, quos in Syriâ Herodes rex Judæorum intra bimatum jussit interfici, filium quoque ejus occisum, ait: melius est, Herodis porcum* (ὗν) *esse quam filium* (υἱὸν).

[22] Vid. Wetstein, Kuinöl, Olshausen in loc. Winer d. A. Herodes.

[23] Fritzsche, Comm. in Matt., p. 93 f.

parents of Jesus at Nazareth was fulfilled the saying of the prophets : *He shall be called a Nazarene.* Now this passage is not to be found in the Old Testament, and unless expositors, losing courage, take refuge in darkness by supposing that it is extracted from a canonical [24] or apocryphal [25] book now lost, they must admit the conditional validity of one or other of the following charges against the evangelist. If, as it has been alleged, he intended to compress the Old Testament prophecies that the Messiah would be despised, into the oracular sentence, He shall be called a Nazarene, *i.e.* the citizen of a despised city,[26] we must accuse him of the most arbitrary mode of expression ; or, if he be supposed to give a modification of נזיר (*nasir*) we must tax him with the most violent transformation of the word and the grossest perversion of its meaning, for even if, contrary to the fact, this epithet were applied to the Messiah in the Old Testament, it could only mean either that he would be a Nazarite,[27] which Jesus never was, or that he would be crowned,[28] as Joseph, Gen. xlix. 26, in no case that he would be brought up in the petty town of Nazareth. The most probable interpretation of this passage, and that which has the sanction of the Jewish Christians questioned on the subject by Jerome, is, that the evangelist here alludes to Isa. xi. 1, where the Messiah is called נֵצֶר יִשַׁי (*surculus Jesse*) as elsewhere צֶמַח.[29] But in every case there is the same violence done to the word by attaching to a mere appellative of the Messiah, an entirely fictitious relation to the name of the city of Nazareth.

§ 35.

ATTEMPTS AT A NATURAL EXPLANATION OF THE HISTORY OF THE MAGI. TRANSITION TO THE MYTHICAL EXPLANATION.

To avoid the many difficulties which beset us at every step in interpreting this chapter after the manner of the supranaturalists, it is quite worth our while to seek for another exposition which may suffice to explain the whole according to physical and psychological laws, without any admixture of supernaturalism. Such an exposition has been the most successfully attempted by Paulus.

How could heathen magi, in a remote country of the east, know anything of a Jewish king about to be born ? This is the first difficulty, and it is removed on the above system of interpretation by supposing that the magi were expatriated Jews. But this, apparently, is not the idea of the evangelist.

For the question which he puts into the mouth of the magi, "*Where is he that is born King of the Jews?*" distinguishes them from that people, and as regards the tendency of the entire narrative, the church seems to have apprehended it more correctly than Paulus thinks, in representing the visit of the magi as the first manifestation of Christ to the Gentiles. Nevertheless, as we have above remarked, this difficulty may be cleared away without having recourse to the supposition of Paulus.

Further, according to the natural explanation, the real object of the journey of these men was not to see the new-born king, nor was its cause the star which they had observed in the east; but they happened to be travelling to Jerusalem perhaps with mercantile views, and hearing far and wide in the land of a new-born king, a celestial phenomenon which they had recently

[24] Chrysostom and others.
[25] Vid. Gratz, Comm. zum Ev. Matth. 1, s. 115.
[26] Kuinöl, ad Matth. p. 44 f.
[27] Wetstein, in loc.
[28] Schneckenburger, Beiträge zur Einleitung in das N. T., s. 42.
[29] Gieseler, Studien und Kritiken, 1831, 3. Heft, s. 588 f. Fritzsche, s. 104. Comp. Hieron. ad Jesai. xi. 1.

observed occurred to their remembrance, and they earnestly desired to see the child in question. By this means, it is true, the difficulty arising from the sanction given to astrology by the usual conception of the story is diminished, but only at the expense of unprejudiced interpretation. For even if it were admissible unceremoniously to transform magi μάγους into merchants, their purpose in this journey cannot have been a commercial one, for their first inquiry on arriving at Jerusalem is after the new-born king, and they forthwith mention a star, seen by them in the east, as the cause not only of their question, but also of their present journey, the object of which they aver to be the presentation of their homage to the new-born child (v. 2).

The ἀστήρ (*star*) becomes, on this method of interpretation, a natural meteor, or a comet,[1] or finally, a constellation, that is, a conjunction of planets.[2] The last idea was put forth by Kepler, and has been approved by several astronomers and theologians. Is it more easy, on any one of these suppositions, to conceive that the star could precede the magi on their way, and remain stationary over a particular house, according to the representation of the text? We have already examined the two first hypotheses; if we adopt the third, we must either suppose the verb προάγειν (v. 9) to signify the disjunction of the planets, previously in apparent union,[3] though the text does not imply a partition but a forward movement of the entire phenomenon; or we must call Süskind's pluperfect to our aid, and imagine that the constellation, which the magi could no longer see in the valley between Jerusalem and Bethlehem, again burst on their view over the place where the child dwelt.[4] For the expression, ἐπάνω οὗ ἦν τὸ παιδίον (v. 9), denotes merely the place of abode, not the particular dwelling of the child and his parents. This we grant; but when the evangelist proceeds thus: καὶ εἰσελθόντες εἰς τὴν οἰκίαν, (v. 9), he gives the more general expression the precise meaning of dwelling-house, so that this explanation is clearly a vain effort to abate the marvellousness of the evangelical narrative.

The most remarkable supposition adopted by those who regard ἀστήρ as a conjunction of planets, is that they hereby obtain a fixed point in accredited history, to which the narrative of Matthew may be attached. According to Kepler's calculation, corrected by Ideler, there occurred, three years before the death of Herod, in the year of Rome 747, a conjunction of Jupiter and Saturn in the sign Pisces. The conjunction of these planets is repeated in the above sign, to which astrologers attribute a special relation to Palestine, about every 800 years, and according to the computation of the Jew Abarbanel (1463) it took place three years before the birth of Moses; hence it is probable enough that the hope of the second great deliverer of the nation would be associated with the recurrence of this conjunction in the time of Herod, and that when the phenomenon was actually observed, it would occasion inquiry on the part of Babylonian Jews. But that the star mentioned by Matthew was this particular planetary conjunction, is, from our uncertainty as to the year of Christ's birth, and also as to the period of the above astrological calculation, an extremely precarious conjecture; and as, besides, there are certain particulars in the evangelical text, for instance, the words προῆγεν and ἔστη, which do not accord with such an explanation,—so soon as another, more congruous with Matthew's narrative, presents itself, we are justified in giving it the preference.

[1] For both these explanations, see Kuinöl, in loc.
[2] Kepler, in various treatises; Münter, der Stern der Weisen; Ideler, Handbuch der mathemat. und technischen Chronologie, 2. Bd. s. 399 ff.
[3] Olshausen, s. 67.
[4] Paulus, ut sup. s. 202, 221.

The difficulties connected with the erroneous interpretations of passages from the Old Testament are, from the natural point of view, eluded by denying that the writers of the New Testament are responsible for the falsity of these interpretations. It is said that the prophecy of Micah is applied to the Messiah and his birth in Bethlehem by the Sanhedrim alone, and that Matthew has not committed himself to their interpretation by one word of approval. But when the evangelist proceeds to narrate how the issue corresponded with the interpretation, he sanctions it by the authoritative seal of fact. In relation to the passage from Hosea, Paulus and Steudel [5] concur in resorting to a singular expedient. Matthew, say they, wished to guard against the offence which it might possibly give to the Jews of Palestine to learn that the Messiah had once left the Holy Land; he therefore called attention to the fact that Israel, in one sense the first-born of God, had been called out of Egypt, for which reason, he would imply, no one ought to be astonished that the Messiah, the son of God in a higher sense, had also visited a profane land. But throughout the passage there is no trace [6] of such a negative, precautionary intention on the part of the evangelist in adducing this prophecy: on the contrary, all his quotations seem to have the positive object to confirm the Messiahship of Jesus by showing that in him the Old Testament prophecies had their fulfilment. It has been attempted with reference to the two other prophecies cited in this chapter, to reduce the signification of the verb πληρωθῆναι (*to be fulfilled*) to that of mere similitude or applicability; but the futility of the effort needs no exposure.

The various directions conveyed to the persons of our narrative by means of visions are, from the same point of view, all explained psychologically, as effects of waking inquiries and reflections. This appears, indeed, to be indicated by the text itself, v. 22, according to which Joseph, hearing that Archelaus was master of Judea, feared to go thither, and not until then did he receive an intimation from a higher source in a dream. Nevertheless, on a closer examination we find that the communication given in the dream was something new, not a mere repetition of intelligence received in waking moments. Only the negative conclusion, that on account of Archelaus it was not advisable to settle at Bethlehem, was attained by Joseph when awake; the positive injunction to proceed to Nazareth was superadded in his dream. To explain the other visions in the above way is a direct interpolation of the text, for this represents both the hostility and death of Herod as being first made known to Joseph by dreams; in like manner, the magi have no distrust of Herod until a dream warns them against his treachery.

Thus, on the one hand, the sense of the narrative in Matt. ii. is opposed to the conception of its occurrence as natural; on the other hand, this narrative, taken in its original sense, carries the supernatural into the extravagant, the improbable into the impossible. We are therefore led to doubt the historical character of the narrative, and to conjecture that we have before us something mythical. The first propounders of this opinion were so unsuccessful in its illustration, that they never liberated themselves from the sphere of the natural interpretation, which they sought to transcend. Arabian merchants (thinks Krug, for example) coming by chance to Bethlehem, met with the parents of Jesus, and learning that they were strangers in distress (according to Matthew, the parents of Jesus were not strangers in Bethlehem), made them presents, uttered many good wishes for their child, and pursued their

[5] Bengel's Archiv. vii. ii. p. 424.
[6] At a later period, it is true, this journey of Jesus was the occasion of calumnies from the Jews, but those were of an entirely different nature, as will be seen in the following chapter.

journey.   When subsequently, Jesus was reputed to be the Messiah, the incident was remembered and embellished with a star, visions, and believing
homage.   To these were added the flight into Egypt and the infanticide ; the
latter, because the above incident was supposed to have had some effect on
Herod, who, on other grounds than those alleged in the text, had caused some
families in Bethlehem to be put to death ; the former, probably because Jesus
had, with some unknown object, actually visited Egypt at a later period.[7]

In this, as in the purely naturalistic interpretation, there remain as so many
garb, the arrival of some oriental travellers, the flight into Egypt, and the
massacre in Bethlehem ; divested, however, of the marvellous garb with which
they are enveloped in the evangelical narrative.   In this unadorned form,
these occurrences are held to be intelligible and such as might very probably
happen, but in point of fact they are more incomprehensible even than when
viewed through the medium of orthodoxy, for with their supernatural embellishments vanishes the entire basis on which they rest.   Matthew's narrative
adequately accounts for the relations between the men of the east and the
parents of Jesus ; this attempt at mythical exposition reduces them to a wonderful chance.   The massacre at Bethlehem has, in the evangelical narrative,
a definite cause ; here, we are at a loss to understand how Herod came
to ordain such an enormity ; so, the journey into Egypt, which had so urgent
a motive according to Matthew, is on this scheme of interpretation totally
inexplicable.   It may indeed be said : these events had their adequate causes
in accordance with the regular course of things, but Matthew has withheld this
natural sequence and given a miraculous one in its stead.   But if the writer
or legend be capable of environing occurrences with fictitious motives and
accessory circumstances, either the one or the other is also capable of fabri-
cating the occurrences themselves, and this fabrication is the more probable,
the more clearly we can show that the legend had an interest in depicting
such occurrences, though they had never actually taken place.

This argument is equally valid against the attempt, lately made from the
supranaturalistic point of view, to separate the true from the false in the evangelical narrative.   In a narrative like this, says Neander, we must carefully
distinguish the kernel from the shell, the main fact from immaterial circumstances, and not demand the same degree of certitude for all its particulars.
That the magi by their astrological researches were led to anticipate the birth
of a Saviour in Judea, and hence journeyed to Jerusalem that they might offer
him their homage is, according to him, the only essential and certain part of
the narrative.   But how, when arrived in Jerusalem, did they learn that the
child was to be born in Bethlehem?   From Herod, or by some other means?
On this point Neander is not equally willing to guarantee the veracity of Matthew's statements, and he regards it as unessential.   The magi, he continues,
in so inconsiderable a place as Bethlehem, might be guided to the child's
dwelling by many providential arrangements in the ordinary course of events ;
for example, by meeting with the shepherds or other devout persons who had
participated in the great event.   When however they had once entered the
house, they might represent the circumstances in the astrological guise with
which their minds were the most familiar.   Neander awards an historical
character to the flight into Egypt and the infanticide.[8]   By this explanation
of the narrative, only its heaviest difficulty, namely, that the star preceded the

[7] Ueber formelle oder genetische Erklärungsart der Wunder.   In Henke's Museum, 1, 3,
399 ff.   Similar essays see in the Abhandlungen über die beiden ersten Kapitel des Matthäus u. Lukas, in Henke's Magazin, 5, 1, 171 ff., and in Matthäi, Religionsgl. der Apostel,
2, s. 422 ff.
[8] L. J. Ch., s. 29 ff.

magi on their way and paused above a single house, is in reality thrown overboard ; the other difficulties remain.   But Neander has renounced unlimited confidence in the veracity of the evangelist, and admitted that a part of his narrative is unhistorical.   If it be asked how far this unhistorical portion extends, and what is its kind—whether the nucleus around which legend has deposited its crystallizations be historical or ideal—it is easy to show that the few and vague data which a less lenient criticism than that of Neander can admit as historical, are far less adapted to give birth to our narrative, than the very precise circle of ideas and types which we are about to exhibit.

§ 36.

THE PURELY MYTHICAL EXPLANATION OF THE NARRATIVE CONCERNING THE MAGI, AND OF THE EVENTS WITH WHICH IT IS CONNECTED.

Several Fathers of the Church indicated the true key to the narrative concerning the magi when, in order to explain from what source those heathen astrologers could gather any knowledge of a Messianic star, they put forth the conjecture that this knowledge might have been drawn from the prophecies of the heathen Balaam, recorded in the Book of Numbers.[1]   K. Ch. L. Schmidt justly considers it a deficiency in the exposition of Paulus, that it takes no notice of the Jewish expectation that a star would become visible at the appearance of the Messiah ; and yet, he adds, this is the only thread to guide us to the true origin of this narrative.[2]   The prophecy of Balaam (Num. xxiv. 17), *A star shall come out of Jacob*, was the cause—not indeed, as the Fathers supposed, that magi actually recognized a newly-kindled star as that of the Messiah, and hence journeyed to Jerusalem—but that legend represented a star to have appeared at the birth of Jesus, and to have been recognized by astrologers as the star of the Messiah.   The prophecy attributed to Balaam originally referred to some fortunate and victorious ruler of Israel ; but it seems to have early received a Messianic interpretation.   Even if the translation in the Targum of Onkelos, *surget rex ex Jacobo et Messias (unctus) ungetur ex Israele*, prove nothing, because here the word *unctus* is synonymous with *rex*, and might signify an ordinary king—it is yet worthy of notice that, according to the testimony of Aben Ezra,[3] and the passages cited by Wetstein and Schöttgen, many rabbins applied the prophecy to the Messiah. The name Bar-Cocheba (*son of a star*), assumed by a noted pseudo-Messiah under Hadrian, was chosen with reference to the Messianic interpretation of Balaam's prophecy.

It is true that the passage in question, taken in its original sense, does not speak of a real star, but merely compares to a star the future prince of Israel, and this is the interpretation given to it in the Targum above quoted.   But the growing belief in astrology, according to which every important event was signalized by sidereal changes, soon caused the prophecy of Balaam to be understood no longer figuratively, but literally, as referring to a star which was to appear contemporaneously with the Messiah.   We have various proofs that a belief in astrology was prevalent in the time of Jesus.   The future greatness of Mithridates was thought to be prognosticated by the appearance of a comet in the year of his birth, and in that of his accession to the throne [4] ;

[1] Orig. c. Cels. i. 60.   Auctor, op. imperf. in Matth. ap. Fabricius Pseudepigr. V. T., p. 807 ff.

[2] Schmidt's Bibliothek, 3, 1, s. 130.

[3] In loc. Num. (Schöttgen, horæ, ii. p. 152) : *Multi Interpretati sunt hæc de Messiâ.*

[4] Justin. Hist. 37.

and a comet observed shortly after the death of Julius Cæsar, was supposed to have a close relation to that event.[5] These ideas were not without influence on the Jews; at least we find traces of them in Jewish writings of a later period, in which it is said that a remarkable star appeared at the birth of Abraham.[6] When such ideas were afloat, it was easy to imagine that the birth of the Messiah must be announced by a star, especially as, according to the common interpretation of Balaam's prophecy, a star was there made the symbol of the Messiah. It is certain that the Jewish mind effected this combination ; for it is a rabbinical idea that at the time of the Messiah's birth, a star will appear in the east and remain for a long time visible.[7] The narrative of Matthew is allied to this simpler Jewish idea ; the apocryphal descriptions of the star that announced the birth of Jesus, to the extravagant fictions about the star said to have appeared in the time of Abraham.[8] We may therefore state the opinion of K. Ch. L. Schmidt,[9] recently approved by Fritzsche and De Wette, as the nearest approach to truth on the subject of Matthew's star in the east. In the time of Jesus it was the general belief that stars were always the forerunners of great events; hence the Jews of that period thought that the birth of the Messiah would necessarily be announced by a star, and this supposition had a specific sanction in Num. xxiv. 17. The early converted Jewish Christians could confirm their faith in Jesus, and justify it in the eyes of others, only by labouring to prove that in him were realized all the attributes lent to the Messiah by the Jewish notions of their age—a proposition that might be urged the more inoffensively and with the less chance of refutation, the more remote lay the age of Jesus, and the more completely the history of his childhood was shrouded in darkness. Hence it soon ceased to be matter of doubt that the anticipated appearance of a star was really coincident with the birth of Jesus.[10] This being once presupposed, it followed as a matter of course that the observers of this appearance were eastern magi ; first, because none could better interpret the sign than astrologers, and the east was supposed to be the native region of their science ; and secondly, because it must have seemed fitting that the Messianic star which had been seen by the spiritual eye of the ancient magus Balaam, should, on its actual appearance be first recognized by the bodily eyes of later magi.

This particular, however, as well as the journey of the magi into Judea, and their costly presents to the child, bear a relation to other passages in the Old Testament. In the description of the happier future, given in Isaiah, chap. lx., the prophet foretells that, at that time, the most remote people and kings will come to Jerusalem to worship Jehovah, with offerings of gold and incense

---

[5] Sueton. Jul. Cæs. 88.

[6] Jalkut Rubeni, f. xxxii. 3 (ap. Wetstein) : *quâ horâ natus est Abrahamus, pater noster, super quem sit pax, stetit quoddam sidus in oriente et deglutivit quatuor astra, quæ erant in quatuor cæli plagis.* According to an Arabic writing entitled Maallem, this star, prognosticating the birth of Abraham, was seen by Nimrod in a dream. Fabric. Cod. pseudepigr. V. T. i. s. 345.

[7] Testamentum XII. Patriarcharum, test. Levi, 18 (Fabric. Cod. pseud. V. T. p. 584 f.) : καὶ ἀνατελεῖ ἄστρον αὐτοῦ (of the Messianic ἱερεὺς καινὸς) ἐν οὐρανῷ.—φωτίζον φῶς γνώσεως κ. τ. λ. Pesikta Sotarta, f. xlviii. 1 (ap. Schöttgen, ii. p. 531) : *Et prodibit stella ab oriente, quæ est stella Messiæ, et in oriente versabitur dies XV.* Comp. Sohar Genes. f. 74. Schöttgen, ii. 524, and some other passages which are pointed out by Ideler in the Handbuch der Chronologie, 2 Bd. s. 409, Anm. 1, and Bertholdt, Christologia Judæorum, § 14.

[8] Compare with the passages cited Note 7. Protevang. Jac. cap. xxi. : εἴδομεν ἀστέρα παμμεγέθη, λάμψαντα ἐν τοῖς ἄστροις τούτοις καὶ ἀμβλύνοντα αὐτοὺς τοῦ φαίνειν. Still more exaggerated in Ignat. ep. ad Ephes. 19. See the collection of passages connected with this subject in Thilo, cod. apocr. i. p. 390 f.

[9] Exeg. Beiträge, i. s. 159 ff.

[10] Fritzsche in the paraphrase of chap. ii. *Etiam stella, quam judaica disciplina sub Messiæ natale visum iri dicit, quo Jesus nascebatur tempore exorta est.*

and all acceptable gifts.[11] If in this passage the messianic times alone are spoken of, while the Messiah himself is wanting, in Psalm lxxii. we read of a king who is to be feared as long as the sun and moon endure, in whose times the righteous shall flourish, and whom all nations shall call blessed ; this king might easily be regarded as the Messiah, and the Psalm says of him nearly in the words of Isa. lx., that foreign kings shall bring him gold and other presents. To this it may be added, that the pilgrimage of foreign people to Jerusalem is connected with a risen light,[12] which might suggest the star of Balaam. What was more natural, when on the one hand was presented Balaam's messianic star out of Jacob (for the observation of which magian astrologers were the best adapted) ; on the other, a light which was to arise on Jerusalem, and to which distant nations would come, bringing gifts—than to combine the two images and to say : In consequence of the star which had risen over Jerusalem, astrologers came from a distant land with presents for the Messiah whom the star announced ? But when the imagination once had possession of the star, and of travellers attracted by it from a distance, there was an inducement to make the star the immediate guide of their course, and the torch to light them on their way. This was a favourite idea of antiquity : according to Virgil, a star, *stella facem ducens*, marked out the way of Æneas from the shores of Troy to the west [13] ; Thrasybulus and Timoleon were led by celestial fires ; and a star was said to have guided Abraham on his way to Moriah.[14] Besides, in the prophetic passage itself, the heavenly light seems to be associated with the pilgrimage of the offerers as the guide of their course ; at all events the originally figurative language of the prophet would probably, at a later period, be understood literally, in accordance with the rabbinical spirit of interpretation. The magi are not conducted by the star directly to Bethlehem where Jesus was ; they first proceed to Jerusalem. One reason for this might be, that the prophetic passage connects the risen light and the offerers with Jerusalem ; but the chief reason lies in the fact, that in Jerusalem Herod was to be found ; for what was better adapted to instigate Herod to his murderous decree, than the alarming tidings of the magi, that they had seen the star of the great Jewish king?

To represent a murderous decree as having been directed by Herod against Jesus, was the interest of the primitive christian legend. In all times legend has glorified the infancy of great men by persecutions and attempts on their life ; the greater the danger that hovered over them, the higher seems their value ; the more unexpectedly their deliverance is wrought, the more evident is the esteem in which they are held by heaven. Hence in the history of the childhood of Cyrus in Herodotus, of Romulus in Livy,[15] and even later of Augustus in Suetonius,[16] we find this trait ; neither has the Hebrew legend neglected to assign such a distinction to Moses.[17] One point of analogy be-

---

[11] As in Matt. ii. 11 it is said of the magi τροσήνεγκαν αὐτῷ—χρυσὸν καὶ λίβανον : so in Isa. lx. 6 (LXX.) : ἥξουσί, φέροντες χρυσίον, καὶ λίβανον οἴσουσι. The third present is in Matt. σμύρνα, in Isa. λίθος τίμιος.

[12] V. I. und 3 : קוּמִי אוֹרִי (LXX : 'Ιερουσαλήμ) כִּי בָא אוֹרֵךְ וּכְבוֹד יְהֹוָה עָלַיִךְ זָרָח :—וְהָלְכוּ גוֹיִם לְאוֹרֵךְ וּמְלָכִים לְנֹגַהּ זַרְחֵךְ

[13] Æneid. ii. 693 ff.

[14] Wetstein, in loc.

[15] Herod. i. 108 ff. Liv. i. 4.

[16] Octav. 94 :—*ante paucos quam nasceretur menses prodigium Romæ factum publice, quo denuntiabatur, regem populi Romani naturam parturire. Senatum exterritum, censuisse, ne quis illo anno genitus educaretur. Eos, qui gravidas uxores haberent, quo ad se quisque spem traheret, curasse, ne Senatus consultum ad ærarium deferretur.*

[17] Bauer (über das Mythische in der früheren Lebensper. des Moses, in the n. Theol.

tween the narrative in Exod. i. ii, and that in Matthew, is that in both cases the murderous decree does not refer specially to the one dangerous child, but generally to a certain class of children; in the former, to all new-born males, in the latter to all of and under the age of two years. It is true that, according to the narrative in Exodus, the murderous decree is determined on without any reference to Moses, of whose birth Pharaoh is not supposed to have had any presentiment, and who is therefore only by accident implicated in its consequences. But this representation did not sufficiently mark out Moses as the object of hostile design to satisfy the spirit of Hebrew tradition, and by the time of Josephus it had been so modified as to resemble more nearly the legends concerning Cyrus and Augustus, and above all the narrative of Matthew. According to the later legend, Pharaoh was incited to issue his murderous decree by a communication from his interpreters of the sacred writings, who announced to him the birth of an infant destined to succour the Israelites and humble the Egyptians.[18] The interpreters of the sacred writings here play the same part as the interpreters of dreams in Herodotus, and the astrologers in Matthew. Legend was not content with thus signalizing the infancy of the lawgiver alone—it soon extended the same distinction to the great progenitor of the Israelitish nation, Abraham, whom it represented as being in peril of his life from the murderous attempt of a jealous tyrant, immediately after his birth. Moses was opposed to Pharaoh as an enemy and oppressor; Abraham held the same position with respect to Nimrod. This monarch was forewarned by his sages, whose attention had been excited by a remarkable star, that Tharah would have a son from whom a powerful nation would descend. Apprehensive of rivalry, Nimrod immediately issues a murderous command, which, however, Abraham happily escapes.[19] What wonder then, that, as the great progenitor and the lawgiver of the nation had their Nimrod and Pharaoh, a corresponding persecutor was found for the restorer of the nation, the Messiah, in the person of Herod;—that this tyrant was said to have been apprised of the Messiah's birth by wise men, and to have laid snares against his life, from which, however, he happily escapes? The apocryphal legend, indeed, has introduced an imitation of this trait, after its own style, into the history of the Forerunner; he, too, is endangered by Herod's decree, a mountain is miraculously cleft asunder to receive him and his mother, but his father refusing to point out the boy's hiding-place, is put to death.[20]

Jesus escapes from the hostile attempts of Herod by other means than those by which Moses, according to the mosaic history, and Abraham, according to the Jewish legend, elude the decree issued against them; namely, by a flight out of his native land into Egypt. In the life of Moses also there occurs a flight into a foreign land; not, however, during his childhood, but after he had slain the Egyptian, when, fearing the vengeance of Pharaoh, he takes refuge in Midian (Exod. ii. 15). That reference was made to this flight of the first Goël in that of the second, our text expressly shows, for the words, which it attributes to the angel, who encourages Joseph to

---

Journ. 13, 3) had already compared the marvellous deliverance of Moses with that of Cyrus and Romulus; the comparison of the infanticides was added by De Wette, Kritik der Mos. Geschichte, s. 176.

[18] Joseph. Antiq. ii. ix. 2.

[19] Jalkut Rubeni (cont. of the passage cited in Note 6): *dixerunt sapientes Nimrodi: natus est Tharæ filius hâc ipsâ horâ, ex quo egressurus est populus, qui hæreditabit præsens et futurum seculum; si tibi placuerit, detur patri ipsius domus argento auroque plena, et occidat ipsum.* Comp. the passage of the Arabic book quoted by Fabric. Cod. pseudepigr. ut sup.

[20] Protev. Jacobi, c. xxii. f.

return out of Egypt into Palestine, are those by which Moses is induced to return out of Midian into Egypt.[21]   The choice of Egypt as a place of refuge for Jesus, may be explained in the simplest manner : the young Messiah could not, like Moses, flee *out of* Egypt ; hence, that his history might not be destitute of so significant a feature as a connexion with Egypt, that ancient retreat of the patriarchs, the relation was reversed, and he was made to flee *into* Egypt, which, besides, from its vicinity, was the most appropriate asylum for a fugitive from Judea.   The prophetic passage which the evangelist cites from Hosea xi. 1, *Out of Egypt have I called my son*—is less available for the elucidation of this particular in our narrative.   For the immediate proofs that the Jews referred this passage to the Messiah are very uncertain ;[22] though, if we compare such passages as Ps. ii. 7, in which the words בְּנִי אַתָּה (*thou art my son*) are interpreted of the Messiah, it cannot appear incredible that the expression לְבְנִי (*my son*) in Hosea was supposed to have a messianic signification.

Against this mythical derivation of the narrative, two objections have been recently urged.   First, if the history of the star originated in Balaam's prophecy, why, it is asked, does not Matthew, fond as he is of showing the fulfilment of Old Testament predictions in the life of Jesus, make the slightest allusion to that prophecy ?[23]   Because it was not he who wove this history out of the materials furnished in the Old Testament ; he received it, already fashioned, from others, who did not communicate to him its real origin.   For the very reason that many narratives were transmitted to him without their appropriate keys, he sometimes tries false ones ; as in our narrative, in relation to the Bethlehem massacre, he quotes, under a total misconception of the passage, Jeremiah's image of Rachel weeping for her children.[24]   The other objection is this : how could the communities of Jewish Christians, whence this pretended mythus must have sprung, ascribe so high an importance to the heathen as is implied in the star of the magi ?[25]   As if the prophets had not, in such passages as we have quoted, already ascribed to them this importance, which, in fact, consists but in their rendering homage and submission to the Messiah, a relation that must be allowed to correspond with the ideas of the Jewish Christians, not to speak of the particular conditions on which the heathen were to be admitted into the kingdom of the Messiah.

We must therefore abide by the mythical interpretation of our narrative, and content ourselves with gathering from it no particular fact in the life of Jesus, but only a new proof how strong was the impression of his messiahship left by Jesus on the minds of his contemporaries, since even the history of his childhood received a messianic form.[26]

Let us now revert to the narrative of Luke, chap. ii., so far as it runs parallel with that of Matthew.   We have seen that the narrative of Matthew

---

[21] Ex. iv. 19, LXX :
βάδιζε, ἄπελθε εἰς Αἴγυπτον, τεθνήκασι γὰρ πάντες οἱ ζητοῦντές σου τὴν ψυχήν.

Matt. ii. 20 :
ἐγερθεὶς—πορεύου εἰς γῆν Ἰσραήλ· τεθνήκασι γὰρ οἱ ζητοῦντες τὴν ψυχὴν τοῦ παιδίου.

We may remark that the inappropriate use of the plural in the evangelical passage, can only be explained on the supposition of a reference to the passage in Exod. See Winer, N. T. Gramm. s. 149.   Comp. also Exod. iv. 20 with Matt. ii. 14, 21.

[22] Vide e. g. Schöttgen, Horæ, ii. p. 209.

[23] Theile, zur biographie Jesu, § 15, Anm. 9.   Hoffmann, s. 269.

[24] Comp. my Streitschriften, i. 1, s. 42 f. ; George, s. 39.

[25] Neander, L. J. Ch. s. 27.

[26] Schleiermacher (Ueber den Lukas, s. 47), explains the narrative concerning the magi as a symbolical one ; but he scorns to take into consideration the passages from the O. T. and other writings, which have a bearing on the subject, and by way of retribution, his exposition at one time rests in generalities, at another, takes a wrong path.

M

does not allow us to presuppose that of Luke as a series of prior incidents :
still less can the converse be true, namely, that the magi arrived before the
shepherds : it remains then to be asked, whether the two narratives do not
aim to represent the same fact, though they have given it a different garb ?
From the older orthodox opinion that the star in Matthew was an angel, it
was an easy step to identify that apparition with the angel in Luke, and to
suppose that the angels, who appeared to the shepherds of Bethlehem on the
night of the birth of Jesus, were taken by the distant magi for a star vertical
to Judea,[27] so that both the accounts might be essentially correct.   Of late,
only one of the Evangelists has been supposed to give the true circumstances,
and Luke has had the preference, Matthew's narrative being regarded as an
embellished edition.

According to this opinion, the angel clothed in heavenly brightness, in
Luke, became a star in the tradition recorded by Matthew, the ideas of angels
and stars being confounded in the higher Jewish theology ; the shepherds
were exalted into royal magi, kings being in antiquity called the shepherds
of their people.[28]   This derivation is too elaborate to be probable, even were
it true, as it is here assumed, that Luke's narrative bears the stamp of historical credibility.   As, however, we conceive that we have proved the
contrary, and as, consequently, we have before us two equally unhistorical
narratives, there is no reason for preferring a forced and unnatural derivation
of Matthew's narrative from that of Luke, to the very simple derivation which
may be traced through Old Testament passages and Jewish notions.   These
two descriptions of the introduction of Jesus into the world, are, therefore,
two variations on the same theme, composed, however, quite independently
of each other.

§ 37.

CHRONOLOGICAL RELATION BETWEEN THE VISIT OF THE MAGI, TOGETHER
WITH THE FLIGHT INTO EGYPT, AND THE PRESENTATION IN THE TEMPLE
RECORDED BY LUKE.

It has been already remarked, that the narratives of Matthew and Luke
above considered at first run tolerably parallel, but afterwards widely diverge ;
for instead of the tragical catastrophe of the massacre and flight, Luke has
preserved to us the peaceful scene of the presentation of the child Jesus in
the temple.   Let us for the present shut our eyes to the result of the preceding inquiry—the purely mythical character of Matthew's narrative—and ask :
In what chronological relation could the presentation in the temple stand to
the visit of the magi and the flight into Egypt ?

Of these occurrences the only one that has a precise date is the presentation
in the temple, of which it is said that it took place at the expiration of the
period appointed by the law for the purification of a mother, that is, according to Lev. xii. 2–4, forty days after the birth of the child (Luke ii. 22).   The
time of the other incidents is not fixed with the same exactness ; it is merely
said that the magi came to Jerusalem, τοῦ Ἰησοῦ γεννηθέντος ἐν Βηθλεὲμ (Matt.
ii. 1)—how long after the birth the Evangelist does not decide.   As, however,
the participle connects the visit of the magi with the birth of the child, if not
immediately, at least so closely that nothing of importance can be supposed
to have intervened, some expositors have been led to the opinion that the

---

[27] Lightfoot, Horæ, p. 202.
[28] Schneckenburger, Ueber den Ursprung des ersten kanonischen Evangeliums, s. 69 ff.

visit ought to be regarded as prior to the presentation in the temple.[1]   Admitting this arrangement, we have to reconcile it with one of two alternatives; either the flight into Egypt also preceded the presentation in the temple; or, while the visit of the magi preceded, the flight followed that event.   If we adopt the latter alternative, and thrust the presentation in the temple between the visit of the magi and the flight, we come into collision at once with the text of Matthew and the mutual relation of the facts.   The Evangelist connects the command to flee into Egypt with the return of the magi, by a participial construction (v. 13) similar to that by which he connects the arrival of the oriental sages with the birth of Jesus; hence those, who in the one instance hold such a construction to be a reason for placing the events which it associates in close succession, must in the other instance be withheld by it from inserting a third occurrence between the visit and the flight.   As regards the mutual relation of the facts, it can hardly be considered probable, that at the very point of time in which Joseph received a divine intimation, that he was no longer safe in Bethlehem from the designs of Herod, he should be permitted to take a journey to Jerusalem, and thus to rush directly into the lion's mouth.   At all events, the strictest precautions must have been enjoined on all who were privy to the presence of the messianic child in Jerusalem, lest a rumour of the fact should get abroad.   But there is no trace of this solicitous incognito in Luke's narrative; on the contrary, not only does Simeon call attention to Jesus in the temple, unchecked either by the Holy Spirit or by the parents, but Anna also thinks she is serving the good cause, by publishing as widely as possible the tidings of the Messiah's birth (Luke ii. 28 ff. 38).   It is true that she is said to have confined her communications to those who were like-minded with herself (ἐλάλει περὶ αὐτοῦ πᾶσι τοῖς προσδεχομένοις λύτρωσιν ἐν Ἰερουσαλήμ), but this could not hinder them from reaching the ears of the Herodian party, for the greater the excitement produced by such news on the minds of those *who looked for redemption*, the more would the vigilance of the government be aroused, so that Jesus would inevitably fall into the hands of the tyrant who was lying in wait.

Thus in any case, they who place the presentation in the temple after the visit of the magi, must also determine to postpone it until after the return from Egypt.   But even this arrangement clashes with the evangelical statement; for it requires us to insert, between the birth of Jesus and his presentation in the temple, the following events: the arrival of the magi, the flight into Egypt, the Bethlehem massacre, the death of Herod, and the return of the parents of Jesus out of Egypt—obviously too much to be included in the space of forty days.   It must therefore be supposed that the presentation of the child, and the first appearance of the mother in the temple, were procrastinated beyond the time appointed by the law.   This expedient, however, runs counter to the narrative of Luke, who expressly says, that the visit to the temple took place at the legal time.   But in either case the difficulty is the same; the parents of Jesus could, according to Matthew's account, as little think of a journey to Jerusalem after their return from Egypt, as immediately previous to their departure thither.   For if Joseph, on his return from Egypt, was warned not to enter Judea, because Archelaus was Herod's successor in that province, he would least of all venture to Jerusalem, the very seat of the redoubted government.

On neither of the above plans, therefore, will the presentation in the temple bear to be placed after the visit of the magi, and the only remaining alterna-

---

[1] Thus, e. g. Augustin de consensu evangelistarum, ii. 5.   Storr, opusc. acad. iii. s. 96 ff. Süskind, in Bengel's Archiv. i. 1, s. 216 ff.

tive, which is embraced by the majority of commentators,[2] is to make the
incident noticed by Luke, precede both those narrated by Matthew.   This is
so far the most natural, that in Matthew there is at least an indirect intimation of a considerable interval between the birth of Jesus and the arrival of
the magi.   For we are told that Herod's decree included all the children in
Bethlehem up to the age of two years; we must therefore necessarily infer,
that even if Herod, to make sure of his object, exceeded the term fixed by
the magi, the star had been visible to these astrologers for more than a year.
Now the narrator seems to suppose the appearance of the star to have been
cotemporary with the birth of Jesus.   Viewing the narratives in this order,
the parents of Jesus first journeyed from Bethlehem, where the child was
born, to Jerusalem, there to present the legal offerings; they next returned
to Bethlehem, where (according to Matt. ii. 1 and 5) they were found by the
magi; then followed the flight into Egypt, and after the return from thence,
the settlement at Nazareth.   The first and most urgent question that here
suggests itself is this: What had the parents of Jesus to do a second time in
Bethlehem, which was not their home, and where their original business
connected with the census must surely have been despatched in the space of
forty days?   The discussion of this question must be deferred, but we can
find an ample substitute for this argument, drawn from the nature of the fact,
in one which rests on the words of the evangelical narrative.   Luke (v. 39)
says, in the most definite manner, that after the completion of the legal
observance, the parents of Jesus returned to Nazareth, as to their proper
home, not to Bethlehem, which, according to him, was merely a temporary
residence.[3]   If, then, the magi arrived after the presentation in the temple,
they must have met with the parents of Jesus in Nazareth, and not in
Bethlehem, as Matthew states.   Moreover, had the arrival of the magi really
been preceded by the presentation in the temple, together with the attention
which must have been excited by the language of Simeon and Anna; it is
impossible that at the period of that arrival the birth of the messianic child
could have been so much a secret in Jerusalem, that the announcement of it
by the magi should be, as Matthew relates, a source of general astonishment.[4]

   If, then, the presentation of Jesus in the temple can have taken place
neither earlier nor later than the visit of the magi and the flight into Egypt;
and if the flight into Egypt can have taken place neither earlier nor later than
the presentation in the temple; it is impossible that both these occurrences
really happened, and, at the very utmost, only one can be historical.[5]

   To escape from this dangerous dilemma, supranaturalism has lately been
induced to take a freer position, that by the surrender of what is no longer
tenable, the residue may be saved.   Neander finds himself constrained to
admit, that neither did Luke know anything of what Matthew communicates
concerning the childhood of Jesus, nor did the Greek editor of Matthew (to
be distinguished from the apostle) know anything of the events detailed by
Luke.   But, he contends, it does not therefore follow that both the different
series of incidents cannot have happened.[6]   By giving this turn to the matter,

---

[2] E.g. Hess, Geschichte Jesu, 1, s. 51 ff. Paulus, Olshausen, in loc.

[3] Süskind, ut sup. s. 222.

[4] The same difference as to the chronological relation of the two incidents exists between
the two different texts of the apocryphal book : Historia de nativitate Mariæ et de inf. Serv.,
see Thilo, p. 385, not.

[5] This incompatibility of the two narratives was perceived at an early period by some
opponents of Christianity.   Epiphanius names one Philosabbatius, together with Celsus and
Porphyry (hæres. li. 8).

[6] Neander, L. J. Ch. s. 33, Anm.

the difficulties arising from the words of the Evangelist are certainly avoided; not so, the difficulties arising from the nature of the facts. The first Evangelist ranges in close succession the visit of the magi and the flight into Egypt, as though no change of place had intervened; the author of the third Gospel represents the parents of Jesus as returning with the child, after the presentation in the temple, directly to Nazareth. We cannot, on this ground, argue from one evangelist against the other; for it is inadmissible to maintain that certain events never happened, because they were unknown to a remote narrator. But viewing the two narratives in another light, we perceive how improbable it is that, after the scene in the temple, the birth of the messianic child should be so entirely unknown in Jerusalem as the conduct of Herod on the arrival of the magi implies; how incredible (reversing the order of the events) that Joseph should be permitted to go to Jerusalem, with the child which Herod had just sought to kill; how inconceivable, finally, that the parents of Jesus should have returned to Bethlehem after the presentation in the temple (of which more hereafter). All these difficulties, lying in the nature of the facts, difficulties not less weighty than those connected with the words of the Evangelists, still subsist in Neander's explanation, and prove its inadequacy.

Thus the dilemma above stated remains, and were we compelled to choose under it, we should, in the present stage of our inquiry, on no account decide in favour of Matthew's narrative, and against that of Luke; on the contrary, as we have recognized the mythical character of the former, we should have no resource but to adhere, with our modern critics,[7] to the narrative of Luke, and surrender that of Matthew. But is not Luke's narrative of the same nature as that of Matthew, and instead of having to choose between the two, must we not deny to both an historical character? The answer to this question will be found in the succeeding examination.

§ 38.

THE PRESENTATION OF JESUS IN THE TEMPLE.

The narrative of the presentation of Jesus in the temple (Luke ii. 22) seems, at the first glance, to bear a thoroughly historical stamp. A double law, on the one hand, prescribing to the mother an offering of purification, on the other, requiring the redemption of the first-born son, leads the parents of Jesus to Jerusalem and to the temple. Here they meet with a devout man, absorbed in the expectation of the Messiah, named Simeon. Many expositors hold this Simeon to be the same with the Rabbi Simeon, the son of Hillel, his successor as president of the Sanhedrim, and the father of Gamaliel; some even identify him with the Sameas of Josephus,[1] and attach importance to his pretended descent from David, because this descent makes him a relative of Jesus, and helps to explain the following scene naturally; but this hypothesis is improbable, for Luke would hardly have introduced so celebrated a personage by the meagre designation, ἄνθρωπός τις, (a certain man).[2] Without this hypothesis, however, the scene between the parents of Jesus and Simeon, as also the part played by Anna the prophetess, seems to admit of a very natural explanation. There is no necessity for supposing, with the

---

[7] Schleiermacher, Ueber den Lukas, s. 47. Schneckenburger, ut sup.
[1] Antiq. xiv. ix. 4, xv. i. 1 and x. 4.
[2] The Evang. Nicodemi indeed calls him, c. xvi. ὁ μέγας διδάσκαλος, and the Protev. Jacobi, c. xxiv. makes him a priest or even high priest, vid. Varr. ap. Thilo Cod. Apocr. N. T. 1, s. 271, comp. 203.

author of the Natural History,[3] that Simeon was previously aware of the hope cherished by Mary that she was about to give birth to the Messiah; we need only, with Paulus and others, conceive the facts in the following manner. Animated, like many of that period, with the hope of the speedy advent of the Messiah, Simeon receives, probably in a dream, the assurance that before his death he will be permitted to see the expected deliverer of his nation. One day, in obedience to an irresistible impulse, he visited the temple, and on this very day Mary brought thither her child, whose beauty at once attracted his notice; on learning the child's descent from David, the attention and interest of Simeon were excited to a degree that induced Mary to disclose to him the hopes which were reposed on this scion of ancient royalty, with the extraordinary occurrences by which they had been called into existence. These hopes Simeon embraced with confidence, and in enthusiastic language gave utterance to his messianic expectations and forebodings, under the conviction that they would be fulfilled in this child. Still less do we need the supposition of the author of the Natural History with respect to Anna, namely, that she was one of the women who assisted at the birth of the infant Jesus, and was thus acquainted beforehand with the marvels and the hopes that had clustered round his cradle; she had heard the words of Simeon, and being animated by the same sentiments, she gave them her approval.

Simple as this explanation appears, it is not less arbitrary than we have already found other specimens of natural interpretation. The evangelist nowhere says, that the parents of Jesus had communicated anything concerning their extraordinary hopes to Simeon, before he poured forth his inspired words; on the contrary, the point of his entire narrative consists in the idea that the aged saint had, by virtue of the spirit with which he was filled, instantaneously discerned in Jesus the messianic child, and the reason why the co-operation of the Holy Spirit is insisted on, is to make it evident how Simeon was enabled, without any previous information, to recognise in Jesus the promised child, and at the same time to foretel the course of his destiny. Our canonical Gospel refers Simeon's recognition of Jesus to a supernatural principle resident in Simeon himself; the *Evangelium infantiæ arabicum* refers it to something objective in the appearance of Jesus [4]—far more in the spirit of the original narrative than the natural interpretation, for it retains the miraculous element. But, apart from the general reasons against the credibility of miracles, the admission of a miracle in this instance is attended with a special difficulty, because no worthy object for an extraordinary manifestation of divine power is discoverable. For, that the above occurrence during the infancy of Jesus served to disseminate and establish in more distant circles the persuasion of his Messiahship, there is no indication; we must therefore, with the Evangelist, limit the object of these supernatural communications to Simeon and Anna, to whose devout hopes was vouchsafed the special reward of having their eyes enlightened to discern the messianic child. But that miracles should be ordained for such occasional and isolated objects, is not reconcileable with just ideas of divine providence.

Thus here again we find reason to doubt the historical character of the narrative, especially as we have found by a previous investigation that it is annexed to narratives purely mythical. Simeon's real expressions, say some commentators, were probably these: Would that I might yet behold the newborn Messiah, even as I now bear this child in my arms!—a simple wish

---

[3] 1 Th. s. 205 ff.
[4] Cap. vi. *Viditque illum Simeon senex instar columnæ lucis refulgentem, cum Domina Maria virgo, mater ejus, ulnis suis eum gestaret,—et circumdabant eum angeli instar circuli, celebrantes illum*, etc. Ap. Thilo, p. 71.

which was transformed *ex eventu* by tradition, into the positive enunciations now read in Luke[5]. But this explanation is incomplete, for the *reason* why such stories became current concerning Jesus, must be shown in the relative position of this portion of the evangelical narrative, and in the interest of the primitive Christian legend. As to the former, this scene at the presentation of Jesus in the temple is obviously parallel with that at the circumcision of the Baptist, narrated by the same evangelist; for on both occasions, at the inspiration of the Holy Spirit, God is praised for the birth of a national deliverer, and the future destiny of the child is prophetically announced, in the one case by the father, in the other by a devout stranger. That this scene is in the former instance connected with the circumcision, in the latter with the presentation in the temple, seems to be accidental; when however the legend had once, in relation to Jesus, so profusely adorned the presentation in the temple, the circumcision must be left, as we have above found it, without embellishment.

As to the second spring in the formation of our narrative, namely, the interest of the Christian legend, it is easy to conceive how this would act. He who, as a man, so clearly proved himself to be the Messiah, must also, it was thought, even as a child have been recognisable in his true character to an eye rendered acute by the Holy Spirit; he who at a later period, by his powerful words and deeds, manifested himself to be the Son of God, must surely, even before he could speak or move with freedom, have borne the stamp of divinity. Moreover if men, moved by the Spirit of God, so early pressed Jesus with love and reverence in their arms, then was the spirit that animated him not an impious one, as his enemies alleged; and if a holy seer had predicted, along with the high destiny of Jesus, the conflict which he had to undergo, and the anguish which his fate would cause his mother,[6] then it was assuredly no chance, but a divine plan, that led him into the depths of abasement on the way to his ultimate exaltation.

This view of the narrative is thus countenanced positively by the nature of the fact,—and negatively by the difficulties attending any other explanation. One cannot but wonder, therefore, how Schleiermacher can be influenced against it by an observation which did not prevent him from taking a similar view of the history of the Baptist's birth, namely, that the narrative is too natural to have been fabricated[7]; and how Neander can argue against it, from exaggerated ideas of the more imposing traits which the mythus would have substituted for our narrative. Far from allowing a purification for the mother of Jesus, and a redemption for himself, to take place in the ordinary manner, Neander thinks the mythus would have depicted an angelic appearance, intended to deter Mary or the priest from an observance inconsistent with the dignity of Jesus.[8] As though even the Christianity of Paul did not maintain that Christ was *born under the law* γενόμενος ὑπὸ νόμον (Gal. iv. 4); how much more then the Judaic Christianity whence these narratives are derived! As though Jesus himself had not, agreeably to this view of his position, submitted to baptism, and according to the Evangelist whose narrative is in question, without any previous expostulation on the part of the

---

[5] Thus E. F. in the treatise, on the two first chapters of Matth. and Luke. In Henke's Mag. 5 bd. s. 169 f. A similar half measure is in Matthäi, Synopse der 4 Evan. s. 3, 5 f.

[6] With the words of Simeon addressed to Mary : καὶ σοῦ δὲ αὐτῆς τὴν ψυχὴν διελεύσεται ῥομφαία (v. 35) comp. the words in the messianic psalm of sorrow, xxii. 21 : ῥῦσαι ἀπὸ ῥομφαίας τὴν ψυχήν μου.

[7] Schleiermacher, Ueber den Lukas, s. 37. Compare on the other hand the observations in § 18, with those of the authors there quoted, Note 19.

[8] Neander here (s. 24 f.) mistakes the apocryphal for the mythical, as he had before done the poetical.

Baptist ! Of more weight is Schleiermacher's other observation, that supposing this narrative to be merely a poetical creation, its author would scarcely have placed by the side of Simeon Anna, of whom he makes no poetical use, still less would he have characterized her with minuteness, after designating his principal personage with comparative negligence. But to represent the dignity of the child Jesus as being proclaimed by the mouth of two witnesses, and especially to associate a prophetess with a prophet—this is just the symmetrical grouping that the legend loves. The detailed description of Anna may have been taken from a real person who, at the time when our narrative originated, was yet held in remembrance for her distinguished piety. As to the Evangelist's omission to assign her any particular speech, it is to be observed that her office is to spread abroad the glad news, while that of Simeon is to welcome Jesus into the temple: hence as the part of the prophetess was to be performed behind the scenes, her precise words could not be given. As in a former instance Schleiermacher supposes the Evangelist to have received his history from the lips of the shepherds, so here he conceives him to have been indebted to Anna, of whose person he has so vivid a recollection ; Neander approves this opinion—not the only straw thrown out by Schleiermacher, to which this theologian has clung in the emergencies of modern criticism.

At this point also, where Luke's narrative leaves Jesus for a series of years, there is a concluding sentence on the prosperous growth of the child (v. 40) ; a similar sentence occurs at the corresponding period in the life of the Baptist, and both recall the analogous form of expression found in the history of Samson (Judg. xiii. 24 f.).

§ 39.

RETROSPECT. DIFFERENCE BETWEEN MATTHEW AND LUKE AS TO THE ORIGINAL RESIDENCE OF THE PARENTS OF JESUS.

In the foregoing examinations we have called in question the historical credibility of the Gospel narratives concerning the genealogy, birth, and childhood of Jesus, on two grounds : first, because the narratives taken separately contain much that will not bear an historical interpretation ; and secondly, because the parallel narratives of Matthew and Luke exclude each other, so that it is impossible for both to be true, and one must necessarily be false ; this imputation however may attach to either, and consequently to both.   One of the contradictions between the two narratives extends from the commencement of the history of the childhood to the point we have now reached ; it has therefore often come in our way, but we have been unable hitherto to give it our consideration, because only now that we have completely reviewed the scenes in which it figures, have we materials enough on which to found a just estimate of its consequences. We refer to the divergency that exists between Matthew and Luke, in relation to the original dwelling-place of the parents of Jesus.

Luke, from the very beginning of his history, gives Nazareth as the abode of Joseph and Mary ; here the angel seeks Mary (i. 26) ; here we must suppose Mary's house οἶκος, to be situated (i. 56); from hence the parents of Jesus journey to Bethlehem on account of the census (ii. 4) : and hither, when circumstances permit, they return as to their own city πόλις αὐτῶν (v. 39). Thus in Luke, Nazareth is evidently the proper residence of the parents of Jesus, and they only visit Bethlehem for a short time, owing to a casual circumstance.

In Matthew, it is not stated in the first instance where Joseph and Mary resided. According to ii. 1, Jesus was born in Bethlehem, and since no extraordinary circumstances are said to have led his parents thither, it appears as if Matthew supposed them to have been originally resident in Bethlehem. Here he makes the parents with the child receive the visit of the magi ; then follows the flight into Egypt, on returning from which Joseph is only deterred from again seeking Judea by a special divine admonition, which directs him to Nazareth in Galilee (ii. 22). This last particular renders certain what had before seemed probable, namely, that Matthew did not with Luke suppose Nazareth, but Bethlehem, to have been the original dwelling-place of the parents of Jesus, and that he conceived their final settlement at Nazareth to have been the result of unforeseen circumstances.

This contradiction is generally glided over without suspicion. The reason of this lies in the peculiar character of Matthew's Gospel, a character on which a modern writer has built the assertion that this Evangelist does not contradict Luke concerning the original residence of the parents of Jesus, for he says nothing at all on the subject, troubling himself as little about topographical as chronological accuracy. He mentions the later abode of Joseph and Mary, and the birth-place of Jesus, solely because it was possible to connect with them Old Testament prophecies ; as the abode of the parent of Jesus prior to his birth furnished no opportunity for a similar quotation, Matthew has left it entirely unnoticed, an omission which however, in his style of narration, is no proof that he was ignorant of their abode, or that he supposed it to have been Bethlehem.[1] But even admitting that the silence of Matthew on the earlier residence of the parents of Jesus in Nazareth, and on the peculiar circumstances that caused Bethlehem to be his birth-place, proves nothing ; yet the above supposition requires that the exchange of Bethlehem for Nazareth should be so represented as to give some intimation, or at least to leave a possibility, that we should understand the former to be a merely temporary abode, and the journey to the latter a return homeward. Such an intimation would have been given, had Matthew attributed to the angelic vision, that determined Joseph's settlement in Nazareth after his return from Egypt, such communications as the following : Return now into the land of Israel and into your native city Nazareth, for there is no further need of your presence in Bethlehem, since the prophecy that your messianic child should be born in that place is already fulfilled. But as Matthew is alleged to be generally indifferent about localities, we will be moderate, and demand no positive intimation from him, but simply make the negative requisition, that he should not absolutely exclude the idea, that Nazareth was the original dwelling-place of the parents of Jesus. This requisition would be met if, instead of a special cause being assigned for the choice of Nazareth as a residence, it had been merely said that the parents of Jesus returned by divine direction into the land of Israel and betook themselves to Nazareth. It would certainly seem abrupt enough, if without any preamble Nazareth were all at once named instead of Bethlehem : of this our narrator was conscious, and for this reason he has detailed the causes that led to the change (ii. 22). But instead of doing this, as we have shown that he must have done it had he, with Luke, known Nazareth to be the original dwelling-place of the parents of Jesus, his account has precisely the opposite bearing, which undeniably proves that his supposition was the reverse of Luke's. For when Matthew represents Joseph on his return from Egypt as being prevented from going to Judea solely by his fear of Archelaus, he ascribes to him an inclina-

[1] Olshausen, bibl. Comm. 1. s. 142 f.

tion to proceed to that province—an inclination which is unaccountable if the affair of the census alone had taken him to Bethlehem, and which is only to be explained by the supposition that he had formerly dwelt there. On the other hand as Matthew makes the danger from Archelaus (together with the fulfilment of a prophecy) the sole cause of the settlement of Joseph and Mary at Nazareth, he cannot have supposed that this was their original home, for in that case there would have been an independently decisive cause which would have rendered any other superfluous.

Thus the difficulty of reconciling Matthew with Luke, in the present instance, turns upon the impossibility of conceiving how the parents of Jesus could, on their return from Egypt, have it in contemplation to proceed a second time to Bethlehem unless this place had formerly been their home. The efforts of commentators have accordingly been chiefly applied to the task of finding other reasons for the existence of such an inclination in Joseph and Mary. Such efforts are of a very early date. Justin Martyr, holding by Luke, who, while he decidedly states Nazareth to be the dwelling-place of the parents of Jesus, yet does not represent Joseph as a complete stranger in Bethlehem (for he makes it the place from which he lineally sprang), seems to suppose that Nazareth was the dwelling-place and Bethlehem the birth-place of Joseph,[2] and Credner thinks that this passage of Justin points out the source, and presents the reconciliation of the divergent statements of our two Evangelists.[3] But it is far from presenting a reconciliation. For as Nazareth is still supposed to be the place which Joseph had chosen as his home, no reason appears why, on his return from Egypt, he should all at once desire to exchange his former residence for his birth-place, especially as, according to Justin himself, the cause of his former journey to Bethlehem had not been a plan of settling there, but simply the census—a cause which, after the flight, no longer existed. Thus the statement of Justin leans to the side of Luke and does not suffice to bring him into harmony with Matthew. That it was the source of our two evangelical accounts is still less credible; for how could the narrative of Matthew, which mentions neither Nazareth as a dwelling-place, nor the census as the cause of a journey to Bethlehem, originate in the statement of Justin, to which these facts are essential? Arguing generally, where on the one hand, there are two diverging statements, on the other, an insufficient attempt to combine them, it is certain that the latter is not the parent and the two former its offspring, but vice versâ. Moreover, in this department of attempting reconciliations, we have already, in connection with the genealogies, learned to estimate Justin or his authorities.

A more thorough attempt at reconciliation is made in the *Evangelium de nativitate Mariæ*, and has met with much approval from modern theologians. According to this apocryphal book, the house of Mary's parents was at Nazareth, and although she was brought up in the temple at Jerusalem and there espoused to Joseph, she returned after this occurrence to her parents in Galilee. Joseph, on the contrary, was not only born at Bethlehem, as Justin seems to intimate, but also lived there, and thither brought home his betrothed.[4] But this mode of conciliation, unlike the other, is favourable to

---

[2] Dial. c. Trypho, 78 : Joseph came from Nazareth, *where he lived*, to Bethlehem, *whence he was*, to be enrolled, ἀνεληλύθει (᾽Ιωσὴφ) ἀπὸ Ναζαρὲτ, ἔνθα ᾤκει, εἰς Βηθλεὲμ, ὅθεν ἦν, ἀπογράψασθαι. The words ὅθεν ἦν might however be understood as signifying merely the place of his tribe, especially if Justin's addition be considered : *For his race was of the tribe of Judah, which inhabits that land*, ἀπὸ γὰρ τῆς κατοικούσης τὴν γῆν ἐκείνην φυλῆς ᾽Ιούδα τὸ γένος ἦν.

[3] Beiträge zur Einleit. in das N. T. I. s. 217. Comp. Hoffmann, s. 238 f. 277 ff.

[4] C. I. 8. 10.

Matthew and disadvantageous to Luke. For the census with its attendant circumstances is left out, and necessarily so, because if Joseph were at home in Bethlehem, and only went to Nazareth to fetch his bride, the census could not be represented as the reason why he returned to Bethlehem, for he would have done so in the ordinary course of things, after a few days' absence. Above all, had Bethlehem been his home, he would not on his arrival have sought an inn where there was no room for him, but would have taken Mary under his own roof. Hence modern expositors who wish to avail themselves of the outlet presented by the apocryphal book, and yet to save the census of Luke from rejection, maintain that Joseph did indeed dwell, and carry on his trade, in Bethlehem, but that he possessed no house of his own in that place, and the census recalling him thither sooner than he had anticipated, he had not yet provided one.[5] But Luke makes it appear, not only that the parents of Jesus were not yet settled in Bethlehem, but that they were not even desirous of settling there ; that, on the contrary, it was their intention to depart after the shortest possible stay. This opinion supposes great poverty on the part of Joseph and Mary ; Olshausen, on the other hand, prefers enriching them, for the sake of conciliating the difference in question. He supposes that they had property both in Bethlehem and Nazareth, and could therefore have settled in either place, but unknown circumstances inclined them, on their return from Egypt, to fix upon Bethlehem until the divine warning came as a preventive. Thus Olshausen declines particularizing the reason why it appeared desirable to the parents of Jesus to settle in Bethlehem ; but Heydenreich [6] and others have supplied his omission, by assuming that it must have seemed to them most fitting for him, who was pre-eminently the Son of David, to be brought up in David's own city.

Here, however, theologians would do well to take for their model the honesty of Neander, and to confess with him that of this intention on the part of Joseph and Mary to settle at Bethlehem, and of the motives which induced them to give up the plan, Luke knows nothing, and that they rest on the authority of Matthew alone. But what reason does Matthew present for this alleged change of place ? The visit of the magi, the massacre of the infants, visions in dreams—events whose evidently unhistorical character quite disqualifies them from serving as proofs of a change of residence on the part of the parents of Jesus. On the other hand Neander, while confessing that the author of the first Gospel was probably ignorant of the particular circumstances which, according to Luke, led to the journey to Bethlehem, and hence took Bethlehem to be the original residence of the parents of Jesus, maintains that there may be an essential agreement between the two accounts though that agreement did not exist in the consciousness of the writers.[7] But, once more, what cause does Luke assign for the journey to Bethlehem? The census, which our previous investigations have shown to be as frail a support for this statement, as the infanticide and its consequences for that of Matthew. Hence here again it is not possible by admitting the inacquaintance of the one narrator with what the other presents to vindicate the statements of both ; since each has against him, not only the ignorance of the other, but the improbability of his own narrative.

But we must distinguish more exactly the respective aspects and elements of the two accounts. As, according to the above observations, the change of residence on the part of the parents of Jesus, is in Matthew so linked with the unhistorical data of the infanticide and the flight into Egypt, that without

---

[5] Paulus, exeg. Handb. I, a, s. 178.
[6] Ueber die Unzulässigkeit der mythischen Auffassung u. s. f. I, s. 101.
[7] L. J. Ch. s. 33.

these every cause for the migration disappears, we turn to Luke's account, which makes the parents of Jesus resident in the same place, both after and before the birth of Jesus.   But in Luke, the circumstance of Jesus being born in another place than where his parents dwelt, is made to depend on an event as unhistorical as the marvels of Matthew, namely the census.   If this be surrendered, no motive remains that could induce the parents of Jesus to take a formidable journey at so critical a period for Mary, and in this view of the case Matthew's representation seems the more probable one, that Jesus was born in the home of his parents and not in a strange place.   Hitherto, however, we have only obtained the negative result, that the evangelical statements, according to which the parents of Jesus lived at first in another place than that in which they subsequently settled, and Jesus was born elsewhere than in the home of his parents, are destitute of any guarantee ; we have yet to seek for a positive conclusion by inquiring what was really the place of his birth.

On this point we are drawn in two opposite directions.   In both Gospels we find Bethlehem stated to be the birth-place of Jesus, and there is, as we have seen, no impediment to our supposing that it was the habitual residence of his parents ; on the other hand, the two Gospels again concur in representing Nazareth as the ultimate dwelling-place of Joseph and his family, and it is only an unsupported statement that forbids us to regard it as their original residence, and consequently as the birth-place of Jesus.   It would be impossible to decide between these contradictory probabilities were both equally strong, but as soon as the slightest inequality between them is discovered, we are warranted to form a conclusion.   Let us first test the opinion, that the Galilean city Nazareth was the final residence of Jesus.   This is not supported barely by the passages immediately under consideration, in the 2nd chapters of Matthew and Luke ;—it rests on an uninterrupted series of data drawn from the Gospels and from the earliest church history.   The Galilean, the Nazarene—were the epithets constantly applied to Jesus.   As Jesus of Nazareth he was introduced by Philip to Nathanael, whose responsive question was, Can any good thing come out of Nazareth?   Nazareth is described, not only as the place where he was brought up, οὗ ἦν τεθραμμένος (Luke iv. 16 f.), but also as his country ; πατρὶς (Matt. xiii. 34, Mark vi. 1).   He was known among the populace as Jesus of Nazareth (Luke xviii. 37.), and invoked under this name by the demons (Mark i. 24).   The inscription on the cross styles him a Nazarene (John xix. 19), and after his resurrection his apostles everywhere proclaimed him as Jesus of Nazareth (Acts ii. 22), and worked miracles in his name (Acts iii. 6).   His disciples too were long called Nazarenes, and it was not until a late period that this name was exclusively applied to a heretical sect.[8]   This appellation proves, if not that Jesus was born in Nazareth, at least that he resided in that place for a considerable time ; and as, according to a probable tradition (Luke iv. 16 f. parall.), Jesus, during his public life, paid but transient visits to Nazareth, this prolonged residence must be referred to the earlier part of his life, which he passed in the bosom of his family.   Thus his family, at least his parents, must have lived in Nazareth during his childhood ; and if it be admitted that they once dwelt there, it follows that they dwelt there always, for we have no historical grounds for supposing a change of residence : so that this one of the two contradictory propositions has as much certainty as we can expect, in a fact belonging to so remote and obscure a period.

Neither does the other proposition, however, that Jesus was born in Beth-

<hr>

[8] Tertull. adv. Marcion iv. 8.   Epiphan. hær. xxix. 1.

lehem, rest solely on the statement of our Gospels; it is sanctioned by an expectation, originating in a prophetic passage, that the Messiah would be born at Bethlehem (comp. with Matt. ii. 5 f., John vii. 42). But this is a dangerous support, which they who wish to retain as historical the Gospel statement, that Jesus was born in Bethlehem, will do well to renounce. For wherever we find a narrative which recounts the accomplishment of a long-expected event, a strong suspicion must arise, that the narrative owes its origin solely to the pre-existent belief that that event would be accomplished. But our suspicion is converted into certainty when we find this belief to be groundless; and this is the case here, for the alleged issue must have confirmed a false interpretation of a prophetic passage. Thus this prophetic evidence of the birth of Jesus in Bethlehem, deprives the historical evidence, which lies in the 2nd chapters of Matthew and Luke, of its value, since the latter seems to be built on the former, and consequently shares its fall. Any other voucher for this fact is however sought in vain. Nowhere else in the New Testament is the birth of Jesus at Bethlehem mentioned; nowhere does he appear in any relation with his alleged birth-place, or pay it the honour of a visit, which he yet does not deny to the unworthy Nazareth; nowhere does he appeal to the fact as a concomitant proof of his messiahship, although he had the most direct inducements to do so, for many were repelled from him by his Galilean origin, and defended their prejudice by referring to the necessity, that the Messiah should come out of Bethlehem, the city of David (John vii. 42).[9] John does not, it is true, say that these objections were uttered in the presence of Jesus;[10] but as, immediately before, he had annexed to a discourse of Jesus a comment of his own, to the effect that the Holy Ghost was not yet given, so here he might very suitably have added, in explanation of the doubts expressed by the people, that they did not yet know that Jesus was born in Bethlehem. Such an observation will be thought too superficial and trivial for an apostle like John: thus much however must be admitted; he had occasion *repeatedly* to mention the popular notion that Jesus was a native of Nazareth, and the consequent prejudice against him; had he then known otherwise, he must have added a corrective remark, if he wished to avoid leaving the false impression, that he also believed Jesus to be a Nazarene. As it is, we find Nathanael, John i. 46, alleging this objection, without having his opinion rectified either mediately or immediately, for he nowhere learns that the *good thing* did not really come out of Nazareth, and the conclusion he is left to draw is, that even out of Nazareth something good can come. In general, if Jesus were really born in Bethlehem, though but fortuitously (according to Luke's representation), it is incomprehensible, considering the importance of this fact to the article of his messiahship, that even his own adherents should always call him the Nazarene, instead of opposing to this epithet, pronounced by his opponents with polemical emphasis, the honourable title of the Bethlehemite.

Thus the evangelical statement that Jesus was born at Bethlehem is destitute of all valid historical evidence; nay, it is contravened by positive historical facts. We have seen reason to conclude that the parents of Jesus lived at Nazareth, not only after the birth of Jesus, but also, as we have no counter evidence, prior to that event, and that, no credible testimony to the contrary existing, Jesus was probably not born at any other place than the home of his parents. With this twofold conclusion, the supposition that Jesus was born at Bethlehem is irreconcileable: it can therefore cost us no further effort to

[9] Comp. K. Ch. L. Schmidt, in Schmidt's Bibliothek, 3, 1, s. 123 f.; Kaiser, bibl. Theol. I, s. 230.
[10] On this Heydenreich rests his defence, Ueber die Unzulässigkeit. I. s. 99.

decide that Jesus was born, not in Bethlehem, but, as we have no trustworthy indications that point elsewhere, in all probability at Nazareth.

The relative position of the two evangelists on this point may be thus stated. Each of their accounts is partly correct, and partly incorrect: Luke is right in maintaining the identity of the earlier with the later residence of the parents of Jesus, and herein Matthew is wrong; again, Matthew is right in maintaining the identity of the birth-place of Jesus with the dwelling-place of his parents, and here the error is on the side of Luke. Further, Luke is entirely correct in making the parents of Jesus reside in Nazareth before, as well as after, the birth of Jesus, while Matthew has only half the truth, namely, that they were established there after his birth; but in the statement that Jesus was born at Bethlehem both are decidedly wrong. The source of all the error of their narratives, is the Jewish opinion with which they fell in, that the Messiah must be born at Bethlehem; the source of all their truth, is the fact which lay before them, that he always passed for a Nazarene; finally, the cause of the various admixture of the true and the false in both, and the preponderance of the latter in Matthew, is the different position held by the two writers in relation to the above data. Two particulars were to be reconciled—the historical fact that Jesus was universally reputed to be a Nazarene, and the prophetic requisition that, as Messiah, he should be born at Bethlehem. Matthew, or the legend which he followed, influenced by the ruling tendency to apply the prophecies, observable in his Gospel, effected the desired reconciliation in such a manner, that the greatest prominence was given to Bethlehem, the locality pointed out by the prophet; this was represented as the original home of the parents of Jesus, and Nazareth merely as a place of refuge, recommended by a subsequent turn of events. Luke, on the contrary, more bent on historic detail, either adopted or created that form of the legend, which attaches the greatest important to Nazareth, making it the original dwelling-place of the parents of Jesus, and regarding the sojourn in Bethlehem as a temporary one, the consequence of a casual occurrence.

Such being the state of the case, no one, we imagine, will be inclined either with Schleiermacher,[11] to leave the question concerning the relation of the two narratives to the real facts undecided, or with Sieffert,[12] to pronounce exclusively in favour of Luke.[13]

[11] Ueber den Lukas, s. 49. There is a similar hesitation in Thelte, Biographie Jesu, § 15.
[12] Ueber den Ursprung u. s. w., s. 68 f. u. s. 158.
[13] Comp. Ammon. Fortbildung, 1, s. 194 ff.; De Wette, exeget. Handb. 1, 2, s. 24 f.; George, s. 84 ff. That different narrators may give different explanations of the same fact, and that these different explanations may afterwards be united in one book, is proved by many examples in the O. T. Thus in Genesis, three derivations are given of the name of Isaac; two of that of Jacob (xxv. 26. xxvii. 16), and so of Edom and Beersheba (xxi. 31. xxvi. 33). Comp. De Wette, Kritik der mos. Gesch., s. 110. 118 ff. and my Streitschriften, 1, 1, s. 83 ff.

CHAPTER V.

THE FIRST VISIT TO THE TEMPLE, AND THE EDUCATION OF JESUS.

§ 40.

JESUS, WHEN TWELVE YEARS OLD, IN THE TEMPLE.

THE Gospel of Matthew passes in silence over the entire period from the return of the parents of Jesus out of Egypt, to the baptism of Jesus by John : and even Luke has nothing to tell us of the long interval between the early childhood of Jesus and his maturity, beyond a single incident—his demeanour on a visit to the temple in his twelfth year (ii. 41–52). This anecdote, out of the early youth of Jesus is, as Hess has truly remarked,[1] distinguished from the narratives hitherto considered, belonging to his childhood, by the circumstance that Jesus no longer, as in the latter, holds a merely passive position, but presents an active proof of his high destination ; a proof which has always been especially valued, as indicating the moment in which the consciousness of that destination was kindled in Jesus.[2]

In his twelfth year, the period at which, according to Jewish usage, the boy became capable of an independent participation in the sacred rites, the parents of Jesus, as this narrative informs us, took him for the first time to the Passover. At the expiration of the feast, the parents bent their way homewards ; that their son was missing gave them no immediate anxiety, because they supposed him to be among their travelling companions, and it was not until after they had accomplished a day's journey, and in vain sought their son among their kinsfolk and acquaintance, that they turned back to Jerusalem to look for him there. This conduct on the part of the parents of Jesus may with reason excite surprise. It seems inconsistent with the carefulness which it has been thought incumbent on us to attribute to them, that they should have allowed the divine child entrusted to their keeping, to remain so long out of their sight ; and hence they have on many sides been accused of neglect and a dereliction of duty, in the instance before us.[3] It has been urged, as a general consideration in vindication of Joseph and Mary, that the greater freedom permitted to the boy is easily conceivable as part of a liberal method of education ;[4] but even according to our modern ideas, it would seem more than liberal for parents to let a boy of twelve years remain out of their sight during so long an interval as our narrative supposes ; how far less reconcileable must it then be with the more rigid views of education held by the

---

[1] Hess, Geschichte Jesu, I, s. 110.
[2] Olshausen, bibl. Comm. I, s. 145 f.
[3] Olshausen, ut sup. I. 150.
[4] Hase, Leben Jesu, § 37.

ancients, not excepting the Jews? It is remarked however, that viewing the case as an extraordinary one, the parents of Jesus knew their child, and they could therefore very well confide in his understanding and character, so far as to be in no fear that any danger would accrue to him from his unusual free-dom;[5] but we can perceive from their subsequent anxiety, that they were not so entirely at ease on that head. Thus their conduct must be admitted to be such as we should not have anticipated; but it is not consequently incredible nor does it suffice to render the entire narrative improbable, for the parents of Jesus are no saints to us, that we should not impute to them any fault.

Returned to Jerusalem, they find their son on the third day in the temple, doubtless in one of the outer halls, in the midst of an assembly of doctors, en-gaged in a conversation with them, and exciting universal astonishment (v. 45 f.). From some indications it would seem that Jesus held a higher position in the presence of the doctors, than could belong to a boy of twelve years. The word καθεζόμενον (sitting) has excited scruples, for according to Jewish records, it was not until after the death of the Rabbi Gamaliel, an event long subse-quent to the one described in our narrative, that the pupils of the rabbins sat, they having previously been required to stand [6] when in the school; but this Jewish tradition is of doubtful authority.[7] It has also been thought a diffi-culty, that Jesus does not merely hear the doctors, but also asks them ques-tions, thus appearing to assume the position of their teacher. Such is indeed the representation of the apocryphal Gospels, for in them Jesus, before he is twelve years old, perplexes all the doctors by his questions,[8] and reveals to his instructor in the alphabet the mystical significance of the characters;[9] while at the above visit to the temple he proposes controversial questions,[10] such as that touching the Messiah's being at once David's Son and Lord (Matt. xxii. 41), and proceeds to throw light on all departments of knowledge.[11] If the expressions ἐρωτᾶν and ἀποκρίνεσθαι implied that Jesus played the part of a teacher in this scene, so unnatural a feature in the evangelical narrative would render the whole suspicious.[12] But there is nothing to render this interpreta-tion of the words necessary, for according to Jewish custom, rabbinical teach-ing was of such a kind that not only did the masters interrogate the pupils, but the pupils interrogated the masters, when they wished for explanations on any point.[13] We may with the more probability suppose that the writer in-tended to attribute to Jesus such questions as suited a boy, because he, appar-ently not without design, refers the astonishment of the doctors, not to his questions, but to that in which he could best show himself in the light of an intelligent pupil—namely, to his answers. A more formidable difficulty is the statement, that the boy Jesus sat *in the midst of the doctors*, ἐν μέσῳ τῶν διδασ-κάλων. For we learn from Paul (Acts xxii. 3) the position that became a pupil, when he says that he was brought up *at the feet* (παρὰ τοὺς πόδας) of Gamaliel: it being the custom for the rabbins to be placed on chairs, while their pupils sat on the ground,[14] and did not take their places among their masters. It has indeed been thought that ἐν μέσῳ might be so explained as

[5] Heydenreich, über die Unzulässigkeit u. s. f. 1, s. 103.
[6] Megillah, f. 21, apud Lightfoot, in loc.
[7] Vid. Kuinöl, in Luc. p. 353.
[8] Evang. Thomæ, c. vi. ff. Ap. Thilo. p. 288 ff. and Evang. infant. arab. c. xlviii. p. 123, Thilo.
[9] Ibid.
[10] Evang. infant. arab. c. l.
[11] Ibid. c. l. and li.; comp. ev. Thomæ, c. xix.
[12] Olshausen confesses this, s. 151.
[13] For proofs (e g. Hieros. Taanith, lxvii. 4) see Wetstein and Lightfoot, in loc.
[14] Lightfoot, Horæ, p. 742.

to signify, either that Jesus sat between the doctors, who are supposed to have been elevated on chairs, while Jesus and the other pupils are pictured as sitting on the ground between them,[15] or merely that he was in the company of doctors, that is, in the synagogue ;[16] but according to the strict sense of the words, the expression καθέζεσθαι ἐν μέσῳ τινῶν appears to signify, if not as Schöttgen believes,[17] *in majorem Jesu gloriam*, a place of pre-eminent honour, at least a position of equal dignity with that occupied by the rest. It need only be asked, would it harmonize with the spirit of our narrative to substitute καθεζόμενον παρὰ τοὺς πόδας τῶν διδασκάλων for καθ. ἐν μέσῳ τ. δ.? the answer will certainly be in the negative, and it will then be inevitable to admit, that our narrative places Jesus in another relation to the doctors than that of a learner, though the latter is the only natural one for a boy of twelve, however highly gifted. For Olshausen's position,[18]—that in Jesus nothing was formed from without, by the instrumentality of another's wisdom, because this would be inconsistent with the character of the Messiah, as absolutely self-determined, —contradicts a dogma of the church which he himself advances, namely, that Jesus in his manifestation as man, followed the regular course of human development. For not only is it in the nature of this development to be gradual, but also, and still more essentially, to be dependent, whether it be mental or physical, on the interchange of reception and influence. To deny this in relation to the physical life of Jesus—to say, for example, that the food which he took did not serve for the nourishment and growth of his body by real assimilation, but merely furnished occasion for him to reproduce himself from within, would strike every one as Docetism ; and is the analogous proposition in relation to his spiritual development, namely, that he appropriated nothing from without, and used what he heard from others merely as a voice to evoke one truth after another from the recesses of his own mind—is this anything else than a more refined Docetism ? Truly, if we attempt to form a conception of the conversation of Jesus with the doctors in the temple according to this theory, we make anything but a natural scene of it. It is not to be supposed that he taught, nor properly speaking that he was taught, but that the discourse of the doctors merely gave an impetus to his power of teaching himself, and was the occasion for an ever-brightening light to rise upon him, especially on the subject of his own destination. But in that case he would certainly have given utterance to his newly acquired knowledge ; so that the position of a teacher on the part of the boy would return upon us, a position which Olshausen himself pronounces to be preposterous. At least such an indirect mode of teaching is involved as Ness subscribes to, when he supposes that Jesus, even thus early, made the first attempt to combat the prejudices which swayed in the synagogue, exposing to the doctors, by means of good-humoured questions and requests for explanation, such as are willingly permitted to a boy, the weakness of many of their dogmas.[19] But even such a position on the part of a boy of twelve, is inconsistent with the true process of human development, through which it behoved the God-Man himself to pass. Discourse of this kind from a boy must, we grant, have excited the astonishment of all the hearers ; nevertheless the expression ἐξίσταντο πάντες οἱ ἀκούοντες αὐτοῦ (v. 47), looks too much like a panegyrical formula.[20]

[15] Paulus, s. 279.
[16] Kuinöl, s. 353 f.
[17] Horæ, ii. p. 886.
[18] Bibl. Comm. p. 151.
[19] Geschichte Jesu, I, s. 112.
[20] In the similar account also which Josephus gives us of himself when fourteen, it is easy to discern the exaggeration of a self-complacent man. Life, 2 : *Moreover, when I was a*

N

The narrative proceeds to tell us how the mother of Jesus reproached her son when she had found him thus, asking him why he had not spared his parents the anguish of their sorrowful search? To this Jesus returns an answer which forms the point of the entire narrative; he asks whether they might not have known that he was to be sought nowhere else than in the house of his Father, in the temple? (v. 48 f.) One might be inclined to understand this designation of God as τοῦ πατρὸς generally, as implying that God was the Father of all men, and only in this sense the Father of Jesus. But this interpretation is forbidden, not only by the addition of the pronoun μοῦ, the above sense requiring ἡμῶν (as in Matt. vi. 9), but still more absolutely by the circumstance that the parents of Jesus did not understand these words (v. 50), a decided indication that they must have a special meaning, which can here be no other than the mystery of the Messiahship of Jesus, who as Messiah, was υἱὸς θεοῦ in a peculiar sense. But that Jesus in his twelfth year had already the consciousness of his Messiahship, is a position which, although it may be consistently adopted from the orthodox point of view, and although it is not opposed to the regular human form of the development of Jesus, which even orthodoxy maintains, we are not here bound to examine. So also the natural explanation, which retains the above narrative as a history, though void of the miraculous, and which accordingly supposes the parents of Jesus, owing to a particular combination of circumstances, to have come even before his birth to a conviction of his Messiahship, and to have instilled this conviction into their son from his earliest childhood,—this too may make it plain how Jesus could be so clear as to his messianic relation to God; but it can only do so by the hypothesis of an unprecedented coincidence of extraordinary accidents. We, on the contrary, who have renounced the previous incidents as historical, either in the supernatural or the natural sense, are unable to comprehend how the consciousness of his messianic destination could be so early developed in Jesus. For though the consciousness of a more subjective vocation, as that of a poet or an artist, which is dependent solely on the internal gifts of the individual (gifts which cannot long remain latent), may possibly be awakened very early; an objective vocation, in which the conditions of external reality are a chief co-operator, as the vocation of the statesman, the general, the reformer of a religion, can hardly be so early evident to the most highly endowed individual, because for this a knowledge of cotemporary circumstances would be requisite, which only long observation and mature experience can confer. Of the latter kind is the vocation of the Messiah, and if this is implied in the words by which Jesus in his twelfth year justified his lingering in the temple, he cannot have uttered the words at that period.

In another point of view also, it is worthy of notice that the parents of Jesus are said (v. 50) not to have understood the words which he addressed to them. What did these words signify? That God was his Father, in whose house it behoved him to be. But that her son would in a specific sense be called a υἱὸς θεοῦ had been already made known to Mary by the annunciating angel (Luke i. 32, 35), and that he would have a peculiar relation to the temple she might infer, both from the above title, and from the striking reception which he had met with at his first presentation in the temple, when yet an infant. The parents of Jesus, or at least Mary, of whom it is repeatedly noticed that she carefully kept in her heart the extraordinary communications concerning her son, ought not to have been in the dark a single moment as

child, and about fourteen years of age, I was commended by all for the love I had to learning, on which account the high priests and principal men of the city came there frequently to me together, in order to know my opinion about the accurate understanding of points of the law.

to the meaning of his language on this occasion. But even at the presentation in the temple, we are told that the parents of Jesus marvelled at the discourse of Simeon (v. 33), which is merely saying in other words that they did not understand him. And their wonder is not referred to the declaration of Simeon that their boy would be a cause, not only of the rising again, but of the fall of many in Israel, and that a sword would pierce through the heart of his mother (an aspect of his vocation and destiny on which nothing had previously been communicated to the parents of Jesus, and at which therefore they might naturally wonder); for these disclosures are not made by Simeon until after the wonder of the parents, which is caused only by Simeon's expressions of joy at the sight of the Saviour, who would be the glory of Israel, and a light even to the Gentiles. And here again there is no intimation that the wonder was excited by the idea that Jesus would bear this relation to the heathens, which indeed it could not well be, since this more extended destination of the Messiah had been predicted in the Old Testament. There remains therefore as a reason for the wonder in question, merely the fact of the child's Messiahship, declared by Simeon; a fact which had been long ago announced to them by angels, and which was acknowledged by Mary in her song of praise. We have just a parallel difficulty in the present case, it being as inconceivable that the parents of Jesus should not understand his allusion to his messianic character, as that they should wonder at the declaration of it by Simeon. We must therefore draw this conclusion: if the parents of Jesus did not understand these expressions of their son when twelve years old, those earlier communications cannot have happened; or, if the earlier communications really occurred, the subsequent expressions of Jesus cannot have remained incomprehensible to them. Having done away with those earlier incidents as historical, we might content ourselves with this later want of comprehension, were it not fair to mistrust the whole of a narrative whose later portions agree so ill with the preceding. For it is the character, not of an historical record, but of a marvellous legend, to represent its personages as so permanently in a state of wonder, that they not only at the first appearance of the extraordinary, but even at the second, third, tenth repetition, when one would expect them to be familiarized with it, continually are astonished and do not understand—obviously with the view of exalting the more highly the divine impartation by this lasting incomprehensibleness. So, to draw an example from the later history of Jesus, the divine decree of his suffering and death is set forth in all its loftiness in the evangelical narratives by the circumstance, that even the repeated, explicit disclosures of Jesus on this subject, remain throughout incomprehensible to the disciples; as here the mystery of the Messiahship of Jesus is exalted by the circumstance, that his parents, often as it had been announced to them, at every fresh word on the subject are anew astonished and do not understand.

The twofold form of conclusion, that the mother of Jesus kept all these sayings in her heart (v. 51), and that the boy grew in wisdom and stature, and so forth, we have already recognised as a favourite form of conclusion and transition in the heroic legend of the Hebrews; in particular, that which relates to the growth of the boy is almost verbally parallel with a passage relating to Samuel, as in two former instances similar expressions appeared to have been borrowed from the history of Samson.[21]

[21] 1 Sam. ii. 26 (LXX) :
καὶ τὸ παιδάριον Σαμουὴλ ἐπορεύετο μεγαλυνόμενον, καὶ ἀγαθὸν καὶ μετὰ Κυρίου καὶ μετὰ ἀνθρώπων.

Luc. ii. 52 :
καὶ Ἰησοῦς προέκοπτε σοφία καὶ ἡλικία, καὶ χάριτι παρὰ θεῷ καὶ ἀνθρώποις.

Compare also what Josephus says Antiq. ii. ix. 6 of the χάρις παιδικὴ of Moses.

§ 41.

THIS NARRATIVE ALSO MYTHICAL.

Thus here again we must acknowledge the influence of the legend; but as the main part of the incident is thoroughly natural, we might in this instance prefer the middle course, and after disengaging the mythical, seek to preserve a residue of history. We might suppose that the parents of Jesus really took their son to Jerusalem in his early youth, and that after having lost sight of him (probably before their departure), they found him in the temple, where, eager for instruction, he sat at the feet of the rabbins. When called to account, he declared that his favourite abode was in the house of God;[1] a sentiment which rejoiced his parents, and won the approbation of the bystanders. The rest of the story we might suppose to have been added by the aggrandizing legend, after Jesus was acknowledged as the Messiah. Here all the difficulties in our narrative,—the idea of the boy sitting in the midst of the doctors, his claiming God as his father in a special sense, and the departure of the parents without their son, would be rejected; but the journey of Jesus when twelve years old, the eagerness for knowledge then manifested by him, and his attachment to the temple, are retained. To these particulars there is nothing to object negatively, for they contain nothing improbable in itself; but their historical truth must become doubtful if we can show, positively, a strong interest of the legend, out of which the entire narrative, and especially these intrinsically not improbable particulars, might have arisen.

That in the case of great men who in their riper age have been distinguished by mental superiority, the very first presaging movements of their mind are eagerly gleaned, and if they are not to be ascertained historically, are invented under the guidance of probability, is well known. In the Hebrew history and legend especially, we find manifold proofs of this tendency. Thus of Samuel it is said in the old Testament itself, that even as a boy he received a divine revelation and the gift of prophecy (1 Sam. iii.), and with respect to Moses, on whose boyish years the Old Testament narrative is silent, a subsequent tradition, followed by Josephus and Philo, had striking proofs to relate of his early development. As in the narrative before us Jesus shows himself wise beyond his years, so this tradition attributes a like precocity to Moses;[2] as Jesus, turning away from the idle tumult of the city in all the excitement of festival time, finds his favourite entertainment in the temple among the doctors; so the boy Moses was not attracted by childish sports, but by serious occupation, and very early it was necessary to give him tutors, whom, however, like Jesus in his twelfth year, he quickly surpassed.[3]

According to Jewish custom and opinion, the twelfth year formed an epoch in development to which especial proofs of awakening genius were the rather attached, because in the twelfth year, as with us in the fourteenth, the boy was regarded as having outgrown the period of childhood.[4] Accordingly it

---

[1] Gabler neuest. theol. Journal 3, 1, s. 39.

[2] Joseph. Antiq. ii. ix. 6.

[3] Philo, de vita Mosis, Opp. ed. Mangey, Vol. 2. p. 83 f. οὐχ οἷα κομιδῇ νήπιος ἥδετο τωθασμοῖς καὶ γέλωσι καὶ παιδιαῖς—ἀλλ' αἰδῶ καὶ σεμνότητα παραφαίνων, ἀπούσμασι καὶ θεάμασιν, ἃ τὴν ψυχὴν ἔμελλεν ὠφελήσειν προσεῖχε. διδάσκαλοι δ' εὐθὺς, ἀλλαχόθεν ἄλλος, παρῆσαν·—ὧν ἐν οὐ μακρῷ χρόνῳ τὰς δυνάμεις ὑπερέβαλεν, εὐμοιρίᾳ φύσεως φθάνων τὰς ὑφηγήσεις.

[4] Chagiga, ap. Wetstein, in loc. *A XII anno filius censetur maturus.* So Joma f. lxxxii. 1. Berachoth f. xxiv. 1; whereas Bereschith Rabba lxiii. mentions the 13th year as the critical one.

was believed of Moses that in his twelfth year he left the house of his father, to become an independent organ of the divine revelations.[5] The Old Testament leaves it uncertain how early the gift of prophecy was imparted to Samuel, but he was said by a later tradition to have prophesied from his twelfth year;[6] and in like manner the wise judgments of Solomon and Daniel (1 Kings iii. 23 ff., Susann. 45 ff.) were supposed to have been given when they were only twelve.[7] If in the case of these Old Testament heroes, the spirit that impelled them manifested itself according to common opinion so early as in their twelfth year, it was argued that it could not have remained longer concealed in Jesus; and if Samuel and Daniel showed themselves at that age in their later capacity of divinely inspired seers, Solomon in that of a wise ruler, so Jesus at the corresponding period in his life must have shown himself in the character to which he subsequently established his claim, that namely, of the Son of God and Teacher of Mankind. It is, in fact, the obvious aim of Luke to pass over no epoch in the early life of Jesus without surrounding him with divine radiance, with significant prognostics of the future; in this style he treats his birth, mentions the circumcision at least emphatically, but above all avails himself of the presentation in the temple. There yet remained according to Jewish manners one epoch, the twelfth year, with the first journey to the passover; how could he do otherwise than, following the legend, adorn this point in the development of Jesus as we find that he has done in his narrative? and how could we do otherwise than regard his narrative as a legendary embellishment of this period in the life of Jesus,[8] from which we learn nothing of his real development,[9] but merely something of the exalted notions which were entertained in the primitive church of the early ripened mind of Jesus?

But how this anecdote can be numbered among mythi is found by some altogether inconceivable. It bears, thinks Heydenreich,[10] a thoroughly historical character (this is the very point to be proved), and the stamp of the highest simplicity (like every popular legend in its original form); it contains no tincture of the miraculous, wherein the primary characteristic of a mythus (but not of every mythus) is held to consist; it is so remote from all embellishment that there is not the slightest detail of the conversation of Jesus with the doctors (the legend was satisfied with the dramatic trait, *sitting in the midst of the doctors :* as a dictum, v. 49 was alone important, and towards this the narrator hastens without delay); nay, even the conversation between Jesus and his mother is only given in a fragmentary aphoristic manner (there is no

---

[5] Schemoth R. ap. Wetstein : *Dixit R. Chama : Moses duodenarius avulsus est a domo patris sui etc.*

[6] Joseph. Antiq. v. x. 4 : Σαμούηλος δὲ πεπληρωκὼς ἔτος ἤδη δωδέκατον, προεφήτευς.

[7] Ignat. ep. (interpol.) ad Magnes. c. iii. : Σολομῶν δὲ—δωδεκαετὴς βασιλεύσας, τὴν φοβερὰν ἐκείνην καὶ δυσερμήνευτον ἐπὶ ταῖς γυναιξὶ κρίσιν ἕνεκα τῶν παιδίων ἐποιήσατο.—Δανιὴλ ὁ σοφὸς δωδεκαετὴς γέγονε κάτοχος τῷ θείῳ πνεύματι, καὶ τοὺς μάτην τὴν πολιὰν φέροντας πρεσβύτας συκοφάντας καὶ ἐπιθυμητὰς ἀλλοτρίου κάλλους ἀπήλεγξε. *But Solomon, . . . being king at the age of twelve years, gave that terrible and profound judgment between the women with respect to the children. . . . Daniel, the wise man, when twelve years old, was possessed by the divine spirit, and convicted those calumniating old men who, carrying gray hairs in vain, coveted the beauty that belonged to another.* This, it is true, is found in a Christian writing, but on comparing it with the above data, we are led to believe that it was drawn from a more ancient Jewish legend.

[8] This Kaiser has seen, bibl. Theol. I, 234.

[9] Neither do we learn what Hase (Leben Jesu § 37) supposes to be conveyed in this narrative, namely, that as it exhibits the same union with God that constituted the idea of the later life of Jesus, it is an intimation that his later excellence was not the result of conversion from youthful errors, but of the uninterrupted development of his freedom.

[10] Ueber die Unzulassigkeit u. s. f. 1, s. 92.

trace of an omission); finally, the inventor of a legend would have made Jesus speak differently to his mother, instead of putting into his mouth words which might be construed into irreverence and indifference. In this last observation Heydenreich agrees with Schleiermacher, who finds in the behaviour of Jesus to his mother, liable as it is to be misinterpreted, a sure guarantee that the whole history was not invented to supply something remarkable concerning Jesus, in connexion with the period at which the holy things of the temple and the law were first opened to him.[11]

In combating the assertion, that an inventor would scarcely have attributed to Jesus so much apparent harshness towards his mother, we need not appeal to the apocryphal *Evangelium Thomæ*, which makes the boy Jesus say to his foster-father Joseph : *insipientissime fecisti ;* [12] for even in the legend or history of the canonical gospels corresponding traits are to be found. In the narrative of the wedding at Cana, we find this rough address to his mother : τί ἐμοὶ καὶ σοὶ γύναι (John ii. 4); and in the account of the visit paid to Jesus by his mother and brethren, the striking circumstance that he apparently wishes to take no notice of his relatives (Matt. xii. 46). If these are real incidents, then the legend had an historical precedent to warrant the introduction of a similar feature, even into the early youth of Jesus ; if, on the other hand, they are only legends, they are the most vivid proofs that an inducement was not wanting for the invention of such features. Where this inducement lay, it is easy to see. The figure of Jesus would stand in the higher relief from the obscure background of his contracted family relations, if it were often seen that his parents were unable to comprehend his elevated mind, and if even he himself sometimes made them feel his superiority—so far as this could happen without detriment to his filial obedience, which, it should be observed, our narrative expressly preserves.

§ 42.

ON THE EXTERNAL LIFE OF JESUS UP TO THE TIME OF HIS PUBLIC APPEARANCE.

What were the external conditions under which Jesus lived, from the scene just considered up to the time of his public appearance? On this subject our canonical gospels give scarcely an indication.

First, as to his place of residence, all that we learn explicitly is this : that both at the beginning and at the end of this obscure period he dwelt at Nazareth. According to Luke ii. 51, Jesus when twelve years old returned thither with his parents, and according to Matthew iii. 13, Mark i. 9, he, when thirty years old (comp. Luke iii. 23), came from thence to be baptized by John. Thus our evangelists appear to suppose, that Jesus had in the interim resided in Galilee, and, more particularly, in Nazareth. This supposition, however, does not exclude journeys, such as those to the feasts in Jerusalem.

The employment of Jesus during the years of his boyhood and youth seems, from an intimation in our gospels, to have been determined by the trade of his father, who is there called a τέκτων (Matt. xiii. 55). This Greek word, used to designate the trade of Joseph, is generally understood in the sense of *faber*

,[11] Ueber den Lukas, s. 39 f.
[12] Cap. v. In the Greek text also the more probable reading is καὶ μάλιστα οὐ σοφῶς, vid. Thilo, p. 287.

lignarius (carpenter) ;[1] a few only, on mystical grounds, discover in it a *faber ferrarius (blacksmith)*, *aurarius (goldsmith)*, or *cæmentarius (mason)*.[2] The works in wood which he executed are held of different magnitude by different authors : according to Justin and the *Evangelium Thomæ*,[3] they were *ploughs and yokes*, ἄροτρα καὶ ζυγὰ, and in that case he would be what we call a wheel-wright; according to the *Evangelium infantiæ arabicum*,[4] they were doors, milk-vessels, sieves and coffers, and once Joseph makes a throne for the king ; so that here he is represented partly as a cabinet-maker and partly as a cooper. The *Protevangelium Jacobi*, on the other hand, makes him work at *buildings*, οἰκοδομαῖς,[5] without doubt as a carpenter. In these labours of the father Jesus appears to have shared, according to an expression of Mark, who makes the Nazarenes ask concerning Jesus, not merely as in the parallel passage of Matthew : *Is not this the carpenter's son ?* οὐκ οὗτός ἐστιν ὁ τοῦ τέκτονος υἱός ; but *Is not this the carpenter ?* οὐκ οὗτός ἐστιν ὁ τέκτων (vi. 3). It is true that in replying to the taunt of Celsus that the teacher of the Christians was a carpenter by trade, τέκτων ἦν τὴν τέχνην, Origen says, he must have forgotten *that in none of the Gospels received by the churches is Jesus himself called a carpenter*, ὅτι οὐδαμοῦ τῶν ἐν ταῖς ἐκκλησίαις φερομένων εὐαγγελίων τέκτων αὐτὸς ὁ Ἰησοῦς ἀναγέγραπται.[6] The above passage in Mark has, in fact, the various reading, ὁ τοῦ τέκτονος υἱός, which Origen must have taken, unless he be supposed altogether to have overlooked the passage, and which is preferred by some modern critics.[7] But here Beza has justly remarked that *fortasse mutavit aliquis, existimans, hanc artem Christi majestati parum convenire;* whereas there could hardly be an interest which would render the contrary alteration desirable.[8] Moreover Fathers of the Church and apocryphal writings represent Jesus, in accordance with the more generally accepted reading, as following the trade of his father. Justin attaches especial importance to the fact that Jesus made ploughs and yokes or scales, as symbols of active life and of justice.[9] In the *Evangelium infantiæ Arabicum*, Jesus goes about with Joseph to the places where the latter has work, to help him in such a manner that if Joseph made anything too long or too short, Jesus, by a touch or by merely stretching out his hand, gave to the object its right size, an assistance which was very useful to his foster-father, because, as the apocryphal text naïvely remarks : *nec admodum peritus erat artis fabrilis.*[10]

Apart from these apocryphal descriptions, there are many reasons for believing that the above intimation as to the youthful employment of Jesus is correct. In the first place, it accords with the Jewish custom which pre-scribed even to one destined to a learned career, or in general to any spiritual occupation, the acquisition of some handicraft; thus Paul, the pupil of the rabbins, was also a tent-maker, σκηνοποιὸς τὴν τέχνην (Acts xviii. 3). Next, as our previous examinations have shown that we know nothing historical of

---

[1] Hence the title of an Arabian apocryphal work (according to the Latin translation in Thilo, I, p. 3) : *historia Josephi, fabri lignarii.*

[2] Vid. Thilo, Cod. Apocr. N. T. p. 368 f. not.

[3] Justin. Dial. c. Tryph. 88. According to him Jesus makes these implements, doubtless under the direction of Joseph. In the *Evang. Thomæ* c. xiii. Joseph is the workman.

[4] Cap. xxxviii. ap. Thilo, p. 112 ff.

[5] C. ix. and xiii.

[6] C. Cels. vi. 36.

[7] Fritzsche, in Marc. p. 200.

[8] Vid. Wetstein and Paulus, in loc. ; Winer, Realwörterbuch, I, s. 665. Note ; Neander, L. J. Chr. s. 46 f. Note.

[9] Ut sup. : ταῦτα γὰρ τὰ τεκτονικὰ ἔργα εἰργάζετο ἐν ἀνθρώποις ὢν, ἄροτρα καὶ ζυγά. διὰ τούτων καὶ τὰ τῆς δικαιοσύνης σύμβολα διδάσκων, καὶ ἐνεργῆ βίον.

[10] Cap. xxxviii.

extraordinary expectations and plans on the part of the parents of Jesus in relation to their son, so nothing is more natural than the supposition that Jesus early practised the trade of his father. Further, the Christians must have had an interest in denying, rather than inventing, this opinion as to their Messiah's youthful occupation, since it often drew down upon them the ridicule of their opponents. Thus Celsus, as we have already mentioned, could not abstain from a reflection on this subject, for which reason Origen will known nothing of any designation of Jesus as a τέκτων in the New Testament; and every one knows the scoffing question of Libanius about the carpenter's son, a question which seems to have been provided with so striking an answer, only *ex eventu*.[11] It may certainly be said in opposition to this, that the notion of Jesus having been a carpenter, seems to be founded on a mere inference from the trade of the father as to the occupation of the son, whereas the latter was just as likely to apply himself to some other branch of industry; nay, that perhaps the whole tradition of the carpentry of Joseph and Jesus owes its origin to the symbolical significance exhibited by Justin. As however the allusion in our Gospels to the trade of Joseph is very brief and bare, and is nowhere used allegorically in the New Testament, nor entered into more minutely; it is not to be contested that he was really a carpenter; but it must remain uncertain whether Jesus shared in this occupation.

What were the circumstances of Jesus and his parents as to fortune? The answer to this question has been the object of many dissertations. It is evident that the ascription of pressing poverty to Jesus, on the part of orthodox theologians, rested on dogmatical and æsthetic grounds. On the one hand, they wished to maintain even in this point the *status exinanitionis*, and on the other, they wished to depict as strikingly as possible the contrast between the μορφὴ θεοῦ (*form of God*) and the μορφὴ δούλου (*form of a servant*). That this contrast as set forth by Paul (Phil. ii. 6, ff.), as well as the expression ἐπτώχευσε, which this apostle applies to Christ (2 Cor. viii. 9) merely characterizes the obscure and laborious life to which he submitted after his heavenly pre-existence, and instead of playing the part of king which the Jewish imagination attributed to the Messiah, is also to be regarded as established.[12] The expression of Jesus himself, *The Son of man hath not where to lay his head*, ποῦ τὴν κεφαλὴν κλίνῃ (Matt. viii. 20), may possibly import merely his voluntary renunciation of the peaceful enjoyment of fortune, for the sake of devoting himself to the wandering life of the Messiah. There is only one other particular bearing on the point in question, namely, that Mary presented, as an offering of purification, doves (Luke ii. 24),—according to Lev. xii. 8, the offering of the poor: which certainly proves that the author of this information conceived the parents of Jesus to have been in by no means brilliant circumstances;[13] but what shall assure us that he also was not induced to make this representation by unhistorical motives? Meanwhile we are just as far from having tenable ground for maintaining the contrary proposition, namely, that Jesus possessed property: at least it is inadmissible to adduce the coat without seam [14] (John xix. 23), until we shall have inquired more closely what kind of relation it has to the subject.

[11] Theodoret. H. E. iii. 23.
[12] Hase, Leben Jesu, § 70; Winer, bibl. Realw. 1, s. 665.
[13] Winer, ut sup.
[14] This is done by both the above-named theologians.

§ 43.

THE INTELLECTUAL DEVELOPMENT OF JESUS.

Our information concerning the external life of Jesus during his youth is very scanty : but we are almost destitute of any concerning his intellectual development. For the indeterminate phrase, twice occurring in Luke's history of the childhood, concerning the increase of his spiritual strength and his growth in wisdom, tells us no more than we must necessarily have presupposed without it ; while on the expectations which his parents cherished with respect to him before his birth, and on the sentiment which his mother especially then expressed, no conclusion is to be founded, since those expectations and declarations are themselves unhistorical. The narrative just considered, of the appearance of Jesus in the temple at twelve years of age, rather gives us a result—the early and peculiar development of his religious consciousness,—than an explanation of the causes and conditions by which this development was favoured. But we at least learn from Luke ii. 41 (what however is to be of course supposed of pious Israelites), that the parents of Jesus used to go to Jerusalem every year at the Passover. We may conjecture, then, that Jesus from his twelfth year generally accompanied them, and availed himself of this excellent opportunity, amid the concourse of Jews and Jewish proselytes of all countries and all opinions, to form his mind, to become acquainted with the condition of his people and the false principles of the Pharisaic leaders, and to extend his survey beyond the narrow limits of Palestine.[1]

Whether or in what degree Jesus received the learned education of a rabbin, is also left untold in our canonical Gospels. From such passages as Matt. vii. 29, where it is said that Jesus taught *not as the scribes*, οὐχ ὡς οἱ γραμματεῖς, we can only infer that he did not adopt the method of the doctors of the law, and it does not follow that he had never enjoyed the education of a *scribe* (γραμματεὺς). On the other hand, not only was Jesus called ῥαββὶ and ῥαββουνὶ by his disciples (Matt. xxvi. 25, 49 ; Mark ix. 5, xi. 21, xiv. 45. John iv. 31, ix. 2, xi. 8, xx. 16 : comp. i. 38, 40, 50), and by supplicating sufferers (Mark x. 5), but even the pharisaic ἄρχων Nicodemus (John iii. 2) did not refuse him this title. We cannot, however, conclude from hence that Jesus had received the scholastic instruction of a rabbin ;[2] for the salutation Rabbi, as also the privilege of reading in the synagogue (Luke iv. 16 ff.), a particular which has likewise been appealed to, belonged not only to graduated rabbins, but to every teacher who had given actual proof of his qualifications.[3] The enemies of Jesus explicitly assert, and he does not contradict them, that he had never learned letters : πῶς οὗτος γράμματα οἶδε μὴ μεμαθηκὼς (John vii. 15) ; and the Nazarenes are astonished to find so much wisdom in him, whence we infer that he had not to their knowledge been a student. These facts cannot be neutralized by the discourse of Jesus in which he represents himself as the model of a scribe well instructed unto the kingdom of heaven [4] (Matt. xiii. 52), for the word γραμματεὺς here means a doctor of the law in general, and not directly a doctor qualified in the schools. Lastly, the intimate acquaintance with the doctrinal traditions, and the abuses of the rabbins, which Jesus exhibits,[5] especially in the sermon on the mount and the anti-pharisaic discourse

---

[1] Paulus, exeget. Handb. 1, a, s. 273 ff.
[2] Such, however, are the arguments of Paulus, ut sup. 275 ff.
[3] Comp. Hase, Leben Jesu, § 38 ; Neander, L. J. Chr. s. 45 f.
[4] Paulus, ut sup.
[5] To this Schöttgen appeals, *Christus rabbinorum summus*, in his horæ, ii. p. 890 f.

Matt. xxiii. he might acquire from the numerous discourses of the Pharisees to the people, without going through a course of study under them.   Thus the data on our present subject to be found in the Gospels, collectively yield the result that Jesus did not pass formally through a rabbinical school; on the other hand, the consideration that it must have been the interest of the Christian legend to represent Jesus as independent of human teachers, may induce a doubt with respect to these statements in the New Testament, and a conjecture that Jesus may not have been so entirely a stranger to the learned culture of his nation.   But from the absence of authentic information we can arrive at no decision on this point.

Various hypotheses, more or less independent of the intimations given in the New Testament, have been advanced both in ancient and modern times concerning the intellectual development of Jesus : they may be divided into two principal classes, according to their agreement with the natural or the supernatural view.   The supernatural view of the person of Jesus requires that he should be the only one of his kind, independent of all external, human influences, self-taught or rather taught of God ; hence, not only must its advocates determinedly reject every supposition implying that he borrowed or learned anything, and consequently place in the most glaring light the difficulties which lay in the way of the natural development of Jesus ;[6] but, the more surely to exclude every kind of reception, they must also be disposed to assign as early an appearance as possible to that spontaneity which we find in Jesus in his mature age.   This spontaneous activity is twofold : it is theoretical and practical.   As regards the theoretical side, comprising judgment and knowledge, the effort to give as early a date as possible to its manifestation in Jesus, displays itself in the apocryphal passages which have been already partly cited, and which describe Jesus as surpassing his teachers long before his twelfth year, for according to one of them he spoke in his cradle and declared himself to be the Son of God.[7]   The practical side, too, of that superior order of spontaneity attributed to Jesus in his later years, namely, the power of working miracles, is attached by the apocryphal gospels to his earliest childhood and youth.   The *Evangelium Thomæ* opens with the fifth year of Jesus the story of his miracles,[8] and the Arabian *Evangelium Infantiæ* fills the journey into Egypt with miracles which the mother of Jesus performed by means of the swaddling bands of her infant, and the water in which he was washed.[9]   Some of the miracles which according to these apocryphal gospels were wrought by Jesus when in his infancy and boyhood, are analogous to those in the New Testament—cures and resuscitations of the dead ; others are totally diverse from the ruling type in the canonical Gospels—extremely revolting retributive miracles, by which every one who opposes the boy Jesus in any matter whatever is smitten with lameness, or even with death, or else mere extravagancies, such as the giving of life to sparrows formed out of mud.[10]

The natural view of the person of Jesus had an opposite interest, which was also very early manifested both among Jewish and heathen opponents of Christianity, and which consisted in explaining his appearance conformably to the laws of causality, by comparing it with prior and contemporaneous

---

[6] As e. g. Reinhard does, in his Plan Jesu.

[7] Evang. infant. arab. c. i. p. 60 f. ap. Thilo, and the passages quoted § 40 out of the same Gospel and the Evang. Thomæ.

[8] Cap. ii. p. 278, Thilo.

[9] Cap. x. ff.

[10] E. g. Evang. Thomæ, c. iii.–v.   Evang. infant. arab. c. xlvi. f.   Evang. Thomæ, c. ii. Evang. inf. arab. c. xxxvi.

facts to which it had a relation, and thus exhibiting the conditions on which Jesus depended, and the sources from which he drew. It is true that in the first centuries of the Christian era, the whole region of spirituality being a supernatural one for heathens as well as Jews, the reproach that Jesus owed his wisdom and seemingly miraculous powers, not to himself or to God, but to a communication from without, could not usually take the form of an assertion that he had acquired natural skill and wisdom in the ordinary way of instruction from others.[11] Instead of the natural and the human, the unnatural and the demoniacal were opposed to the divine and the supernatural (comp. Matt. xii. 24), and Jesus was accused of working his miracles by the aid of magic acquired in his youth. This charge was the most easily attached to the journey of his parents with him into Egypt, that native land of magic and secret wisdom, and thus we find it both in Celsus and in the Talmud. The former makes a Jew allege against Jesus, amongst other things, that he had entered into service for wages in Egypt, that he had there possessed himself of some magic arts, and on the strength of these had on his return vaunted himself for a God.[12] The Talmud gives him a member of the Jewish Sanhedrim as a teacher, makes him journey to Egypt with this companion, and bring magic charms from thence into Palestine.[13]

The purely natural explanation of the intellectual development of Jesus could only become prevalent amid the enlightened culture of modern times. In working out this explanation, the chief points of difference are the following : either the character of Jesus is regarded in too circumscribed a view, as the result of only one among the means of culture which his times afforded, or more comprehensively, as the result of all these combined ; again, in tracing this external influence, either the internal gifts and self-determination of Jesus are adequately considered, or they are not.

In any case, the basis of the intellectual development of Jesus was furnished by the sacred writings of his people, of which the discourses preserved to us in the Gospels attest his zealous and profound study. His Messianic ideas seem to have been formed chiefly on Isaiah and Daniel : spiritual religiousness and elevation above the prejudices of Jewish nationality were impressively shadowed forth in the prophetic writings generally, together with the Psalms.

Next among the influences affecting mental cultivation in the native country of Jesus, must be reckoned the three sects under which the spiritual life of his fellow-countrymen may be classified. Among these, the Pharisees, whom Jesus at a later period so strenuously combated, can apparently have had only a negative influence over him ; yet along with their fondness for tradition and legal pedantry, their sanctimoniousness and hypocrisy, by which Jesus was repelled from them, we must remember their belief in angels and in immortality, and their constant admission of a progressive development of the Jewish religion after Moses, which were so many points of union between them and

[11] Yet some isolated instances occur, vid. Semler, Baumgarten's Glaubenslehre, 1, s. 42, Anm. 8.

[12] Orig. c. Cels. 1. 28 : καὶ (λέγει) ὅτι οὗτος (ὁ Ἰησοῦς) διὰ πενίαν εἰς Αἴγυπτον μισθαρνήσας, κἀκεῖ δυνάμεων τίνων πειραθεὶς, ἐφ᾽ αἷς Αἰγύπτιοι σεμνύνονται, ἐπανῆλθεν, ἐν ταῖς δυνάμεσι μέγα φρονῶν, καὶ δι᾽ αὐτὰς θεὸν αὐτὸν ἀνηγόρευσε.

[13] Sanhedr. f. cvii. 2 : R. Josua f. Perachja et ישו Alexandrian Aegypti profecti sunt —— ישו ex illo tempore magiam exercuit, et Israëlitas ad pessima quœvis perduxit. (An important anachronism, as this Josua Ben Perachja lived about a century earlier. See Jost, Geschichte des Isr., 2, s. 80 ff. and 142 of the Appendices.) Schabbath f. civ. 2 : Traditio est, R. Elieserem dixisse ad viros doctos : annon f. Satdae (i.e. Jesus) magiam ex Aegypto adduxit per incisionem in carne suâ factam ? vid. Schöttgen, horæ, ii. p. 697 ff. Eisenmenger, entdecktes Judenthum, 1, s. 149 f.

Jesus. Still as these tenets were only peculiar to the Pharisees in contradis-
tinction to the Sadducees, and, for the rest, were common to all orthodox
Jews, we abide by the opinion that the influence of the Pharisaic sect on the
development of Jesus was essentially negative.

In the discourses of Jesus Sadduceeism is less controverted, nay, he agrees
with it in rejecting the Pharisaic traditions and hypocrisy ; hence a few of the
learned have wished to find him a school in this sect.[14] But the merely
negative agreement against the errors of the Pharisees,—an agreement which,
moreover, proceeded from quite another principle in Jesus than in the Sadducees,—is more than counterbalanced by the contrast which their religious
indifference, their unbelief in immortality and in spiritual existences, formed
with the disposition of Jesus, and his manner of viewing the world. That
the controversy with the Sadducees is not prominent in the Gospels, may be
very simply explained by the fact that their sect had very slight influence on
the circle with which Jesus was immediately connected, the adherents of
Sadduceeism belonging to the higher ranks alone.[15]

Concerning one only of the then existing Jewish sects can the question
seriously arise, whether we ought not to ascribe to it a positive influence on
the development and appearance of Jesus—the sect, namely, of the Essenes.[16]
In the last century the derivation of Christianity from Essenism was very much
in vogue ; not only English deists, and among the Germans, Bahrdt and
venturini, but even theologians, such as Stäudlin, embraced the idea.[17] In
the days of freemasonry and secret orders, there was a disposition to transfer
their character to primitive Christianity. The concealment of an Essene
lodge appeared especially adapted to explain the sudden disappearance of
Jesus after the brilliant scenes of his infancy and boyhood, and again after
his restoration to life. Besides the forerunner John, the two men on the
Mount of Transfiguration, and the angels clothed in white at the grave, and on
the Mount of Ascension, were regarded as members of the Essene brotherhood,
and many cures of Jesus and the Apostles were referred to the medical traditions
of the Essenes. Apart, however, from these fancies of a bygone age, there
are really some essential characteristics which seem to speak in favour of an
intimate relation between Essenism and Christianity. The most conspicuous
as such are the prohibition of oaths, and the community of goods : with the
former was connected fidelity, peaceableness, obedience to every constituted
authority ; with the latter, contempt of riches, and the custom of travelling
without provisions. These and other features, such as the sacred meal par-
taken in common, the rejection of sanguinary sacrifices and of slavery, constitute so strong a resemblance between Essenism and Christianity, that even
so early a writer as Eusebius mistook the Therapeutæ, a sect allied to the
Essenes, for Christians.[18] But there are very essential dissimilarities which
must not be overlooked. Leaving out of consideration the *contempt of marriage*, ὑπεροψία γάμου, since Josephus ascribes it to a part only of the Essenes ;
the asceticism, the punctilious observance of the Sabbath, the purifications,
and other superstitious usages of this sect, their retention of the names of the
angels, the mystery which they affected, and their contracted, exclusive devo-

[14] E. g. Des Côtes, Schutzschrift für Jesus von Nazaret, s. 128 ff.
[15] Neander, L. J. Chr. s. 39 ff.
[16] Vid. Joseph. B. j. ii. viii. 2–13. Antiq. xviii. i. 5. Comp. Philo, *quod omnis probus liber* and *de vita contemplativa*.
[17] This opinion is judiciously developed by Stäudlin, Geschichte der Sittenlehre Jesu, I, s. 570 ff. ; and in a romantic manner in the Geschichte des Grossen Propheten von Nazaret, I. Band.
[18] H. E. ii. 16 f.

tion to their order, are so foreign, nay so directly opposed to the spirit of Jesus, that, especially as the Essenes are nowhere mentioned in the New Testament, the aid which this sect also contributed to the development of Jesus, must be limited to the uncertain influence which might be exercised over him by occasional intercourse with Essenes.[19]

Did other elements than such as were merely Jewish, or at least confined to Palestine, operate upon Jesus? Of the heathens settled in *Galilee of the Gentiles*, Γαλιλαία τῶν ἐθνῶν, there was hardly much to be learned beyond patience under frequent intercourse with them. On the other hand, at the feasts in Jerusalem, not only foreign Jews, some of whom, as for example the Alexandrian and Cyrenian Jews, had synagogues there (Acts vi. 9), but also devout heathens were to be met with (John xii. 20); and that intercourse with these had some influence in extending the intellectual horizon of Jesus, and spiritualizing his opinions, has, as we have already intimated, all historical probability.[20]

But why do we, in the absence of certain information, laboriously seek after uncertain traces of an influence which cotemporary means of development may have exercised on Jesus? and yet more, why, on the other side, are these labours so anxiously repudiated? Whatever amount of intellectual material may be collected, the spark by which genius kindles it, and fuses its various elements into a consistent whole, is neither easier to explain nor reduced in value. Thus it is with Jesus. Allow him to have exhausted the means of development which his age afforded: a comprehensive faculty of reception is with great men ever the reverse side of their powerful originality; allow him to have owed far more to Essenism and Alexandrianism, and whatever other schools and tendencies existed, than we, in our uncertainty, are in a condition to prove:—still, for the reformation of a world these elements were all too little; the leaven necessary for this he must obtain from the depth of his own mind.[21]

But we have not yet spoken of an appearance to which our Gospels assign a most important influence in developing the activity of Jesus—that of John the Baptist. As his ministry is first noticed in the Gospels in connexion with the baptism and public appearance of Jesus, our inquiry concerning him, and his relation to Jesus, must open the second part.

[19] Comp. Bengel, Bemerkungen über den Versuch. das Christenthum aus dem Essäismus abzuleiten, in Flatt's Magazin, 7, s. 126 ff. ; Neander, L. J. Chr. s. 41 ff.

[20] This is stated with exaggeration by Bahrdt, Briefe über die Bibel, zweites Bändchen, 18ter, 20ster Brief ff. 4tes Bändchen, 49ster Brief.

[21] Comp. Paulus ut sup. 1, a, 273 ff. Planck, Geschichte des Christenthums in der Periode seiner ersten Einführung 1, s. 84. De Wette, bibl. Dogm. § 212. Hase L. J. § 38. Winer, bibl. Realw. s. 677 f. Neander, L. J. Chr. s. 38 ff.

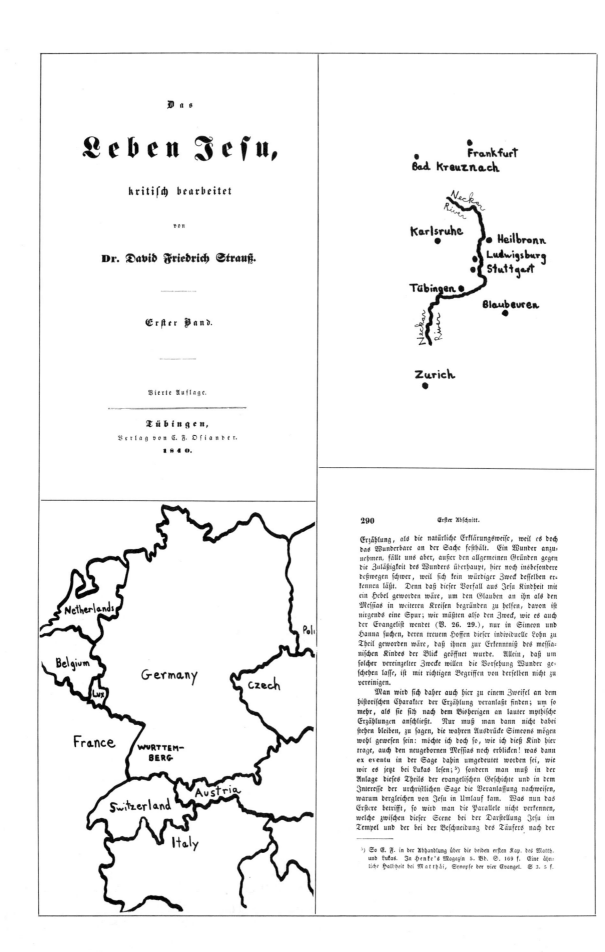

Das

Leben Jesu,

kritisch bearbeitet

von

Dr. David Friedrich Strauß.

Erster Band.

Vierte Auflage.

Tübingen,
Verlag von C. F. Osiander.
1840.

Erzählung, als die natürliche Erklärungsweise, weil es doch das Wunderbare an der Sache festhält. Ein Wunder anzunehmen, fällt uns aber, außer den allgemeinen Gründen gegen die Zulässigkeit des Wunders überhaupt, hier noch insbesondere deßwegen schwer, weil sich kein würdiger Zweck desselben erkennen läßt. Denn daß dieser Vorfall aus Jesu Kindheit mit ein Hebel geworden wäre, um den Glauben an ihn als den Messias in weiteren Kreisen begründen zu helfen, davon ist nirgends eine Spur; wir müßten also den Zweck, wie es auch der Evangelist wendet (V. 26. 29.), nur in Simeon und Hanna suchen, deren treuem Hoffen dieser individuelle Lohn zu Theil geworden wäre, daß ihnen zur Erkenntniß des messianischen Kindes der Blick geöffnet wurde. Allein, daß um solcher vereinzelter Zwecke willen die Vorsehung Wunder geschehen lasse, ist mit richtigen Begriffen von derselben nicht zu vereinigen.

Man wird sich daher auch hier zu einem Zweifel an dem historischen Charakter der Erzählung veranlaßt finden; um so mehr, als sie sich nach dem Bisherigen an lauter mythische Erzählungen anschließt. Nur muß man dann nicht dabei stehen bleiben, zu sagen, die wahren Ausdrücke Simeons mögen wohl gewesen sein: möchte ich doch so, wie ich dieß Kind hier trage, auch den neugebornen Messias noch erblicken! was dann ex eventu in der Sage dahin umgedeutet worden sei, wie wir es jetzt bei Lukas lesen;[5] sondern man muß in der Anlage dieses Theils der evangelischen Geschichte und in dem Interesse der urchristlichen Sage die Veranlassung nachweisen, warum dergleichen von Jesu in Umlauf kam. Was nun das Erstere betrifft, so wird man die Parallele nicht verkennen, welche zwischen dieser Scene bei der Darstellung Jesu im Tempel und der bei der Beschneidung des Täufers nach der

[5] So C. F. in der Abhandlung über die beiden ersten Kap. des Matth. und Lukas. In Henke's Magazin 5. Bd. S. 169 f. Eine ähnliche Halbheit bei Matthäi, Synopse der vier Evangel. S 3. 5 f.